South of the Sahara

South of the Sahara: Development in African Economies

Edited by Sayre P. Schatz

TEMPLE UNIVERSITY PRESS Philadelphia

Temple University Press, Philadelphia 19122

Published 1972. Printed in Great Britain

International Standard Book Number: 0-87722-014-X
Library of Congress Catalog Card Number: 72-84173

Contents

Preface

Interest in Africa on the part of American economists is recent. Before 1960, relatively few American economists were concerned with Africa and relatively little high quality work was done. During the 1960s, however, there was a rapid acceleration of interest in Africa and in both the quantity and average quality of the work done. It was this increase in quantity and quality which made it possible to draw together such a sizeable group of worthwhile papers at a conference on African economic development at Temple University toward the end of the decade. These are essays which are based on research in the field, which match in vigor and competence studies being carried out in other fields of economics, and which are of continuing interest because they are analyses of continuing development processes and problems.

The editor wishes to express his appreciation to those who participated in the conference. He thanks Mrs. Grace Tappert for cheerful secretarial help, and Dwight Stewart for his management of conference logistics, as well as his graduate assistant, Tapan Roy, who compiled the Index. He also thanks Dean Seymour L. Wolfbein of the Temple University School of Business Administration for encouragement and financial support of the conference.

SAYRE P. SCHATZ

Part I

Indigenous Entrepreneurship and Trade

The forces that have kept African enterprises relatively small, and in many countries few in number, have occupied the attention of many Africanist economists. Entrepreneurial shortcomings have usually been considered the main limiting factor, but in recent years this view has been questioned. For example, in 1963 the editor ventured the thesis that the importance of entrepreneurial deficiencies had been exaggerated and that the major obstacle to indigenous business growth lay in the economic environment, i.e., in the conditions the entrepreneur encountered. This view was challenged by several economists who believed that entrepreneurial inadequacies were in fact the major barrier.

The first four articles in this section carry on this debate. In doing so, they enhance our understanding of the restraints on the growth of African enterprise (or so it appears to the editor who, as one of the participants, may not be able to view the debate objectively). All the papers go beyond a simple paucity-of-entrepreneurship explanation.

Harris and Nafziger present a possible resolution of the disagreement by means of supply-and-demand analyses of entrepreneurship which encompass both sides of the debate. The supply side includes entrepreneurial qualities and capacities and indicates the possibility that these attributes may be either scarce or abundant. The demand side encompasses the economic environment, which may be either adverse or congenial, thus providing few or many profitable business opportunities. In the Harris and Nafziger approach, the nature of the supply of and demand for entrepreneurship determines the pace of business expansion.

Harris is largely concerned with *developing* this supply-and-demand analytical framework, which he believes is flexible enough to apply to widely differing circumstances and countries. He presents fourteen specific hypotheses regarding the rate of expansion of entrepreneurship and industry in less-developed economies, and relates these to his research in Nigeria. Nafziger is more concerned with *applying* his supply-and-demand approach. He concentrates on presenting and interpreting his findings on the factors affecting the supply of entrepreneurship in Nigeria.

The editor's article deals with the economic environment. It consists mainly of a delineation of the special difficulties in the African environment which limit the scope of profitable business opportunities. In the Harris and Nafziger analyses the economic environment would constitute the demand side of the entrepreneurial equation. However, the Schatz paper argues that the economic environment cannot be correctly integrated into the entrepreneurial supply-and-demand framework and that such a framework cannot encompass the factors governing the development of indigenous private enterprise.

Garlick's article also deals with factors other than the supply of entrepreneurial capability in explaining the tendency of African traders in Ghana to remain small. That they have not generally chosen to reinvest their profits and enlarge their trading businesses may well have been a rational decision. Reinvestment in trade involved many difficulties and was relatively risky compared to investments in other sources of income such as cocoa farms and urban rental housing. Moreover, these other investments as well as outlays for such things as houses in their home villages, other durable goods, and education for promising members of the family fulfilled social obligations as well as economic purposes.

Miracle deals with a different aspect of African business activity: the degree of competition in African internal trade. Descriptions of the colonial period before World War II suggest the prevalence of collusion and price control. However, economists writing of the years of decolonization and independence after the war depict a high degree of competition in marketing. Miracle suggests that this latter view is based on superficial examination and is incorrect. He argues that cartel arrangements tend to be more effective in the African context than in advanced economies and that considerable restriction on competition prevails in the marketing of virtually all major commodities in Africa.

Chapter 1

On the Concept of Entrepreneurship, with an Application to Nigeria

John R. Harris

The term "entrepreneurship" has been used rather differently by various authors and, at least in the economic literature, distinctions have been made (or glossed over) among invention, innovation, imitation, and risk-taking. As a result there has been some fruitless controversy arising from semantic rather than substantive differences. Also, most discussion of entrepreneurship has implicitly revolved around an individual who can be identified as "the entrepreneur." It has thereby failed to consider the entrepreneurial function in institutional settings other than that of the relatively small-scale private enterprise which marked the industrial beginnings of western economies.

It seems more useful to define entrepreneurship in terms of its common functions, which are in large part independent of the specific institutional settings. The function common to most of the definitions of entrepreneurship found in the literature is that of making the decision to engage in production – a decision that can be made by an individual or by a group. It may involve innovational activities like producing novel goods or finding new means of producing familiar goods. The decision may also entail considerable risk, since it usually involves creating additional productive capacity prior to actually undertaking production. The types of decisions needed range from complex to simple, from "once in a lifetime" to routine. The entrepreneurial function can in fact include:

1. Perceiving production opportunities;
2. Gaining control over other factors of production;

3. Organizing productive facilities; and
4. Managing the continuing operation of the productive unit.[1]

It is obvious that entrepreneurship cannot function in a vacuum; indeed its essence is that of exploiting potential opportunities for economic gain. It is therefore important to separate factors determining the potential opportunities (the demand for entrepreneurship) from the response to those opportunities (the supply of entrepreneurship).

Viewed in this framework, most of the variables which receive attention from economists, such as stocks of productive factors, technology, effective demand, foreign trade possibilities, prices, interest rates, alternative sources of income, and institutional arrangements, are seen to develop relevance through their determination of the set of potentially profitable opportunities. On the other hand, the variables which have received attention from psychologists, sociologists, anthropologists, and historians, and which include personality characteristics and social structure and values, affect the response (or supply) side through determination of the willingness of individuals to respond to entrepreneurial opportunities.

However, mere willingness to engage in entrepreneurial activity is not enough. Individuals (or groups) must also have the ability to respond, and this is influenced by such variables as education, occupational experience, and the existence of capital markets.

Economic growth results from the actual exploitation of potential projects which give rise to increased factor productivity and output. The real rate of project exploitation is determined by the simultaneous effects of both the supply-and-demand conditions.[2]

Much of the controversy concerning the economic importance of entrepreneurship can thus be interpreted as arising from differing assumptions about the elasticity of supply of entrepreneurship. Economists who feel that entrepreneurship can be disregarded in favor of such "purely economic" variables as capital formation, foreign trade conditions, etc., tacitly assume both that the supply is positively elastic and that few feasible policy variables can affect it.[3]

In contrast, some economists assert the primacy of entrepreneurship. Hagen states: "In a traditional society in which nothing else has yet occurred to change traditional personality and culture, an increase in the size of the market or in the flow of saving available is not apt to have a great effect in inducing continuing change in technology."[4] He is assuming the supply of entrepreneurship to be extremely inelastic and at a low level. Hirschman states: "If backwardness is due to insufficient number and speed of development decisions . . . then the fundamental problem of development consists in generating and energizing human action in a certain direction."[5] In terms of this analysis, he is saying that the supply of entrepreneurship is both limited and inelastic, and he is recommending a strategy that will improve both conditions.

As with any supply-and-demand analysis, there is an identification problem. If one starts with the proposition that entrepreneurship is vital for growth, it is all too easy to find that in countries with low rates of growth there is a lack of entrepreneurship, and, conversely, that there is an abundance of entrepreneurship in countries which have achieved high rates of growth.[6] Rather than make entrepreneurship important by definition, we must try to identify separately the factors governing supply and demand.

This supply-and-demand framework is capable of accommodating many different experiences. Papanek has reported a high rate of industrial growth in response to economic incentives in Pakistan, where conditions for a vigorous entrepreneurial response seemed relatively lacking.[7] In Greece there has been a long tradition of vigorous entrepreneurship, yet, according to Alexander, industrial growth has been disappointing because of problems in the economic structure.[8] We can also think of examples, such as the United States and England, in which both the economic environment[9] and entrepreneurial supply were conducive to rapid growth, and of examples like Burma, where both factors seem prejudiced to growth.

In a somewhat similar vein, Papanek has aptly pointed out:

> The development of industrial entrepreneurs results from the interaction of three forces – the strength of economic incentives; the values, institutions and political situation in the society as a whole; and the motivations of the potential

entrepreneurs. The more favorable for the development of industrial entrepreneurs one or two of these factors, the less favorable can be the other one or two without affecting the results.[10]

A careful examination of this general model and extant empirical studies (which this writer has made elsewhere) suggests the following fourteen specific hypotheses (each to be interpreted as a ceteris paribus statement).

1. The rate of expansion of industry and of entrepreneurship will be higher in industries yielding higher current rates of profit. (The underlying assumption is that expectations adapt to realizations.)
2. The rate of expansion will be higher in industries with lower risk.
3. The rate of expansion will be higher in industries with less complex technology.
4. The rate of expansion will be higher in industries in which economies of scale are not great; these require less complex organization and provide a lower capital threshold for entry.
5. The rate of expansion will be higher in industries in which technological communication between the country and the rest of the world is most easily facilitated.
6. Entrepreneurs with greater access to credit (or other means of raising capital) will be more successful.
7. Entrepreneurial performance will vary among ethnic groups. (Ethnicity is expected to reflect differences in social structure, sanctions, and child-rearing practices, which in turn condition an individual's possible entry into entrepreneurial activity.)
8. Entrepreneurs will exhibit a high degree of geographic mobility.
9. Entrepreneurs will exhibit a high degree of social mobility.
10. Entrepreneurs will exhibit a high degree of occupational mobility (both inter- and intra- generational).
11. Entrepreneurial success will be conditioned by occupational experience. In particular, individuals coming from backgrounds in large-scale trade will be more successful than others.

12. Formal education will be positively related to entrepreneurial success. (Note that both education and occupational experience should condition the individual's ability to perceive opportunities as well as to provide specific skills needed to exploit any opportunity perceived.)
13. Successful entrepreneurs will be relatively cut off from traditional relationships and obligations. (The assumption here is that traditional values and obligations inhibit entrepreneurship. Successful entrepreneurs are likely to rebel against the traditional order.)
14. Successful entrepreneurs will be active in politics or at least have significant political affiliations.

In order to test these propositions, lengthy interviews were conducted during 1965 among 269 Nigerian owners of industrial enterprises with more than ten employees. Data were collected on the history, activities, and current financial structure of each firm, including management structure, sources of capital and technical information, future plans, and special obstacles which had been encountered. A detailed biography of the entrepreneur was also recorded.[11]

Two major problems arise in interpreting the results of these interviews in order to provide tests of the hypotheses. First, each of the hypotheses has been framed as a ceteris paribus statement. It is extremely difficult to disentangle the various underlying determinants when all that can be observed are cases in which entrepreneurial services are actually being provided in specific projects. Just as in conventional supply-and-demand analysis, all that can be observed are actual transactions which presumably lie on both the supply-and-demand curves; additional information is needed if the two schedules are to be identified. This will always be true of interdependent systems.

Suppose, for instance, that the extent of formal education and entrepreneurial success are found to be positively correlated. What then can be inferred? At least two interpretations are possible. If education affects the ability of an individual to perceive opportunities because of his greater literacy, his appreciation of general principles, etc., it is then likely that people with more education will have exploited the more profitable opportunities primarily because they are more difficult to identify. Innovative activity may be considered in this light. Thus the observed correlation implies that greater education increases general responsiveness to any given set of opportunities.

An alternative interpretation arises from the observation that education imparts particular skills. Specific projects which require these skills will then be potentially more profitable to individuals possessing the skills than to those who lack them. The first interpretation involves the supply side, while the second involves the demand side of the suggested entrepreneurship model. The prediction of association is the same in either interpretation, although for purposes of policy prescription a knowledge of the causal mechanism may be crucial.

The second major problem is that of measurement. The term "entrepreneurial success' was used in several of the hypotheses. What is it and how can it be measured? At least three possible measures come to mind: size of enterprise; growth of enterprise; and entrepreneurial income. The first is derived from the notion that a larger scale of operation requires more entrepreneurial input; hence an individual controlling a large firm must be supplying more entrepreneurship than does an individual controlling a smaller firm. The second arises from the observation that resource constraints may limit the absolute size of a firm at any point of time, but that a more able or effective entrepreneur will be able to expand his firm. The third measure is derived from the notion that entrepreneurial income is a residual (receipts less all payments to other factors of production). The size of this residual is presumably related directly to the entrepreneur's ability to choose profitable lines of activity and to combine factors in an efficient manner. None of the three measures is entirely satisfactory; the writer is forced to consider each of them and to examine the sensitivity of the conclusions to the choice of the measure.

EMPIRICAL FINDINGS IN NIGERIA

The evidence from detailed studies of the sawmilling, furniture, rubber-processing, printing and garment-making industries tends to confirm the first six hypotheses. Large numbers of Nigerians have been highly responsive to economic opportunities and incentives within the limits imposed by their particular technical, commercial, and managerial skills. Industries characterized by simple technologies and low investment thresholds have been expanded rapidly – more rapidly, in fact, than would appear to be economically optimal, since most are working at rather low levels of capacity utilization. On the other hand, there has been relatively little private African participation in large-scale industrial activities undertaken by expatriates and, to an increasing extent, by governments.

This general responsiveness is consistent with historical evidence which suggests that traditional social structures and values in several important Nigerian societies have not inhibited response to pecuniary incentives. As LeVine has stated:

> Rather than thinking of Africans as tradition-directed people perpetuating an ancient and stagnant culture, we might more accurately regard them as pragmatic frontiersmen with a persistent history of migration, settlement and resettlement of new lands, and of responding to the challenge of intertribal wars and the slave trade. In this historical perspective, Africans were experienced in adapting to and taking advantage of change, instability and movement, so that they were more prepared to adopt new paths of advancement offered by European institutions than were the populations of some of the more stable non-Western societies.[12]

Yet a serious problem remains. How can the coexistence of high responsiveness to small-scale industrial opportunities and minimal entry into large-scale operations (which at the same time are attractive to expatriates) be explained?

Two possible lines of approach seem plausible. The first is to note that social structures and values (either working directly by role expectations and sanctions, or by mediating child-rearing practices, thus affecting individual personality) may be both conducive to individualistic creative aspects of entrepreneurship, and inhibitory to the cooperative element of entrepreneurship which Hirschman has described as "the ability to bring and hold together an able staff, to delegate authority, to inspire loyalty, to handle successfully relations with labor and the public, and a host of other managerial talents."[13] The extended family system may also encourage high levels of consumption spending, thereby reducing the capacity of entrepreneurs to reinvest and expand their businesses into large-scale units. Furthermore, emphasis on money-making as such may also lead individuals to opt for the easy life as soon as they have made enough money to sustain the consumption patterns to which they aspire. Successful entrepreneurs elsewhere are usually thought to have been motivated by desire for achievement for its own sake or for power or for some other similar motive, money being merely the symbol of success rather than the ultimate goal.[14] The other approach is to note that few Nigerians possess the requisite technical and managerial skills for operating large-scale industries because they have had little experience in such activities and because the educational system, with its emphasis on purely literary skills, has failed to impart technical or managerial skills. Furthermore, imperfections in the capital market preclude the necessary agglomeration of capital. Opportunities that appear profitable to expatriate entrepreneurs with their experience, skills, and access to capital markets are not therefore potentially profitable to the would-be Nigerian entrepreneur.

Undoubtedly there are elements of truth in both explanations. Instances of conflict between traditional relationships and the authority patterns required for administration of large-scale enterprises have been documented and appear to present a somewhat serious problem.[15] Traditional mores, suspicion of outsiders, and unwillingness to invest in firms over which the individual does not exercise direct control have been shown by Nyhart to be serious obstacles to the formation of large-scale business units in Nigeria.[16] On the other hand, many Nigerians, after being sent overseas for periods of formal technical and managerial training along with on-the-job experience, are presently performing high-level managerial functions quite successfully in several expatriate and government enterprises.[17] Such training is expensive, and expatriate firms have resorted to it only because of considerable governmental pressure. Yet the results have been quite impressive. The conclusion to be drawn is that cultural or social forces have not prevented effective performance by Nigerians in large-scale organizations when they have had opportunities to gain the requisite training and experience.

Nigeria is at a very early stage of industrial development; "modern" industry was virtually unknown prior to 1950. The emergence of a first generation of small-scale entrepreneurs coming from craftsman origins has also been documented in the Philippines, Greece, India, Turkey, and Lebanon.[18] In each of those countries, the majority of large-scale industrialists came either from second-generation industrialists, from large-scale trading, or from professional activities. The training and background of Nigerian industrialists is strikingly similar to that of the first-generation industrialists (who remained predominantly small-scale) in those other countries. If the analogy is legitimate, one would be led to expect that although cultural factors may well condition the character of entrepreneurial response,[19] a second generation of Nigerian industrialists, with more formal technical and managerial training, greater experience in large-scale organizations, greater contact with the "outside world," and reared in an industrial environment, will emerge capable of undertaking large-scale enterprises.[20] The institutional basis for improved capital markets is presently being formed; it can be expected that with the emergence of Nigerians possessing the requisite skills for establishing and operating large-scale enterprises, the problem of capital agglomeration will also recede.

It is useful at this juncture to note critically the kind of evidence used to reach these conclusions. Data (of widely varying quality) on the extent of Nigerian participation, rates of return, expansion, sources of technological information, credit, and capacity utilization were gathered industry by industry. In addition, historical and ethnological data were used to establish some characteristics of Nigerian societies, and comparisons were made with studies of entrepreneurship in other developing economies. Another piece of evidence consists of data collected from respondents about their previous occupations, and that of their fathers and of their grandfathers; this is reproduced in Table 1.

Examination of Table 1 reveals considerable intergenerational and individual occupational mobility. Coming from a group of grandfathers who were preponderantly farmers or chiefs, and from fathers who were farmers, craftsmen, or traders, these men started their economic lives as craftsmen, clerks, small-scale

TABLE 1
Occupational Background of Entrepreneurs

Occupation	*Grand-father's occupation*	%	*Father's occupation*	%	*Own first occupation*	%	*Own previous occupation*	%
Subsistence farmer	92	44.0	66	25.1	7	2.6	0	0.
Cash Crop farmer	39	18.7	51	19.4	3	1.1	1	0.4
Small-Scale trader	9	4.3	11	4.2	16	6.0	10	3.7
Large-Scale trader	24	11.5	46	17.5	3	1.1	37	13.9
Employed artisan	1	0.5	10	3.8	74	27.8	31	11.6
Self-Employed artisan, contractor or transporter	12	5.7	44	17.0	46	18.5	116	45.5
Clerk	0	0	4	1.5	59	22.2	19	7.1
Teacher	0	0	2	0.8	32	12.0	6	2.2
Government employee	2	1.0	14	5.4	17	6.4	30	11.5
Professional worker	4	1.9	5	1.6	6	2.3	10	3.7
Traditional activity high rank	26	12.4	9	3.4	0	0	1	0.4
TOTAL	209	100.0	262[a]	100.0	263[a]	100.0	261[a]	100.0

[a] Totals of fewer than 269 result from nonresponse.

traders, and government servants, and were primarily self-employed as craftsmen, contractors, transporters, and large-scale traders prior to founding their industrial enterprises. It is particularly significant to note the movement of these individuals from "modern" occupations, such as clerical work and teaching, into self-employment.

Still another piece of corroborative evidence relates to status mobility. The writer's data indicate that although there is a significant positive association between father's and entrepreneur's status (Goodman–Krushkal's Gamma=.493, $p<.001$), yet entrepreneurial activity has been an avenue of upward status mobility for most of the individuals, since 122 of the respondents were of higher status and only 42 of lower status than their fathers.

So far the analysis has concentrated principally on the demand side. The evidence suggests that there is response to differences in opportunity; the supply schedule must be in some sense elastic, but no systematic explanation of the determinants of this schedule has been presented. The previous observation of minimal response to large-scale or technically complex opportunities strongly suggests a systematic supply element. A priori considerations of the influence of education, relevant occupational experience, and cultural values give rise to suggested alternative explanations of the phenomenon. However, all that could be observed were Nigerians engaged in relatively small-scale activities and Europeans in large-scale firms. The Europeans and Nigerians differed with respect to education, experience, connections with parent companies, and access to capital markets, as well as with respect to culture; hence it is impossible to differentiate empirically between the alternative explanations.

Psychological and sociological theories of entrepreneurship have gained wide currency. The writer has already indicated that such factors should affect the supply of entrepreneurial activity. Since Nigeria is marked by a number of ethnic (or tribal) groups which differ with respect to social structure and organization, values, and child-rearing practices, one would expect psychological or sociological differences to be reflected in differential ethnic responses.

It seems reasonable that correlation between measures of entrepreneurial success and ethnic group membership should provide a test of the importance of these factors. However, interpretation of the findings is beclouded by several problems.

First, even though occupational and status mobility may be high in Nigeria, geographic mobility is extremely limited in industrial activities, as indicated in Table 2. A further analysis of the respondents outside of Lagos indicates that more than 65 percent operate businesses in their *province* of birth, and another 15 percent in an immediately adjacent province.[21] Since ethnic group and place of birth are almost perfectly correlated, it becomes difficult to distinguish between effects of ethnicity and effects specific to a geographical area. The set of opportunities varies from area to area because of different natural resource endowments, availability of skilled labor, markets, and governmental policies with respect to credit and education.

LeVine's recent measurement of *n*-Achievement among Nigerian high school students is consistent with theories of

TABLE 2

Region in Which Business Is Located

Region of birth	*Greater Lagos*	*Western*	*Mid-West*	*Eastern*	*Northern*	*Total*
Greater Lagos	34	0	0	0	0	34
Western	92	35	0	1	2	130
Mid-West	12	0	16	0	0	28
Eastern	22	0	0	38	2	62
Northern	3	0	0	0	7	10
TOTAL	163	35	16	39	11	264

traditional status mobility patterns, population pressure, withdrawal of group status respect, and contemporary status mobility patterns, all of which predict significant differences between ethnic groups with respect to achievement motivation.[22] The predicted level of *n*-Achievement decreased in order of Ibo, Yoruba, and Hausa. LeVine's measurement of differences also accords with popular stereotypes which depict Ibos as ambitious, enterprising, and "pushful." There is also general agreement that the Hausas are relatively more backward, notwithstanding the almost ubiquitous Hausa traders selling goods throughout West Africa. Yorubas have long been active in commerce, government, and the professions, but are popularly regarded as having less drive and aggressiveness than do the Ibos.

Other important ethnic groups, for the purpose of this study, are the Edo group, comprised of the Bini, Urhobo, Itsekiri, and related peoples of the former Midwest region, and the Ibibio, Efik, and Ijaw peoples of the coastal areas of the former Eastern region. In social structure, the Edo closely resemble the Yoruba, although hereditary status may be relatively more important; on the other hand, the Ibibio, Efik, and Ijaw peoples resemble the Ibo in lacking centralized traditional institutions. These groups, however, were among the first to have contact with the Europeans, were active in the slave (and later the oil) trade, and were exposed to western education quite early.[23]

The purpose of the foregoing few paragraphs has been to indicate that both psychological and sociological theories of entrepreneurship predict considerable variation in entrepreneurial responsiveness among Nigeria's different ethnic groups. The order of responsiveness (ranged from high to low) would probably be: Ibo, Ibibio, Yoruba, Edo, and Hausa. The explanatory power of these theories can be examined in terms of the sample.

In Table 3, the relative proportions of entrepreneurs from each ethnic group are examined in conjunction with the distribution of ethnic groups within the entire Nigerian population.

TABLE 3

Distribution of Entrepreneurs by Ethnic Grouping Compared with That of the Nigerian Population

Ethnic group	*% of entrepreneurs*	*% of Nigerian population (1952–53) census*	*Index of representation (1)/(2)*
Ibo	21.6	17.9	1.2
Ibibio, Efik, and Ijaw	1.9	2.5	0.8
Yoruba	63.5	16.6	3.8
Edo	9.3	1.5	6.2
Hausa–Fulani	2.6	18.2	0.2
Other ethnic groups	1.1	43.3	0.03
TOTAL	100.0	100.0	

The table indicates that the Edo, Yoruba, and Ibo groups are overrepresented in the sample; Ibibio, Efik, and Ijaw, Hausa–Fulani, and other groups are underrepresented. The order of representation is: Edo, Yoruba, Ibo, Ibibio, Efik, Ijaw, Hausa–Fulani, and other groups. Although this ranking is inconsistent with prediction based on psychological and sociological theories, caution must be exercised in interpreting this "test." The census is out of date and of questionable reliability, though it is unlikely that errors in the census would change these findings. Our sampling procedure, however, does not permit any confidence in the ethnic distribution of entrepreneurs. The investigation was restricted to a limited number of industries in major urban areas; it cannot be said with confidence, therefore, that this is a representative sample of all Nigerian industry. Even if this claim could be made, it would not be a significant test of the hypothesis. Industry represents a small part of the Nigerian economy; it cannot be claimed that participation in industry is an appropriate test of entrepreneurial responsiveness. Trade, transport, and services are all quantitatively more important outlets for entrepreneurial energy at this time. Moreover, geographic differences are confounded with ethnic groupings. For example, the Edo are concentrated entirely in rubber processing and sawmilling; the area in which they live is the principal area of high forest and rubber cultivation.

Qualitative differences between entrepreneurial performance of different ethnic groups might shed more light on the hypothesis under question. Table 4 presents a cross-classification between ethnic groupings and size of firm (measured by number of employees). Although there is clearly some tendency for the Ibibio, Edo, and Ibo entrepreneurs to have larger firms than do the Yoruba or Hausa, the relationship is not statistically significant (after further grouping, a chi-square test was not significant at the .10 level).

TABLE 4

Ethnic Group of Entrepreneur and Number of Employees in Firm

	Number of employees											
	Fewer than 20		*21–30*		*31–50*		*51–100*		*More than 100*		*Total*	
Ethnic group	%	*no.*	%	*no.*	%	*no.*	%	*no.*	%	*no.*	%	*no.*
Ibo	39.7	23	13.8	8	13.8	8	20.7	12	12.1	7	100	58
Ibibio, Efik, and Ijaw	20.0	1	20.0	1	20.0	1	20.0	1	20.0	1	100	5
Yoruba	52.4	88	18.5	31	13.1	22	10.1	17	6.0	10	100	168
Edo	29.1	7	8.3	2	25.0	6	25.0	6	12.5	3	100	24
Hausa	14.3	1	57.1	4	14.3	1	0.0	0	14.3	1	100	7
Other	66.6	2	0.0	0	0.0	0	33.3	1	0.0	0	100	3
TOTAL	46.1	122	17.4	46	14.3	38	14.0	37	8.3	22	100	265

One of the obvious difficulties that arises in evaluating Table 4 is whether or not size of firm is an appropriate measure of entrepreneurial performance; a measure of firm growth and/or profitability might be better. A rough index of success was constructed on the basis of the rate of growth of assets and profitability. Because of the state of the records of the firms, the data were not particularly accurate for either growth or profitability. Nevertheless, the index gives a reasonably accurate and useful ordering of the firms with regard to these variables. Sixteen of the firms could not be evaluated because they were too new or because major reorganizations had recently been made. Table 5 shows the distribution of entrepreneurs by success and ethnic groups.

TABLE 5

Ethnic Group of Entrepreneur and Success of the Firm

Ethnic group	*Index of success*											
	Very successful		*Successful*		*Average*		*Marginal*		*Un-successful*		*Total*	
	%	*no.*	%	*no.*	%	*no.*	%	*no.*	%	*no.*	%	*no.*
Ibo	22.6	12	41.5	22	24.5	13	5.7	33	5.7	3	100	53
Ibibio, Efik, and Ijaw	20.0	1	60.0	3	0.0	0	20.0	1	0.0	0	100	5
Yoruba	14.1	23	35.0	57	25.8	42	20.2	33	4.9	8	100	163
Edo	14.3	3	33.3	7	9.5	2	38.1	8	4.8	18	100	21
Hausa	0.0	0	60.0	3	20.0	1	20.0	1	0.0	0	100	5
Other	33.3	1	0.0	0	33.3	1	33.3	1	0.0	0	100	3
TOTAL	16.0	40	36.8	92	23.6	59	18.8	47	4.8	12	100	250

Inspection of Table 5 reveals that Ibo and Ibibio entrepreneurs tended to be relatively more successful than did Yorubas and Edos. Hausas performed about the same as the average of all groups, although the small number makes this difficult to interpret. Application of a chi-square test for association reveals that the relationship in Table 5 is even weaker than that in Table 4. Other measures of differential entrepreneurial performance such as innovation, changes made within the firm since founding, and plans for future expansion revealed that in each case Ibibios and Ibos ranked higher than did the other groups, but that Hausas were significantly higher than Yorubas or Edos. The most highly significant relationship was found for innovation, as shown in Table 6.

TABLE 6

Ethnic Group and Innovation

Ethnic group	*Innovated* %	*no.*	*Non-innovated* %	*no.*	*Total* %	*no.*
Ibo	29.3	17	70.7	41	100	58
Ibibio, Efik, and Ijaw	60.0	3	40.0	2	100	5
Yoruba	12.1	20	87.9	145	100	165
Edo	8.3	2	91.7	22	100	24
Hausa	71.4	5	28.6	2	100	7
Other	33.3	1	66.7	2	100	3
TOTAL	18.3	48	81.7	214	100	262

Chi-square = 29.968, 5 d.f., $p < .001$

However, both size of firm and measure of success may well be correlated with the particular industry and with access to credit, both of which may be importantly influenced by the economic structure of the particular region. Given the relative geographic immobility of the entrepreneurs, a better test of the hypothesis that entrepreneurial performance is related to psychological and social variables would be an examination of the ethnic distribution of entrepreneurs by size of firm and success, in Lagos only. Tables 7 and 8 show these data.

Both tables reveal a tendency for a greater proportion of Ibos to have larger and more successful businesses than is the case for Yorubas, but the relationship is even less strong than it was for the entire sample. Further tests were performed in which the particular industry was controlled, and in which both region and particular industry were also controlled. In each case, the relationship was in the same direction: Ibos and Ibibios higher than Yorubas and Edos, with Hausas occupying an intermediate position. However, the effect of controlling for the additional variables was to weaken the relationship further.

TABLE 7

Ethnic Group of Entrepreneur and Number of Employees in Firm (Lagos Only)

Ethnic group	*Number of Employees*											
	Fewer than 20		*21–30*		*31–50*		*51–100*		*More than 100*		*Total*	
	%	*no.*	%	*no.*	%	*no.*	%	*no.*	%	*no.*	%	*no.*
Ibo	60.8	14	8.7	2	8.7	2	17.4	4	4.3	1	100	23
Yoruba	58.8	74	15.6	20	11.7	15	9.4	12	5.5	7	100	128
Bini	37.5	3	25.0	2	25.0	2	12.5	1	0.0	0	100	8
All others[a]	60.0	3	20.0	1	0.0	0	20.0	1	0.0	0	100	5[a]
TOTAL	57.3	94	15.2	25	11.6	19	11.0	18	4.9	8	100	164

[a] "All others" consists of two Ibibio or Efik and three "others."

TABLE 8

Ethnic Group of Entrepreneur and Success of the Firm (Lagos Only)

Ethnic group	*Index of Success*											
	Very successful		*Successful*		*Average*		*Marginal*		*Un-successful*		*Total*	
	%	*no.*	%	*no.*	%	*no.*	%	*no.*	%	*no.*	%	*no.*
Ibo	23.8	5	28.6	6	33.3	7	14.3	3	0.0	0	100	21
Yoruba	16.0	20	36.0	45	23.2	29	20.0	25	4.8	6	100	125
Bini	12.5	1	25.0	2	25.0	2	37.5	3	0.0	0	100	8
All others[a]	20.0	1	40.0	2	20.0	1	20.0	1	0.0	0	100	5
TOTAL	17.0	27	34.6	55	24.5	39	20.1	32	3.8	6	100	159[a]

[a] Five Lagos entrepreneurs could not be rated on the success scale because of recent changes in the firm.

In summary, the following ordering of entrepreneurial performance by ethnic grouping is predicted on the basis of social structure and psychological testing: Ibo, Ibibio, Yoruba, Edo, and Hausa. The data do not contradict this prediction, but neither do they lend any support to it. An alternative hypothesis, that the differences in economic structure of the regions, exposure to western education, and "modern" occupational experience are responsible for the observed ethnic differences, cannot be rejected.

CONCLUSION

The fundamental methodological point stressed repeatedly here is the necessity for identifying separately the demand for entrepreneurial services (or structure of opportunities) and the supply of those services (or response to available opportunities). Given the limited number of situations which could be observed in the Nigerian context, it was impossible to distinguish confidently among social, psychological, and economic theories of entrepreneurial supply, since individuals from different ethnic groups (exhibiting somewhat different social and psychological characteristics) have had differential opportunities to obtain certain strategic skills and experience, and face rather different sets of potential opportunities. What is needed is the opportunity to observe groups of individuals from diverse social or ethnic backgrounds, with similar opportunities to obtain skills and experience and facing identical sets of potential entrepreneurial opportunities.[24] In the meantime, we must be content with the inconclusive observation that the evidence is largely consistent with either social and psychological or economic theories of entrepreneurial supply.[25] This deficiency is not inconsequential, since the policy implications of these theories are rather different.

The writer would like to go one step further, to suggest a plausible, eclectic interpretation. Both social and economic theories point to necessary but hardly sufficient conditions. Attractive economic opportunities may abound, yet remain unexploited if social or psychological attributes preclude individuals' responding to them. On the other hand, even though a number of individuals are prepared to enter entrepreneurial activity, there must be attractive economic potentialities for them to exploit. However, in the first case, entrepreneurship may be undertaken by foreigners or local pariah groups if the political structure allows, while in the second case only a change in the "objective" economic environment will be of any avail. It must, however, be recognized that there are important interrelationships among these variables. A lack of entrepreneurship can interact with an unfavorable economic environment to perpetuate a vicious circle of stagnation; similarly, changes in social or psychological variables, giving rise to the exercise of entrepreneurship, change the economic environment. This in turn brings about further changes in social and psychological variables leading on in a virtual circle. Just as one of the frequently mentioned functions of entrepreneurship is innovation which changes the economic environment, so economic change is capable of inducing substantial social change.[26]

The observations here, taken in conjunction with the several studies of entrepreneurship in other developing countries, suggest that changes in the economic environment can be sufficient to elicit a substantial quantity of entrepreneurial services, given the existence of groups within the society familiar with market-oriented activities.[27] The less favorable the social climate and the less transferable the skills and experience, the higher will be the price that must be paid to elicit a given quantity of entrepreneurship. Thus, in Pakistan, India, Turkey, and the Philippines, restrictions on foreign exchange made industry enormously profitable; the response to these new opportunities was rapid indeed.

Personality requirements for entrepreneurship seem to be quite specific. Willingness to forego immediate satisfaction for future gains, a degree of thrift, the desire to succeed, and the capacity for hard and continuing work are common attributes of most successful entrepreneurs. However, the number of such individuals needed to start a backward economy on the road to growth may be very small. In our sample, no industrialists were identified as coming from ethnic groups comprising over half the population of Nigeria. Nevertheless, from the standpoint of economic development it is relatively unimportant that several of these groups are almost entirely outside the cash economy and have social structures which are probably inimical to the exercise of entrepreneurship. What is important is that there are significant groups which have been engaged in the money economy for some period of time, and which have some individuals oriented to pecuniary incentives; and also that social structures are not wholly inhibitory to entrepreneurial activities. It would be surprising to find any African country in which no individuals possess the requisite personality characteristics to become entrepreneurs. The point to be made is that economic development can begin with a rather small cadre of entrepreneurs: as growth proceeds, changes will occur to draw additional groups into the nexus of the cash economy and to increase the supply of potential entrepreneurs through which growth can be maintained or accelerated.

NOTES

The author acknowledges support from the SSRC/ACLS Foreign Area Fellowship Program, the Northwestern University Council for Intersocial Research, the Nigerian Institute of Social and Economic Research, and the Computation Centers of Northwestern University and the Massachusetts Institute of Technology. He also expresses appreciation for helpful comments and suggestions from Professors H. F. Williamson, Sr., George Dalton, and J. R. T. Hughes of Northwestern University, and for the collaboration at several stages in the study of Mrs. Mary P. Rowe. The paper was drawn principally from Dr. Harris' doctoral dissertation, "Industrial Entrepreneurship in Nigeria" (Northwestern University, 1967).

1. This definition is essentially similar to what Frederick Harbison calls "organization" in "Entrepreneurial Organization as a Factor in Economic Development," *Quarterly Journal of Economics* 70: 3 (August 1956), or A. O. Hirschman's "ability to made development decisions," in *The Strategy of Economic Development* (New Haven: Yale University Press, 1958), p. 24.
2. The writer has developed two models which treat these concepts at length; he has surveyed the psychological, sociological,and historical literature on entrepreneurship in detail in "Industrial Entrepreneurship in Nigeria," chap. 2. See also W. Glade, "Approaches to a Theory of Entrepreneurial Formation," *Exploration in Economic History* (*EEH*, second series) 4: 3 (Spring 1967): and A. Alexander, "The Supply of Industrial Entrepreneurship," *EEH* (second series) 4: 2 (Winter 1967), pp. 136–49.
3. For one example, see N. S. Buchanan and H. S. Ellis, *Approaches to Economic Development* (New York: Twentieth Century Fund, 1955), pp. 74–87, quoted by A. H. Cole, *Business Enterprise*, who says: "No more economistic statement could be found. It seems to envisage a one-punch set of 'cultural changes' and it surely suggests that a dosage of capital is, to some extent, required in all alterations of social thought and practices."
4. E. E. Hagen, *On the Theory of Social Change* (Homewood, Ill.: The Dorsey Press, 1964), p. 239.
5. A. O. Hirschman, *The Strategy of Economic Development*, p. 25.
6. Both David Landes in "French Entrepreneurship and Industrial Growth in the Nineteenth Century," *Journal of Entrepreneurial History* (May 1949) and F. Harbinson and C. Myers in their book, *Management in the Industrial World – An International Analysis* (New York: McGraw-

Hill, 1959) appear to fall into the trap of making entrepreneurship important by definition. On the other hand, most of the growth models with which economists have been preoccupied concentrate exclusively on capital formation and population growth.

An illuminating controversy arose among Landes, Sawyer, and Gerschenkron. See D. Landes, "French Business and Businessmen in Social and Cultural Analysis," in E. Earle, ed., *Modern France* (Princeton N.J.: Princeton University Press, 1951), pp. 334–53; A. Gerschenkron, "Social Attitudes, Entrepreneurship, and Economic Development: A Comment," *EEH* (first series, May 1954); and J. Sawyer, "The Entrepreneur and the Social Order: France and the United States," in W. Miller (ed.), *Men in Business* (Cambridge, Mass.: Harvard University Press, 1952). The writer sides with Gerschenkron on this issue.

T. H. Burnham and G. O. Hoskins, *Iron and Steel in Britain, 1870–1930* (London: George Allen and Unwin, 1943), p. 271, attributed the decline of the British iron-and-steel industry to a failure of entrepreneurship by reasoning that: "If a business deteriorates it is of no use blaming anyone except those at the top. . . ." The error of such a simple-minded approach is clearly pointed out by P. Temin in "The Relative Decline of the British Steel Industry, 1880–1913," pp. 140–57 in H. Rosovsky (ed.) *Industrialization in Two Systems* (New York: John Wiley & Sons, 1966).

7. G. Papanek, "The Development of Entrepreneurship," *American Economic Review* 52: 2 (May 1962), pp. 46–58.
8. A. Alexander, *Greek Industrialists* (Athens: Center of Planning and Economic Research, 1965).
9. The concept of the economic environment is also discussed, though not as the demand for entrepreneurship, in the essay in this volume by Sayre P. Schatz, "Development in an Adverse Economic Environment." See also his earlier article, "Economic Environment and Private Enterprise in West Africa," *The Economic Bulletin* (Ghana) 7: 4 (December 1963).
10. G. Papanek, "Government and Private Enterprise in Pakistan." (Unpublished manuscript, Harvard University, 1964.)
11. The author conducted interviews with 101 firms outside of Lagos, and Mrs. Mary P. Rowe interviewed 168 Lagos firms. It is estimated that the combined sample contains more than 80 percent of the indigenous firms with more than twenty employees and approximately 35 percent of those with more than ten and fewer than twenty employees.

    In the earlier section of the paper it is stated that an operational definition of entrepreneurship should be applicable to many institutional settings. In this part of the study attention is focused only on individual capitalist-proprietors, although another part of the larger study considered expatriate and governmental firms to determine the locus of entrepreneurial function in large organizations.
12. Robert LeVine, *Dreams and Deeds* (Chicago: University of Chicago Press, 1966), p. 3.

13. A. O. Hirschman, *The Strategy of Economic Development*, p. 17.
14. See David McClelland, *The Achieving Society* (Princeton, N.J.: D. Van Nostrand Co., Inc., 1961), p. 238.
15. An article by Dr. Ademola Banjo, "The Image of Management," *Management in Nigeria* 1 : 2 (1965) contains several interesting examples.
16. J. D. Nyhart, "Notes on Entrepreneurship in Africa." (Unpublished manuscript, Center for International Affairs, Harvard University, November 11, 1961.) This study deals with the problem at length.
17. The United Africa Company, Shell BP, and Nigerian Tobacco Company have particularly successful management training schemes for Nigerians, several of whom are now functioning in senior positions in these firms.
18. G. Papanek, *American Economic Review* 52: 2 (May 1962): Alexander, *Greek Industrialists*; "Industrial Entrepreneurship in Turkey: Origins and Growth," *Economic Development and Cultural Change* 8: 4 (July 1960); John J. Carroll, *The Filipino Manufacturing Entrepreneur: Agent and Product of Change* (Ithaca, N.Y.: Cornell University Press, 1965); Yusif Sayigh, *Entrepreneurs of Lebanon* (Cambridge, Mass.: Harvard University Press, 1962); James J. Berna, *Industrial Entrepreneurship in Madras State* (London: Asia Publishing House, 1960); Thomas C. Cochran, *The Puerto Rican Businessmen: A Study in Cultural Change* (Philadelphia, Pa.: University of Pennsylvania Press, 1959). Each of these works is an empirical investigation of entrepreneurship in a developing economy.
19. One of the most dramatic examples of traditional influence on the character of "modern" activity is provided by Japan.
20. Several Nigerian industrialists have sons who have trained overseas and are beginning to reorganize the management of their firms in a manner which will allow orderly expansion. It is to be expected that as other second-generation industrialists come into control, many of the present organizational barriers to growth will be reduced.
21. This pattern of geographical immobility in industry is strikingly different from patterns of mobility in trade and transport. Two recent unpublished papers (presented to a conference on problems of integration and disintegration in Nigeria held at Northwestern University in March 1967), Robert H. T. Smith's "Interregional Trade in Nigeria – A Constraint on National Unity?" and E. W. Nafziger's "Interregional Economic Relations in Nigeria: The Case of the Footwear Industry," provide evidence of considerable interregional mobility of traders and transporters. However, both papers demonstrate that direct commercial contacts between ethnic groups are minimal. According to Nafziger, trading networks dealing in footwear can be identified as Ibo, Yoruba, or Hausa. Evidence is strong that credit extension between the ethnic groupings is relatively rare. Thus the mobility of individuals tends to be restricted to trading enclaves. Given the relatively easy transportability of inventories or vehicles, an individual remains fairly well protected against arbitrary action or expropriation.

    In industry, the situation is quite different. The essence of industrial production is that a fairly large investment is required in fixed assets which are not readily transportable. Hence an individual establishing an industry in an area occupied by "strangers" is extremely vulnerable to harassment. Furthermore, negotiating for raw materials, dealing with labor, and establishing distribution channels may be much easier for an individual with good local contacts and established position in the community.

22. Levine, *Dreams and Deeds.*
23. K. Onwuka Dike, *Trade and Politics in the Niger Delta 1830–1885* (Oxford: The Clarendon Press, 1956). This is a fascinating account of the decline of the slave trade and the rise of traffic in palm oil during the early period of European contact. Entrepreneurial drive was much in evidence on the part of the Delta residents, who fought to maintain their position as middlemen for all trade between the coast and the interior.
24. See W. Glade, "Approaches to a Theory of Entrepreneurial Formation."
25. For example, the Hausa's limited entry into industrial activity can be at least partly explained by their low levels of western education and experience in "modern" industrial undertaking. This lack of education and experience, however, can be attributed in part to deliberate colonial policy which, through indirect rule, limited the extent of western acculturation; but it can also be explained by cultural and psychological barriers to acculturation.

    It should be recalled that for Lagos alone more of the ceteris paribus assumptions are valid, so that the significance of ethnicity is reduced.
26. The several cases of traditional élites which turned to "modern" entrepreneurial activities in response to changed economic environment are interesting. See C. Geertz, *Peddlers and Princes* (Chicago, Ill.: University of Chicago Press, 1963) for a particularly illuminating account of one such group in Indonesia. See W. Moore, *Social Change* (Englewood Cliffs, N.J.: Prentice Hall, 1963), chap. 1. This contains an excellent discussion of the cumulative nature of change.
27. See footnote 18 for a partial list of references to the other studies.

Chapter 2

Development in an Adverse Economic Environment

Sayre P. Schatz

The impediments to the expansion of private business, and thus to economic development in countries relying on private enterprise to generate growth, can be divided into three categories: shortage of capital; deficiencies in entrepreneurial capacity (i.e. in the economic capability of the businessman himself, reflecting his knowledge, experience, skill and his inherent and/or socially-determined personal qualities); and difficulties in the economic environment. The term economic environment refers here to all the factors impinging upon the operation of a business other than the availability of capital and the ability of the businessman himself – problems in securing the proper equipment in reasonable time and in good working order, problems of human resources, of infrastructure, of supplies, of adequate markets, etc. This paper suggests that special difficulties are encountered in the economic environment of an underdeveloped economy, and that because of these an African businessman having adequate capital and a reasonable degree of entrepreneurial ability will have a considerably more difficult time in business than his equally well financed and talented counterpart in a more developed economy. Many of the environmental adversities hinder impartially all firms in Africa, whether foreign or indigenously owned. Many others apply largely or wholly to indigenous entrepreneurs alone.

This essay undertakes to present the concept of the economic environment as an obstacle to economic development; to set forth the hypothesis that it is one of the major impediments to development in Africa; and to support this hypothesis by delineating the special difficulties in the economic environment in Africa.[1] This delineation of the nature and scope of the environmental difficulties constitutes the bulk of the paper, and in carrying it out I refine and extend an earlier discussion of the economic environment.[2] The final section of the essay discusses the significance of the economic environment and revises an earlier statement regarding its paramount importance.

THE ALIEN SOCIAL MILIEU OF BUSINESS

Even in non-settler economies like Nigeria's, African businessmen operate in a significantly alien economic network. They may sell to or buy from foreign-owned enterprises; they may compete with such enterprises; they may export or import; they may seek financing from expatriate[3] banks; they may deal with foreign managers, engineers, accountants or other consultants and even with foreign personnel in the African government. Even if they are not in direct contact with foreigners, African businessmen have to deal with companies and government agencies that are run by modern (i.e. expatriate rather than traditional) standards. The rules and procedures of the economy, the personnel to a significant extent, the unspoken and unconscious presumptions and judgments, and even the language are of alien origin. Problems arising out of the alien character of the social milieu in which indigenous business must function are discussed in this section and those arising out of the alien economic milieu are discussed in the following section.

1. African businessmen miss out on opportunities for lack of social contact. In the relatively small expatriate business communities in African countries, foreign businessmen are likely to know one another personally or to have mutual friends. Even when not personally acquainted, "they share a common culture and a common knowledge of their society. Dress, manner, background, personal history are mutually intelligible. . . .There are also clubs and informal social networks which facilitate and reinforce business relations."[4] For the African businessman the

absence of this kind of rapport is an impediment. It is important, for example, in making sales, and is particularly important when (as is frequently the case in Africa) those making the purchasing decisions lack the expertise required for judging the quality of many of the goods and services they have to buy, and therefore rely on personal relationships. In general, many kinds of assistance, advice, and information, from bankers, suppliers, and other business colleagues, tend to flow less freely when business relationships are unlubricated by the camaraderie of ethnic similarity.

2. Non-involvement in the social milieu also results in discrimination against capable African businessmen. Leaving aside blatant prejudice – which exists, but whose adverse effects on the indigenous entrepreneur require no elucidation – there is also a more subtle form of discrimination, which may be called *probabilistic discrimination*. This may be practiced by men of good will toward Africans. More important, given the disparate social networks, it may be commercially justified.

Because of the social separateness, "all Africans look alike" in a figurative sense to many foreign firms, especially those without long experience in Africa. They find it extremely difficult to differentiate – to distinguish among the many Africans with business aspirations who may be inefficient, incapable of turning out a product of uniform quality and making regular deliveries, less than punctilious in meeting business obligations, etc., and those indigenous entrepreneurs who run their businesses capably and carefully. In these circumstances, African businessmen (including the capable ones) tend to be passed over in various business dealings simply on the basis of probabilities.

Thus, an outstanding Nigerian firm that rewound electrical generators was passed over in this way. Although its work was as good as or better than that of any other firm in the country,[5] some foreign-owned firms that were potential customers were unaware or skeptical of this, or simply ignored this firm. Acting in accord with the general probability, they gave their work to an expatriate rewinder. (The proprietor, at the time of my most recent information, was trying to meet this problem by creating an image of a firm substantially capitalized and run by foreigners.) In foreign trade, too, probabilistic discrimination has handicapped Nigerians. In timber and rubber, Levantine exporters have had a slight marketing advantage over Nigerians because the former have been scrupulous in all their dealings, while many Nigerians have not;[6] this has undermined the reputations even of those Nigerians who have been blameless. Discrimination based on probabilities also affects bank credit, viz. the case of a Nigerian firm that could not get overdraft privileges from an expatriate bank despite its solid business record until a foreigner (and thus a distinct individual with a clearly defined identity) made the arrangements. Even consumers, including Nigerian consumers, share this prejudice; they are predisposed in favor of imported rather than domestically produced goods.

3. The fact that the language of commerce and government is a foreign tongue (English or French in most African countries) sometimes causes problems. Some African businessmen have not mastered the language; this is one of the reasons why few Northern Nigerian merchants have engaged in exporting or importing. Even for those who are relatively proficient in the language of commerce, communication is not always as clear or conclusive as it should be. Thus, one Nigerian company encountered delays in the construction of a building it needed, and had to devote valuable managerial time to the process, because the expatriate architect and the African contractor were not always able to make themselves clear to one another. The managers of the firm acquiring the building had to participate in the planning and decision-making process every step of the way.

It might be mentioned that language problems also arise between Nigerians. While complex and delicate relationships can be sustained among businessmen of the same tribe, language barriers sometimes complicate dealings between different ethnic groups. In Nigeria's kola trade, for example, the many intricate matters of storing, packing, shipping the kola nut, of securing credit, and of mutual confidence among those engaged in the trade are "made more difficult and complicated by the differences in language and cultural tradition between the centres of consumption in the North and the centres of production in the South – more specifically between Hausa and Yoruba respectively."[7]

THE ALIEN ECONOMIC MILIEU

The economic milieu of business, like the social milieu, is significantly alien in Africa. Many of the conditions and parameters of the economy have been established by and adjusted to foreign participation. Being required to operate in this alien economic network entails difficulties for African businessmen.

1. There are personnel problems. To the extent that an indigenous firm requires upper- or even middle-level manpower, it has been faced with salary and perquisite levels arising mainly out of the colonial situation and subsequent political developments, and inappropriate to the economic conditions of poor countries. Earnings have been based upon the relatively high inducements that were required during the colonial period to persuade Europeans to work and live in the tropics. Under conditions of nationalist agitation for independence it was politically impossible to do anything but institute the same rewards for Africans and then to carry the relative salary standards over into the post-colonial era. Expatriate firms have also been willing to pay high salaries for upper-level Africans because, under nationalist pressure, they have been buying not only managerial or other skill but also good public relations and political acceptability.[8] The cost and difficulty of hiring capable personnel have been further increased by the sanguine expectations of Africans in government or expatriate firms. Africanization of the civil service and in foreign companies has resulted in abundant opportunities for special training and exhilarating possibilities of rapid advancement in government and foreign enterprises, opportunities which indigenous firms cannot match.[9]

2. Economic patterns developed by or adapted to foreign enterprises hamper African businesses in other ways. For example, they make it more difficult for Nigerian firms to get credit, entirely aside from any matter of discrimination. Short-term bank loans in Nigeria are not ordinarily very profitable, and such credit is dispensed partially as an accommodation to firms with numerous overseas transactions, for banks earn attractive commissions on these. Most African firms, however, have relatively few overseas transactions; they therefore do not fall into the category of favored customers and so have low-priority claims on bank credit. Another example is

provided by welfare legislation. Labor costs are raised for the successful African firm because, as it grows, it encounters labor and social welfare codes designed for expatriate enterprises. African employers find it hard to meet standards regarding working conditions, minimum wages, vacations, hospitalization, etc. originally intended for large foreign firms.[10]

3. Then there is the special competitive problem that arises from the necessity of competing in the alien economic network. Compared with foreign-owned companies, indigenous firms suffer from entrepreneurial shortcomings and from differential economic-environmental difficulties, i.e. those difficulties which have a more pronounced impact on indigenous than on expatriate firms.

Even in an economy without competition from expatriate firms, the entrepreneurial and environmental problems would constitute a heavy drag on the indigenous businesses. They would increase costs, reduce receipts, and render unattractive a broad margin of projects that would be profitable in the absence of these problems. Still, there would be many ventures that indigenous firms could undertake profitably. Returns would be lower than they might otherwise be, but nevertheless the undertakings would be viable. Since expatriate firms do in fact compete with indigenous firms, however, many of the projects that the latter could otherwise profitably undertake are pre-empted or are rendered more precarious by the superior competitive power of the former. The indigenous firm may be likened to an infant industry facing competition with mature foreign companies; but since the foreign competitors operate within the borders of the less developed country, no tariff protection is possible.[11]

SEVERE INDIGENOUS COMPETITION

The competition faced by Nigerian businessmen is – even aside from expatriate competition – often unusually severe.

The problem arises from the large number of eager entrants into most lines of business, hopeful of earning even a small income. There can be little doubt that Nigerians display an abundance of "entrepreneurial spirit" – if we mean by this a willingness to venture, to work hard, to seek far and wide and to take chances in the quest for profit.[12] This abundance of entrepreneurial spirit is manifested in the rush of hopeful Nigerian businessmen into any line in which some pioneers are prospering.[13] This rush is caused not by imitativeness, as is frequently said, but by the pressure of innumerable hopeful entrepreneurs looking for profit opportunities. Aspiring Nigerian businessmen also press out in all directions. Any venture that has the remotest prospect of profit attracts aspiring entrepreneurs. Applicants to government loans boards have applied for loans for a vast variety of different business ventures.[14] Nigerian entrepreneurs are not wedded to any particular kind of venture; they are willing to seek fortune wherever it may require them to go. Thus in an unpublished government survey of 626 very small-scale producers in Western Nigeria, 216 responded in the affirmative when asked if they would abandon their present businesses for another which appeared more promising.

Excessive entry puts great pressure on all businessmen in the industry. A competitive equilibrium is reached, economic theory tells us, when pure profits disappear and the entrepreneur earns only a competitive return on his own inputs – his capital, labor, and managerial services. In the absence of profit prospects, further entry is inhibited. Under Nigerian conditions, however, the minimum acceptable "wage of management" is so low that entry continues long after it would stop in an advanced economy. Moreover, imperfect knowledge often causes continued entry even when minimum wages of management can no longer be earned. Under these circumstances, the competition sometimes becomes almost pathological.[15]

The erosion of profits affects not only businessmen who approximate pure competitors, but also those who have managed to secure a pure profit by differentiating their output or by superior efficiency or some other competitive superiority. Excessive entry affects even the large expatriate firms.[16]

ACQUIRING CAPITAL GOODS AND SUPPLIES

Enterprises operating in Africa encounter many cost-increasing difficulties in acquiring the capital goods, intermediate goods, and raw materials they need.

1. Frequently ordering at long distance and without good contacts and buying in a world that generally does not design equipment for African conditions, African firms often find it virtually impossible to order the best equipment for their purposes. Thus, a Nigerian printing firm, in which an American management adviser and investor had a substantial interest, placed an order for a sizeable package of interrelated printing equipment from an American manufacturer. The precise kinds of equipment to order were carefully decided in close consultation by the Nigerian entrepreneur, the American management adviser, and the representative in Nigeria of the equipment manufacturer. Fortunately, before the equipment order was filled, the American (for reasons not related to the equipment purchase) made a trip back to the United States and took the opportunity to visit the manufacturer of the equipment. When he discussed the order there in the same way that he had discussed it with the manufacturer's representative in Nigeria, he was informed that he had not ordered the best equipment for the printing firm's purposes. Following the manufacturer's advice, he was able to purchase equipment that was not only more suitable but that also saved approximately 15 percent on the original £180,000 purchase. Most African firms, however, are not able to rectify mistakes of this nature by discussing their orders with the head offices of the supplying companies. One of Nigeria's leading indigenous industrial firms, for example, ordered a machine for producing camelback, a necessary component in the tire-retreading process, that they were told was large enough to supply all three of their plants. After laying out the money for the equipment (and after a series of expensive difficulties in setting up and installing the equipment), the firm discovered that the capacity of the machine was actually insufficient for even one of its factories. The firm therefore had to undertake the additional expense (£28,000) of ordering more equipment.

A firm operating in Africa often has less precise knowledge of and control over the exact nature of imported supplies than does a firm operating in an advanced economy where it is aided by highly developed international marketing facilities. As a result the entrepreneur in Africa is more likely to order supplies that are not fully suited to his purposes.[17] An example is provided by the Nigerian factory for rubber-soled shoes, established with the latest plant and equipment in 1959, which suffered expensive and protracted delays because the raw material imports proved unsatisfactory.

2. Whether or not he ordered suitable equipment or other inputs, the businessman operating in Africa has not uncommonly found that the goods specified were not delivered or did not arrive in good condition. A river transport firm, e.g., ran into serious difficulty because the launch it ordered from the United Kingdom was damaged during transit, and the damage was not fully covered by insurance.[18] Damage or deterioration during transit is a common problem. Moreover, the equipment the entrepreneur finally gets may not be exactly what he desires or specified – as in the case of a printer who found that the machine he understood was earmarked for him had been sold, with the result that he purchased an alternate costing 50 percent more.

3. The African firm, particularly the indigenous one, tends to pay a high price for its equipment and other inputs, even aside from importing costs. The printing firm mentioned above, whose American participant fortunately paid a visit to the equipment manufacturer, saved approximately £25,000 on an original order of £180,000. The African entrepreneur also loses out on the chance for special bargains that occasionally present themselves to a buyer on the spot. The ability of the indigenous firm to get special discounts, to buy below list price, to receive extra services that in effect shave the price a little, is very limited compared to that of firms operating in advanced economies – it is in fact more limited than that of foreign-owned firms operating in Africa, for these firms have extensive contacts in the equipment-producing countries.

The cost of constructing appropriate premises may also be very high. While the construction of standard types of structures has not been expensive, costs soar tremendously if anything unusual is to be done. For example, while standard steel window frames are manufactured in Nigeria, frames of a special size or finish must be imported. If carpentry is required except for doors and windows, little finished lumber is delivered to the job, and the labor force must square and plane this material before use. Factors of this nature may easily double or triple construction costs per square foot.[19]

4. Inordinate delays in getting equipment once it has been ordered also increase costs. This has been a common problem, and not only for businessmen but for government undertakings as well; the pumps required for the Aba urban water system evidently took more than two years to arrive.[20] For more complicated projects that require estimates, the orders themselves are sometimes delayed because indigenous entrepreneurs cannot interest potential suppliers in submitting the estimates until they can demonstrate that they already have a firm assurance of the funds.[21]

5. Delays in getting ancillary equipment or other appurtenances necessary to start operating the machinery are sometimes more excruciating than the wait for the basic equipment itself. Thus, a printer who bought a stitching machine from a local supplier found that the supplier did not have the wire necessary for operating the machinery. The printer, at considerable cost to himself, had the supplier order the wire by air and received it in two weeks. This wire was found to be the wrong kind. Another delay ensued while work was piling up. During the entire period before the correct stitching wire arrived, the equipment dealer maintained that he was not responsible for the wire needed for the stitching machine, just as a car dealer is not responsible for the petrol needed for a car.

6. Equipment ordered from abroad encounters many expensive installation difficulties in Africa. For example, the boilers for Textile Printers of Nigeria, a United Africa Company subsidiary, weighed forty-five tons instead of the expected thirty-seven tons. As a result, the intended means of transporting them across the Niger proved inadequate, and it took a full month rather than two days to get the boilers across. During this period, wage and similar costs continued to accrue. Another large textile firm that did not supervise carefully enough found that its looms had been improperly installed and, partially for this reason, scrapped them and purchased new ones.[22] The printing firm with the American partner, already mentioned, also incurred unexpectedly high installation costs. Continuous and close consultation between the architect and the machinery supplier was impossible, for the former was in Nigeria while the latter was overseas. As a result, the building was not designed with precisely the right clearances for the

machinery, and expensive changes in construction were subsequently required. Equipment of any size or complexity often requires the importing firm to bring in an engineer or technician from the supplying country. This is not only costly but may cause delays until properly qualified personnel in the supplying country can be spared. Moreover, the technicians available for such overseas assignments are often not of the requisite ability. One large indigenous firm, for example, found after ten costly months that the German engineer hired to set up their German equipment was incapable of doing the job, and the firm therefore had to hire other technical personnel to do the installation properly.

Because of the difficulties and delays in getting, installing, and beginning operation of equipment, starting a project in Nigeria requires, in the words of one expatriate, "substantially more capital, especially working capital" than in a more developed economy.

7. Once the equipment has started operating, there are problems in getting the supplies and replacement parts necessary to keep it operating. For one thing, slow and irregular deliveries and the frequent unavailability of substitutes force the producer in Africa to sink more capital than his advanced-economy counterpart into large stocks. When the enterprise operates on a small scale, as is usually the case, and when at the same time a fairly large number of different materials and intermediate goods are used, this is an expensive burden. This is particularly true when the firm has to import its supplies directly (e.g. an indigenously-owned printing firm with specialized photogravure equipment, which was the sole importer of the specialized reels of paper and photogravure inks) and especially when the firm's orders are small (for small orders are harder to handle at the docks and are subject to especially long delays). Supplies from domestic sources, incidentally, need stocking just as much as do imports. A steady flow of uniform quality goods can no more be relied upon from domestic producers than from foreign suppliers.

Still, firms often find that their stocks have been inadequate to prevent idling of equipment or even complete cessation of production. Some interruptions in supplies are of a nature or duration that cannot be foreseen. In one case a special battery used in a dictaphone went dead. The owner found that neither the local nor the national branches of the firm that supplied the dictaphone had the batteries. The firm had given up the agency for the product. From its stock it could still supply the entire machine, complete with batteries, but not the batteries separately. The supplier's head office in England replied to a query that such matters were handled in Nigeria. Finally, the manufacturer in Germany agreed to send the necessary batteries on receipt of the correct payment. Unfortunately the machine had stood idle so long in the humid climate by the time the batteries arrived that it had deteriorated and no longer worked. To the outside observer, this case was painful but funny. In a more serious case encountered by this writer during one of his visits to a successful Nigerian mattress producer, the shop was completely idle except for a few women combing out coir fiber by hand. The workers were there (and drawing their pay); the demand for the products of the firm was sufficient; the equipment was in good working order. The trouble was that the stock of a seemingly insignificant ribbon used to bind the seams of the mattresses had run out. According to the entrepreneur, the ribbon had been ordered from abroad in plenty of time, with a substantial leeway for delays in delivery. However, due to difficulties which the entrepreneur did not yet fully understand, delivery of the ribbon had been delayed so long that the firm's supply was exhausted and production petered out to virtually nothing. The firm had made efforts to secure a substitute locally but these had not been successful.

8. The life expectancy of equipment is frequently shorter in tropical Africa than in the more developed areas. The humid climate, the lack of skill and experience of the operators, the less expert maintenance services, and similar factors all tend to shorten the working life of machinery. This life is often shortened also by careless handling. An outstanding Nigerian businessman told me, for example, that he figures on only six months of service from his delivery vans although the same kind of vans operating in the United Kingdom last an average of two years. Poor maintenance and poor roads are partly responsible, but the biggest factor, he says, is poor and reckless driving. In a six-month period in 1961, he lost through accidents seven vehicles out of a modest-sized fleet. He was compensated by

insurance for only three of these; the other four accidents were the fault of his drivers; he says that for that reason he got no compensation.

HUMAN RESOURCES

The African firm's human resource difficulties – problems regarding the productivity, responsibility, availability, etc. of human inputs – take many forms.

1. The literature on African unskilled and semi-skilled labor is voluminous, so that this issue will merely be touched upon here. Despite what may be called European folklore to the contrary, careful studies suggest that it is not high-unit-cost labor. Peter Kilby, who has done considerable interesting work in this area, has concluded that "we may dismiss a number of problems commonly claimed to be impeding the progress of industrialization in Africa. These include problems of labor recruitment, commitment to wage-earning, adverse effects of labour migration, impaired productive capacity as a result of excessive absenteeism, and barriers to the development of a skilled labour force as a result of labour instability."[23]

This is not to say that African labor productivity may not often be low – partly because of managerial and supervisory deficiencies,[24] and partly because of inexperience, illiteracy, language problems which hamper communication with fellow nationals of different ethnic groups and with Europeans, intertribal friction, debilitating diseases and malnutrition, and other problems. Lower productivity, however, is usually counterbalanced by lower wages. For example, while Nigeria's labor productivity in textiles was approximately half of Britain's, unit labor costs were lower because the hourly wage was one-sixth that of Britain.[25]

2. Higher-level manpower constitutes, however, a serious problem. Skilled labor is in short supply and tends to be inferior because of deficiencies in training, education, and the problems mentioned in the preceding paragraph.

Supervisory and managerial personnel involve an even more serious problem. The supply of secondary school graduates, the usual source of such personnel, has been limited relative to the demands of government and business and the beckoning opportunities for higher education. There has been rapid turnover, and the educational drain has created a negative selection process which has left a high proportion of those in business, particularly with indigenous firms, of mediocre quality.[26] "With few exceptions among firms employing over twenty-five, the inadequacy of Nigerian supervisory performance was reported by management to be their chief problem in the labour field."[27] The unpredictable nature of some of the problems is illustrated by the experience of a Lagos electronics firm. Their production was interrupted by their production control supervisor who, after several quarrels with the foreman, petulantly withheld parts from the assembly line.[28] With respect to Nigerian managerial personnel, there is virtually universal testimony by businessmen, indigenous and foreign, as well as by scholars that it is deficient in supply and inadequate in quality.[29]

3. Overseas sources of higher-level personnel are often resorted to, but such sources have been generally unsatisfactory. For one thing, they are "fiendishly expensive."[30] As an inducement for overseas work, salaries of such personnel tend to be high; estimates range from an average of 50 percent to 100 percent greater than home-country salaries. Travel and other allowances must be paid. And there are other expenses as well. For example, the cost of constructing housing for the expatriate personnel of a proposed company to be set up in Northern Nigeria was actually expected to be 50 percent greater than the cost of the proposed factory building. The housing amounted to approximately 40 per cent of the total fixed capital of the firm.

Hiring foreign personnel involves substantial drawbacks besides the direct expense, especially for indigenous firms. Expatriates working for African firms are not so conscientious or so interested in the success of the enterprise as those working for European-owned firms. Their careers and personal interests are not usually so firmly bound up with those of an indigenous firm as with those of an expatriate firm. Foreigners working for African firms expect to return to their own countries, often within two or three years' time,[31] and then will probably sever their connections with the indigenously owned firm, unlike employees of large expatriate companies who are doing a tour of service in Africa. This may mean a devastating loss of managerial familiarity with the particular circumstances of the indigenous firm. In one case, a Nigerian-owned firm hired a British technician for £1800, £700 more than he was getting in England. His salary was increased to £2300. Gradually the business was built around him. After a few years, however, he decided he wanted to leave Nigeria. The last information the author had was that the employer had offered a £3000 salary, but did not yet know whether this would be sufficient to induce the expatriate to stay. The quality of foreign personnel is often, even usually, disappointing. Indigenous firms, having limited contacts overseas, have often hired people who proved incompetent. Several successful Nigerian businessmen have told me of such experiences, and some have forsworn foreign personnel completely. Nafziger also relates the case of a Nigerian footwear manufacturing firm that "out of reaction to the ineptness of foreign managers in [another firm] . . . decided to rely only on Nigerian entrepreneurs."[32] Technical personnel can sometimes be secured for a limited period on secondment from an equipment-supplying firm. But if the Nigerian firm wants a permanent technical employee or a manager, it finds that the persons available "are often second-rate, but yet have to be paid very highly."[33]

4. The shortage of higher-grade manpower sometimes imposes substantial training expenses upon firms operating in Nigeria. For example, a Nigerian company which purchased complex photogravure rotary printing equipment had to send some of its employees to England for a year's study. The training expenses were, of course, considerably greater than those that would have been incurred by a British firm, even assuming that the latter could not have employed workers already capable of operating the equipment. Some firms find it necessary to establish expensive training facilities that they would not need in advanced economies. The cost of these programs has been enhanced by the substantial difficulty firms in Nigeria have had in retaining their trainees. They are not only lured away by other employers, but a great many have used their additional training and savings from enhanced incomes as a springboard for entry into universities.

5. From the vantage point of the firm, the human-resource

problems discussed so far are primarily internal, but there are also difficulties that are mainly external. The problems of servicing and repair of equipment may be either, depending on whether such jobs are performed by employees or outside firms. In any case, it is difficult to find competent personnel for servicing or repair jobs that are somewhat out of the ordinary. I have seen cases in which equipment breakdowns have idled entire plants for more than a week. Larger firms sometimes turn to the expensive alternative of hiring foreigners for maintenance and servicing at salaries far above their remuneration at home.[34]

6. Consultants, specialists, subsidiary services of all kinds, and sources of advice and information are often lacking altogether in Africa, and when available they are frequently of low quality and are more expensive than in more developed economies. Market research services are inadequate; capable accounting services may be unavailable; consulting engineers and architects are few. These services are often crucial for firms operating in the difficult economic environment of Africa.[35]

A substantial array of subsidiary sources of information and advice available, and often free, to businessmen in developed economies may be unavailable in Africa. Financial institutions in advanced economies have "usually provided technical advice and maintained close continuing relations with the enterprises in which they invested."[36] Suppliers of machinery and materials are often in close contact with their domestic customers and offer useful advice and information. Managers in advanced economies benefit from the counsel of expert and broadly experienced directors and advisers.[37] Many entrepreneurs in advanced economies receive a great deal of highly useful information from trade and business associations.[38] Universities, government agencies and other organizations in advanced economies also provide valuable advice and information.[39] Unfortunately, assistance from these sources is usually unobtainable in Africa.

The lack of technical expertise and advice is perhaps the most keenly felt. Modest technical jobs may be prohibitively expensive. A small Nigerian businessman producing simple science equipment for schools cited examples in which local costs were literally fifty times greater than those in advanced economies. The choice between alternate sets of equipment has to be made blindly. The most important obstacle to business success in Nigerian sawmilling, according to Harris, may be the difficulty of "obtaining technical information that will enable the entrepreneur to select the appropriate equipment and supervise its operation." This difficulty "explains a good bit of the low quality of sawing and poor maintenance of equipment."[40]

Foreign consultants, like managerial personnel, have proven costly and unsatisfactory. An internal report on the Nigerian Public Works Department (applicable to the private sector as well) delineates some of the problems. First, foreign consultants "insist on high standards in order to maintain their professional reputations and tend to impose European standards" inappropriately. Second, they "need to be briefed by [busy local personnel] with a knowledge of the local background and needs." Third, "all the knowledge and experience of local conditions gained from their work . . . departs with them . . ." Fourth, "their recommendations at all stages normally take the form of alternatives," and overworked local personnel must then take the time to make the decisions. Foreign consultants have often given bad advice.[41] Sometimes they simply have been unwilling to allot enough time to do an effective job.[42]

GOVERNMENTAL PROBLEMS

1. Attitudes of government personnel in new countries are frequently unaccommodating or impeditive. A survey of business revealed strong feelings on this score:[43]

> Both internal and external business would be much facilitated if departmental staffs (particularly those junior grades with whom the public has most contact) were to be made to understand the importance of business to the life of the country. The usual attitude at present varies between disinterestedness and deliberate obstruction. The question seems to be not "How can I help this person?" but "What can I do (exceeding the limits of my authority if necessary) to hold up this transaction?"

As a result, the simplest piece of business takes more time

> and trouble than it should and frequently requires the attention of a senior instead of a junior employee before it can be done at all. This adds considerably to the actual cost of operating a business and involves uneconomic use of manpower.

This comment, while coming from a foreign firm, expresses African feeling as well. In Ghana, the chairman of the Ghana National Liberation Council, General Ankrah, reflected similar resentments in castigating civil servants for "slipshodness, laziness, apathy, improper practices, lack of integrity, and ineptitude seriously rampant among public servants."[44]

2. Governmental fractiousness has been intensified by – or perhaps it is simply a reflection of – national and class differences. In the colonial period a substantial gulf frequently existed between foreign officials and African businessmen. Even after independence one encounters numerous examples of profound misunderstanding and antagonism between expatriate civil servants and indigenous entrepreneurs. This problem rapidly diminishes with Africanization and with changes in the attitudes of foreigners working for African governments, but has been partially replaced by a different, and narrower, gulf between African officials and African businessmen. While the Africans who hold managerial positions with large concerns have considerable influence in dealing with their former schoolmates, personal friends and social peers who are the government officials, independent Nigerian businessmen are usually from a different social class and tend to encounter governmental contrariety. Foreign businessmen also find that friction and misunderstanding with African officials interfere with investment-incentive measures. Delays and palaver with respect to tax incentives, land acquisition, immigration quotas, etc. are commonplace and well known.

3. Even when civil servants are friendly, Nigerian businessmen find government unwilling to extend business-incentive provisions to them. Government concessions to investors are intended for relatively large, hence almost invariably foreign, investors. Although indigenous businessmen often feel that this involves an infuriating kind of neo-colonialist discrimination against Africans, government policy-makers are probably correct in believing that the benefits to be derived from

administering these complex programs for small business would not justify the costs.[45]

4. Finally, two widely discussed governmental problems deserve at least brief mention. The capability of the young governments in Africa is often still limited. This "in some instances . . . constitutes the most serious of all obstacles to economic development."[46] There generally has not been sufficient time to establish a solid government apparatus, manned by competent, experienced personnel, and free of serious staff shortages. Bungling often results. For example, the Nigerian Ports Authority, in what businessmen consider a typically feckless fashion, introduced new regulations governing the handling of dangerous and hazardous goods, but neglected to give advance notice to users of the port facilities. Considerable unnecessary expense and inconvenience resulted from the abrupt imposition of the new regulations.[47] Another common syndrome in newly developing countries – undergoing rapid social transformation, discarding old values and patterns before fully developing new ones, exposed to the personal gain philosophy that is the mainspring of capitalism – is a proliferation of corruption and favoritism. Most small businessmen believe that they suffer from such practices.

INFRASTRUCTURAL PROBLEMS

The fact that inadequate infrastructures in less developed economies increase costs and reduce potential receipts is thoroughly familiar and needs no extended discussion. Still, the following announcement may serve as vivid reminder of the impact of infrastructural deficiencies in Africa: "The Nigerian Cement Company Ltd. regrets to announce that due to the failure of the Electricity Corporation of Nigeria to supply sufficient power to the cement works at Nkalagu, production of cement has been drastically reduced . . . Effective immediately and until further notice, sales . . . are suspended. The Electricity Corporation of Nigeria is at present unable to give a firm date for resumption of full power to Nkalagu. We are therefore unable to give any indication as to when production will be back to normal."[48]

The frustration and rage generated by these difficulties is

sometimes explosive. Citing a case in which seven wagon carloads of gari were completely spoiled because they had been delayed for weeks by the railroad, the Kaduna Branch of the Northern Nigerian Gari Traders Union demanded that the Federal Minister of Transport institute a full-scale inquiry into the Nigerian Railway Corporation's "deliberate infliction of losses to gari traders."[49]

OTHER COST-INCREASING PROBLEMS

There are many other cost-increasing problems. Some will be mentioned in this section and there are undoubtedly others which have not come to my attention.

There are site problems. As a direct or indirect result of traditional land-tenure relations, it is sometimes difficult to make satisfactory arrangements regarding a business site. There are often an assortment of time-consuming legal problems and lawsuits.[50] A Nigerian construction and civil engineering firm, which received a Federal Loans Board loan of £11,000 to finance expansion, ran into such problems, despite assistance from a sympathetic government agency. More than three years after the loan was approved, a government report stated that the project "did not materialize owing to the inability of the company to obtain a good site. The original site obtained is being contested . . ." The project was being abandoned and the company was repaying the loan.[51] Delays of this nature also occur, as a result of locally-instituted court actions, even when a firm leases land from government.

There are credit problems. Long-standing customers, under strain because of social change, may suddenly and unexpectedly default on credit.[52]

There are knowledge problems. Aside from the already discussed problems in making information available, little may be known about the countries' natural resources and their manufacturing and processing qualities, and about the applicability of various techniques of production under African climatic conditions.

THE MARKET

The size of the market has always been considered critical in the literature on economic development. For Adam Smith it governed the division of labor and thus the level of technology. Rosenstein-Rodan stressed the pivotal role of market magnitude in a seminal article published at the very beginning of the contemporary revival of interest in development.[53] Nurkse stated his "modern variant" of Smith's thesis: "The inducement to invest is limited by the size of the market."[54] Many others have amplified the point.[55] In Africa, of course, it hardly needs saying that the small-market handicap is endemic.

Leaving aside considerations of aggregate market size, the market may also be niggardly relative to the productive capacity existing at any given time. This has been the case in Nigeria; considerable excess capacity has been common during the 1960s.[56] In visits to indigenously owned enterprises, it was commonplace to see workers and equipment, some of it modern and technologically advanced, standing idle for lack of demand for the firm's output. I have encountered this in printing, cushions, pillows and mattresses, wooden furniture, rubber-soled shoes, leather shoes, sawmilling, gramophone recording, car servicing and repairing, tailoring, hotels, soap, modern production of chickens and eggs, baking, and other lines. Others, in intensive studies of particular industries, have made similar observations. In sawmilling, John Harris concluded "that demand is the most serious problem facing the industry today" and that "expansion [of productive capacity] has been faster than the growth of . . . markets."[57] In modern wooden furniture, he also found that marketing has been the major problem, and that (although there were conceptual difficulties of measurement) there appeared to be underutilization of capacity.[58] Nafziger similarly found that idle capacity because of demand limitations was important in the shoe industry.[59]

It is worth mentioning that problems are caused by limited markets for by-products as well as for a firm's principal product. Thus, groundnut crushers in Northern Nigeria have been handicapped because, unlike foreign crushers, they have had virtually no local market for the groundnut cake left after the oil is extracted. Local farmers do not feed their cattle groundnut cake because it is cheaper to graze their cattle around the countryside.[60]

MARKETING CHANNELS

The underdeveloped marketing network impedes the expansion of domestic firms. Producers trying to reach the domestic market can generally do so adequately only through one of the large national trading companies. For many reasons, however, these organizations have been reluctant to handle new locally produced goods. The regular suppliers of their big-selling, well-known lines tend to be antagonistic. The trading firms may lack the facilities to stock or display a larger variety of brands[61] and they may be reluctant to sink money into larger inventories. Particularly in the case of indigenously produced goods, they may have found that quality was uneven and delivery was uncertain.[62] Officials who have tried to persuade the large sales outlets to deal with Nigerian suppliers have had little success.

Capable salesmen, sales agents, or other dealers are hard to find. For example, a Nigerian firm signed a contract with a "van promotion contractor" who used sound-equipped vans to promote sales in "up-country" villages. The van salesman, however, tried to demonstrate the radios during the day in areas which received only inadequate daytime transmission. He therefore did more harm than good, for the audiences thought that the radios were defective.[63] Sometimes the sales agents cannot be trusted. When Nigerian entrepreuneurs were asked about obstacles to the formation of joint ventures with other Nigerian businessmen, 74 percent of those surveyed spoke of financial untrustworthiness.[64]

There are other marketing problems. Insurance of goods in transit is not yet highly developed although the risks are substantial.[65] Advertising costs have been estimated to be triple those of similar advertising in the United States and, moreover, there is a widely-held belief (or guess) that advertising is not very effective.[66] Even the pattern of consumer preferences may inhibit expansion. Kilby has maintained that there is an extremely strong preference for the cheapest product even if it is of substantially poorer quality. "A producer must turn out a product whose quality is markedly greater than those of his competitors before the consumer is willing to pay a higher price."[67] If this is true, it tends to impede at least one method of expansion, through producing a higher quality product.

Inadequacy of the marketing network is in many cases an important factor limiting expansion. It has been one of the decisive factors restricting the growth of Nigerian shoe factories.[68] Feeble marketing systems have hampered entrepreneurs in the sawmilling and wooden furniture industries.[69] Marketing control problems have been a critical factor curtailing company growth in the bread industry.[70] A leading indigenous druggist and distributor of pharmaceutical products was unable, on more than one occasion, to take up advantageous opportunities to become the sole distributor for Nigeria of imported pharmaceuticals because of the nonexistence of a national marketing network. This firm could handle distribution for all of Western Nigeria, but the foreign pharmaceutical firms wanted a single distributing agent with countrywide coverage, and this could be provided only by the large expatriate chains. The existence of a marketing organization is so important, in fact, that it even tends to determine the kinds of goods the largest firm in West Africa will undertake to produce. All but one of the twenty-eight industrial projects of the United Africa Company are directly related to already established marketing facilities of the company.[71]

UNEXPECTED DIFFICULTIES

There is a fervent consensus among virtually all who have actually taken part in establishing businesses in Nigeria that when one initiates a project, a rich and multivarious and enormously frustrating assortment of unexpected difficulties arises. Participants have commented on this ever since experience started to accumulate on setting up modern industries in Nigeria. An early government report speaks several times of "the exceptional expense and hazards of starting new industries under local conditions."[72] "Projects may look wonderful on paper, but all kinds of unexpected difficulties come up."[73] "Setting up an industry here is incredibily difficult." There are "so many snags that never occur elsewhere." Because of the unexpected problems, "One does become more cautious as he accumulates experience."[74] Unforeseen difficulties emerge at every stage: in getting a preliminary project description to a point at which an intelligent decision can be made on going ahead; in constructing the facilities, purchasing and installing the equipment, and setting up the enterprise; and in producing and marketing once operations are underway.

These burdens sometimes submerge an enterprise. The long procession of unlooked-for complications that have bogged down attempts to establish what originally appeared to be the simple operation of manufacturing gari have been described by Kilby.[75] In fact, the sanguine expectations of government in undertaking a whole series of efforts to initiate domestic processing went unfulfilled; with the benefit of hindsight Kilby concludes that "a majority of the projects in the field of processing, canning and preserving of foodstuffs should not have been undertaken."[76] Even experienced businessmen are sometimes overwhelmed: for example, a number of European and other foreign entrepreneurs who were successful in the shoe industry in their home countries, but who failed in Nigeria,[77] or the well-known Lebanese businessman who invested in equipment for culling out "hand-selected" peanuts for the confection trade. Perhaps the most striking example of an experienced firm being struck by an unforeseen disaster occurred in the sugar growing and processing operation established in Nigeria with the participation and under the management of Bookers, one of the most experienced companies in the world. When they cut the cane and brought it to the mill, it was found to be completely dessicated. They had unknowingly waited too long to harvest the crop. In Nigeria ripe cane looks different from cane elsewhere.

The cumulative impact of the improbable inflictions was epitomized by a businessman running a very large and very successful textile plant near Lagos. In response to a query about why he did not expand further, he replied that if he had known what he had to go through to build the plant, he would not have done it, and he would not do it again. He had aged five years in two!

CONCLUSION

So far the special difficulties found in the African economic environment have been delineated. Finally, let us concern ourselves with the significance of that environment.

I find it necessary to revise an earlier formulation. My studies had led me to the conclusion (which I still affirm) that a shortage of capital funds is not generally a critical impediment to indigenous private investment in Africa.[78] And of the two remaining possible impediments, I maintained that the economic environment was more serious than entrepreneurial shortcomings. This emphasis was criticized. Gerald Helleiner,[79] Peter Kilby,[80] and Wayne Nafziger[81] took the position that my formulation exaggerated the importance of environmental adversities, and that entrepreneurial shortcomings in fact constitute the major inhibitor of indigenous private investment. A similar criticism is also implicit in the supply-and-demand analyses of entrepreneurship presented by Harris and Nafziger.[82]

Although I cannot accept the converse emphasis on the primary importance of entrepreneurial inadequacies, I withdraw my proposition on the primacy of the environmental obstacle to indigenous private investment and maintain instead simply that the economic environment constitutes a major barrier.

There are two reasons for the change in formulation. First, it appears impossible to measure the relative investment-inhibiting effects of economic environment and entrepreneurial capacity. One cannot describe them in measurable enough terms to say with any clear or easily-agreed-upon meaning that one is more important than the other. For example, there is no clear meaning in the statement that, say, a greater increase in investment will result from an X percent improvement in the economic environment than from a like improvement in entrepreneurship. Or, if we assume that some improvement in the economic environment will generate as big an increase in investment as some improvement in entrepreneurship, one cannot say that the improvement in one was greater than the improvement in the other.

Second, I have become dubious of the legitimacy of conceiving of the economic environment and entrepreneurship as separate and distinct matters. The more entrepreneurship there is, or in other words the more businesses of all sorts there are in an underdeveloped economy and the better they are run, the better is the economic environment. The exercise of entrepreneurship constitutes one facet of the economic environment for other entrepreneurs, and this creates difficulties for an approach which compares the importance of the two.

This essay's proposition regarding the inhibiting effect of the economic environment might be seen – although I will argue that such an interpretation is incorrect – as one that harmonizes with and fits into a more general supply-and-demand approach, such as that of Harris and Nafziger. In that sort of approach, the economic environment (or something like it) is conceived of as determining the set of opportunities or the demand for entrepreneurship, whereas what has been referred to in this essay as entrepreneurship refers only to the supply side of the equation. In this perspective, the delineation of the environmental difficulties is an elaboration of the demand side of the supply-demand relationship. There are, however, weaknesses in the supply-and-demand formulation which call for separate discussion of entrepreneurship and economic environment.

First, the formulation in terms of demand and supply of (and thus the determination of the price and quantity of) entrepreneurship squeezes into too narrow an arena the phenomena being analyzed. What is actually being examined in the demand-supply analysis is a process that is broader and more crucial than the determination of the price and quantity of a factor of production, even a unique and strategic factor. Being analyzed are, on the one hand, the entire economic environment, which determines the availability of profitable investment opportunities, and, on the other hand, the response to those opportunities. These are the determinants of private investment. And the investment process, particularly in underdeveloped economies, generates much more than the bare accumulation of capital. It generates also the entrepreneurial inputs for the new undertakings, the utilization, enskillment, and modernization of labor inputs drawn from the traditional economy, the improvement of the economic environment as the business network becomes more substantial and modern, and all the other externalities that may be created – in other words, the entire process of economic development insofar as it is carried out in the private sector.[83] The issues are too broad to be confined to the arena of entrepreneurial supply and demand.

Second, viewed as a determinant of demand, the economic environment determines more than the demand for entrepreneurship. It determines also the demand for labor and for capital. Holding entrepreneurship constant, an improvement in the economic environment (and thus an increase in profitable investment opportunities) raises the marginal value product of labor, thereby increasing the demand for labor, and raises the marginal efficiency of investment and marginal productivity of capital, thereby increasing the demand for capital.

Third, the supply-demand schematism equates by definition the process of development with the expansion of entrepreneurship. The supply-demand formulation regards the interplay between the economic environment and entrepreneurial capability as constituting the market for entrepreneurship. The preceding paragraph but one states that this very same interplay largely determines the rate of private-sector development. If the latter point is correct, then the supply-demand formulation characterizes the process of development as an increase in the supply of and/or demand for, and the consequent increase in the quantity of entrepreneurship.

Finally, application of supply-and-demand analysis to entrepreneurship is clumsy because entrepreneurship has the unique quality of being a self-selecting factor. In any particular instance, the demand comes into being when an entrepreneur decides to undertake some economic action; at the same time, and by the same action, the supply of entrepreneurship also comes into being. The single act of a single economic actor creates both demand and supply. Moreover, the analysis is also impeded because, as has already been mentioned, the supply of entrepreneurship is a facet of the economic environment (and thus helps to determine demand).

For these reasons, it appears useful to conceive of the economic environment not simply as the demand for entrepreneurship, but as a broader set of conditions with broader implications. In particular, this view of the economic environment has policy implications. If entrepreneurial inadequacy is considered the main barrier, then development policy will deal with ways of improving entrepreneurship and of coping with entrepreneurial deficiencies. If the economic environment is stressed, policy will tend to focus on means of improving and coping with that environment.

NOTES

The author expresses his appreciation for financial aid and other assistance in carrying out his African research to the Nigerian Institute of Social and Economic Research, the Ford Foundation, and the Social Science Research Council.

1. Sources comprise visits to indigenous and foreign-owned enterprises; interviews with owners and other business personnel, with officials of Nigerian and other African governments, and with a wide range of economic, business, technical, and other advisers in many African countries; government files and other internal government materials; and published materials. In general, the writer is precluded by the terms on which he approached the interviewees from citing them and from mentioning the names of specific businesses. Where possible, he has tried to use published materials, so that a source can be cited.
2. Sayre P. Schatz, "Economic Environment and Private Enterprise in West Africa," *The Economic Bulletin* (*Ghana*) (December 1963). The illustrations used in this paper are drawn mainly from Nigeria, but the thesis is believed to be generally applicable in Africa.
3. The term "expatriate" is used as in Africa in this essay to mean non-African.
4. Peter Marris, "The Social Barriers to African Entrepreneurship," *Journal of Development Studies* 5: 1 (October 1968).
5. This represents the judgment of a knowledgeable foreign businessman.
6. I am indebted to John R. Harris for this information.
7. Abner Cohen, "Politics of the Kola Trade," in Edith H. Whethem and Jean I. Currie (eds.), *Readings in the Applied Economics of Africa*, vol. 1: *Micro-Economics* (London: Cambridge University Press, 1967).
8. E. Wayne Nafziger, *Nigerian Entrepreneurship: A Study of Indigenous Businessmen in the Footwear Industry*, unpublished Ph.D. dissertation, University of Illinois, 1967, p. 156.
9. See, e.g., Theodore Geiger and Winifred Armstrong: *The Development of African Private Enterprise* (Washington, D.C.: National Planning Association, 1964), p. 54: "African entrepreneurs have difficulty in recruiting sufficient employees in this latter category [middle managerial and technical personnel], particularly since the great majority of them do not offer opportunities for training and advancement commensurate with those provided by many government agencies and some foreign firms."
10. See, e.g., ibid., pp. 99–100. ". . . these codes are often intended for large

enterprises and do not take into account the inability of small entrepreneurs to meet the same wage and social benefit standards. In addition, compliance with these codes often involves a large amount of paper work, which may be burdensome for small entrepreneurs."

11. This is certainly not to say that the presence of expatriate firms necessarily has a negative overall effect on development.
12. As Margaret Katzin has remarked: "The search for new ways of earning a profit is unremitting." ("The Role of the Small Entrepreneur," unpublished manuscript, Northwestern University, n.d., p. 15.)
13. Speaking of Eastern Nigeria, the credit manager of the Eastern Nigeria Development Corporation says: "Private capital in developing areas can be surprisingly quick to follow a successful lead, so that strong local competition may be encountered within a short space of time." *Development: ENDC Quarterly Magazine* (April–June 1962), p. 27.
14. Sayre P. Schatz, *Development Bank Lending: The Federal Loans Board of Nigeria* (Ibadan and London: Oxford University Press, 1964), pp. 71–72.
15. The Secretary of the Nigerian Petroleum Operators Union vividly described to me the competition among Nigerian-run gasoline stations in the Kaduna area in 1965. The main forms of competition were sales at discount and on credit. Agreements to refrain from these practices were quickly violated and broke down. Between the reduced profit margins, the time spent chasing after collectible debts, and the losses on bad debts, the frazzled operators were in despair. (Of course, "cut-throat" or "destructive" competition is not confined to underdeveloped economies.)
16. See Peter Kilby, *Industrialization in an Open Economy: Nigeria 1945–1966* (Cambridge, England and New York: Cambridge University Press, 1969), pp. 61–63 for a brief discussion of the way that, for large merchant firms, "entry of new sellers has far more than offset the growth in demand with consequent pressure on profit margins."
17. This particularly affects the businessman who is setting up modern operations. "A modernized and expanded enterprise may require raw materials of a type or quality different from that of a very small company. A cobbler can use leather of a quality unacceptable to a shoe factory. Yarn imperfections that would be permissible for a hand loom would not be tolerated by a power loom." Joseph E. Stepanek, *Managers for Small Industry: An International Study* (Glencoe, Ill.: The Free Press, 1960), p. 72.
18. Eastern Regional Development Board, *Second Annual Report, 1950–51* (Enugu: published by the Board, n.d.), p. 11.
19. Arthur D. Little, Inc., *Manufacturing Opportunities for Construction Products in Nigeria*, Report to the Ministry of Commerce and Industry, Federal Republic of Nigeria, April 1964, pp. 28–32.
20. For a description of this problem in Pakistan, see Nathaniel H. Engle, *Industrial Development Banking in Action: A Study of the Organisation, Operations and Procedure of Private Development Banks in India, Iran, Pakistan, Turkey*, Pakistan Industrial Credit and Investment Corporation Ltd., mimeo., 1962, p. 102.

21. Nigeria, Eastern Region, *Eastern House of Assembly Debates, 1956*, (Enugu: Government Printer, 1957), p. 536.
22. Kilby, *Industrialization in an Open Economy*, pp. 161–62.
23. Ibid., p. 213. See also Robert Ward, "Economic Spotlight on Nigeria," *SAIS Review* (Spring 1967), p. 23: "where systems of production are similar, there has been nothing to suggest that the Nigerian [unskilled or semi-skilled] worker is less capable than his counterpart in Europe. Most industrialists in Nigeria feel that with adequate training, supervision, and incentive payments, Nigerian labour can be about as productive as labour in Europe or the United States in repetitive and routine jobs." Ward then presents examples.
24. Kilby, *Industrialization in an Open Economy*, pp. 225 ff. and "African Labour Productivity Reconsidered," *Economic Journal* 71: 282 (June 1961).
25. Ibid., p. 124; labor costs are discussed on pp. 123–28.
26. T. M. Yesufu, "Nigerian Manpower Problems (A Preliminary Assessment)," *Nigerian Journal of Economic and Social Studies* (November 1962), p. 221.
27. Kilby, *Industrialization in an Open Economy*, p. 224; author's italics. See also F. A. Wells and W. A. Warmington, *Studies in Industrialization: Nigeria and the Cameroons* (Ibadan and London: Oxford University Press, 1962), p. 88.
28. Robert Waite, *Establishing an Electronics Industry in Nigeria*, unpublished M.B.A. thesis, New York University, 1964, p. 104. African Electronics is a pseudonym.
29. See, e.g., Nafziger, *Nigerian Entrepreneurship*, pp. 149–50, 171; Harris, *Industrial Entrepreneurship*, chap. 5, p. 13; Kilby, *Industrialization in an Open Economy*, pp. 224–33; and sources cited in the preceding footnotes.
30. The phrase of the chairman of the Commonwealth Development Corporation in an interview with the author.
31. The leading Nigerian manpower economist confirms that ". . . a high rate of turnover has become characteristic of expatriate staff. . . .' Yesufu, p. 207.
32. Nafziger, *Nigerian Entrepreneurship*, p. 27.
33. Yesufu, *Nigerian Manpower Problems*, p. 207. Testimony regarding the high cost and unsatisfactory nature of foreign high-level personnel comes from all sources: the largest expatriate companies, virtually all Nigerian firms large enough to employ foreigners, Nigerian government officials, foreign government personnel concerned with Nigerian economic affairs, and internationally financed development organizations. Written sources include Yesufu; John R. Harris, *Industrial Entrepreneurship in Nigeria*, unpublished Ph.D. dissertation, Northwestern University, chap. 5, p. 13; Nafziger, *Nigerian Entrepreneurship*, pp. 151–52, 155–57; Charles H. Olmstead, "Private Investment In Nigeria," in Warren H. Hausman (ed.), *Managing Economic Development in Africa*, (Cambridge, Mass.: M.I.T. Press, 1963), p. 97; *British Aid – 1, Survey and Comment* (London, Overseas Development Institute Ltd., 1963), p. 49; and my own "Crude Private Neo-Imperialism: A New Pattern

in Africa," *Journal of Modern African Studies* (December 1969), pp. 681–85.

34. Wells and Warmington, *Studies in Industrialization*, p. 38.
35. W. Arthur Lewis, e.g., mentions the need to provide consulting services for small businessmen in less-developed economies, *Development Planning: the Essentials of Economic Policy* (New York: Harper and Row, 1966), p. 271.
36. William Diamond, *Development Banks*, Baltimore, published for the International Bank for Reconstruction and Development by the Johns Hopkins Press, 1957.
37. See Everett E. Hagen, "The Allocation of Investment in Underdeveloped Countries," in Massachusetts Institute of Technology, Center for International Studies, *Investment Criteria and Economic Growth*, mimco., 1954, pp. 63–64.
38. "Many businessmen look on these associations as their most important sources of information." L. J. Crampton and Stewart F. Schweizer, *A Study of the Information Needs and Problems of Small Businessmen* (Boulder, Colo.: Bureau of Business Research, University of Colorado), summarized in Small Business Administration, *Management Research Summary* (February 1962). Of the businessmen surveyed, 38 percent belonged to one or more associations.
39. Stepanek, *Managers for Small Industry*, p. 63.
40. Harris, *Industrial Entrepreneurship*, chap. 4, p. 35. See also C. C. Onyemelukwe, *Problems of Industrial Planning and Management in Nigeria* (New York: Columbia University Press, 1966), p. 25 on the difficulties of securing existing information required for industrial development.
41. See, e.g., G. K. Helleiner, "New Forms of Foreign Investment in Africa," *Journal of Modern African Studies* 6: 1 (May 1968), pp. 21–22 and Schatz, "Crude Private Neo-imperialism," pp. 681–85. For a specific case, see the statement that one of the reasons for the difficulties of a relatively large ceramics firm in Western Nigeria was "that the expert advice [by foreigners] given to them on the outset did not allow for special circumstances of this country," Nigeria, Federation, *Proceedings of Commission of Inquiry into the Affairs of Certain Statutory Corporations* (*Coker Hearings*), mimeo., Lagos, 1962, Day 34, p. 23.
42. Waite, *Establishing an Electronics Industry*, pp. 92–93. In contrast, Crampon and Schweizer, *Information Needs of Small Businessmen*, found that most of the surveyed firms (in the United States) that used consultants were satisfied with the results.
43. See Sayre P. Schatz and S. I. Edokpayi, "Economic Attitudes of Nigerian Businessmen," *Nigerian Journal of Economic and Social Studies* (November, 1962), p. 262.
44. Statement upon receipt of the report of a government commission that investigated the operations of the civil service. *West Africa* (January 13, 1968), p. 49.
45. See, e.g., Sayre P. Schatz, "The High Cost of Aiding Businesses in Developing Economies: Nigeria's Loans Programmes," *Oxford Economic Papers* 20: 3 (November 1968).

46. A. H. Hanson, *Public Enterprise and Economic Development* (London: Routledge and Kegan Paul, 1959), p. 52. See also Guy Hunter, *The New Societies of Tropical Africa* (London and Ibadan: Oxford University Press, 1962), p. 188 for a brief discussion of the bureaucratic problems of African countries; and A. L. Adu, *The Civil Service in New African States* (London: Allen and Unwin, 1965), pp. 228–29 for an interesting discussion of problems of African civil servants related to the problem discussed here.
47. Lagos Chamber of Commerce, *Quarterly Review* (September 1961), p. 4. Business complaints are discussed in many issues of this publication (later called the *Quarterly Review of the Lagos Chamber of Commerce and Industry*). See, e.g., complaints about shortages of imported spare parts (June 1968), p. 2.
48. *West Africa* (August 20, 1966), p. 951. For another interesting example, see R. A. Akinola, "Factors Affecting the Location of a Textile Industry – The Example of the Ikeja Textile Mill," *Nigerian Journal of Economic and Social Studies* (November 1965), p. 255.
49. *Lagos Daily Times*, August 16, 1963, p. 13.
50. See, e.g., Paul O. Proehl, *Foreign Enterprise in Nigeria* (Chapel Hill, N.C.: University of North Carolina Press, 1965), chap. 7. For a discussion of changes in land tenure under the impact of economic development, see Sayre P. Schatz, "Implications of Economic Development," in John H. Hallowell (ed.), *Development: for What?* (Durham, N.C.: Duke University Press, 1964), pp. 59–64.
51. Federal Loans Board, *Annual Report, 1960–61* (Lagos, Government Printer, 1962), and internal materials.
52. Cf. Hunter, *The New Societies of Tropical Africa*, p. 140.
53. Paul N. Rosenstein-Rodan, "Problems of Industrialization in Eastern and South-Eastern Europe," *Economic Journal* 53: 210–11 (June–September 1943), p. 205.
54. Ragnar Nurske, *Problems of Capital Formation in Underdeveloped Economies* (New York: Oxford University Press, 1967), p. 6. See also chaps. 1 and 4.
55. For a quite interesting historical analysis, see H. J. Habbakuk, "The Historical Experience on the Basic Conditions of Economic Progress," in Leon H. Dupriez, ed., *Economic Progress: Papers and Proceedings of a Round Table Conference held by the International Economic Association* (Louvain, Institut de Recherches Economiques et Sociales, 1955), p. 153.
56. The demands generated by the Civil War considerably increased the utilization of capacity during the latter part of the 1960s. Sayre P. Schatz, Rudolph H. Blythe, Jr., and Warren O. Williams, "Nigeria: A Look at the Balance Sheet," *Africa Report* (January 1970), pp. 19–20.
57. Harris, *Industrial Entrepreneurship*, chap. 4, pp. 19, 42.
58. Ibid., chap. 7, pp. 7–8.
59. Nafziger, *Nigerian Entrepreneurship*, pp. 134–35.
60. "Processing Nigeria's Agricultural Products – Ground Nut Oil Milling," *Nigerian Trade Journal* (January–March 1962), p. 12.
61. See, e.g., Waite, *Establishing an Electronics Industry*, p. 110.
62. One of the major trading firms gave a deliberate margin of preference

to Nigerian-produced goods for political and public relations reasons, but it stopped this practice after a while.

63. Waite, *Establishing an Electronics Industry*, pp. 108–9.
64. Schatz and Edokpayi, "Economic Attitudes of Nigerian Businessmen," pp. 262–63.
65. Cohen, "Politics of the Kola Trade," p. 156.
66. Waite, *Establishing an Electronics Industry*, p. 113.
67. Peter Kilby, *The Development of Small Industry in Eastern Nigeria*, Lagos, USAID (United States Agency for International Development), 1962, p. 9.
68. "It is rare for a footwear firm in Nigeria to have the requisite marketing knowledge and organization to warrant the establishment of a plant in which the value of assets is £100,000 or more." Nafziger, *Nigerian Entrepreneurship*, p. 135.
69. Harris, *Industrial Entrepreneurship*, chap. 4, p. 20; chap. 7, p. 7.
70. Kilby, *African Enterprise: The Nigerian Bread Industry* (Stanford, Calif.: Stanford University Press, 1965), p. 86.
71. Kilby, *Industrialization in an Open Economy*, p. 78. This point was also made to me by the director of the United Africa Company.
72. Nigeria, Federation, *Statement on the Activities of the Department of Commerce and Industries* (Lagos: Government Printer, 1953), p. 17.
73. An industrial development adviser of a foreign government aid mission.
74. The foreign manager of a regional development corporation.
75. Kilby, *Industrialization in an Open Economy*, pp. 191–95.
76. Ibid., p. 195.
77. Nafziger, *Nigerian Entrepreneurship*, pp. 24–25.
78. Cf. my "The Capital Shortage Illusion," *Oxford Economic Papers* 17: 2 (July 1965), and *Development Bank Lending*, chap. 6. See, however, the criticism by E. Wayne Nafziger, "A Reconsideration of 'Capital Surplus' in Nigeria," *The Nigerian Journal of Economic and Social Studies* (March 1968).
79. Gerald K. Helleiner, *Peasant Agriculture, Government, and Economic Growth in Nigeria* (Homewood, Ill.: Richard D. Irwin, Inc., 1966), pp. 265–66.
80. Kilby, *Industrialization in an Open Economy*, pp. 340–42.
81. Nafziger, *Nigerian Entrepreneurship*, p. 150.
82. In order to avoid possible misinterpretation, I feel impelled to repeat a point I have made previously, that a paucity of profitable business ventures does not necessarily signify a paucity of economically worthwhile investments in the directly productive sphere of the economy. Investment may engender external benefits and/or involve savings in real costs which cause them to yield a net economic benefit, even though pecuniarily unprofitable. Policies can and should be adopted to bring such investments into being. Ibid., chap. 6; John R. Harris, *Industrial Entrepreneurship*, chap. 2.
83. Cf. Sayre P. Schatz, "The Role of Capital Accumulation in Economic Development," *Journal of Development Studies* 5: 1 (October 1968).

Chapter 3

The Market for Nigerian Entrepreneurs

E. Wayne Nafziger

In studies of economic growth, attention has been focused upon expansion of the supply of productive factors and upon the rate of technical change. Recently some economists have shifted the emphasis away from the growth of physical capital to increases in high-level manpower, such as entrepreneurship, as the major determinant of the rate of economic growth. In part, this shift has been a result of empirical studies based on American economic development, which suggest that increases in the supply of physical capital explain no more than a fraction of growth in aggregate output.[1] In part, the shift has resulted from the increased use of the other social sciences in the theory of economic development.[2]

From the perspective of the economic analyst, the entrepreneur is a factor of production. In the study of this factor, an analysis of the market is important. Although economists have analyzed the factor markets for labor and capital, they have, because of conceptual problems, been reluctant to discuss the market for entrepreneurs. This paper attempts to analyze the market, and particularly the supply side of the market, for entrepreneurs of indigenous firms in Nigeria.[3] Starting with data on the quantity and remuneration of entrepreneurs, and with additional information and a few assumptions, it offers some generalizations about the nature of the supply of and the demand for entrepreneurs of Nigerian firms.[4] Additional empirical and theoretical studies are needed before a more general theory of the market for entrepreneurs can be developed.

The analysis is based primarily on the author's research on Nigerian entrepreneurs in 107 indigenous manufacturing firms during the year preceding the January 1966 coup. Entrepreneurs are defined in this study as those who make and execute decisions concerning the employment and organization of the factors of production of the firm. This implies that various aspects of management of an existing enterprise would be included as a part of the entrepreneurial function.

DATA ON THE MARKET FOR ENTREPRENEURS

In 1965 the modal salary for the foreign major entrepreneur in an indigenous manufacturing firm with a net worth of £75,000–£125,000 and 100–200 workers was about £2,500 yearly.[5] International travel and fringe benefits cost the firm an additional £1,500 per annum. The modal salary for an indigenous top entrepreneur of a firm of the same size was about £800 per year plus training costs and fringe benefits, which frequently were substantial.

The 1965 monthly wages for top entrepreneurs in firms of about £3,000 net worth and employing twenty persons were about £15 in the East, £20 in the West, and Lagos, and £25 in the North.[6] For purposes of comparison, 1965 wages in Nigeria for a typist, an automobile driver, a school nurse, an unskilled worker, and a journeyman were £20, £17, £17, £7, and £4 per month respectively.[7]

Available data indicate that the number of industrial entrepreneurs (and firms) in Nigeria relative to the population was low.[8] Nigeria, with an official population of 55.7 million,[9] had fewer than 1000 industrial firms with twenty-five or more employees, and fewer than 400 with fifty or more engaged in 1963.

Figures in Table 1, based primarily on official data, give some indication of the scarcity of industrial entrepreneurs.[10] (Virtually all the entrepreneurs of manufacturing firms are listed as managerial or professional personnel.)

In 1963, there were about 1,400 indigenous and 1,900 foreign managerial and professional personnel in the approximately seven hundred industrial firms with twenty-five or more workers. Probably no more than 1,000 indigènes and 1,200

TABLE 1

Estimates of Professional and Managerial Employees in Manufacturing Firms Engaging Ten or More Persons
1962, 1963

(Size of firm by number of persons engaged)	Number of indigenous firms		Number of foreign firms		Total number of firms		Number of indigenous professional and managerial personnel in indigenous firms		Number of indigenous professional and managerial personnel in foreign firms		Number of foreign professional and managerial personnel in all manufacturing firms		Number of professional and managerial personnel in all manufacturing firms	
	1962	1963	1962	1963	1962	1963	1962	1963	1962	1963	1962	1963	1962	1963
10–24	1,519	1,887	31	38	1,550	1,925	2,543	2,993	52	60	130	180	2,725	3,233
25–49	196	244	65	81	261	325	360	401	120	133	194	266	674	800
50–99	76	95	51	63	127	158	186	188	124	125	286	392	596	705
100–199	46	57	46	57	92	114	128	124	127	124	284	389	539	637
200–499	22	27	32	40	54	67	87	81	127	120	292	398	506	599
500–999	5	6	11	13	16	19	27	22	58	49	141	183	226	254
1,000–1,999	3	3	3	4	6	7	22	15	22	19	90	115	134	149
2,000 & over	2	3	3	3	5	6	16	14	25	14	105	140	146	168
TOTAL	1,869	2,322	242	299	2,111	2,621	3,369	3,838	655	644	1,522	2,063	5,546	6,545

foreigners held entrepreneurial responsibility in these firms. In the same year, there were about 900 indigenous and about 1,600 foreign managerial and professional personnel in the 350–400 firms with 50 or more persons working, of which it is unlikely that more than 600 indigenous and 1,000 foreign personnel held entrepreneurial or managerial responsibility. Thus, the number of industrial entrepreneurs in Nigeria – especially among the indigenous population – has been very small.

Nigeria's low per-capita gross domestic product originating in the manufacturing sector also suggests a paucity of industrial entrepreneurs. In 1962 in Africa, the continent with the lowest level of industrial development, Nigeria ranked fifteenth out of seventeen countries in per-capita value-added in manufacturing.[11] Nigeria was tied with the Sudan as ninth out of eleven African countries in value-added in manufacturing as a percentage of gross domestic product.[12]

On the other hand, the survey of rural household enterprises by the Nigerian Office of Statistics[13] and other government sources[14] suggests that small firms and entrepreneurs number in the hundreds of thousands.

ON THE SCARCITY OF ENTREPRENEURSHIP

We now turn to the question: how can we explain the smallness of the number of functioning industrial entrepreneurs? One can look for the explanation in terms of either demand or supply. The demand for entrepreneurship may be thought of as a schedule of income-earning possibilities that could be reaped from potential entrepreneurial activities.

Schatz has contended that the smallness of the number of functioning entrepreneurs stems primarily from impediments in the economic environment (i.e. lack of demand for entrepreneurship), rather than from a lack of entrepreneurial capacity (i.e., lack of entrepreneurial supply).[15] Schatz maintains that even with entrepreneurial ability comparable to the developed economies, profit opportunities would be limited because of an unfavorable economic environment.[16]

The author concurs with Schatz's contention that numerous impediments in the economic environment restrain the demand for entrepreneurship. Demand is also dampened by the relatively small endowment of capital.[17] Among African countries, Nigeria, with a ratio of 12 percent, ranked tenth among twelve countries in the ratio of gross fixed investment to gross national product in 1958; and with a ratio of 13 percent, ranked eighth among ten countries in 1962–63.[18] Another factor reducing demand is the inadequacy of social overhead capital, such as schools, transportation facilities, and public utilities. There are also the slow and irregular deliveries (and unsatisfactory service when something goes wrong) of much of the equipment, materials, and supplies – often purchased abroad.[19] The scarcity of high- and intermediate-level manpower (consultants, technicians, supervisors, and foremen, etc.) is another impediment to demand.[20] In addition, access to technical knowledge is limited, partly because of the lack of programs and personnel to assist in the transfer of technology from abroad.[21] The small size of the Nigerian market resulting from low per-capita income is also an obstacle. Finally, the perception by prospective industrialists, whether valid or not, that government officials are frequently indifferent, obstructionist, inefficient, discriminatory, and corrupt in their dealings with business decreases the demand for entrepreneurs.[22]

On the other hand, Gerald K. Helleiner argues that the fact that foreign-owned-and-managed enterprises (which encounter the same economic environment as indigenous firms) have been generally much more successful than have Nigerian enterprises suggests that the explanation may lie in lack of entrepreneurial capacity and experience.[23] Thus, Helleiner's view is that the lack of entrepreneurship is largely a result of a lack of supply rather than of a deficiency in demand.

Since both Nigerian and foreign entrepreneurs are placed in the same economic setting, one might expect the marginal productivity of (and demand for) both types of entrepreneurial inputs to be the same, if the inputs are assumed to be of identical quality. However, as a result of the heterogeneity of input quality resulting from the fact that training, education, experience, and sociocultural milieu are more conducive to the development of entrepreneurship in Western countries, the schedule of expected returns to (or demand for) foreign entrepreneurs is greater than for Nigerian entrepreneurs. In addition, the fact that the foreign entrepreneur may have access to more capital, advanced techniques, and highly skilled manpower frequently results in a higher marginal productivity of entrepreneurial units. While exchange restrictions, immigrant quotas, and pressures for Nigerianization restrain the demand for foreign entrepreneurs, one would expect, on balance, the demand for foreign entrepreneurs to exceed that for indigenous entrepreneurs.

In the light of the relatively low remuneration and quantity of indigenous large-scale entrepreneurs, it is most consistent to conclude that the lack of supply discussed below is combined with a demand for Nigerian entrepreneurs that is not very keen. This weak demand, together with an abundant supply of small-scale entrepreneurs, can explain the relatively low remuneration and relatively high quantity of small-scale entrepreneurs. On the other hand, the relatively high remuneration of foreign entrepreneurs indicates that the limited supply is combined with a demand somewhat greater than that for indigenous entrepreneurs.

SUPPLY OF ENTREPRENEURSHIP

Foreign Entrepreneurs

Despite the fact that £2,500 annually, plus fringe benefits, is competitive compensation for comparable positions in Europe, it is still difficult to lure foreign personnel into indigenous Nigerian firms. A man from abroad wants decidedly increased income if he is to give up his home environment and its securities, assume added costs of travel and dislocation, and subject himself and his family to a less satisfactory environment in terms of health facilities and education, not to mention possible political insecurities.

Frequently the position with the Nigerian firm proves temporary. After one to three years, the firm may have indigènes trained to assume management. The manager who returns home may then find difficulty in locating a satisfactory position, and if he returns to his former position, he may have lost opportunities for promotion, retirement benefits, and professional contacts.

Because of the reluctance of foreign entrepreneurs to move,

some large Nigerian industrial firms have made arrangements with foreign firms to supply entrepreneurial personnel. However, it is unlikely that a foreign firm would send promising managerial material abroad, unless there is a major financial inducement, as when the foreign firm's assistance is tied to the supplying of machinery. However, there are obvious drawbacks for the Nigerian firm in this arrangement; for example, the foreign firm's personnel might have an interest in advising the Nigerian firm to acquire more machinery than optimal.

A Nigerian, perceiving his business knowledge and experience to be deficient, may seek a partnership with a foreigner who has the proper expertise. However, it is difficult for an indigenous entrepreneur to attract foreign capital and expertise to the firm.[24] Expected returns must be lucrative indeed to induce foreigners to invest in an underdeveloped country like Nigeria, without majority control.[25]

Another option is for the Nigerian firm to obtain the entrepreneurial services of personnel from a Western consulting firm.[26] The consulting firm might make a feasibility study, carry out the initial decisions, find a management staff for the first few years, assist in training it, and begin a program to improve the entrepreneurial, managerial, and technical skills of the initiating entrepreneurs and high-level Nigerians in the firm. Professional consultants would have a greater motivation than do personnel of machinery firms to act in the interest of the Nigerian firm. For the Nigerian entrepreneur, however, the problem remains of evaluating the consulting firm – especially with respect to its ability to handle problems requiring knowledge of the Nigerian culture and economy.[27]

Indigenous Entrepreneurs of Large Firms

The lack of indigenous industrial entrepreneurship is a result partly of a lack of supply. Even though foreign managers are far more expensive than Nigerians of the same skill,[28] a majority of the managerial personnel in these firms are foreigners.[29] A number of interrelated factors account for the deficiency in supply of indigenous entrepreneurs for large firms.

A major factor impeding supply of entrepreneurship to indigenous firms is high salaries in occupations requiring a comparable level of skills, such as employment in foreign firms and government. The demand for (and salary of) indigenous managers in foreign firms is increased by public and political pressure to obtain Nigerian managers. For government officials and high-ranking civil servants, salaries, additional allowances, fringe benefits, and working conditions are quite attractive.[30] In addition, the civil servant enjoys much more job security than does the entrepreneur in an indigenous firm. It is not surprising that high-level manpower "turns to the high and certain salary, immediate prestige, and other perquisites offered by the civil service or expatriate corporations rather than to entrepreneurial activity with its relatively low mean and high variance of expected earnings."[31]

The 1965 annual salaries of high-level civil servants and government officials generally exceed £2,000 and are much higher than entrepreneurial incomes mentioned in Section 1.[32]

Another restrictive factor is the low level of educational attainment in Nigeria. The average educational level of the seventeen major entrepreneurs of large industrial firms in the sample is 10.2 years. Statistics on age structure and education[33] and figures on enrollment rates[34] indicate that around 1964–65 no more than 25 percent of the population (seven years of age or older) had four or more years of schooling and no more than 3 percent of the population had a minimum of a secondary-school certificate. Of the seventeen large-scale entrepreneurs in the sample, sixteen had completed primary school; and eleven had also received a secondary school certificate.

Entrepreuneurs in large complex firms need skills possessed generally only by persons with some secondary education. The supply of Nigerian manpower with the necessary education is sparse.

The lack of training adapted to the development of entrepreneurial skills needed in large industry also reduces supply. Until recently, "the need for high-level managerial institutional training was completely neglected in the higher institutions."[35] The technical and vocational schools, which might be an alternative source of supply of trained entrepreneurs, accounted for only 3 percent of the 1959–63 enrollment in post-primary schools below the university level.[36] Moreover, the technical and trade schools and centers also suffer low-quality instruction, irrelevant training programs, and an approach meant for workers rather than managers.

Other educational factors impeding the supply of indigenous entrepreneurs for large firms are the shortage of secondary graduates with mathematics and science training, the unduly lengthy training period required in most technical and trade institutes, and the low prestige associated with technical training compared with the high prestige of university training.

The inexperience of Africans in business, especially in manufacturing, has dampened the supply of entrepreneurs. This is suggested by the positive relationship between the entrepreneurial and managerial experience of the major entrepreneur and the value of output of the firm among the seventeen large firms in our sample.[37] Obstructionism, ineffectiveness, and antipathy toward business in government service not only shift the schedule of expected returns from entrepreneurship downward, but also impede the supply of entrepreneurship.[38]

Indigenous Entrepreneurs of Small Firms

Let us now consider the supply of small entrepreneurs.

The Nigerian economy is characterized by a multiplicity of petty businessmen. Small industry receives a large supply of these as a result of the minimal barriers to entry and the low opportunity cost of labor. A small firm can be started with meager skill and perhaps as little as £25. The high rate of unemployment and underemployment serves as a further inducement to the establishment of small enterprises.

The supply of small entrepreneurs is not hindered appreciably by the low average education level in Nigeria. Callaway's study of 5,135 small manufacturing entrepreneurs in Ibadan indicates that only 36 percent of the entrepreneurs had some primary education[39] compared with about 30–35 percent of the population of the city with the same age distribution.[40] Because of the low skill requirements of small industry and the fact that an apprentice training may be more closely related to business occupations, the lack of formal education does not seem to be a significant barrier to entrepreneurial activity in small firms.

The supply of entrepreneurs is not hampered significantly by deficiencies in the availability of capital, since the initial outlay needed is small. Frequently the extended family provides the funds needed for apprentice training and the establishment of the firm, if the entrepreneur lacks sufficient capital. Although entrepreneurs encounter more problems in raising the capital for the expansion of the firm, most successful firms have access to retained earnings.[41]

The nature of government policies reduces the supply of small entrepreneurs just as it does that of large entrepreneurs. In fact, small entrepreneurs, lacking political power, suffer even more from government apathy and red tape than do large entrepreneurs.

There are significant supply differences between the regions of Nigeria. Work this writer has done indicates that entrepreneurial income in small industrial firms is greater in the North than in the East. Monthly wages for top entrepreneurs in firms of about £3,000 net worth and employing twenty persons ranged from £180 per annum in the East to £300 per annum in the North. The major determinant of the supply of small entrepreneurs is the supply of apprentice course graduates. Whereas the number of these graduates in the North was relatively small,[42] the number in the East was relatively large. With a relatively large supply of small entrepreneurs in the East, individual wages were relatively low.

These interregional differences in wages to small entrepreneurs persisted because of barriers to migration. There has been almost no interregional or socioethnic group area migration among manufacturing entrepreneurs.[43] Among 107 entrepreneurs interviewed in 1965, only four were operating businesses in a region other than that of birth,[44] and only three were operating businesses in an area dominated by another ethnic group.[45] These minority-group entrepreneurs continually encountered pressure to leave the area – whether it was cultural and language barriers, the power of economic restriction and discrimination by local authorities, or the direct physical threat arising from intertribal conflict or a political crisis.

Interregional differences in wages for top managers in large firms were not significant. The availability of foreigners, who have been more mobile between regions than have Nigerians, has made the domestic market less segmented.

Of course, sociopolitical barriers to migration not only widen the regional differentials in the supply of entrepreneurs, but also decrease their aggregate supply.

Some Implications of the Analysis

If the critical bottleneck impeding the development of more industrial firms lies in the inadequacy of the supply of entrepreneurs, then training is important. Most entrepreneurs of small and craft firms are trained in the indigenous system, whereby a boy, usually fourteen to eighteen years old, enrolls for a two- to five-year course with the proprietor of such a firm and learns the trade on the job. The supply of small and craft entrepreneurs is largely a function of the supply of apprentice course graduates.

A small entrepreneur expanding his firm into a medium industrial firm will need to upgrade his technical and entrepreneurial skills. Organization of an expanded firm becomes more complex, with need for delegation of responsibility, advance planning, and a communications system. Although other productive resources tend to substitute for each other, entrepreneurship is complementary to other production factors. The more other resources are available, the more entrepreneurship is required to combine them. The Nigerian small firm can grow to the point that no additional capital can be absorbed without a substantial increase in entrepreneurial skills.

Few training programs for small entrepreneurs in Nigeria are designed with the market for entrepreneurs in mind. One or two post-apprentice courses are probably optimal in training small entrepreneurs for medium industrial firms. Such courses should be offered only to experienced persons most likely to benefit from them, priority being given to those with a current or prospective entrepreneurial position in a medium industrial firm. Such courses should be less than six months long, to prevent disruption of the firm whose entrepreneur is absent for the training, and also to insure that the courses can compete with two- or three-year post-primary management and technical training institutes that prepare the student for the relatively high salaries in the civil service.

Both technical and managerial training should be stressed. Individual and group instruction are more effective if instructors are familiar with the needs of the firms represented by the students, and if they are already involved with the students in on-the-job training. This is especially true in Nigeria, where instructors are frequently either foreigners unacquainted with the small scale and lack of technical and managerial expertise of many manufacturing enterprises, or indigènes unfamiliar with the operation of industrial firms.

More emphasis should be placed on training programs of large industrial firms, since post-primary technical and administrative training in Nigeria is often not adapted to the needs of large industry. Most large industrial firms send some prospective technicians and managers abroad for training programs. However, there are problems. It might take several years before the returns from the investment in training indigenous managers equals its cost to the firm.[46] If a trained indigenous manager can be retained only for a year to two, it may be more profitable to hire a foreign manager with comparable training and skill. If the skills developed by a trainee are used outside the training firm in his lifetime, the benefit to the economy as a whole exceeds the benefit to the firm. The firm has no incentive to train high-level manpower to the point where the social cost of the program equals its social benefit. It might then be fitting for the government to give a partial subsidy to the firm's training program.[47]

Other things might be done to increase the supply of entrepreneurship in Nigeria. The economics ministries or statutory development corporations could play an active role in evaluating foreign entrepreneurs or consultants. In addition, the Nigerian government might arrange with foreign governments to compile a register of appropriate foreign managerial personnel interested in work in Nigeria.

There are probably more high-level organizational and managerial skills in the public sector than in the private sector. Thus it would make sense for officials in the ministries and statutory corporations to undertake entrepreneurial functions for the private sector: originating the idea for an enterprise, finding local entrepreneurs to establish it, and arranging to obtain the proper skills. Civil servants can sometimes exercise a useful restraining influence on an ill-conceived firm. Government agencies may be able to withhold a land title, rent permit, pioneer firm certificate, or capital until the firm has made arrangements to obtain the necessary technical and managerial skills.

In some instances, the government agency that perceives the need for a new enterprise may try to establish a public firm.

It would appear wise to provide direct entrepreneurial and technical assistance to small- and medium-sized firms. While the alternative wage of a person with high-level technical and entrepreneurial skills is too high for him to be utilized in a small firm, the economic cost per firm is low if such an individual's scarce abilities are used as an input for thirty or forty firms in a year.

The experience of centers in Nigeria providing direct entrepreneurial and technical assistance to firms has shown that successful departments and programs are often tied closely to the skill and drive of one person. Where turnover of personnel is rapid, and the successful adviser soon departs, business expansion may abruptly cease.

NOTES

The author acknowledges his indebtedness to the Midwest Universities Consortium for International Activities and to the Economic Development Institute of the University of Nigeria for funds and facilities to expedite a year of research on Nigerian entrepreneurship. He also expresses appreciation of helpful comments from John F. Due, Peter Kilby, and Edgar Bagley.

1. Edward F. Denison, *The Sources of Economic Growth in the United States and the Alternatives Before Us* (Supplementary Paper Number 13, Committee for Economic Development, New York, 1962); Robert Solow, "Technical Change and the Aggregate Production Function," *Review of Economics and Statistics* 39: 3 (August 1957); Moses Abramovitz, "Resources and Output Trends in the United States Since 1870," *American Economic Association Papers and Proceedings* 46: 2 (May 1956), pp. 5–23; Benton F. Massell, "Capital Formation and Technological Change in United States Manufacturing," *Review of Economics and Statistics* 42: 2 (May 1960), pp. 182–88.
2. See, e.g., David C. McClelland, *The Achieving Society* (Princeton, N.J.: D. Van Nostrand Co., 1961); and Everett E. Hagen, *On the Theory of Social Change: How Economic Growth Begins* (Homewood, Ill.: The Dorsey Press, Inc., 1962).

3. Indigenous firms are those in which at least 50 percent of the capital is Nigerian. "Nigerian" includes only Nigerian citizens of African origin and regional statutory corporations. Other firms are designated as "foreign" firms.
4. Determinants of the supply of entrepreneurs are discussed more fully by the author in "Nigerian Entrepreneurship: A Study of Indigenous Businessmen in the Footwear Industry" (unpublished Ph.D. dissertation, Department of Economics, University of Illinois, May 1967), pp. 9–12; "The Effect of the Nigerian Extended Family on Entrepreneurial Activity," *Economic Development and Cultural Change* 18: 1 (October 1969), pp. 25–33; and "The Relationship Between Education and Entrepreneurship in Nigeria," *Journal of Developing Areas* 4: 3 (April 1970).
5. The Nigerian pound exchanged for $2.80 in 1965, and maintains that rate now.
6. The number of persons "engaged" by a firm includes working proprietors, paid employees, unpaid apprentices, and unpaid family workers.
7. Wage rates for the first three categories of labor are found in Nigeria, *Estimates of the Government of the Federal Republic of Nigeria, 1965–66 (Approved)*, (Lagos: Federal Ministry of Information 1965), pp. 67, 122, 143.
8. Others have noted the sparsity of industrial entrepreneurs in Nigeria. See Peter Kilby, *Development of Small Industries in Eastern Nigeria* (Enugu: Eastern Ministry of Information, 1963), p. 12; Gerald K. Helleiner, *Peasant Agriculture, Government, and Economic Growth in Nigeria* (Homewood, Ill.: Richard D. Irwin, Inc., 1966), p. 265; T. M. Yesufu, "Nigerian Manpower Problems (A Preliminary Assessment)," *The Nigerian Journal of Economic and Social Studies* 4: 2 (May 1959), p. 210; Frederick Harbison, "Human Resources and Economic Development in Nigeria," *The Nigerian Political Scene*, ed. Robert Tilman and Taylor Cole (Durham, N.C.: Duke University Commonwealth Studies Center, 1962), pp. 204–5; P. T. Bauer, *West African Trade: A Study of Competition, Oligopoly, and Monopoly in a Changing Economy* (London: Routledge and Kegan Paul Ltd., 1963), pp. 13–18; Nigeria, *National Development Plan 1962–68* (Lagos: Federal Ministry of Economic Development, n.d.), p. 15; and Nigeria, *Report on the Advisory Committee on Aids to African Businessmen* (Lagos, 1959), pp. 34–35.
9. Nigeria, Office of Statistics, *Digest of Statistics January, 1967* (Lagos: Federal Office of Statistics, 1967), p. 3.
10. Table was computed primarily on the basis of *Industrial Survey, 1962* (Lagos: Office of Statistics, 1965), *Industrial Survey, 1963* (Lagos: Office of Statistics, 1966); and Gerald K. Helleiner, *Peasant Agriculture, Government, and Economic Growth in Nigeria* (Homewood, Ill.: Richard D. Irwin, Inc., 1966), p. 491. The distribution of managerial and professional personnel by firm size and the extent of coverage by the federal industrial surveys were estimated on the basis of the preceding sources and on *Industrial Directory 1964* (Lagos: Ministry of Commerce and

Industry, n.d.), plus an unpublished supplement in 1965; *Eastern Nigeria Industrial Directory* (Enugu: Eastern Nigeria, Ministry of Economic Planning, 1963); *Mid-western Nigeria Industrial Survey, 1964* (Benin: Mid-western Nigeria, n.d.); *Northern Nigeria Industrial Directory* (Kaduna: Northern Nigeria, Ministry of Economic Planning, 1965); Personal Interview, Assistant Trade Officer, Western Nigeria, May 6, 1965; Nigeria, Ministry of Commerce and Industry, Registration of Business Names, Lagos, August 1965; Nigeria, Ministry of Labour, Lagos, August 1965; Peter Kilby, *Development of Small Industry in Eastern Nigeria* (Enugu: Eastern Ministry of Information, 1963); and E. Wayne Nafziger, "Nigerian Entrepreneurship: A Study of Indigenous Businessmen in the Footwear Industry," unpublished Ph.D. dissertation, Department of Economics, University of Illinois, May 1967, pp. 254–71.

11. Computed from United Nations, Department of Economic and Social Affairs, *Statistical Yearbook 1964* (New York, 1965), pp. 23–28, 211–13, and *Yearbook of National Accounts Statistics 1965* (New York, 1966), pp. 493–98. The inadequacies of international comparisons from data from less-developed countries are well known. See Stephen Enke, *Economics for Development* (Englewood Cliffs, N.J.: Prentice-Hall, Inc., 1963), pp. 40–44; and Simon Kuznets, "Levels and Variability of Growth Rates," *Economic Development and Cultural Change* 5: 1 (October 1956), pp. 4–9. Nevertheless, $16, the per-capita value-added in manufacturing in the other sixteen African countries, is so much higher than $4, the figure for Nigeria, that it must be concluded that Nigeria ranks very low among African countries. (Figures on per-capita value-added in manufacturing in selected African countries are: Cameroun, $48; Senegal, $30; Ivory Coast, $23; Congo (Kinshasa), $13; Niger, $9; Sudan, $7; Kenya, $6; Uganda, $4; Tanzania, $2, and Dahomey, $1.)
12. United Nations, Department of Economic and Social Affairs, *Yearbook of National Accounts Statistics 1964* (New York, 1965), pp. 364–69.
13. Lagos, 1965.
14. See the sources cited in the first footnote of the third paragraph in this section – especially the Federal Ministries of Labour and Commerce and Industry, and the Kilby report.
15. Sayre P. Schatz, "Economic Environment and Private Enterprise in West Africa," *Economic Bulletin (Ghana)* 7: 4 (December 1963), pp. 42–56. This article discusses the relative importance of obstacles in the economic environment and the lack of entrepreneurial supply. See, however, the change in formulation in the Schatz essay in this volume.
16. Ibid., pp. 54–56.
17. See S. A. Aluko, "The Educated in Business: The Calabar Home Farm – A Case Study," *Nigerian Journal of Economic and Social Studies* 7: 2 (July 1966), p. 200. Schatz does not support this statement. *Development Bank Lending in Nigeria: The Federal Loans Board* (Ibadan: Oxford University Press, 1965); and "The Capital Shortage Illusion: Government Lending in Nigeria," *Oxford Economic Papers* 17: 2 (July 1965),

pp. 309–16. See, however, the author's discussion of the difference between the concepts of capital "shortage" and "scarcity." *Nigerian Journal of Economic and Social Studies* 10: 1, p. 116.

18. United Nations, *Statistical Yearbook 1964*, pp. 529–35. See also W. Arthur Lewis, *Reflections on Nigeria's Economic Growth* (Paris: Development Centre of the Organization for Economic Co-operation and Development, 1967), p. 27.
19. Schatz, *Economic Bulletin* (*Ghana*) 7: 4 (December 1963), pp. 43–45, 47–48.
20. Ibid., pp. 45–47; Helleiner, pp. 330–31; T. M. Yesufu, *Nigerian Journal of Economic and Social Studies* 9: 3 (May 1959), p. 210; Harbison, *The Nigerian Political Scene*, ed. Tilman and Cole, pp. 204–13; and Nigeria, *National Development Plan 1962–68*, p. 15.
21. See Aluko, *Nigerian Journal of Economic and Social Studies* 8: 2, pp. 200–201.
22. Schatz, *Economic Bulletin* (*Ghana*) 7: 4 (December 1963), pp. 48–49; and Schatz and S. I. Edokpayi, "Economic Attitudes of Nigerian Businessmen," *Nigerian Journal of Economic and Social Studies* 4: 3 (November 1962), pp. 257–68.
23. Helleiner, p. 265; and John R. Harris, "Industrial Entrepreneurship in Nigeria," unpublished Ph.D. dissertation, Department of Economics, Northwestern University, August 1967, chap. 7, p. 41.
24. Cases where foreign capitalists have over 50 percent of equity capital are not discussed, since by definition the firm is not indigenous.
25. Schatz and Edokpayi's study indicates that Nigerians believe lack of knowledge and experience on the part of Nigerians to be one of the foreigner's major objections to forming a partnership with a Nigerian. Sayre P. Schatz and S. I. Edokpayi, "Economic Attitudes of Nigerian Businessmen," *Nigerian Journal of Economic and Social Studies* 4: 3 (November 1962), p. 266. This is assuming, as intimated, that the lack of capital on the part of the Nigerian is not an obstacle to the partnership.
26. This would not be an appropriate option if, as in a majority of the cases in the United Kingdom, the consulting firm concentrates on analysis at the shop level of the organization rather than on a broader perspective of the management of the firm. David Granick, The European Executive (Garden City, N.Y.: Doubleday and Co., Inc., 1962), pp. 255–56.
27. Some consulting firms do have personnel who are specialists in management problems in West Africa, or even in Nigeria specifically.
28. Wolfgang Stolper, *Planning Without Facts: Lessons in Resource Allocation From Nigeria's Development* (Cambridge, Mass.: Harvard University Press, 1966), p. 301; Schatz, *Economic Bulletin* (*Ghana*) 7: 4, pp. 46–47; and F. A. Wells and W. A. Warmington, *Studies in Industrialization: Nigeria and the Cameroons* (London: Oxford University Press, 1962), p. 88.
29. One can assume that in part because of the political pressure on foreign firms to obtain indigenous high-level personnel, the percentage of foreign professionals and managers is as high in indigenous firms as

in foreign firms. If the data in Table 1 are also assumed, it follows that the majority of professional and managerial personnel in large indigenous industrial firms are foreigners.

30. See "The Civil Service," *Nigerian Opinion* 1: 8 (August 1965), pp. 3–4; and Richard Burghart, "Ministerial Emoluments in Nigeria," *Nigerian Opinion* 7: 8 (August 1965), pp. 10–12.
31. Harris, "Industrial Entrepreneurship in Nigeria," chap. 8, pp. 31–32.
32. To go fully into the reasons for the high salaries of top-ranking government bureaucrats is beyond the scope of this study. The major reasons are probably institutional rigidities that maintained intact the high salaries required to induce qualified Britons to take civil service positions in the colonial period, and the concentration of oligopolistic power in the hands of government officials and civil servants. Hugh H. Smythe and Mabel M. Smythe, *The New Nigerian Elite* (Stanford, Calif.: Stanford University Press, 1960), pp. 132–33, see high government salaries as a psychological necessity for the Nigerian government élite, in order to retain the status attached to government positions under the British.
33. Nigeria, *Annual Abstract 1964*, pp. 13–14.
34. Kilby, "Technical Education in Nigeria," *Bulletin of the Oxford University Institute of Economics and Statistics* (May 1964), p. 182; and Nigeria, *Annual Abstract of Statistics 1963* (Lagos: Federal Office of Statistics, 1963), p. 25.
35. S. A. Aluko, "The Educated in Business: The Calabar Home Farm – A Case Study," *Nigerian Journal of Economic and Social Studies* 8: 2 (July 1966), p. 198.
36. Ibid., and Nigeria, *Statistics of Education in Nigeria – 1963* 3: 1 (Lagos: Federal Ministry of Education, 1965), pp. 11–13.
37. If X equals the number of years the major entrepreneur has held an entrepreneurial or managerial position in a manufacturing or trading firm with three or more workers engaged and Y 1964 value of output, $Y = 54{,}327 + 668X$. If the T-test is used, the regression coefficient is significant at the 1/10 percent level ($T = 5.17$).
38. See Schatz, *Nigerian Journal of Economic and Social Studies* 4: 3, pp. 257–68; also *Economic Bulletin (Ghana)* 4: 4 (December 1963), pp. 48–49; and Nafziger, "Nigerian Entrepreneurship," pp. 27–47, 136–39, and 177–78.
39. Callaway, "From Traditional Crafts to Modern Industries," *Odu: University of Ife Journal of African Studies* 2: 1 (July 1965), p. 36.
40. Kilby, *Bulletin of the Oxford Institute of Economics and Statistics* 26, p. 182; Nigeria, *Annual Abstract 1964*, pp. 12, 14; Helleiner, pp. 305–6; and Callaway, *Odu* 2: 1, pp. 28–51.
41. Nafziger, "The Effect of the Nigerian Extended Family on Entrepreneurial Activity," and Harris and Rowe, "Entrepreneurial Patterns in the Nigerian Sawmilling Industry," *The Nigerian Journal of Economic and Social Studies* 8: 1 (March 1966), pp. 67–96. See also Schatz, *Development Bank Lending in Nigeria*, pp. 89–101.
42. Archibald Callaway, "Nigeria's Indigenous Education: The Apprentice

System," *Odu: University of Ife Journal of African Studies* 1: 1 (July 1964), p. 12.

43. In 1965, the relatively cosmopolitan city of Lagos, where non-Yoruba entrepreneurs established enterprises in some sectors, might be considered an exception to this statement.
44. For the purpose of this analysis, Lagos is included with the Western Region.
45. Harris, pp. viii–5 found only five of the 101 manufacturing entrepreneurs in his sample operating businesses in regions outside of their birth.
46. The more successful the training is, the higher the manager's alternative price is and the more expensive it is to retain him. (See Schatz, *Economic Bulletin (Ghana)* 7: 4 (December 1963), p. 46.) The extent to which long-term indentures can counter this difficulty is limited.
47. There are problems in distinguishing the "investment" component of training from the "current cost" component, on the one hand, and "learning by experience," on the other hand. See Fritz Machlup, *The Production and Distribution of Knowledge in the United States* (Princeton, N.J.: Princeton University Press, 1962), pp. 58–60, 63–64. The argument above is consistent with the subsidization of the "investment" component of training.

Chapter 4

African Traders and Economic Growth: A Case Study in Ghana

Peter C. Garlick

The scene is Ghana, principally its two largest towns, Accra and Kumasi. This study centers on the largest permanently established African firms trading in imported goods in these towns, and their growth problems.[1] It is in the trading sector of the Ghana economy that African private-enterprise activities outside farming are most evident. The studies in these towns are not of statistically based samples of African traders. An attempt was made to cover the activities of all the biggest traders there, on the assumption that these firms, having already achieved a measure of growth, were likely to yield useful information about the background of growth and their problems in further development. The material was collected chiefly through interviews – hundreds of them – all over Ghana, covering other kinds of businesses, expatriate businessmen and bankers, farmers, and former traders who had retired. About ninety interviews with Ghanaian traders in Kumasi and one hundred and twenty in Accra were of a detailed nature. A primary objective at the time was to assist Ghanaian businessmen to play a larger role in their country's economic development. This objective was not realized, partly because of the political philosophy of Nkrumah, then leading the nation, and partly because it was not evident that the businessmen studied were able to play the sort of role envisioned.

TYPE OF TRADERS INTERVIEWED

In the 1960 census, Ghana had a population of approximately 6.7 million, of whom 44 percent were Akan-speaking. The largest individual Akan tribes were the Ashanti (895,000), and the Fanti (708,000). The Akan are closely related linguistically and culturally, almost all observing matrilineal descent in their social organization. Apart from the northern tribes, there were two other major groups in Ghana: the Ga-Adangme (560,000), which includes the people of the Accra region to the Volta river, and the Ghanaian Ewe (876,000) across the Volta. There are more Ewe across the Togo frontier, which arbitrarily divides the Ewe people.

In Kumasi, located in the Ashanti area, the biggest traders were found to be predominantly Ashanti. In Accra, by way of contrast, few of the biggest traders were local Accra people. Most of them were also Akan, but from a small tribal group called Kwahu, sixty or seventy miles east of Kumasi.[2] In Kumasi, only 10 percent of the traders had no formal education. In Accra the percentage was nearly four times as great, reflecting the predominance at this level of the Kwahu "strangers." In both Accra and Kumasi, most of the traders – over 80 percent – had built up their starting capital from previous occupations. Most of the rest had started with gifts or loans from relatives. Over 80 percent of their businesses were sole proprietorships, but many of the partnerships and limited companies or corporations were virtually sole proprietorships, in that one person, in fact, provided both the capital and the management. In these latter cases, it was not always clear why a form of organization other than sole proprietorship had been sought, especially where the partners or shareholders were members of the family, and sometimes minors. It was widely alleged by Ghanaian entrepreneurs that they could not associate in business, and the reason most frequently given was an unwillingness to trust prospective business associates. Certainly there was no shortage of examples offered by traders to justify this attitude. It is interesting that, in the census of enterprises carried out by the Central Bureau of Statistics, which kindly permitted access to its files, the proportions of sole proprietorships, partnerships, and limited companies were roughly the same for those larger Ghanaian traders whom it had sought out as for the Levantine trading firms in Ghana.

How big were the biggest African businesses? Stores were

relatively small – "petty traders grown large," in Guy Hunter's phrase.[3] Net profit, the figure the development economist would perhaps most like to know, thinking in terms of capital formation, was not surprisingly the least likely figure to be disclosed. Information was obtained about other possible criteria of size: turnover (i.e. the share of the market); number of employees; physical size of business premises. None was completely satisfactory, but turnover figures seemed to give the most reliable guide. An annual turnover of £50,000 was big; one of £100,000 exceptional.

The structure of businesses was analyzed in considerable detail: business costs, ownership of capital assets, specialization in trading, diversification of business interests, sources of credit, sources of supply of goods, and identification of customers.

The general impression was that for many, if not most, commodities most of the time, competition was keen.[4] Its intensity at the petty wholesale and retail levels, where comparatively little capital was required to start trading, could be seen in the big urban markets. There was a wide margin of traders at the end of the chain who moved in when trade was good and moved out when trade was poor. At the hawking level, school children after school hours and children who did not attend school joined the existing multitudes, chiefly of women and girls, seeking rewards from the pettiest of petty trading. It was not apparent how some store owners with poorly stocked shelves survived. Some small traders with market stalls, seeking short-term advantages, changed their range of goods frequently, one trader sometimes copying another. The larger trader, similarly, tended to display considerable flexibility in adapting to market variations the range of goods he supplied.

The structure of trading in imported goods in Ghana was pyramidal. At the apex were the large interterritorial firms, and in the 1960s, the state-owned Ghana National Trading Corporation, and it was here that most of the import trade was concentrated; at the base of the pyramid were the thousands of petty and itinerant African traders; between these groups were a few fairly large or medium-sized Indian and Levantine firms, and many smaller Indian, Levantine, and African firms. It was the African traders in this last group who were the main concern of these studies.

Most of the bigger African traders were concerned to reduce competition, first of all by reducing the activities of non-Africans. In the late 1950s the big expatriate firms were already well advanced in evacuating the retail field, so that, during the period of these studies, attention was focused on the Levantines. There was certainly plenty of evidence of hostility to them, and African traders voiced their complaints to the government. But it was widely believed that nothing would come of Ghanaian representations because some of Nkrumah's ministers found the Levantines a useful source of income. The Ollennu Report (April 1967) later provided evidence of such ministerial corruption.

THE SEARCH FOR SECURITY

Businessmen – and not only traders – were always complaining that they had too little capital to develop their businesses and thus to offer some competition to the larger commercial enterprises. Yet, at the same time, they were building houses or establishing cocoa farms. There were a few businessmen in these surveys who said that their only concern was the development of their businesses, but in fact it seems that there were none who did not draw off money from business for the construction of houses or the creation of farms, or both. Smaller businessmen, who were still developing their businesses, expressed intentions to build and to make farms. It was difficult to understand such apparently paradoxical behavior. How could a man expect to succeed in business if he were not plowing back his profits? It was only after a great deal of probing and questioning on this point over many months that the explanation of this behavior gradually became clear.

From the trader's point of view, in terms of organizing his resources to provide for his own immediate and future needs and those of the family, his behavior was comprehensible, and, indeed, completely rational. A major consideration was the provision of other sources of income. This was possible from urban residential property and farming, particularly cocoa farming. Provision for family costs, including food, clothing, accommodation, medical and (notably) education expenses, was thought of – where resources made planning possible – in long-period terms. Building in one's "home town" usually provided no income, but apart from the possible needs of the family, it was intended to meet the requirements of old age. A farm provided additional sources of income, perhaps some employment for relatives, and an occupation for retirement.

The striving for material security was a feature of the society with which these studies were concerned. More economically advanced countries must create state organizations for unemployment, old-age, and other social benefits, but for Ghana these were still largely future aspirations. For the most part, the family constituted the social security system. Family obligations could be onerous, and the successful man had to carry a substantial share of these burdens (though there appeared to be some compensation in the status he assumed in the family). Family costs had to be met with money. Success, therefore, could be measured in money terms.

It was generally true that only when a trader's business was new and still being built up would profits be plowed back. Profits otherwise were for investment elsewhere, perhaps in other types of business enterprise, but especially in farming and housing. In general, this was a businessman's long-run view of his economic activities. If this is not how developed capitalist society works, the difference is perhaps one only of degree. Individual endeavor in Ghana, as elsewhere, responded to the institutions and the opportunities in society. Thus, the businessman was not displaying improvident behavior. On the contrary, he was making a calculated, planned effort to meet his own needs and those of his family.

The widespread emphasis on the education of children in the family indicated in these studies reflected the intention that education should do more than provide a child with a job for his own fulfillment. The child was expected to shoulder his share of the family burden when he started earning. A family often cooperated to send a bright child for advanced education; less-favored children had to seek their fortune as best they could. The family combined communal responsibilities and individual enterprise.

The returns from business were uncertain and irregular.

A business life was full of anxieties. The tendency for a business to depend on one man, no matter what the formal organization of the firm, is clear from these studies. If this principal figure were ill, a wife or other relative was sometimes able to keep the business going, but there was rarely anyone to take over completely. If a business were to decline or fail because times were hard, or because of sickness or death, there might be nothing to show after years of work. In general, the difficulty of finding reliable subordinates limited the development of a firm to the size which an entrepreneur could control himself. Not least, the family might make demands on his stocks if he were a trader.

Business tended, therefore, to be regarded as ephemeral, expected to last only for a man's working life. The purpose of trading was not primarily to develop a business of size (though this might also be possible) but to provide for immediate and future personal and family needs, particularly by the acquisition of real property. If a man built houses in Accra or Kumasi, or established cocoa farms with money from his business, he created assets which would yield him income for the rest of his life, in sickness, and in retirement. This income would be independent of fluctuation in his business fortunes, and on his death his houses and farms would not perish, as his business probably would, but could be handed on to the family. A business was tied to the life of its creator; real property would endure with the family.

A house in a major urban area might yield an annual rent of 10 percent or even as much as 20 percent of the outlay, and the deeds could be used as security for bank accommodation. A man who built a big house in his "home town" might be acting less obviously in his best interests. Building there for the family and for his old age did not always appear to the outsider to require the size and prestige of a house costing several thousands of pounds. Indeed several African businessmen said that they regretted spending so much on building such large family houses in their home towns (when smaller houses would have served the purpose) instead of building somewhere else for gain.

An African trader often built first in his home town to be sure of satisfying various needs, before he built elsewhere as a commercial proposition. A house built in a village or a small town had little resale value, probably could not be let, and therefore yielded no rent. Neither was it acceptable as security for a bank loan. The property might be used, at least for the time being, only on festival or family occasions if most of the family lived and worked elsewhere; additionally, the owner might have to pay a caretaker.

It can be observed in passing that while Levantines apparently built more for reward than did Africans, Lebanese informants said that Lebanese traders, some retired from Ghana, had built houses in their home country for reasons similar to those given by Ghanaians.

Until the cocoa trees grew, there was revenue only from the food crops on a new cocoa farm – or possibly there were no returns at all, if roads and markets were too far away. A new house in an area where there was a demand for accommodation gave immediate returns much higher than those from a farm. A farm in one's own home area provided an occupation for retirement. At that stage of life, the personal collection of rents and the supervision of buildings might present problems of incapacity or distance, though scattered farms would present similar problems. But the reasons for establishing farms and for building houses were much the same: the desire for the permanence of real property and for income-yielding assets which were additional to a man's business, and which would survive both it and himself.

If, after establishing a house and farm or two, a businessman had then concentrated on his business, his behavior would perhaps have been similar to that of a small businessman in Europe and America. The comparison need not be pushed, beyond saying that in Europe a small business may grow into a large one. In Ghana, the indications were that the chances of such a development were much smaller, for it appeared that, with more profits from business, more houses were built and more cocoa farms established. Such investment indeed might be made not only from profits but sometimes at the cost of withdrawing capital from a business. The evidence indicated a tendency for more money to be shifted by traders from business into farming than from farming into business. Given the framework of society and the trader's responsibilities, it is worth repeating that this seemed entirely comprehensible behavior.

Viewed in the context of social responsibilities and the need for security, as well as against the background of economic institutions and opportunities, some of the reasons for the failure of small-business loan schemes (such as that of the Guarantee Corporation) become clearer. Such assistance did not create larger business units because traders had different objectives, about which they themselves were not articulate. It was not a question of deception. The objectives of growth were understood well enough and often formed the language of their expressed intentions. But their actual behavior could not conform because social realities were different, and were either not understood or ignored in legislation modeled on Western "norms" of business, which did not quite fit. Yet clearly such legislation was intended to improve the prospect and opportunites for the development of small businessmen. Schatz's argument, based on the experience of the Nigeria Federal Loans Board, that there is a large "false demand" for capital based upon unsound projects, but that capital shortage is less an impediment to Nigerian private business investment than is the shortage of commercially viable undertakings,[5] seems to fit the experience of the Guarantee Corporation, and helps to explain both the extent of the demand for loans and the rate of failure.

GROWTH PROSPECTS

The general argument from these studies is that, with few exceptions, the size of private African businesses, including enterprises outside trade, was unlikely to increase for a number of reasons. In both economic and social terms it made more sense for these traders to put business profits into farms and houses. The problems of finding business associates and reliable subordinates, the demands of the family, and indeed the whole social structure and ethos reinforced this tendency to hold businesses to a size manageable by one man, and, at least as important, to channel profits into areas where the risk of loss was substantially lower. The apparent conspicuous consumption sometimes observed was no doubt partly just that; but a car, like a house, was not in cash form, and therefore was not consumable by relatives. The greater achievement was in real property, not in stocked store shelves. The one survived; the other did not.

These studies do not point with much optimism to substantial participation by private African enterprise in Ghana's economic development. However, there is evidence since the fall of Nkrumah not only of a resurgence of African business, but also of the emergence of new businessmen with ambition and with greater opportunities than ever before. Here may be the vanguard of a new force for economic change in Ghana.

NOTES

1. This paper represents some of the conclusions reached in Dr. Garlick's book: *African Traders and Economic Development in Ghana*, (Oxford: The Clarendon Press, 1971).
2. Most of the cocoa production in Ghana is in Akan hands, so that Akan people are among the richest of the national community.
3. Guy Hunter, *The New Societies of Tropical Africa* (London, New York, and Ibadan: Oxford University Press, 1962), p. 135.
4. Cf. the paper in this volume by Marvin Miracle, "Market Structure and Conduct in Tropical Africa: A Survey." However, Dr. Miracle's study deals largely with primary products whereas the concern here is with imported goods.
5. Sayre P. Schatz, "The Capital Shortage Illusion" (London, New York, and Ibadan: *Oxford Economic Papers* 17: 2 (July 1965). See also his *Development Bank Lending in Nigeria: The Federal Loans Board* (London, New York, and Ibadan: Oxford University Press, 1964), particularly chap. 6.

Chapter 5

Market Structure and Conduct in Tropical Africa: A Survey

Marvin P. Miracle

As is often true, the sort of data needed for analysis of market structure, conduct, and performance in tropical Africa are difficult to obtain, usually fragmentary, and often of questionable reliability. In fact, anything on performance is extremely hard to find, and what can be uncovered is so untrustworthy that in this writer's view it would be unwise to attempt to draw inferences from it at this juncture. A careful search of the literature will suggest, however, that something can be inferred about market structure and conduct; consequently, the emphasis here is limited to these matters. Particularly interesting is the contrast between the portrait of competitive behavior that emerges for the pre-colonial period and the assumptions usually made about competition in contemporary Africa.

Evidence of market structure and conduct in the pre-colonial period is first briefly summarized; current thinking on the subject is then reviewed; and finally, evidence of both organized and unorganized collusion is surveyed and evaluated.

THE PRE-COLONIAL PERIOD

The tribal economies that colonial administrators found when they imposed their rule a little over half a century ago appear commonly to have been dominated by guilds. (Most of the data here are on West Africa, where trade was probably most active, but the little evidence for other areas suggests that restrictive practices may have been common everywhere. What we can reconstruct about the economic conditions then prevailing gives reason to expect this.)

Polyani tells us that in southern Dahomey prices were set by producers' or sellers' organizations.[1] In Whydah and Porto Novo vendors of the same commodity belonged to a trade association called a *sodudo* which fixed prices. In addition to regulating competition the *sodudo* was a mutual aid society with certain social functions at times of illness or death in the family.

Hodder and Lloyd suggest that among the Yoruba, guilds were found for all crafts, with similar trade guilds organized along commodity lines.[2] Membership in these guilds usually was compulsory, and they were run by a powerful head.

Likewise among the Nupe of northern Nigeria, crafts and trading were organized through guilds;[3] M. G. Smith's description of the economic organization of the Hausa[4] and the accounts of Dubois and Miner of Timbuctoo[5] indicate the same pattern farther north. The greatest detail is given on the craft guilds, and, as in the south, guilds had powerful leaders and controlled prices; they may also have regulated the economic activities of members in other ways.

Skinner and Radbury discuss craft guilds in Benin, and Skinner also mentions them for Djenne, Senegal, Sierra Leone, Guinea, Liberia, and northern Ivory Coast.[6, 7] It is not unlikely that similar organizations were also found among commodity traders in all these areas.

Restriction of competition is also suggested by Binger's report in 1892 (cited in Skinner) that in parts of the Ivory Coast a secret society controlled the trade in kola nuts (one of the mainstays of commerce in that area then as now) and tried to block access to areas of production by other traders.[8]

Similar restrictive practices may have been common in other areas. Coastal chiefs or trading groups are reported to have similarly monopolized trade between European companies and inland supply zones in many areas. According to Allan McPhee, chiefs and heads of trading groups frequently closed roads and streams connecting the inland areas and the coast in Nigeria in order to establish themselves as the sole sellers dealing with European firms, and he notes that in Ghana the Ashanti finally fought their way to the coast to break the monopolistic power of coastal groups there.[9] Similar situations are reported elsewhere along the coast as far south as Angola.[10]

Considering the prevailing economic conditions, restrictive practices are not surprising. Most economic relationships were highly personal, with a keen awareness of mutual dependence prevailing among ethnic and kinship groups. Capital was scarce and largely controlled by merchants. There is nothing to suggest a banking system through which savings might be transmitted impersonally from savers to borrowers. Once inequality of wealth developed there was little scope for a relatively poor individual to challenge the holders of economic power. Those without power were obliged to join with the relatively wealthy, or to band together. There were strong pressures for group action.

THE POST-WORLD WAR II PERIOD

Since World War II, opinions about the amount and nature of competition in tropical Africa have been strongly influenced by the pioneering work of P. T. Bauer, particularly through his *West African Trade*, a controversial book because of its fierce attack on marketing boards.[11] Bauer gives relatively little attention to the organization of internal trade either in this book or in articles dealing with Africa,[12] but he does argue that domestic marketing is fairly competitive. His comments that nearly everyone in West Africa is involved in some sort of trade, his view that there are rarely barriers to entry of any significance, and his opinion that as trade is now organized, good use is made of available resources, all leave the impression that he sees internal trade as fairly competitive, in contrast to the oligopolistic and oligoponistic conditions he found among importers and exporters. Bauer does note in the final chapter of *West African Trade* that restrictive associations have been reported in southern Nigeria for cattle, fish, and "staple foodstuffs" but he dismisses this as of little significance on the grounds that such organizations cannot effectively enforce attempts at price maintenance.[13]

Similar views seem to be based on numbers of individuals seen in marketplaces. S. La Anyane, Dean of Agriculture at the University of Ghana, writes of Ghana: "Comparatively restrictive tendencies are ineffective. Crowds of buyers bargain freely with the large number of sellers of similar commodities. . . ."[14] Harold Riley states: "An atomistically competitive structure exists in West African markets for products produced and consumed domestically."[15] Edward and Mildred Marcus comment ". . . the multiplicity of traders in the larger centers (of tropical Africa) makes the outsider wonder whether this isn't competition carried to its most vicious extreme."[16] Tardits writes of Dahomey: "Competition is hard in Dahomean markets. Merchants sell either the same goods or products for which there are ready substitutes."[17] Edwin Dean, speaking of marketplaces in Brazzaville and southern Malawi, where he attempted to measure selling behavior, states: "The markets concerned were competitive."[18]

These modern generalizations suggest enormous changes in patterns of competition during the colonial period. If so what were the causes? Did economic relationships for some reason become greatly less personal? Did available capital dramatically increase? Were there sufficiently rapid economic growth and expansion of markets to eliminate barriers to entry?

The answer to all these possibilities is, this writer believes, clearly no. We have little reason to think that there were sufficient changes in the African economies to cause replacement of restrictive by competitive arrangements.

Economic relationships are still highly personal and ethnic, and kinship bonds continue to be impressively strong. Binet, speaking of Guinea, emphasizes such ties in saying that ". . . the profession of commerce is relatively closed . . . it is not necessarily hereditary in that sons inherit from fathers, but one does find a large proportion of kinsmen together."[19] In Nigeria and Ghana the cattle and kola nut trade is almost exclusively in the hands of Hausa. In the southern Ivory Coast the charcoal sellers are entirely Bambara, the hardware sellers almost exclusively Yoruba, the African producers of "French type" bread are Senegalese. In Accra wholesale plantain traders are mainly Ga; wholesale grain traders are almost entirely from Niamey. Polly Hill refers to the "strangle-hold" the Goa ex-carriers had over the Kumasi yam trade until they were expelled in 1958.[20] Garlick's survey of 113 Ghanaian firms in Accra showed "more than one-third" to be Kwahus, an

Akan group from the hill country sixty miles east of Kumasi.[21] Despois reports that the Bamileke control the fish trade in southern Cameroun.[22] According to Comhaire-Sylvain's study of Lagos traders in 1948, most of the cloth sellers were Yoruba but foodstuff traders were Ibo, except for garri, for which most were also Yoruba.[23]

Capital is still scarce, capital markets are weak and organized in such a manner that capital problems can easily be a barrier to entry. There has clearly been considerable economic growth, particularly with discovery of exploitable mineral deposits and expansion of export crop production, but there is nothing to suggest that in Africa growth of markets alone suffices to explain replacement of guilds or cartels with the highly competitive selling described by Bauer and others.

Thus once account is taken of the history of African economies, doubt arises about the validity of prevailing views that African economies are highly competitive. Scrutiny of Bauer's data and other evidence in the literature also suggests that African economies are not nearly so competitive as has been asserted.

Economy-wide statements about the amount of competition, such as those cited earlier, are not likely to be meaningful, since competition may be different for each commodity sold, and different from one market to another for the same commodity. Nevertheless, evidence available does suggest that, despite prevailing assertions to the contrary, severe departures from atomistic competition are in fact found for a wide variety of goods and services, and are common for the starchy-staples and the major sources of proteins which together account for over 90 percent of calories consumed in tropical Africa.

ORGANIZED COLLUSION

There are details on the operation of several cartels found in major commodities in West Africa. For a number of other sellers' associations, data are incomplete but what is available suggest that they are likely to be cartels.

The most detailed information to be presented in this section concerns cartels that the writer has investigated in the Ivory Coast and Ghana. Among these, the plantain cartel in Grand

Bassam, Ivory Coast, is particularly interesting. Plantain is probably the major starch-staple sold in Grand Bassam. In July 1965 the plantain cartel had about forty members, all women. The organization was composed principally of retailers and was directed by a wholesaler who was the sole supplier of the other members, selling to them on credit at the price she dictated. New members could join only with permission of the cartel head, might have to pay an entry fee, and had to agree to abide by cartel rules. Members caught selling below the retail price set by the cartel leader were fined $8.15 and could be expelled from the organization if the offense became habitual. The cartel leader was said to be the wealthiest member of the group.

Another fairly detailed account was obtained at Makessim, Ghana. Although contact was made with a number of heads of sellers' associations – there called "queens" if women, "chiefs" if men – only a former queen of the maize association was willing to talk freely. Her account of operations is much like that for the plantain cartel in Grand Bassam and for other cartels described by members of cartels operating in Takoradi and Kumasi. The queen is the wholesaler; she finances the other members, settles disputes arising between members, allocates available supplies among them in times of shortage, and maintains price discipline by fines.

Other cartels the writer has investigated, but on which he could get less information, are those among wholesale cattle dealers and ocean fish traders in Abidjan; charcoal sellers in Grand Bassam, Ivory Coast; transporters in the Ivory Coast and Ghana; yam dealers in Kumasi; plantain wholesalers in Accra; cattle dealers in Ho, Ghana; kola nut wholesalers in Ouagadougou; millet wholesalers in Niamey; and cattle dealers in Umuahia, Nigeria. Most of these cartels seem to impose entrance fees on new members (as high as $11.75 in some instances); to use fines as one means of maintaining discipline;[24] and to offer a mutual savings scheme. The cartels all seem to be viewed by the members as important vehicles for mutual aid.

Victor Du Bois reports that prostitutes in Abidjan belong to one of three or four associations founded along ethnic lines, each of which has a head who acts as ". . . a combination of mother superior and banker. . . ."[25] The principal function he lists for these organizations is determination of prices to be charged.

Rowena Lawson states that market queens exist "in all but the smallest towns" in Ghana and that they form price rings and allocate supplies in time of shortage.[26] Ione Acquah lists a number of trade associations in Accra for 1953 and suggests that price control is one of their major functions, but does not provide details.[27]

Polly Hill, in an article on Ghana published in 1963, suggests that restrictions to competition are common in referring to farmers' acceptance of ". . . institutional price-fixing and limitations on competition (which) seem so natural in West African economies generally." In the same article she refers to refusal of women plantain retailers to compete with their sister sellers by cutting prices; and she also comments on the practice of one member of a marketing association bargaining for the whole group when buying supplies.[28] However, she may have changed her mind about all this later. In reply to a letter by Rowena Lawson in *West Africa* which discussed, among other things, the power and functions of so-called market queens, Polly Hill says: "I disagree emphatically with most of what she (Rowena Lawson) states in her letter . . ."[29]

Additional suggestion of organized collusion in Ghana is to be found in James Christensen's comment that among the Fanti there is little variation in price of particular goods on a single day due to agreement between sellers.[30]

M. G. Wygant's description of associations of women traders in Togo strongly suggests they have cartels. He says that within associations ". . . matters are discussed affecting their interests – such as collective buying, and organizing a 'hold-up' or boycott of certain goods . . ."[31] Charbonneau gives no details but similarly reports that in Togo the market women are organized into "trusts."[32]

Herskovits indicates that organized collusion is common in Dahomey: "Price-fixing is done in various ways. On the coast, trade associations fix the price for the commodities sold by their members. A refusal to pay an established price results in concerted physical action against one who insists on taking goods for less." He reports that in the interior, retailers are organized in that they in effect let wholesalers set prices for some commodities. In others, price cutters are fined as on the coast: ". . . every woman must sell her pots at the stated price under fear of penalties exacted by her fellows . . . Native cloth, woven and sold by men who constitute a closed guild, must bring a stated return . . . The name of each pattern, with its selling price, is known to the weavers, and here again penalties are exacted if the agreed price is cut."[33]

Tardits provides a little additional information on Dahomey with his reference to a secret association called *Zangebto*, found among the Gunu of Porto-Novo and the Iong of Abomey.[34] This association reportedly can fine sellers as much as 1,000 CFA francs ($4.08) for failure to follow prices it sets.

There are several references to strong sellers' organizations in Western Nigeria and there is considerable evidence to suggest that they are often cartels. The writer has never been able to get details of their operations from members of these organizations, but one informant states that the maize association her mother-in-law belongs to is run by a powerful head who sets the prices for members and bargains for the group where they buy supplies. This particular association buys maize on the Dahomey border where all the bargaining is done between the head of the Dahomean maize sellers and the leader of the Nigerian buyers. Bargaining between these two women reportedly goes on often for several hours before a satisfactory price is finally negotiated.

In 1958 when the writer was doing field work in Western Nigeria, farmers frequently said they were excluded from marketplaces by assocations of traders. Lloyd and Hodder both refer to market guilds, but do not discuss their importance or how they operate.[35] Comhaire-Sylvain tells us that in Lagos ". . . the commerce in foodstuffs is in the hands of women and they have long been powerfully organized. Each section (fish, garri, cloth, etc.) is directed by a head." Although she points out that "the members of each commodity meet regularly . . . (and that) there is a strict discipline among them, the differences between sellers being taken before commodity heads . . ." she also makes the hard-to-believe comment that they have not used their power to fix prices. However she later points out that the organization of fish sellers prevents fishermen from selling in marketplaces, although this is not the case with the sale of crabs and snails.[36]

Abner Cohen's discussion of cattle trade in Nigeria suggests that a cartel is found among Ibadan butchers and among the cattle dealers who supply them. Dealers may put pressure on a butcher who is delinquent in paying his debts by refusing to sell to any member of the association to which he belongs until his credit position is improved.[37]

Lloyd reports a transport cartel in Western Nigeria which, like those in the Ivory Coast and Ghana, fixes passenger and freight fares on all major roads.[38]

M. G. Smith reports that among the Hausa there is a head of sellers of various commodity groups – e.g., butchers, grain sellers, blacksmiths, and brokers. One of the principal duties of the head of butchers is to buy supplies for the group and to "organize cooperation among butchers to sell supplies quickly." One of the responsibilities of the head of the grain sellers is ". . . maintenance of fair measures and prices."[39] Smith refers to use of fines by the head of prostitutes to maintain discipline but neither confirms nor denies the use of fines by other groups.[40]

Bauer and Yamey describe a complex cartel among Levantine peanut buyers in northern Nigeria, but argue that despite a system of fines for breaking cartel agreements, members of the cartel behaved fairly competitively.[41]

Delane Welsch says the Abakaliki Rice Mill Owners Association in Eastern Nigeria has as its objective restriction of milling hours and maintenance of minimum milling charges.[42] By using coercion it was successful in restricting milling hours, although apparently there was failure at times during the slack season to enforce the minimum milling charges.

Binet suggests that organized collusion is common in Guinea with his comment that "the merchants seem to form relatively tight groups . . . I can cite a number of instances of a single family controlling a vast zone . . ."[43]

I. M. Lewis indicates there is a great deal of collusion in Somalia and that it is organized along clan lines. He says: "It is typical of the lineage character of Somali trading interests that a peace settlement reached at one stage in a long train of conflict between two clans contending for access to water and pasturage, should include a clause defining the trading rights of each to the disputed areas."[44]

In a discussion of produce trading in Tanzania, Hawkins says that in most areas ". . . there are not more than five or six large produce buyers, often only one or two, and they usually seem to be able to come to an agreement not to cut each other's throat."[45] Alvis reports that in Kenya "wholesalers in potato-growing areas practice little price competition. In small towns and villages they would meet at intervals and agree among themselves on the prices to be offered to growers of potatoes."[46]

Evidence on organized collusion is fascinating but economists tend to be reluctant to accept it. Because of our usual assumptions about cartels, we find it easy to believe that they are difficult to organize and often of limited effectiveness because of discipline problems. One of the basic points of cartel theory is that cartels tend to be unstable because any one member can realize highly tempting gains by secretly breaking discipline, with the result that effective cartels are hard to form and are not likely to be long-lived if attempted.

But the discipline problem is quite different in Africa. A major difference between African cartels and those from our own traditions relates to social factors and shortage of capital. Members of African cartels are bound together by social ties that assure mutual aid in times of illness, bereavement, or other needs. These ties are sometimes, but not always, reinforced by ethnic bonds, since "stranger" traders in a foreign, if not hostile, community find cooperation with others of their ethnic group advisable, if not mandatory.

But social pressure aside, most traders appear unable to operate without credit, and given a thin capital market in which commodity traders are the major, if not the dominant, lenders, and blacklisting appears to be a common practice, the choice appears not infrequently to be to conform or to be forced out of worthwhile trade. The gains from delinquent behavior must be weighed against the deficits of cutoff from credit and reduction to much less lucrative petty trade where labor can be largely substituted for capital.

If the cost of delinquency is high, one must next consider, as Bauer does, the probability of a delinquent seller being caught.

Bauer concedes "Market women's unions are ubiquitous in southern Nigeria and the Gold Coast," but goes on to argue that they are ineffective in maintaining price because "there are crowds of customers milling around the large number of sellers all of whom sell by volume . . ."[47] He thus seems to be arguing that price surveillance is so difficult in crowded marketplaces that price cutting is easy.

This is questionable on several grounds. Sellers are nearly always grouped in marketplaces by commodity. The writer has never seen such a crush of buyers that it was impossible for sellers to observe the activities of neighboring sellers. When there is some slack, there is always a possibility that momentarily unoccupied sellers will keep an eye on the others. And even when all sellers are simultaneously occupied it is quite possible to have spies planted in the guise of customers.

Cartels of sellers try to maintain a minimum price.[48] One sees bargaining because a member who can get more than the minimum from a buyer is entitled to his windfall. How long it takes a buyer to determine the minimum cartel price is of no interest to other members of the cartel so long as the price at the end of the negotiations is not below that dictated by the cartel.

Selling by volume rather than by weight presents no problem at all. In fact, if anything, it makes easier a check from a distance on the price being paid. Selling by volume simply means that the price is fixed while the amount of the commodity received varies. It is easier to tell whether the agreed three plantains or the stipulated five cigarette tins of rice is being given for, say, twenty-five francs than to determine whether it was twenty-four, twenty-five, or twenty-six francs paid for a kilo and whether the seller actually weighed exactly one thousand grams or a little more.

In summary, considering (1) the nature of capital markets; (2) the strength of social ties and pressures in cartels; (3) the prominence of guilds and cartels in the traditions of African peoples; and (4) the fact that infractions of cartel discipline can be fairly easily detected, one should expect organized collusion to be widespread in tropical Africa and to be resilient once established.

SELLER CONCENTRATION AND APPARENTLY UNORGANIZED COLLUSION

Given the state of data on marketing in Africa, it is certainly possible that much organized collusion is undetected, or is reported as something else. In some cases, the only data available are on the number of sellers, with no evidence one way or the other on their behavior.

A dramatic illustration of how deceptive appearances can be in this regard is provided by the plantain cartel in Grand Bassam referred to earlier. The author had been working in the Grand Bassam area five months, visiting the marketplace for two or three hours almost every day, when he discovered its existence. He had supposed that plantain selling was highly competitive since his records showed more than forty sellers.

The number of sellers may be deceptive not only because of collusive arrangements, but also because of the common practice of employing paid assistants or relatives to help with selling. Ten vendors may represent only three or four decision-makers. Thus when there are few vendors, one can be certain that there is no more competition than would be consistent with the apparent concentration ratio; on the other hand, when there are many sellers, no inference can be drawn without eivdence regarding actual conduct.

In tropical Africa, despite statements about crowds of sellers, there are often only a few sellers of a given commodity in a given market. The aggregate number of sellers is indeed often as large as the word "crowd" suggests, but there are also many commodities and grades of the same commodity. The correct portrayal, therefore, would be many apparent sellers of some items and few sellers of others.

In Grand Bassam, Ivory Coast, a town of about twelve thousand, there were typically fewer than eight apparent sellers for fifteen of the thirty-seven more important commodities sold in the marketplace between May and the end of October 1965. For Timbuctoo, with some five thousand inhabitants in 1940 when Miner studied it, there were at that time seventeen sellers of tobacco and the same number for milk; fifteen butchers; twelve vendors of shea butter or kola nuts; ten flour merchants; but only two cloth sellers.[49]

According to Couty's study of the fish trade in Cameroun there were fewer than ten wholesale buyers in twenty-two of the forty-six markets he surveyed.[50] Allen and Chaux found only six fish wholesalers in Kinshasa.[51]

Antonio says that there are few yam wholesalers in Ibadan but he comments that nevertheless "price collusion was not heard of as such." A later comment suggests that the same wholesalers may at least tacitly allocate market shares, for he refers to the fact that "an unconscious area specialization develops as wholesalers acquire enough capital and experience." This is further suggested by his comment at another point that bargaining between the wholesaler and the farmer is "reasonably close to a case of bilateral monopoly with the farmer in a weaker bargaining position."[52]

Polly Hill notes that in Kumasi there were forty cattle dealers in April and May 1964 but that the seven largest of these handled three-fourths of the trade.[53]

Crutchfield's study of the fish trade in Uganda suggests considerable geographic variation in the concentration of economic power.[54] He found as few as three wholesale buyers in some areas and indications of collusion, but as many as twenty-five to thirty apparent sellers at some points in the marketing chain. Mukwaya reports that when a truck arrives in marketplaces in Kampala, only one wholesale buyer bargains at a time, which suggests collusion, but unfortunately he does not elaborate.[55] Anne Martin, however, is of the view that marketing is competitive in Uganda, but it is not entirely clear what her evidence is.[56]

It is this writer's strong impression from field work that sellers keenly feel their mutual interdependence and that informal collusion is common even when there are as many as twenty sellers. Most attempts to inquire about selling behavior revealed either organized collusion or a reluctance to talk about business operations, leaving it unclear whether there was collusion. Not a few sellers emphasized how competitive they were, but in many such cases, when their statements were checked, their versions were refuted and specific examples of their collusive behavior were cited by other sellers or observers. Those reluctant to discuss collusion *per se* often gave the impression, in talking about other matters, that a keen sense of interdependence is found among sellers.

This interdependence results in large measure from the conditions under which they must do business, conditions found throughout tropical Africa. Therefore, although the writer's own observations are primarily for parts of the Ivory Coast, Mali, Upper Volta, Ghana, Niger, Congo (Kinshasa), Zambia, and Malawi, the same collusive tendencies should be expected elsewhere in tropical Africa as well.

African sellers can be expected to be reluctant to take actions that would antagonize fellow sellers because, with no insurance available and with credit difficult, they never know when assistance from a competitor may be badly needed. When asked what actions might be taken if a competitor were selling at a lower price, the first response by many informants who claimed to be competitive was that, individually or collectively, they would go to the price-cutter and plead with him to raise his price back to the level charged by the rest of the sellers, pointing out to him that he was "spoiling" the market and injuring his neighbors. Repeatedly, informants have stressed the value of good will of fellow sellers because of the possibility that sellers might have to pool resources for purchase of supplies or to rely on each other for short-term credit to ride out temporary crises.

BUYER ATTACHMENT[57]

If price competition is frequently avoided, for major commodities at least, one might expect a good deal of non-price competition, and this in fact is suggested by the evidence.

A limiting case, perhaps, is the practice reported by some cartels studied by the writer of dividing up supply zones so that farmers have little or no choice in determining who buys their produce. This practice is also suggested for yam wholesalers in Ibadan.[58] Somewhat less restrictive, but important, is the practice of traders giving farmers advances on their unharvested crops and thereby gaining a measure of control over supplies.

In areas of the Ivory Coast and Ghana where the writer has worked, this is widely reported. Dorjahn states that in Sierra Leone rural traders make such advances to farmers but that the traders, in turn, are operating largely with credit they were given by large trading firms in urban areas, while they themselves are committed to sell export crops they collect, such as palm kernels, to the supplier of credit.[59] Daryl Forde indicates that the same credit ties are common in northern Nigeria; he reports that farmers often pay their taxes through advances on crops.[60] Alvis discusses a similar practice in parts of Kenya.[61] Mark Karp reports that traders in Somalia commonly give loans to farmers as a means of obligating producers to sell crops to them;[62] and René Dumont says this practice is common in Madagascar, Senegal, and the Ivory Coast, though he does not provide details.[63]

The reverse credit relationship – producers financing traders – is not unknown, however. Gloria Marshall reports that Yoruba farmers sometimes extend credit to buyers.[64] Informants indicate that yam farmers in the Brong-Ahafo area of Ghana may at times give yam buyers credit, and Dorjahn reports the same practice among fishermen in Sierra Leone when they have an unusually large catch.[65] The Fulani often give credit to cattle buyers providing that it is guaranteed by the broker handling the deal.[66]

For most, if not all, major commodities, credit is likely to be a part of selling strategy each time the good changes hands. According to I. M. Lewis, provision of credit is a major means of attracting customers in Somalia.[67] Marris states that in Lagos credit is a common means of tying customers and that the maxim "No credit, no trade" was often repeated to him.[68] Gloria Marshall reports extension of credit is also a principal means of tying customers among the Yoruba.[69]

There is little information on other means of achieving buyer or seller attachment, but provision of free lodging, gifts, assistance in securing transportation or storage are all clearly of some importance.

CONCLUSIONS

Although there are great gaps in the evidence on market structure and conduct in tropical Africa, there is some basis for generalizing. The most competitive selling is likely to be in supply zones. In areas where a given commodity is produced, producers may be able to enter the ranks of sellers if supernormal profits are being earned. However, we already have sufficient examples of vigorous and successful attempts to keep producers from selling directly to consumers in tropical Africa to know that easy access to supplies is clearly not a sufficient condition to assure competitive selling. Once the commodity is beyond the producer, and storage or transport costs must be added, competition seems to be easily restricted by shortage of capital alone. Finally, once bulk is broken at retail, the capital required of an individual retailer may be relatively small so that a relatively larger number of potential entrants is likely.

Thus, given that a large proportion of the major commodities – even the starchy-staples – seem to move over a hundred, and in some cases several hundred, miles from producer to consumer it is, this observer would argue, highly likely that there are considerable restrictions to competition somewhere in the marketing chain of all major commodities in tropical Africa.

NOTES

Note: The following abbreviations are used below:

FAO	Food and Agriculture Organization of the United Nations
IBRD	International Bank for Reconstruction and Development
NISER	Nigerian Institute of Social and Economic Research
ORSTOM	Office de la Recherche Scientifique et Technique Outre-Mer (France)
SEDES	Société d'Études pour le Développement Économique et Social

1. Karl Polyani, *Dahomey and the Slave Trade* (Seattle: University of Washington Press, 1966), p. 87.
2. B. W. Hodder, "The Yoruba Rural Market," in *Markets in Africa*, Paul Bohannan and George Dalton, eds. (Evanston, Ill.: Northwestern University Press, 1962), p. 144. See also P. C. Lloyd, "The Yoruba Town Today," *The Sociological Review*, New Series 7: 1, p. 52.
3. S. F. Nadel, *A Black Byzantium* (New York: Oxford University Press, 1942), pp. 92, 294, 330.
4. M. G. Smith, "Exchange and Marketing Among the Hausa," in Bohannan and Dalton, eds., *Markets in Africa*.
5. Felix Dubois, *Timbuctoo the Mysterious* (New York: Longmans, Green, & Co., 1966). See also Horace Miner, *The Primitive City of Timbuctoo* (Princeton, N.J.: Princeton University Press, 1953).
6. Elliot P. Skinner, "West African Economic Systems," in M. J. Herskovits and M. Harwitz, eds., *Economic Transition in Africa* (Evanston, Ill.: Northwestern University Press, 1964), pp. 83–85.

   R. E. Radbury, "The Kingdom of Benin," in Daryle Ford and P. M.

Koberry, *West African Kingdoms in the Nineteenth Century* (London: Oxford University Press, 1967), p. 24.

8. E. P. Skinner, "West African Economic Systems," p. 93.
9. Allan McPhee, *The Economic Revolution in British West Africa* (London: G. Routledge & Son, Ltd., 1928), pp. 88–89.
10. Pierre Kalck, *Réalités oubanquiennes* (Paris: Éditions Berger-Levrault, 1959), p. 72.
11. P. T. Bauer, *West African Trade* (Cambridge, England: Cambridge University Press, 1954).
12. Bauer, "Concentration in Tropical Trade: Some Aspects and Implications of Oligopoloy," *Economica* 20: 80 (November 1953).
13. Bauer, *West African Trade*, pp. 391–92.
14. S. La Anyane, "Agriculture in the General Economy," in *Agriculture and Land Use in Ghana*, J. B. Wills, ed. (London: Oxford University Press, 1962), pp. 194–95). But by 1967 La Anyane appears to have changed his view. See S. La Anyane, "Three Leading Issues in Agricultural Policy," *The Legon Observer* 2: 26 (Sept. 29–Oct. 12, 1967). In that article, La Anyane refers to the fact that market women ". . . have formed themselves into monopolistic groups or rings at the wholesale level, which explains much of the high consumer prices of local foodstuffs and the poor quality of produce."
15. Harold M. Riley, "Marketing Patterns and Problems in Domestic Markets of Countries in the Early Stages of Economic Development" (Mimeographed paper, Michigan State University Library, East Lansing, Michigan, 1964), p. 8.
16. Edward and Mildred R. Marcus, *Investment and Development Possibilities in Tropical Africa* (New York: Brookman Associates, 1960), p. 166.
17. Claude and Claudine Tardits, "Traditional Market Economy in South Dahomey," in Bohannan and Dalton, *Markets in Africa*, p. 97.
18. Edwin R. Dean, "Studies in Price Formation in African Markets," *The Rhodes-Livingstone Journal*, no. 31, 1962, p. 13.
19. Jacques Binet, "Marchés en pays Soussou," *Cahiers d'Études Africaines* 2: 4 cahier, 1962, p. 110.
20. Polly Hill, "Some Characteristics of Indigenous West African Enterprise," Nigerian Institute of Social and Economic Research (NISER) *Conference Proceedings*, Ibadan, March 1962, p. 118. Peter Garlick made the same point earlier (see Peter C. Garlick, "The Gao in Kumasi," *Economic Bulletin* (*Ghana*) (November 1958).
21. P. C. Garlick, "African and Levantine Trading Firms in Ghana," NISER, *Conference Proceedings*, Ibadan, 1960, p. 120.
22. J. Despois, "Des Montagnards en pays tropical Bamiléké et Bamoun," *Rev. Géog. Alpine*, vol. 33, p. 622.
23. Suzanne Comhaire-Sylvain, "Le Travail des femmes à Lagos, Nigeria," *Zaïre* (February 1951), p. 178.
24. Alan Thodey says that sellers' associations in western Nigeria are often not effective in trying to discipline members: ". . . because of the size of most markets and the number of traders in each commodity, it is generally difficult for a trade association to enforce its will on

traders . . ." (Alan R. Thodey, *Marketing of Staple Foods in Western Nigeria*, Stanford Research Institute, Project No. 4: 5586, 2: pp. viii–104, Menlo Park, Calif., 1968). He does not present evidence to show that the number of traders is large, and his analysis gives no indication that he is aware of troublesome problems of measuring seller concentration, such as difficulties of defining commodities and determining which sellers are decision-makers and which are employees (Ibid, vol. 2: chap. 8 and appendices 8.2–8.4; cf. Marvin P. Miracle, "Market Structure in Commodity Trade and Capital Accumulation in West Africa," in Reed Moyer and Stanley C. Hollander, eds., *Markets and Marketing in Developing Economies* (Homewood, Ill.: Richard D. Irwin, 1968), pp. 218–19.

There are also other reasons to doubt Thodey's generalization. The author interviewed the heads and members of several sellers' associations in the Ivory Coast, Ghana, Upper Volta, and Niger who claim that those breaking price or market-sharing agreements can be fairly easily forced to conform; and this seems reasonable, given the control of those holding monopoly power over the supply of available capital, the fact that African businessmen often must turn to rivals for help in times of need, and the fact that rival sellers are often tied by social obligations. Moreover, informants in western Nigeria itself claim that tight discipline is often maintained there. (One of these informants was the daughter-in-law of the head of a large association and should have been in a position to get information not readily given to outsiders.) Considerable control over members in western Nigerian associations is also suggested by Cohen and Comhaire-Sylvain, discussed below (A. Cohen, "The Social Organization of Credit in a West African Cattle Market," *Africa* (January 1965); Suzanne Comhaire-Sylvain, "Le Travail des femmes."

Part of the discrepancy may lie in confusion about the nature of sellers' associations. For some commodities it is difficult to establish cartels in Africa because supply cannot be easily controlled. This would be true for any of the common staples at harvest in the zone where they are produced. It may also be true for commodities for which labor can readily be substituted for capital in transportation, storage, or processing. Some existing associations may be formed among sellers who have little control over their commodity and no hope of substantial collusion. Evidence comes from associations formed among sellers who at least potentially had a great deal of control over supplies. The author argues that where sellers can exercise a good deal of control over supplies of what they sell, associations they form can, and commonly do, tightly regulate the market conduct of members.

25. Victor D. Du Bois, "Prostitution in the Ivory Coast," *American Universities Field Staff Reports*, West Africa Series 10: 2 (Ivory Coast), p. 6.
26. Rowena M. Lawson, "Markets in Ghana," *West Africa* (May 28, 1966), pp. 180–81.
27. Ione Acquah, *Accra Survey* (London: University of London Press, 1958), p. 86.

28. Polly Hill, *Some Characteristics of Indigenous West African Enterprises*, pp. 119, 120.
29. Polly Hill, "Markets in Ghana," *West Africa* (June 4, 1966), p. 622.
30. James B. Christensen, "Marketing and Exchange in a West African Tribe," *The Southwest Journal of Anthropology* 17: 2, 1966.
31. M. G. Wygant, "A Treatise on Commercial Activities in Togo," U.S. Department of State Airgram A-127 (Dec. 8, 1965), p. 3.
32. Jean and René Charbonneau, *Marchés et marchands d'Afrique Noire* (Paris: La Colombé, 1961), p. 137.
33. Melville J. Herskovits, *Economic Anthropology* (New York: W. W. Norton, 1952), pp. 220–21.
34. Tardits, "Traditional Market Economy in South Dahomey," p. 101.
35. P. C. Lloyd, "The Yoruba Town Today," p. 52, and B. W. Hodder, "The Yoruba Rural Market," p. 114.
36. Suzanne Comhaire-Sylvain, "Le Travail des femmes à Lagos, Nigeria," pp. 181, 184.
37. Abner Cohen, "The Social Organization of Credit in a West African Cattle Market," *Africa* (January 1965).
38. Lloyd, "The Yoruba Town Today," p. 52.
39. Smith, "Exchange and Marketing Among the Hausa," p. 307.
40. M. G. Smith, *The Economy of Hausa Communities of Zaria*, Gt. Brit. Col. Office, Colonial Research Studies no. 16 (London, 1955), p. 98.
41. P. T. Bauer and B. S. Yamey, "Competition and Prices: A Study of Groundnut Buying in Nigeria," *Economica*, vol. 19 (February 1952), pp. 33–43.
42. Delane E. Welsch, "Rice Marketing in Eastern Nigeria," *Food Research Institute Studies* 3: 3, 1966, pp. 331–32.
43. Binet, "Marchés en pays Sousson," p. 110.
44. I. M. Lewis, "Trade and Markets in Northern Somaliland," in Bohannan and Dalton, *Markets in Africa*, p. 380.
45. H. C. G. Hawkins, *Wholesale and Retail Trade in Tanganyika* (New York: Praeger, 1965).
46. Vance Q. Alvis, "Marketing Selected Staple Foodstuffs in Kenya," West Virginia University, IP-25 (Morgantown, W. Va.), 1968.
47. Bauer, *West African Trade*, p. 391.
48. Cartels of buyers, or buying rings, on the other hand, try to maintain a level of maximum prices that they will pay, and do not mind if one member can manage to get supplies at lower prices.
49. Horace Miner, *The Primitive City of Timbuctoo* (Princeton: Princeton University Press, 1953), pp. 13, 68.
50. P. Couty, *Le Commerce du poisson dans le Nord Cameroun*, ORSTOM, Mémoires, no. 5 (Paris: ORSTOM, 1964), p. 115.
51. G. R. Allen and J. Chaux, *Some Aspects of the Marketing of Dried Fish in Central and West Africa* (Rome: FAO, 1961), p. 10.
52. Q. B. O. Antonio, "The Supply and Distribution of Yams in Ibadan Markets," *The Nigerian Journal of Economic and Social Studies* 9: 1 (March 1967), pp. 35, 43.
53. Hill, "Markets in Ghana," p. 357.

54. FAO, *Report to the Government of Uganda on Fish Marketing in Uganda*, FAO Report No. 998, based on the work of J. A. Crutchfield (Rome, 1959), pp. 41–54.
55. A. B. Mukwaya, "The Marketing of Staple Foods in Kampala, Uganda," in Bohannan and Dalton, *Markets in Africa*, p. 658.
56. Anne Martin, *The Marketing of Minor Crops in Uganda*, Gt. Brit., Dept. of Tech. Cooperation, Overseas Research Publication no. 1 (London, 1963).
57. The term "buyer attachment" is used here for convenience to refer either to buyers attached to particular sellers, or the reverse, since the two cases are similar for analysis of market structure and conduct.
58. Antonio, "The Supply and Distribution of Yams in Ibadan Markets," p. 35.
59. Vernon R. Dorjahn, "African Traders in Central Sierra Leone," in Bohannan and Dalton, *Markets in Africa*, p. 72.
60. Daryl Forde and R. Scott, *The Native Economies of Nigeria* (London: Faber and Faber, 1946), pp. 167, 169.
61. Alvis, "Marketing Selected Staple Foodstuffs in Kenya," p. 300.
62. Mark Karp, *The Economics of Trusteeship in Somalia* (Boston: Boston University Press, 1960), p. 84.
63. René Dumont, *False Start in Africa* (New York: Praeger, 1966), p. 133.
64. Gloria A. Marshall, "The Marketing of Farm Produce: Some Patterns of Trade Among Women in Western Nigeria," NISER, *Conference Proceedings*, p. 95.
65. Dorjahn, "African Traders in Central Sierra Leone," pp. 67–68.
66. Marguerite Dupire, "Trade and Markets in the Economy of the Nomadic Fulani of Niger (Boro)," in Bohannan and Dalton, *Markets in Africa*, p. 349. See also, Denis Danset, "La Commercialisation du bétail et de la viande du Niger," (mimeo.) (Naimey, 1964), p. 15.
67. Lewis, "Trades and Markets in Northern Somaliland," p. 380.
68. Peter Marris, *Family and Social Change in an African City* (Evanston, Ill.: Northwestern University Press, 1962), p. 72.
69. Marshall, "The Marketing of Farm Produce," p. 95.

Part II

Agriculture and Industry

One of the fundamental economic problems in Africa is that of raising agricultural productivity, an issue to which most of this section's papers are related. One of the major ways of increasing agricultural productivity is through capital formation in commercial agriculture; this is the topic of the first essay. West and Ekpenyong statistically test two hypotheses. One is a version of the accelerator theory, indicating that investment in commercial agriculture is governed largely by the need to increase capacity in response to high, increasing, or prospectively increasing demand for primary-product exports. The other hypothesis is a financial-flow theory indicating that the magnitude of investment is determined largely by the availability of liquid funds, particularly retained earnings and depreciation. The paper's findings suggest that in periods of low and decreasing demand for primary product exports, the financial-flow theory fits the data better, but that most of the time, i.e., in periods of high and increasing demand and to a lesser extent under intermediate conditions, the accelerator theory provides a better fit.

Price also deals with commercial agriculture, presenting a careful statistical analysis of productivity change in Kenyan large-scale agriculture in the dozen years preceding and following independence. He describes the statistical problems he encountered and conscientiously informs the reader of the tentative nature of his findings. These findings are, nevertheless, of considerable interest. They suggest that independence and African rule in Kenya did not interfere with the secular increase in large-scale agricultural efficiency.

Peter McLoughlin's essay is an analysis of the Land Reorganization Scheme in Nyasaland (now Malawi). It discusses the difficulties encountered and the reasons for the failure of the program. One of the problems, not unusual in the African colonial situation, was that government officials expected cultivators to work longer and harder for the vague goals of increased soil fertility and technically better agricultural practices without getting any financial or other reward. Despite the collapse of the scheme, however, McLoughlin indicates that the program may have been of considerable long-run value.

The problems of economic development in the Transkei, the only one of the eight projected self-governing reserves within the Republic of South Africa that actually has a limited form of self-government, give some indication of the incipient development problems in all the areas. Attracted by higher incomes, large numbers of Transkei Africans live and work outside the Transkei. The South African government, however, is committed to a program of strengthening apartheid by industrializing in and near the Transkei, thereby reducing the number of Africans outside the reserve. Maintaining that such industrialization first requires agricultural development, Rutman discusses the low level of agricultural output and its causes, and the possibilities of and impediments to revolutionizing agriculture. The required agricultural policies, however, would release large amounts of labor. This leaves three possible alternatives within the prevailing policy orientation. First, subsidization (presumably heavy) of industrial development in and near the Transkei as a means of increasing the degree of economic self-sufficiency. Second, perpetuation of the existing subsistence economy with its dependence upon migration for cash income. Third, a permanent mass exodus of Africans from the reserve.

Massell is concerned with demand rather than supply in the agricultural sector. He presents a method of estimating rural expenditure elasticities in African conditions, where calculation is complicated by the existence of a partial subsistence economy. His main finding is that income, rather than household size or the ratio of subsistence income to total income, is the overwhelming determinant of the allocation of family spending between different types of goods. High income elasticities for a number of food items indicate substantial improvement in the quality of the diet as income increases. Massell presents reasons for thinking that the expenditure elasticities he found may be useful for projecting demand for rural Kenya as a whole, and (it seems to the editor) perhaps for many other areas of rural Africa as well.

Chapter 6

Agricultural Exports and Agricultural Capital Formation: The Congo Experience

Robert L. West and E. E. Ekpenyong

Many of the cardinal issues in the contemporary debate about international economic relations are rooted in differing conceptions of the relationship between production of primary commodities for export and the attainment of economic growth and stability in developing countries. The resolutions submitted and the irresolution of issues debated at the recent UNCTAD Conference testify to the importance of studying the interaction of primary production with economic development and balance-of-payments policies. These questions are of particular moment to the analysis of development in Africa. More unequivocally than any other continent, Africa constitutes the archetype of economic structure shaped by foreign trade and development dependent on the export of primary commodities.

AGRICULTURAL EXPORTS

Although African countries are important suppliers of minerals and petroleum, Africa is principally an agricultural producer. By a very wide margin, agriculture is the most important occupation. More than half of the continent's exports consist of the primary products of agriculture, animal husbandry, and forestry. Historically, the cash crops produced in Africa have been chiefly for export. More recently, with the growth of urban centers, food crops for sale in the cities have grown in importance. With respect to provisioning the internal demand for food and fibers, supply has generally been highly elastic. Unlike other less-developed areas, African countries have thus far experienced few urban food-supply bottlenecks; the growth of demand which has accompanied expansion of mining, processing, manufacturing, and services has been met largely by the transfer of resources out of subsistence agriculture into cash cropping for local sale. It has not generally resulted in the transfer of resources out of production of agricultural products for export.

Several circumstances have contributed to the persistent growth of agricultural exports from Africa, uninterrupted by the relatively more rapid expansion of other economic sectors. The weakening and the termination of colonial administration were often accompanied by the evasion or abolition of constraints on African production of export crops, and of regulations on resource-use designed to secure local self-sufficiency in foodstuffs (legacies of famine prevention in an earlier era of primitive transportation and limited administrative budgets). At the same time the extension of roads and other improvements in transportation, the introduction of improved methods and materials, disease and pest control, and the evolution of land-use practices were contributories to the rapid expansion of production for the market. Response to local market demand has been sufficiently vigorous in many parts of Africa that the prices of food in urban areas have declined over the past fifteen or twenty years. The terms of trade between agricultural products for export and for local markets do not appear to have moved to the disadvantage of production for export.

At least some market forces combined with agricultural improvement programs to encourage growth of exports. Market incentives may have significant application in this context, although it is fashionable to question their relevance in analyzing resource allocation in an era of ambitious planning and the extension of public control and management in other sectors of African economies. Virtually all agricultural export production in Africa is carried out in the private sector, and the decisions to purchase capital assets are made by private producers or managers. Moreover, while African small-holders are responsible for a large and growing proportion of export production, a significant part of the sector producing agricultural commodities for export is organized on modern, commercial, entrepreneurial lines. In the case of the Congo, discussed in this study, organization of the latter kind predominated. For ranching and for the production of such crops as palm oil, palm kernels, and tea, the most important organizations were plantations – usually of large scale, on extensive land tracts, with resident, settled labor and professional managers, and generally consisting of several similar units. In the cultivation of coffee, pyrethrum, and cereal crops, the typical organization was a single unit, smaller, usually managed by the owner or lessee (including nearly ten thousand private settlers). Similar organizations for agricultural export production are important in much of Eastern, Southern, and Central Africa, and in some Francophonic West African countries. If expatriate enterprises of these kinds are of declining relative importance in the independence period, their sensitivity to market forces and other characteristics are frequently adopted by their successors.

In discussion of the relationship between production of agricultural commodities for export and the growth and stability of African economies, the framework of the market economy appears to have substantial relevance. Since the rate of capital formation and its determinants are central to both theories of economic growth and of fluctuations in market economies, it is surprising to discover how little attention has been given to assembling evidence about the relationship between production for export and capital formation in African agriculture. The effect of trends and fluctuations in quantities and unit values of agricultural exports on foreign exchange earnings has been closely studied, generally in an aggregative model relating a balance-of-payments bottleneck to limitations on total effective demand or total investment expenditures. But little work has been done to establish the parameters, in an African economy, associating export demand or external earnings with the growth of output, the decisions to purchase fixed capital assets, or the propensities relevant to investment in agriculture.

Evidence on these relationships is needed to guide development strategies and a wide variety of economic policies. To cite a few examples: the introduction of marketing boards and determination of their management principles are carried out with little knowledge about the impact on capital formation in the industry controlled by the marketing board of either the level, or changes in the level, of producers' earnings. Export duties and subsidies, income and capital taxes, are all introduced and varied with only notional insight into expected effects on investment in the sector which earns the greater part of Africa's foreign exchange and makes the largest contribution of value-added. Land banks and agricultural financing institutions are inaugurated, often employing substantial resources, without clear evidence of how the availability of financing is related to investment decisions in agriculture. Where marketing board surpluses are the source of agricultural bank capital, it is unclear whether the reduction in producers' earnings associated with accumulation of the board's surplus discourages more investment than is stimulated by the bank's lending. Finally, little guidance is available in the agricultural export industry in selecting the appropriate policy-mix under different conditions of export markets to stimulate growth of capacity or pursue stabilization objectives.

INVESTMENT HYPOTHESES

It is difficult to account for the lack of research interest in this critical link between exports and capital formation in African agriculture, but inquiry is no doubt discouraged by the existence of several theories with conflicting assumptions about the determinants of investment and their relationships. The fact of conflicting theories, together with the applied value of evidence which may be established, suggested an investigation into the process of decisions to purchase fixed capital assets in the export-agricultural sector of the Congo economy.[1]

The procedure followed was to test a large number of variables, suggested by various theories of investment, to determine their association with fixed capital assets purchases (by cross-sectional, zero-order correlation analysis of a sample of Congolese commercial-agricultural producers). Variables which exhibited significant association were retained to evaluate two alternative explanations of the rate of fixed capital formation and its determinants; cross-sectional multiple correlation and regression analysis were employed in this evaluation. The two alternative explanations are a version of the accelerator theory and the financing-flow theory of investment.

The acceleration principle states that the change in capital stock per unit of time is a linear function of the rate of change in output. This principle emphasizes that investment outlays are sensitive to technological relationships between capital stock and output, and may be expressed:

$$I_{(t)} = kX_{(t-1)} - K_{(t-1)} + D_{(t)}$$

where I is gross fixed investment, k is the capital-output ratio of the sector of the economy observed, X is output (since virtually all output of the Congolese export-agricultural sector was sold abroad, it also represents export sales or demand), K is capital stock, and D is replacement of depreciated fixed assets. (For flow variables, the notation (t) indicates the current time period; for stock variables, (t) indicates the end of the current time period and $(t-1)$ indicates the beginning of the current time period.) In this rigid form, the accelerator postulates that investment must occur before added output is forthcoming, that investment is not constrained by inadequate finance, and that producers expect the past trend of demand to persist. The effort to relax these restrictive assumptions has produced a number of revisions and variants of the accelerator theory of investment. The variant employed in this study is a capacity-oriented theory involving the ratio of output to capital stock. In functional notation, the accelerator model evaluated by cross-sectional analysis is:

$$\left\{I_{(t)} = f\{X_{(t-1)}, D_{(t)}, A_{(t-1)}, L_{(t-1)}, S_{(t)}, F, u_{(t)}\}\right\} \frac{1}{K_{(t-1)}}$$

where

I is gross fixed investment;
X is export demand;
D is replacement of depreciated fixed assets;
A is the age of the stock of fixed assets;
L is the stock of net quick liquidity;
S is share capital called;

F is a structural factor to distinguish plantation organizations;

u is a stochastic term representing the influence of unincluded variables;

K is stock of gross fixed capital assets.

The financial-flow theory of investment places emphasis on the volume of internally-generated funds; with an imperfect capital market, investment depends significantly upon the flow of depreciation allowances and retained earnings. Account may be taken of the ready availability of pledged but uncalled share capital, and of the stock of quick liquidity. The financial-flow model evaluated is:

$$\left\{I_{(t)} = f\{R_{(t-1)}, D_{(t-1)}, A_{(t-1)}, L_{(t-1)}, S_{(t)}, F, u_{(t)}\}\right\} \frac{1}{K_{(t-1)}}$$

where R is retained profits to surplus and reserves.

Although derived from purely financial considerations, the financial-flow theory is similar in form to the accelerator theory; in the models employed in this study, the distinction rests on the substitution of retained earnings as an independent variable in the former for export demand in the latter. But the distinction is crucial, as it enables a judgment to be formed whether, or in what circumstances, the decision to invest is governed by the technical need to increase capacity in anticipation of high or rising demand in export markets (the accelerator hypothesis) or by favorable retained earnings and availability of finance (the financial-flow hypothesis).

STATISTICAL PROCEDURES

The evaluation of these hypotheses is based on the behavior of a sample of Congolese commercial-agricultural producers over the decade 1950–59. More than 90 percent of the output of these firms was exported; about 40 percent of the Congo's foreign exchange earnings, in the period studied, was derived from the sales abroad of the population of agricultural enterprises from which this sample was drawn. From a study of enterprises in other industrial sectors of the Congo's market economy, it appears that about one-sixth of all private fixed capital formation (about ten billion Congo francs of a total

61.4 billion francs gross private fixed investment in the decade) took place in commercial agriculture. The investment decisions of these agricultural export-commodity producers resulted in more than doubling the value of the stock of fixed assets (other than land) in ten years, while output increased by 80 percent in the same period.

The sample consists of forty-two registered agricultural firms, from a population of about one hundred and fifty firms which maintained offices abroad as well as operations in the Congo. The firms were highly variable in size, but the sample does not include the largest such firms in the Congo (notably the Unilever plantations) and underrepresents the smallest of such firms. The sample is not random, but inclusion was determined by availability of data. The firms included in the sample, taken together, were responsible for between two-thirds and three-fourths of total capital formation in agriculture, in the monetized sector of the Congolese economy, in each year of the period studied. Eighteen of the firms were registered as plantations, engaged in the cultivation of such crops as palm oil and kernels, tea, cotton, and rubber; the other twenty-four firms were not organized on plantation lines, and included some mixed enterprises engaged in forestry and livestock management as well as cultivation. A study of the two classes of firms shows that the structures were significantly different, with markedly different capital-output ratios. Plantations were therefore represented by a structural variable to distinguish them from non-plantations in the tests described below.

The observations were taken annually for the years 1950 through 1959, for annual operating results or stocks at the beginning and end of the calendar year. Data were obtained from profit-and-loss statements, operating reports, and balance sheets where available, and were supplemented by direct inquiries and interviews where necessary. An effort was made to standardize categories and definitions, but this could not be wholly accomplished with respect to variable practices in writing off some investment expenditures as current outlays, to variable rules for determining depreciation allowances, and to different practices in writing off fully depreciated assets. Nonetheless, the observations of the variables employed in testing are believed to be substantially homogeneous.

Eighteen sets of observations were eliminated from testing because they fell in one or another of three categories. These categories of exclusions were: (1) cases of mergers, reorganizations or modifications of structure, causing large changes in the property accounts not immediately reflected in other variables; (2) newly organized firms in the first two years of existence, where it can be assumed that new investment is not governed by data in the same way as for established firms, but is almost completely autonomous; (3) cases of change in fiscal year.

Since the objective was to employ cross-sectional analysis, to test the association of differences among firms in investment outlays with differences in other (stock and flow) variables, each variable (except for the plantations structural variable) in each annual set of observations was deflated by the value of gross fixed capital (fixed capital stock) at the beginning of the year. Thus the tests consisted of determining the association between the rate of growth of fixed capital stock (investment as a ratio of fixed capital at the beginning of the year) and a variety of other stock and flow variables, also as ratios to fixed capital assets.

The method of testing employed was least-squares correlation and regression analysis.[2] There is a total of 396 annual sets of observations for the period 1950–59; these were grouped into three sub-periods: 1950–53, a period of vigorous and expanding demand, rapid growth of the economy, balance-of-payments surpluses, general optimism, and high general liquidity; 1954–57, a period of high but stable demand, continued but lower rate of growth of the economy, modest balance-of-payments deficits, and diminished liquidity; and 1958–59, a period of declining and low demand, negative growth of the economy, balance-of-payments deficits, and low liquidity. Relationships were tested with annual data for the full period 1950–59, and for each of the three sub-periods; relationships were also tested for averages of annual data for each of the sub-periods.

A large number of lagged and unlagged variables were tested by simple correlation analysis to determine their relationship to investment expenditures. Variables which failed to show a relationship with fixed capital formation at the 5 percent level of significance were rejected. Seven variables which, by one or more tests, did show a relationship with fixed capital formation at the 5 percent level were retained. These seven variables (six used to evaluate each of the accelerator and financing-flow theories) were employed in multiple regression and correlation analysis (annual data and averages of annual data for subperiods). "Beta" coefficients[3] were computed to show the relative contribution of each independent variable to the aggregate relationship found between fixed capital formation and the set of other selected variables. All multiple correlation coefficients proved to be significant at the 1 percent level except one test of the 1954–57 period (significant at the 5 percent level).

SELECTED VARIABLES

The deflator employed for each annual set of observations was value of fixed capital assets at the beginning of the year; in most cases this was book value, at acquisition cost, of fixed assets adjusted to eliminate revaluation (wherever revaluation occurred during the period 1950–59).

Both lagged and unlagged values of some variables were tested, notably for all "liquidity-flow" variables. For all tests except for net receipts in 1958–59, one-year lagged values of both export demand and retained profits showed a higher degree of association with fixed capital formation than did unlagged values. Unlagged values of these variables were therefore eliminated. Conversely, unlagged values of shares called had a higher association with fixed capital formation than did one-year lagged values, and the lagged value was eliminated.

The selected variables were these:

1. *Gross fixed investment*, or fixed capital formation
2. *Export demand*, consisting of gross operating and other receipts of the firm, less operating expenses, but before taxes and depreciation allowances

   This variable, for all forty-two firms taken together, shows a high degree of correlation with gross agricultural export earnings (as reported from customs data), suggesting that increased operating costs over the period 1950–59 were compensated by rising productivity in agriculture. This variable is taken to represent agricultural output and Congo agricultural export earnings; for the individual firm, it represents output and demand for export.

3. *Structural factor* distinguishing plantation from non-plantation firms (In each annual set of observations, plantations are given a value of one and non-plantations a value of zero.)
4. *Age of assets*, measured by the book value of fixed-asset depreciation carried at the beginning of the year on the firm's balance sheet, adjusted for revaluation of assets where appropriate
5. *Depreciation allowance*, declared for the previous year, i.e. allowance charged against previous year's earnings

   The one-year lagged value shows such a high degree of correlation with the current-year value that the former is employed to represent both depreciation allowance as a financing flow and current replacement outlays in the accelerator model.
6. *Liquidity stock*, or net quick liquidity of the firm at the beginning of the year, consisting of cash on hand, plus deposits at banks, plus cash receivables, minus accounts payable
7. *Shares called*, i.e. new share capital called from shareholders on both new and previous issues

   Borrowing from banks and loan financing by financial intermediaries were not a significant source of financing for agricultural firms in the population studied, but both private placements (most often with a parent financial "holding" or investment trust) and public issues of shares were frequently employed to supplement internal flows.
8. *Retained profits*, after taxes, depreciation allowances, royalties, bonuses, and dividends (i.e. undistributed profits or profits transferred to reserves and surplus)

The results are shown in the matrices of correlation and "beta" coefficients in Tables 1 and 2. For the period 1950–59 both annual data and averaged data reveal an association at the 1 percent level of confidence between fixed capital formation in agriculture and export demand. The hypothesis that there existed a significant relationship between export demand and investment in commercialized agriculture in the Congo during the period 1950 through 1959 cannot be rejected. The relationship is also significant at the 1 percent level for the sub-period 1950–53, for both annual and averaged data; this was the period of high and rising demand and of general liquidity. But for the sub-periods 1954–57 and 1958–59, the relationship is not significant at the 5 percent level. Both the zero-order and multiple correlation tests give this result. There appear to be important cyclical variations. During the period of high and rising demand for exports, high export prices, general high liquidity, and overall expansion of the economy, the association of export demand and capital formation in agriculture is significant; but the association is weakened during a period of stability in demand, prices, and overall growth, and when liquidity declines. The association is not significant during a period of recession, low and declining prices of and demand for exports, and illiquidity.

Among the selected independent variables, there are four directly related to the accelerator model: export demand; the structural factor, distinguishing two categories of firms with different capital-output ratios; the age-of-assets variable, representing an age influence on the technological relationship between capital stock and output; and depreciation allowance, a lagged variable highly correlated with current replacement of depreciated assets. For the full period 1950–59 these four variables each make a significant contribution to explaining the inter-firm variance of capital formation; the contribution of each (measured by their respective "beta" coefficients) to the multiple correlation result obtained for the period 1950–53 is significant, both for annual data and averaged data. But they are not all significant for the period 1954–57 or 1958–59.

The other selected independent variables are directly related to the financing-flow of the firms, consisting of one liquidity stock value and three sources of financing. The model substituting retained profits for export demand (i.e. a liquidity flow variable for the output variable) has been tested, as shown in Table 2, and appears to show relatively greater importance of the liquidity variables in the sub-periods 1954–57 and 1958–59 than in the sub-period 1950–53. The measure of total

TABLE 1

Simple Correlation Coefficients

	N	(a) *Export Demand* $X(t-1)$	(a) *Structural Factor* F	(a) *Age of Assets* $A(t-1)$	(a) (f) *Depreciation Allowance* $D(t-1)$	(f) *Liquidity Stock* $L(t-1)$	(f) *Shares Called* $S(t)$	(f) *Retained Profits* $R(t-1)$
Annual data								
1950–59	396	.2224**	.0723	.0138	.3262**	.1368**	.1397**	.2969**
1950–53	147	.3573**	.1014	.0763	.3944**	.2860**	.1577*	.2683**
1954–57	168	.1237	.1705*	.0719	.0416	.1197	.2266**	.0974
1958–59	81	.0000	.2627*	.2110	.1703	.2163*	.7203**	.1334
Averaged data								
1950–53	39	.5222**	.0273	.3118*	.4934**	.2925	.1339	.6045**
1954–57	42	.2656	.2658	.1030	.0521	.2106	.0908	.1373
1958–59	42	.0193	.3782*	.2796	.0709	.2895	.7825**	.1127

(a) Variables associated with accelerator model.
(f) Variables associated with financing model.
* Significant at 5 percent level.
** Significant at 1 percent level.

Table 2

Multiple Correlation and Beta Coefficients

	Multiple Correlation Coefficient	*Export Demand* $X(t-1)$	*Structural Factor* $F(t)$	*Age of Assets* $A(t-1)$	*Depreciation Allowance* $D(t-1)$	*Liquidity Stock* $L(t-1)$	*Shares Called* $S(t)$	*Retained Profits* $R(t-1)$
Financing model								
1950–59	.4700**		.2218	.0933	.2713	.0245	.0895	.3342
1950–53	.4989**		.0337	.1121	.3824	.1395	.1439	.1130
1954–57	.3435**		.2502	.1578	.0443	.0754	.1382	.2210
1958–59	.7730**		.0365	.2130	.1553	.0034	.6988	.1005
Accel. model								
Annual data								
1950–59	.4866**	.4332	.4210	.1160	.2383	.0395	.2033	
1950–53	.5753**	.4646	.2792	.1794	.3877	.0293	.1158	
1954–57	.3320*	.2354	.4008	.0466	.0273	.0528	.3330	
1958–59	.7689**	.0097	.0148	.2229	.1985	.0044	.7052	
Averaged data								
1950–53	.8773**	.6777	.6110	.3545	.4750	.2218	.1686	
1954–57	.4856	.7223	.7526	.4315	.1186	.7690	.3030	
1958–59	.8446**	.0643	.0853	.2595	.2077	.0636	.8183	

* *R* significant at 5 percent level.
** *R* significant at 1 percent level.

association, the multiple correlation coefficient, is higher for the financing-flow model in 1958–59 than for earlier sub-periods, and is higher for the financing-flow model than for the accelerator model in both 1954–57 and 1958–59 (although the difference between coefficients is not statistically significant for either sub-period). In general, the accelerator model appears to give the best fit (i.e. the variables associated with a form of the acceleration theory of investment contribute most to the measure of overall association of the set of independent variables with inter-firm differences in fixed capital formation) during the sub-period 1950–53, while the financing model seems to give the best fit during the sub-periods 1954–57 and 1958–59. Averaged data give a better fit than annual data for the accelerator model. And, finally, there is some evidence from the averaged data test that the stock of liquidity contributed to explanation of variance in investment behavior in the 1950–53 period. This is consistent with the tentative conclusions to be drawn from this inquiry.

CONCLUSIONS

It appears that in the period of high export demand and prices, plentiful liquidity, and general expansion, fixed capital formation in agriculture responded to technological relationships between capital and output in a manner consistent with the acceleration principle: capital formation was related to the growth of output (which means also to growth of export earnings). Plentiful liquidity, i.e. high liquidity stocks and ready availability of supplementary sources of liquidity, appears to have contributed to this relationship.

In the intermediate period, investment outlay may also be sensitive to the kinds of technological relationships between capital and output which are central to the acceleration theories (signaled here by the closer fit of the accelerator model when averaged data rather than annual data were employed).

But when the stock of liquidity falls in the short run, demand weakens or declines, producers' receipts fall, and the general economy is stable or subject to deflationary influences, then the financing-flow variables become more significant. Once liquidity becomes pinched, the availability of funds becomes crucially important as an influence on investment outlays in agriculture. Under these conditions, a financing-flow model seems to provide a more satisfactory explanation of fixed capital formation in agriculture than does an accelerator model, and financial variables become relatively more significant at the expense of capital-output relationships and of variations in export demand.

NOTES

1. These same factors gave impetus to investigation of the capital formation process in the United States by John R. Meyer and Edwin Kuh, *The Investment Decision* (Cambridge, Mass.: Harvard University Press, 1957). The methodology employed in studying capital formation in Congo agriculture follows that in Meyer and Kuh (see especially chaps. 5 and 8. A summary of theories and earlier empirical investigations appears in chap. 2.)
2. For a discussion of least-squares technique when the data are ratios, see Meyer and Kuh, Appendix C, "Correlation and Regression Estimates When the Data Are Ratios."
3. "Beta" coefficients are normalized regression coefficients. The squared "beta" coefficient is the proportion of the dependent variable's variation (differences of investment in proportion to capital stock among firms) explained by the particular independent variables; comparison of "beta" coefficients shows the relative importance of the different explanatory variables.

Chapter 7

Land Reorganization in Malawi, 1950–60: Its Pertinence to Current Development

Peter F. M. McLoughlin

In the middle and late 1940s, the colonial governments of sub-Saharan African nations began to show more positive interest in the agricultural development of those nations. Included in their efforts to develop agriculture were a number of the larger projects, such as the Groundnut Scheme, which achieved some notoriety by their failure. Virtually every country had one or several such large schemes, and Malawi, then Nyasaland, was no exception.

The development of generally overcrowded Malawi was seen to depend upon land consolidation, and the effort to consolidate fragmented land over the decade ending in 1959–60 was without doubt the largest single project that small nation had undertaken. It cost several million pounds and directly affected about one hundred thousand farm families. The implementation of the scheme absorbed the bulk of all natural resource development effort for the decade. Considering Malawi's size then, this was a large scheme.

After summarizing a number of the main characteristics of Malawi agriculture as a frame of reference, the nature and problems of the land reorganization scheme will be outlined here and some suggestions put forward concerning reasons for its failure. The present situation will then be commented on, indicating that, for a number of reasons, these land reform attempts were perhaps not all wasted, but in fact just premature.

Their benefits in some respects are only now beginning to show themselves.

Agricultural problems

Malawi African agriculture is marked by the following characteristics:

1. A considerable range of ecological conditions giving rise to some degree of diversity in traditional crop and animal husbandry patterns and in population densities;
2. Zones of better soil and more favorable climate featuring population densities such that a family may have only from 1.5 to 3.0 acres of arable land – the bulk of the Malawi population living under such crowded conditions, often with well over two hundred homesteads per square mile.
3. Overwhelming importance of maize as a food crop, and the use of practically all agricultural land for the growing of maize.
4. A shortage of adult males, more severe in some places than in others, many of the men in countries to the south or in Malawi cities in wage and salary employment (about 40–50 percent of the nation's adult males are away from their farms at any one time);
5. A system of matrilineal land inheritance for approximately three-quarters of the country's people. Combined with uxorilocal marriage and a high divorce rate, this has resulted in fragmentation and subdivision of holdings and the discouragement of male participation in agricultural development;
6. Lack of a highly remunerative and reliable crop which can be grown by most farmers for either domestic or export markets. While there are certain crops – some varieties of tobacco, tea, cotton, groundnuts, and rice – which are grown by Africans in certain selected areas, such growers are by no means the majority of the nation's farmers;
7. A shortage of livestock and a lack of integration of animal and agricultural husbandry. Mixed farming has not developed on any scale, nor has any but minimal use of oxen as draft animals.

These conditions have given the typical Malawi farmer and the development agencies of government a set of problems with which it is very difficult to cope. The increasing shortage of land per family has caused the gradual use of grazing land and of poorer soils and less accessible areas (such as steep slopes) for the growing of crops; all this has contributed to a growing problem of erosion. It has also meant the abandonment some time ago in many places of the habit of rotating with fallow the land used for cropping and allowing some land to rest. "Shifting" has become "static" cultivation.

As a result, there has been a gradual decline in soil fertility, though this has been more rapid in some areas than in others, and sometimes made too much of. It is often not so severe as claimed – many of the steep Cholo area soils, for example, cropped continuously for decades, are extremely stable. An increasing proportion of all land has had to be used to produce food crops, until now in much of central and southern Malawi there is virtually a monoculture of maize (normally interplanted), a crop which is hard on the soil under monoculture conditions. The typical family requires ten to twelve bags of maize per year. Yields under normal conditions range from three to six bags of maize per acre (though sometimes more, and occasionally less). A household therefore needs, allowing for unusual conditions, three to five acres just for maize. Few families in central and southern Malawi have such acreages at their disposal, and the heavy incidence of adult males out at wage labor can partly be explained on these grounds.

Males have also been discouraged from looking at the farm as a source of income because, for the most part, they have had little or no control over the land. To obtain the use of land a man must not only marry, since it is the women who have the rights to the land, but he must also move to his wife's village to obtain the land. If a man divorces his wife, as frequently happens, then he must relinquish that piece of land and he will not get another until he marries again. On the death of the farmer the rights to cultivate pass through the female line, and a piece of land is often fragmented among several women, usually sisters. A man has little influence over his successor to the land and the land usually has no market value (though this is changing), so that investment of time and money in it is not attractive. Such interplot mobility and the insecurity of the whole system have meant that the typical male has had little interest in developing the land he was using. (The Angoni of northern Malawi are the only major group that are patrilineal and hence are exceptions to the above pattern.)

THE LAND REORGANIZATION PROGRAM

In its effort to cope with these interrelated problems over the years, the Malawi Department of Agriculture has attempted the introduction of a variety of technical and institutional measures. On the technical side it has encouraged all the techniques and methods considered necessary to raise per-acre maize yields with the aim of enabling the family to obtain its basic food supplies from a smaller acreage; the balance of the family land could then be used for other crops, thus simultaneously improving soil fertility and diversifying the diet. The department has encouraged the rotation of crops and fallows and the use of manure and fertilizers. A "Master Farmer" scheme has been devised by which rewards and special extension attention are given to those farmers who make an attempt to develop their property, to practice recommended rotations, and so on. One of the major hurdles to the introduction of better farming practices has been the land tenure situation; as in many other parts of Africa, the fragmentation of land has impeded the devising of farm layouts and effective farm management.

It was therefore decided in the late 1940s and the early 1950s to establish a series of village land-improvement schemes. Under some conditions these have been referred to as village reorganization schemes. The purpose of these schemes was to reorganize completely the land-holding pattern of an area and to give each household one consolidated plot equal in size and quality to the total area of its former collection of pieces and fragments, much the same as has since been done in Central Kenya. The entire village reorganization was to be geared to an overall land utilization plan. This meant that the area was first laid out on sound conservation lines (diversion ditches, drainage ways, contour bunds, terraces, etc.) and the land to be used for each main exploitation pattern was clearly demarcated (arable, grazing, forest, etc.).

After experiments with several cooperative villages in the early 1950s the expansion of village land-improvement schemes became by the mid-1950s a cornerstone of government agricultural development policy. A four-year plan of expansion was drawn up in 1955 with the hope that four hundred thousand acres of land could be reorganized at an estimated cost of 2.25 million. This was the nation's main development effort. By early 1959 there were thirty reorganized areas covering some two hundred thousand acres, each area with its own conservation system, improved water supplies, and roads, and each family on its individual holding with a farm plan and an agreed-upon rotation of crops. It was hoped that these more favorable technical and physical conditions would encourage an increasing number of individuals to become better farmers, and that some would even become Master Farmers.

By the middle of 1960, however, none of these schemes was still operational; they had all collapsed and the farmers involved had reverted to the virtual monocropping of maize and the continued fragmentation of holdings. In late 1963 the writer visited the remnants of a good number of these larger schemes where the only vestiges of years of effort were the stray ends of fencing around some of the grazing areas, and bits and pieces of the ridges and bunds which had not been hoed out. In the space of about eighteen months the work which had absorbed most of the Department of Agriculture, and some other staff, most of the time for nearly a decade, and a large percentage of the development budget, had virtually disappeared.

CAUSES OF FAILURE

The reasons why these schemes failed are both complicated and in many cases unclear; the writer does not presume to know all the answers. The general body of evidence seems to indicate, however, that a combination of several factors was pertinent in greater or less degree, and more important in some village areas than in others.

1. Theoretically, a land reorganization scheme was estab-

lished only when the consent of all in the village involved had been obtained. In practice this normally meant that the government administration tried to persuade the Chief of the area. If the Chief was progressive and on amicable terms with the Department of Agriculture and the district administration, then he might agree quickly and wholeheartedly. Conversely, there apparently were cases where the Chief's agreement was rather reluctantly given. Moreover, agreement was sometimes given not in order to improve agriculture in the community concerned, but purely for selfish or status reasons, the Chief not wanting to lag if his peers had agreed to the introduction of the schemes in nearby villages.

2. The Chief then had to persuade the headman and the villagers that the changes were sound and in their mutual interest. The schemes which lasted the longest (into late 1960) were those in which the Chief had the firmest hold over his people, as well as their respect. Where the Chiefs and headmen had less control, they were less able to get a scheme going at all, to push its progress, or to keep it from falling apart.

3. The strength of these authority relationships was tested during the pre-Independence political stirrings of the late 1950s and early 1960s. In common with many other African countries under equivalent political conditions, agricultural department policies became the prime target of anti-colonial government politicians. Not only were people who followed government advice victimized by house burnings, crop slashings, etc., but, to make matters worse, a good number of the more progressive farmers in the reorganization schemes and many of the Master Farmers were active members of the Rhodesian Federal Party. Such political "enemies" tended to receive especially rough treatment, particularly in the Central Region. Once these political problems emerged, the extension and other officers tried to avoid looking too closely at the Master Farmers or other more progressive people in the reorganization schemes, for fear that this would make things even worse for such farmers. Yet these were the very farmers who had helped to get the schemes going and who had influenced their neighbors to participate.

4. One of the most important factors causing discontent with the schemes was the government's initial insistence on a fixed

rotation. This was not only too sophisticated and complicated for the average cultivator to understand, but it also called for fallowing one-fifth to one-third of the farmer's holding. The insistence upon the fallow in the rotation (which took various forms depending upon the fertility of the land, the type of soil, the type of crops, etc.) resulted from the technical consideration that soil fertility improvement was considered the paramount agricultural need. In the first few years of the schemes, however, it caused some farmers to experience a 20–30 percent reduction in food production so that supplemental food had to be issued.

Government was of course aware that fallow land does not produce food. This was one of the major reasons why only villages of greater-than-average acreage per household were chosen for reorganization. On the other hand, villages where pressure on the land was greatest were ones where a more positive response to land reform might reasonably be expected. But the administrators were overly optimistic in assuming a rapid rate of adoption of better farming methods and consequent rapid increases in food crop productivity on the consolidated holdings. Such results rarely materialized.

This negative experience with the early schemes caused the agricultural department to relax the fallow rule, and in some cases to make it optional; but these unfavorable initial consequences did reduce people's receptivity to the consolidation idea in other areas. Another effect of the reduction in food supply apparently was to push even more men off the land in search of wage employment.

5. There also appears to be a negative relationship between the incidence of men in wage jobs and the success of any particular scheme. The provision of a consolidated holding normally meant a substantial increase in that farm's labor requirements. There were no measurements of labor requirement to guide or condition the advice given. While the area cultivated remained approximately the same, the technically more sophisticated cultivation and management techniques insisted upon by the extension staff (pre-rain hoeing, ridging, weeding schedules, etc.) often meant that the work load at certain periods was more than the women could handle. The more households there were with men away, therefore, the less satisfactory the cultivation and the yields. In addition, a newly

consolidated holding requires considerable development labor, such as fencing and boundary work (and housebuilding in many cases), and the man normally was needed for this – if he wasn't there, or was present only occasionally, then the work didn't get done so quickly.

6. Another source of discontent was the handling of livestock. The reorganized village normally had its grazing land reserved in the "dambo" (the swampier bottom lands), or in areas of poorer soil, or in spots otherwise unsuitable for crop cultivation. The land conservation pattern, on which all these schemes were superimposed, often reserved for forestry, or put out of bounds completely, space such as the steeper slopes that heretofore had been used for grazing. The immediate result was overcrowding of livestock on the smaller reserved grazing areas. Where rotational grazing was established, it was found almost impossible to put the rotation into practice, since child herders preferred overgrazing on clearer areas where they could see their cattle to grazing the animals in denser bush where there was a chance of losing them. A "rocket" from the agricultural officer no doubt was thought preferable to parental discipline. No special arrangements appear to have been made for marketing surplus cattle, nor for coping with abnormal periods such as in years of drought, when the fences around reserved grazing areas would be broken down. Cattle owners, though not very numerous, tend to be among the more influential members of the community, and it may be presumed that their dissatisfaction with the state of affairs meant abnormally negative repercussions.

7. There was insufficient staff at all levels to give the required attention to each farmer. As in other sub-Saharan nations, the lower-level extension workers were not sufficiently trained to understand the new farming systems – most still are not. Many of the more senior expatriate staff found difficulty in communicating with farmers. All apparently had trouble talking agriculture to women, who constituted the majority of the cultivators.

8. In most of the reorganized schemes, there was no satisfactory and remunerative crop which could be sold for cash. This has been one of the major development headaches in Malawi, then and now. If there had been some demonstrable

financial reason (as there was in central Kenya) for the revolutionary changes in land tenure and all the inconvenience, it is felt that a considerable number of men would have stayed with it. There were several areas where cash crop output was increased (mainly tobacco and groundnuts), but these were the exceptions. There usually was little cash incentive; reorganization was normally merely to grow more food. This is not necessarily the fault of the government extension officers.

9. There were also the interrelated questions of women's rights to the land, and the provision of some other form of title to the reorganized and consolidated holdings. There is considerable evidence, although mainly hearsay, that aside from some of the economic and technical factors mentioned above, it was the women who brought down many of these schemes. It is held that it was they who had rights to the family land, not the men (and not the Chiefs and headmen); it was they who should have been the deciding authority (not the headman or the agricultural officer) on who was moved where, and on who got how much. By bringing together separate land fragments, the reorganization submerged the social and psychological identity of each plot, leaving the women with no felt attachment to her new and strange holding which may, in fact, have been previously used by someone she didn't like. Equally important, the reorganization split up sisters: instead of simultaneously cultivating adjoining inherited plots (a social and family affair quite as much as an economic activity), sisters often found themselves at considerable and inconvenient distances from one another. That they would resent the scheme seems entirely plausible.

But connected with this situation was the problem of formalizing rights to the consolidated holdings. The initial government intention was to provide the framework in which the farmer had the physical means to improve himself. Once a sufficient number were advancing rapidly it was hoped that the social climate would be such that some form of individual title might be demanded and be made possible. This idea was eventually abandoned in view of the women's resistance, and the dearth of men demanding such titles. But while this thinking is articulated in numerous government documents, one wonders how much of it was passed along to the villagers.

There seems to have been considerable confusion in people's minds about tenure policy, and about the relationship between physical land reform and the vesting of rights to the reorganized land.

In sum, several very general conclusions may be drawn regarding the lack of success with land consolidation in Malawi when it was first introduced.

1. There was an excessively technical bias. The government's two prime and interrelated concerns were the preservation of land and the maintenance and increase of soil fertility. Conservation and land planning were therefore given precedence, as were such technical factors as the need for fallows and for technically sound rotations.

2. As a consequence, the economics, sociology, and psychology of the land reform were given only minimal weight. The people themselves, particularly the women, were not consulted sufficiently, and the project and its many implications were not discussed thoroughly enough. Reliance was placed, instead, on the use of the more formal administrative channels through Chiefs and headmen, to obtain the peoples' consent. The actual reactions of the people to suggestions favoring a reorganization scheme were in most cases not obtained directly by the senior agricultural field staff.

3. The actual implications of the reform were not examined in terms of the economics of the households involved, especially the question of food supplies and the timing of labor requirements. The labor demands of a consolidated holding following a farm plan are very different from those of the previous agricultural system.

4. Coherent and simple policy objectives were either lacking or, more commonly, not explained fully to the people, especially with reference to land rights.

5. The lack of a new and rewarding cash crop meant that there was no financial incentive to stimulate farmers to change their systems. For many of them it was much less effort to buy their extra bags of maize from their wages. Marketing facilities for food crops were especially underdeveloped. While perhaps little could have been done about this at that time, there was undoubtedly a lack of appreciation of the full import of this aspect of the problem.

One lesson must be that tenure reform is far more than a technical matter. The agricultural officers involved here were experienced and well-intentioned men. They wanted the schemes to succeed in order to raise the living standards of the people. But their training, and the whole framework in which they worked, was such that agricultural development, to them, was almost entirely a technical affair. They did not have the training that would have led them to investigate the social and economic aspects of land reform.

OUTLOOK FOR THE FUTURE

A number of forces and pressures in recent years have changed the agricultural development milieu. Political independence and the break-up of the Central African Federation have brought a different development environment. In a variety of ways the one-party political machine has encouraged the use of local political instruments to persuade farmers that their personal effort is part of the national effort. A problem in Malawi, however, as indeed in many African countries, has been for the leaders to reverse their positions regarding agricultural policy. After having insisted during the years of colonial rule that agriculture policies were "bad," they must now take the opposite stand on many of these issues and advocate many practices that they resisted in the pre-Independence era. This requires considerable political courage, and not all political leaders have yet mustered it. Moreover, recent events have demonstrated that some groups in Malawi are unenthusiastic about the Banda regime, so that political discontent has no doubt hampered the effectiveness of policy implementation in some areas.

Education has spread to a much larger share of Malawi's population, increasing general sophistication, social awareness, and levels of aspiration. Population continues to increase and densities on the land have risen in virtually all areas, intensifying the need to raise per-acre yields to maintain per-capita output.

Perhaps most important of all, however, the countries to the south, to which so many Malawi men customarily have migrated to earn their cash income, have made it extremely difficult for migration of workers to continue on the previous scale. There are thus many thousands of motivated, relatively sophisticated, and by no means unskilled adult males in the rural community who now, to maintain the cash income level they desire and to which they have become accustomed, must achieve that income from agriculture. It is this group, primarily, which is stimulating the local community, and insisting that government help to raise the cash income derived from their farms. (This phenomenon, incidentally, is very general these days in many countries where non-farm job opportunities are not keeping pace with the number of persons who want such jobs.)

It is persons like the former migrant workers who are now going ahead with voluntary land consolidation schemes, exchanging land fragments in an increasing number of villages. They already know, because they have experienced them, many of the changes required, and many of the agricultural and farm management techniques demanded by a more intensive system of land use. Government still needs to assist, of course, with some planning, credit, marketing facilities, and so on. But the basic knowledge on the part of the farmer is there – or at least an awareness of the possibility that there are people in government who may have some of the answers; this is mainly the result of the previous land consolidation efforts.

The government of Malawi has found the outlook sufficiently promising to induce it to apply to the World Bank for a loan, to rationalize this consolidation effort in the Lilongwe area. Here is another example of the way a sound scheme or approach may fail because it reflected the limited outlook of the technically trained natural-resource officer and was premature in terms of the felt needs of the people of the area. It can only be hoped that new projects in land reform will avoid some of the problems of the previous efforts.

Chapter 8

Regional Development in Southern Africa, with Special Reference to the Transkei

Gilbert L. Rutman

The African and European regions of the southern part of the African continent form a common labor market with a common currency. This market comprises the Republic of South Africa, including South West Africa, the three former British territories of Lesotho, Botswana, and Swaziland, and the eight African reserves within the Republic, which are supposed to be granted limited forms of self-government. By 1969, however, only the Transkei reserve had achieved limited self-government,[1] and thus was the only African reserve with legal powers to influence its own development. This paper is concerned with the problems of developing the Transkei. However, since all the African regions depend like the Transkei upon job opportunities within the white areas of the Republic for at least part of their income, this analysis will indicate some of the problems to be faced in developing all these areas.

The entire region may be divided into two general categories: high income (European) and low income (African) areas. The economic disparity has led to a flow of labor from African to European areas, which slightly mitigates the income differentials. Equalization of income is prevented by the Europeans legally reserving the higher-paying jobs. Political integration is precluded by European immigration laws which treat all Africans, regardless of place of birth, as aliens inside European centers. Thus, the Africans of the three former British territories and eight reserves are legally considered to be permanently domiciled outside the white region, even though they may earn the major portion of their income as migratory workers inside. This paper indicates that the Transkei contains underemployed labor in the sense that higher productivity forms of employment (or higher paying jobs) are available to these Africans within the Republic. The movement of Africans to the Republic results, at least in the short run, in a higher level of income for the people of the Transkei.

The governments of the Transkei and the Republic favor reducing the flow of Africans to industrial centers within the Republic by shifting these centers to areas within or along the borders of the Transkei. These governments have, however, different motives for favoring this shift in industry. The Transkeian political leaders desire industrialization in or near its territory in order to enlarge their economic base; the Nationalist government of South Africa desires it as a means of achieving its objective of racial separation. This is not to imply that South Africa will eliminate all African labor from its European centers; it only wishes to reduce substantially the number separated from what have been designated as their permanent homelands in order to weaken the external and internal pressures for equal political rights for all races.

It is suggested here that a first step in industrializing the Transkei area must be the development of the agricultural sector. Agricultural surpluses may help to attract industry by providing (1) a market for manufactured consumer and capital goods, and (2) a source of industrial crops for processing. It will be pointed out that: (1) the present level of economic activity within the Transkei produces no agricultural surplus; (2) the major source of male employment is in the Republic; (3) output surpluses in agriculture can be achieved only by creating a full-time farm population; and (4) a first step to a full-time farming population must be an increase in the attractiveness or profitability of farming, which necessitates a change in the tribal property structure.

ECONOMIC CONDITIONS IN THE TRANSKEI

The Transkei is located in the southern part of the Republic of South Africa within the Cape Province. The total land area is slightly over 16,500 square miles (approximately the same size as Switzerland) and constitutes about 3.5 percent of the Republic's total land area. One basic liability of its location with respect to attracting industry is that this region lies between two established growth points: East London-Port Elizabeth and Durban.[2]

Presently, there is little mining carried on within this region, or being planned for the foreseeable future. While mineral surveys are being made by the South African government, there seems to be only a slim possibility of discovering commercially exploitable quantities of minerals.

The small size of the market inhibits the growth of consumer industries. The Transkei economy is based on agriculture. For all practical purposes, subsistence farming is the only form of employment available within the area; the Transkei's Labor Department estimated that only about 25,000, or 5 percent of the adult males aged 15 to 49 maintaining permanent residence in the Transkei, were engaged in nonagricultural forms of employment in 1963. Fewer than 1,500 of these 25,000 African men were classified as manufacturing employees.

From this, it seems that the Transkei's main hope for rapid industrialization lies in an agricultural revolution. The amount of land classified as arable in the Transkei is about 900,000 morgen (one morgen equals 2.117 acres), or slightly more than 20 percent of the approximately 4.3 million morgen which is the Transkei's land area.[3] About 5–10 percent of this land is used for social services and residential purposes, and the remainder (about 70 percent) is used as pasturage.

Climatic conditions and soil types are in general favorable for the production of the Transkei's main crop – maize. Government reports have repeatedly claimed that average rainfall in the Transkei exceeds that for the (maize-exporting) Republic as a whole.[4] A minimum of 25 inches per year is required for the successful production of maize;[5] and nearly 75 percent of the Transkei receives an average rainfall of thirty or more inches, while no area receives less than twenty inches per annum.[6]

In spite of these apparently favorable conditions, the Transkei's total crop output falls far short of the minimum consumption requirement of the population. For example in

1964 (a year classified by the Agricultural Department as normal),[7] total crops amounted to about 1,780,000 bags (one bag equals 200 pounds). Of this, approximately 1,706,000 bags, or over 95 percent, was grain. Given a population of 1,452,100 in 1964, average grain output per person was only 1.2 bags, while the minimum grain consumption requirement per person is put at 2.5 to 2.75 bags per annum.[8] This is roughly consistent with the government's estimate that in 1964 over 40 percent of the maize consumed within this area was imported.

This situation is unlikely to change without help from outside, because agricultural output is apparently at its maximum level with the production techniques currently used. A comparison of the six-year averages of grain output for the three periods 1934–39, 1946–51, and 1959–64 indicates that output has remained fairly constant if drought years are excluded. While average output rose by 14 percent between the periods 1934–39 and 1959–64, this increase disappears if drought years are excluded (see Table 1).

TABLE 1

Average Grain Output (Maize and Kaffir-corn)
1934–39, 1946–51, and 1959–64
The Transkei

Years	*Average grain output per year*	*Average grain output per year excluding drought years*
1934–39	1,585,000	1,816,300
1946–51	1,540,909	1,686,189
1959–64	1,805,313	1,805,313

NOTE: Drought years are 1936 and 1949.

SOURCE: Transkei, *Annual Reports of the Department of Agriculture and Forestry, 1961–1964*; Union of South Africa, *Report on Agricultural and Pastoral Production and Sugar Cane, Timber and Nettle Plantations, 1948–1961*; and the Union of South Africa, *The Native Reserves and Their Place*, p. 14.

The same situation exists for livestock, as can be seen by comparing the average size of the cattle and sheep herds of the Transkei for the two periods of 1946–51 and 1959–64. Table 2 shows that average herd size remained approximately the same.

Neither sheep nor cattle herd size was appreciably affected by the sale of livestock. While cattle sales increased about 50 percent, the absolute number sold remained insignificant, about one-half of 1 percent of the total herd. For all practical purposes, no sheep are sold.

TABLE 2
Average Size of Cattle and Sheep Herd,
1946–51 and 1959–64
The Transkei

Years	*Average cattle herd per year*	*Average number of cattle sold per year*	*Average sheep herd per year*
1946–51	1,407,000	4,317	2,366,000
1959–64	1,364,000	6,527	2,182,000

SOURCE: Union of South Africa, *Report on Agricultural and Pastoral Production 1945–46 to 1950–51*, Agricultural Censuses No. 20–25; and Transkei, *Annual Reports of the Department of Agriculture and Forestry, 1961–1964.*

Let us examine the causes of agricultural stagnation by discussing the types of productive factors used and the profitability of investment in agriculture.

African labor: The working population in agriculture consists mainly of unskilled people, both females and males, between the ages of 10 and 49. The age limits used here are merely rough approximations since it is difficult to estimate accurately when people enter and leave the work force. The skill level is that commonly associated with tribal African farming. In general, the tribal authority allocates each family an allotment of land to be used in the cultivation of crops; and labor requirements are supplied mainly by the family.

On the basis of some simplifying assumptions (that the rural population approximates the farm population, that all labor engaged in agriculture is homogeneous, and that everyone has access to arable land for cultivation)[9] the 1960 grain output per farm worker can be estimated at about three bags.[10] As the price of maize was about $4.50 per bag, the monetary income from crop production was about $13.50 per head in this year. This can be compared to the earnings of Africans in wage employment of approximately $210 per year.[11] While this differential considerably overstates the real income gap, it nevertheless explains why a large percentage of the Transkei's male population leaves the Transkei farm work force. In 1960 for example, an estimated 234,000 males[12] were engaged in wage employment at any particular time on a contract basis outside the Transkei. In 1936, the estimated number was 216,000. In both years, the absentee male population ran at about 30 percent of the total male population.

In 1936, average output per worker in the Transkei was almost one bag higher than in 1960.[13] There has been a 20 percent increase in the total rural work force, but total output in the Transkei remained constant (or even decreased). This suggests that surplus labor exists, i.e., the marginal product of a laborer is zero.[14] The opportunity cost of using the labor of women and children is nil. The compensation for their labor is no problem, for it is not based on marginal product or opportunity cost, but is their share of family consumption.

The point can be made that substitution of absentee males for females and children currently doing farming would increase output per worker, because men are more skillful either as farm laborers or farm managers. There is little evidence to support the assertion that men are more effective farm workers. Traditionally crop cultivation has been the function only of women. The Tomlinson Commission states in this connection: "If the name 'farmer' can be applied to the Bantu, the Bantu woman alone can lay claim to it. The Bantu man has so far displayed no inclination at all to become an arable farmer."[15] With respect to the African man's skills as a manager, McLoughlin emphasizes that he is the sole innovator, so that technological progress is retarded by his absence.[16] This observation may be valid, and is generally accepted as true by the Transkei agricultural officials, although here too there is little supporting evidence. But even if it is true that technological progress will not take place without the male's presence, it does not follow that it will occur with his presence unless it is worthwhile for him to make the effort. Under existing conditions, as is pointed out again later, his investment of labor and capital is not profitable.

The return from livestock farming cannot be attributed to

labor, because virtually no labor is used as a factor of production. Africans can migrate each year to wage employment centers within the Republic and still raise livestock in the Transkei. Under the native land-tenure system, the African is allowed to graze his cattle, sheep, and goats on communally owned land without paying a fee; his cattle mingle freely with those of his neighbors. Because of this arrangement, there is no incentive to attempt to improve the quality of one's livestock unless one's neighbors do likewise. It appears that Africans view livestock in much the same way that Europeans might view a savings deposit. The rate of return is the calves; and in fact, the Xhosa word for "interest" is the word "calves."

Land: The land used in agriculture is relatively fixed in quantity; it can be divided into two types: arable and pastoral. The average yield of maize per morgen is low compared to that of the rest of the Republic – about 2.5 bags per morgen (1954–64), while normal yields for the Republic are put at about ten bags per morgen.[17] As the arable land allocated to each family averages about 3.5 morgen, family farms probably produce on the average somewhat less than nine bags of maize per year, or two-thirds of the minimum requirement of an average family of six.

With respect to pasturage, the problem is much the same – a low return to the land. In the short run, maximum returns can be gained under conditions of high intensity grazing; a high ratio of cattle to land means a high cattle weight per unit of land.[18] Because the pastoral land can be used by the individual African at no charge, the range land of the Transkei tends to be overgrazed and overstocked. The main problem arises in the longer run from the overstocking of the range. This causes a long-run deterioration of the land, and thus a reduction in the range's carrying capacity; it also causes a deterioration of the quality of the livestock, as indicated by higher death rates and lower birth rates. The overall result is a reduction in livestock weight per unit of land.

The Tomlinson Commission reported that by the 1930s the maximum carrying capacity of the Transkei range had been reached.[19] That this situation has continued is indicated by the relative stability in the size of the cattle and sheep herds between the 1940s and the 1960s. At the same time, deterioration of the land's quality has caused a decrease in the weight of the livestock per unit of land. In the early 1930s, the Native Economic Commission warned that the overstocking of the range would create, within a relatively short period, desert conditions within the reserves.[20] In 1955, the Tomlinson Commission reported that only 26 percent of the Transkei land was free of soil erosion. The decrease in livestock weight per unit of land is a result so far of a decrease in the weight per animal. Presently, the average weight can be placed at about four hundred pounds, a weight which causes milk yields to approach zero, and makes oxen too weak to do spring plowing.

Capital: As long as land was abundant in the Transkei, i.e., the supply exceeded the demand at a zero price, the African tended to select those production techniques which minimized use of labor effort. Shifting cultivation fulfilled this requirement. This system involves clearing the land, cultivating it for a specified period, and then moving elsewhere to repeat the same process, leaving the land to recuperate the lost fertility under bush fallow. The total land requirement of the family comprised not only the land currently being used but the land formerly used and currently under bush fallow. Colin Clark and Margaret Haswell point out that the amount of labor involved in shifting cultivation is less than that involved in sedentary.[21]

As land is now scarce in the Transkei, shifting cultivation is less effective; Africans still demand land as part of their birthright, and this forces the tribal authorities to reduce the time land can lie under bush fallow. Nevertheless, Africans have not responded by farming their land much more intensively; they have generally not applied a great deal more labor and/or capital to a given area under cultivation. This reluctance is explained by an insufficient return and perhaps sometimes by ignorance.

There are two major suppliers of capital in the Transkei: private European traders and the government. The Africans purchase such capital items as plows and pure seed from trading stores with money earned in wage employment. For example, from 1950 to 1955 the number of plows in the Transkei increased by over 12,300, or slightly more than 10 percent. The increased use of such capital equipment as the plow has not resulted in an increase in grain output, mainly because of the lack of such complementary factors as land. The six-year average from 1951 to 1956 was 1,166,921 bags, or nearly 400,000 bags less than the average from 1934 to 1939 and 1946 to 1951.

Capital goods supplied by the government are of two types: private and collective. The private forms of capital are such items as fertilizer, insecticides, hybrid seeds, and trucks used to transport manure from the kraals to the fields. These items are normally supplied to the African at prices below market level. For example, hybrid seed is sold at the rate of one bag of poor seed for one bag of hybrid. The collective forms of capital, supplied at no direct cost to the Africans, are such conservation works as grass stripping, contour and training banks, dams and boreholes, silt traps, roads, dipping tanks, and the fencing of grazing camps. In conjunction with this program, the government is attempting to instruct farmers in modern production techniques. Such activities as demonstrations, lectures, and agricultural fairs are a part of the extension program. The necessity of such a program is illustrated by the following example: in the early 1950s the government attempted to promote the use of hybrid seed by offering it to Africans in Pondoland at no charge. There was, however, little supervision in its use. The Africans normally obtain seed from their previous crop. As long as they were using pure seed, there was no problem. However, the use of hybrid seed in one year and seed from the harvested crop the next year led to what might be expected: one or two bumper crops followed by five or six poor ones.

SURPLUSES, INVESTMENT, AND ORGANIZATIONAL CHANGE

Government programs could result in the production of an agricultural surplus if there were also a corresponding change in the present organization of production. For example, after public conservation programs are completed, it is estimated that the African would be able to increase his yields per morgen about four times by applying his labor on a full-time basis, and by using such items as fertilizer, hybrid seed, and insecticides. For the Transkei as a whole, this would mean a total grain output of about 7,200,000 bags. This could mean a grain surplus of some three million bags, assuming that each family consumed only its minimum requirement. In the case of livestock, an increase in the carrying capacity of the land could result in increased income through an increase in both the size of the herds and the weight of individual livestock. Some optimistic government officials estimate that the grazing capacity of the Transkei could be increased by 100 percent, with weight increases of approximately 50 percent, through use of fenced grazing camps, culling of old or inferior animals, castration of inferior sires, compulsory anthrax inoculations, selective breeding, and dipping tanks. The average size of the cattle herd between 1959 and 1964 was about 1,364,000 head. If this was doubled and the weight per animal increased from 400 pounds to 600 pounds and if the average price of cattle in the Transkei remained in the 1965 range of $20 to $30 per one hundred weight, then the total increase in the value of cattle would be roughly $270,800,000. If the rate of return was 10 percent (in terms of milk, tractive power, source of supply of fuel, hut material, fertilizer, and hides), this would yield an increase in income of $27,080,000 per year, or about $100 per family. In addition, the average size of the sheep herd from 1959 to 1964 was about 2,182,000 head. If this was doubled and the wool yield per sheep increased three times as predicted, the increase in income per year from wool alone would be about $9,164,400, or about $35 per family, assuming the price of wool to be about 30 cents per pound.[22]

If these hypothetical increases in income could be realized, diversification in agriculture could be promoted as a means of generating a variety of processing activities. The government is presently experimenting in the Transkei with the cultivation of such crops as sugar, coffee, tea, groundnuts, cotton, and pyrethrum. In the case of livestock, the government has already begun several investigations into the profitability of such enterprises as meat deboning and textiles.

A major drawback to any such development program is the existing traditional property structure, which reduces the attractiveness of private investment in farming. More specifically, the tribal authority acts as the caretaker of the land, equally dividing the arable land among the adult tribal males and maintaining the pastoral land as commonage. In the case of livestock production, the African will not individually invest to improve the quality of the range land or livestock unless he has direct control over the use of the land. For example, under the existing system, the African will pay relatively high prices for a heifer, even if it is an inferior beast, because it is a breeder. Government officials note that such an animal is worth about $35 to the European, but as much as $55 to the African. The difference in valuation lies in the fact that his neighbors share the maintenance of this animal; it deprives of food all the other livestock grazed on the commonage. Similar effects can be expected in the case of crop cultivation. Given the alternatives, it is likely to be unprofitable for the African male to invest his labor in farming on a full-time basis. As noted previously, the African male can earn about $210 per year plus subsistence at the mines. At home, he could increase his income from crop cultivation by only about $56.[23] It should be noted that under present arrangements ranch management does not involve the use of African male labor, so that he could work at the mines and still maintain his livestock on the tribe's commonage.

POSSIBLE CHANGES IN ORGANIZATION

Two possible changes in the economic system might be effective in increasing agricultural incomes. First, cooperatives or state-owned enterprises, operated at the village level, might be established. The two activities – crop and livestock production – could then be combined. The village organization could base its decision on what crop mix to produce partly on the basis of which crops provide good livestock feed as a by-product. They might also find it profitable to plant the pasture with a highly productive species in order to increase the meat and milk yields per morgen. Under the present system, it would not pay a single individual to do this. The role of the individual African could be either as a shareholder (under the cooperative system) or as a worker (under the state-owned system). The cooperative venture could be very similar to the villagization schemes in Tanzania; regardless of which organization is chosen, the African's income could be made dependent upon the profits of the enterprise. The important point is that control over economic activity would be in the same hands as the ownership of the land. This would prevent divergences between private and social costs. An alternative suggestion could accomplish the same thing: all the land could be equally divided among the peasants, including the range land, and a land market established for the purpose of allowing the efficient farmers to absorb the resources of the inefficient ones. In this case, the tribal property would be placed in the same hands as the controllers of economic activity.

Both of these suggestions emphasize a reorganization of the system to achieve maximum returns to the factors of production; such a move would undoubtedly free a large percentage of the present farm population. Given modern technology in agriculture, a rough estimate of the amount of excess labor, made by some Transkei agricultural officials, is about three-quarters of the present work force. Based on population estimates in 1964, this amounts to over one million people. While some of this excess would be absorbed by industry created as a result of the agricultural surpluses, it appears unlikely that the Transkei industrialization can be internally generated at a high enough rate to absorb all this excess, at least in the foreseeable future. The government of South Africa, then, if it is to achieve its goal of political separation, would have to encourage border industries by forcing new firms to locate in border areas. These border industries would involve a cost to the Republic in the form of subsidization. It is either this or the alternatives: the perpetuation of the present subsistence economy, dependent upon migrant labor for cash income, or a permanent mass exodus of Africans to the Republic.

NOTES

1. Transkei Constitution Act (Act No. 48 of 1963).
2. For a discussion of this point see T. J. D. Fair and L. P. Green, "Development of the 'Bantu Homelands'," *Optima*, 12 (March 1962), pp. 7–19.
3. Data have been collected from the interdepartmental reports of the Transkei's Agricultural Service at Umtata (Transkei). The source of such data will hereafter be referred to in the following manner:

Transkei, *Annual Report of the Department of Agriculture and Forestry, 1954–64*.

4. For examples, see Union of South Africa, *Report of the Native Affairs Commission for the Year 1936*, U.S. 48, 1937, pp. 6–11; and *Summary of the Report of the Commission for the Socio-Economic Development of the Bantu Areas Within the Union of South Africa*, U.G. 61, 1955, pp. 46–49. This report is referred to simply as the Tomlinson Commission.
5. This refers to dry farming. For a complete discussion of climatic requirements for the successful production of maize see Monica Cole, *South Africa* (London: Methuen and Company, Ltd., 1960), pp. 22–23.
6. Tomlinson Commission, page 51.
7. See Transkei, *Annual Report of the Department of Agriculture and Forestry*, 1964, p. 8.
8. See Tomlinson Commission, page 77; and Union of South Africa, Social and Planning Council, *The Native Reserves and Their Place in the Economy of the Union of South Africa*, U.G. 32, 1946, p. 49.
9. The Transkei does possess a landless class although most of these people have access to the lands of relatives or others.
10. In 1960, maize and kaffir-corn totalled 1,763,283 bags; the rural population of the Transkei between the ages of 10 and 49 was 587,520.
11. The main source of employment for the Transkei migrant is the mines. In the early 1960s, the average yearly earnings of these workers was about R150 (one rand equals $1.40).
12. These calculations can be obtained from the author upon request.
13. Because 1936 was a drought year, the average total output for the years 1934–39 is used. Maize and kaffir-corn amounted to 1,816,300 bags, and the rural population between the ages of 10 and 49 was about 484,000 people. In making this comparison, the six-year average from 1959–64 is used. The maize and kaffir-corn total was 1,805,313 bags while the total rural population in 1960 was 587,500 people.
14. The supply of capital has been increased, and the supply of land is about constant.
15. Tomlinson Commission, p. 73.
16. Peter F. M. McLoughlin, "The Need for a 'Full Employment' and Not a 'Disguised Unemployment' Assumption in African Development Theorizing." *Zeitschrift für Nationalökonomie* (Springer-Verlag, 1963).
17. Monica Cole, *South Africa* (London: Methuen and Company, Ltd., 1960), p. 172.
18. The weight per unit of cattle, however, is lower.
19. Tomlinson Commission, p. 77.
20. Union of South Africa, *Report of Native Economic Commission 1930–1932*, U.G. 22, 1932, paras. 71–73, p. 11.
21. Colin Clark and Margaret Haswell, *The Economics of Subsistence Agriculture* (London: Macmillan and Company, 1964), p. 33.
22. The price of wool in 1965 was only about twenty cents a pound, but it is expected that the introduction of modern methods of clipping the sheep and transporting the wool to market will bring a 50 percent increase in price.

23. The estimate of $56 is calculated in the following manner: Agricultural officers figure that the African could increase his output of crops by 300 percent if he invested in such forms of capital as insecticides, hybrid seed, and fertilizer, and applied his full-time labor during the growing season. Since he is currently farming an average of 3.5 morgen with yields of 2.5 bags per morgen, this would amount to a total increase of 26.25 bags, or, in value terms, of $110.25. The cost of the modern forms of capital to the individual African is estimated at about $15.40 per morgen, or a total of $53.90 for the 3.5 morgens. This leaves a net of about $56 as a return to his capital and labor.

Chapter 9

Productivity Change in Kenyan Agriculture

James E. Price

Opponents of independence for Kenya predicted that African rule would bring a decline in agricultural efficiency. This paper, which describes the construction of an index of agricultural productivity for Kenya for the period 1954–66, casts some light on this apprehension. The study also serves another function. It is frequently argued that single factoral terms of trade[1] are preferable to the net barter terms of trade[2] as evidence for the Prebisch thesis that the less developed economies tend to suffer from a secular decline in their terms of trade. The calculation of the former requires an estimate of total productivity change in the export sector. The productivity index constructed here is for the large farm sector, which is the best possible approximation to the export sector. The index of productivity is the ratio of an output to an input index. The weights for the input index are the estimated coefficients of a cross-sectional production function for 1958.

Most of this paper is devoted to a delineation of the statistical techniques and procedures employed, and some readers may welcome here a brief statement of the tentative findings. Confident conclusions are precluded by the statistical problems described below, but the evidence suggests that the 1954–66 period as a whole displayed a substantial increase in the productivity of large farms. There appeared to be relative stagnation during the few years preceding the establishment of the new government, followed by a sudden spurt in productivity immediately after independence.

CONSTRUCTION OF PRODUCTIVITY INDEX

The data used in this study were obtained from an agricultural census for Kenya which has been conducted annually since 1954. This census has been variously titled. First it was called *Kenya European and Asian Agricultural Census;* then, *Agricultural Census, Scheduled Areas and Coastal Strip;* and finally, *Agricultural Census, Large Farm Areas.* The number of farms involved in the annual census varied from a high of 3,624 in 1961 to a low of 2,760 in 1966. Without pausing for further remarks on the size distribution of the holdings, it is useful to notice that these are large-scale commercial farms. Their average size is over 2,000 acres; the median is just under 1,000 acres.

The census is based on a postal questionnaire directed to the farms of more than twenty acres in the coastal strip and in the agricultural committee districts of the area formerly known as the White Highlands. The returns cover approximately 90 percent of the acreage and a slightly smaller percentage of the farms. The coverage of the returns has fallen over time, and the census has been completed by taking information from the responses of the previous year, and by extrapolation.[3]

Changes made in the census somewhat reduce the value of the data as a consistent time series. The most troublesome change for this study was elimination in 1963 of the schedule concerning continent of origin, age, and sex of the employees. The study is carried through 1966 by using other and only partially appropriate employment data. A second difficulty in the data is that the agricultural committee district boundaries were substantially changed in 1964. (There had been minor changes previously.) A third change is that "Voi" and the "Coast" were added to the census in 1957 and in 1958 respectively. Finally, there are the usual redefinitions and unexplained inconsistencies. These difficulties were either dealt with in a simple way or overlooked.

The index of productivity used in this study is relatively simple: it is the ratio of an output index to an input index. Thus, any changes in output not proportional to the change in a weighted sum of the inputs is ascribed to a change in resource productivity. This measure of productivity change has been borrowed with some modifications from Professor Domar, who in turn borrowed it from Kendrick.[4]

It is not the purpose of this paper to discuss the theoretical issues pertinent to the measure of technological change or total resource productivity. It might, however, be useful to make two major points. Measures of technological change incorporate economies of scale, changes in utilization of inputs, and changes in unspecified inputs. The measure of productivity change used in this paper implicitly assumes a linear homogeneous production function and is otherwise subject to the problems mentioned. It is usual that measures of technological change are based on output and input data expressed in value terms. Thus changes in prices of goods and factors distort the measure. It is preferable that outputs and inputs be expressed in physical terms to avoid this problem. In this study, output is in value terms and the export price index is used as a deflator. The inputs are always expressed in physical terms. Useful to this discussion are two articles by Griliches.[5]

Before turning to the construction of the output and input indices, it might be well to discuss the choice of the base year. The first few years of the census seemed inappropriate, since the census was less comprehensive than it was thereafter. Further, it is possible that factor inputs and their utilization may at that time have been disturbed by the Mau Mau Emergency. On the other hand, the later years are not suitable for several reasons: there was uncertainty on the part of the European farmers after the plans for Kenya's independence became known in late 1959; there was a climatic disruption in 1961 when the seasonal rains failed; the following seasonal rains were excessive; and after that, new land resettlement programs resulted in the already noted reduction in the number of expatriate farms. From these considerations, 1958 emerges as the best choice as the base year for these indices.

Output is measured in value terms, as has already been indicated. The concept used is gross farm revenue. Although gross farm revenue is reported with the census, it is not collected as a part of the census. The concept and the estimation of gross farm revenue is described in the census as follows:

The estimates of gross farm revenue include the value of all crops, livestock, and livestock products sold or used on the farm for seed, animal fodder, or human consumption. It does not include the net value of changes in livestock populations. Valuation difficulties occur when full details of the production of a crop are not available, or when only part of a crop passes through a recognised marketing point and it has been necessary to have recourse to estimates of gross return per acre supplied by the Department of Agriculture in respect of minor crops, and to value the non-marketed portion of a product on the basis of the portion sold through recognised marketing channels (after allowances for estimated differences in quality).[6]

The output index for each year is obtained by dividing the gross farm revenue for the year by that for 1958. It is appropriate to correct for price changes by deflating by a price index. The export price index appears to be the best available for this purpose.

The input index is constructed from physical inputs reported in the agricultural census. The index is the weighted sum of the inputs for each year divided by that for the base year. The weights for this index are the estimated coefficients of a cross-sectional production function for 1958. The index is constructed in two different forms, arithmetic and geometric. The purpose of the two forms is to test whether the results are sensitive to the choice of mathematical form. The two forms of the input index are as follows:

$$I_i^1 = \frac{a + a_1F_{i1} + a_2F_{i2} + \ldots + a_jF_{ij}}{a + a_1F_{o1} + a_2F_{o2} + \ldots + a_jF_{oj}}$$

and

$$I_i^2 = \frac{(F_{i1})^{a_1}\,(F_{i2})^{a_2}\ldots(F_{ij})^{a_j}}{(F_{o1})^{a_1}\,(F_{o2})^{a_2}\ldots(F_{oj})^{a_j}}$$

where I_i is the input index for the ith year,
F_{ij} is the jth factor input in the ith year,
F_{oj} is the jth factor input in 1958,
a is the constant term,
a_j is the weight of the jth factor.

In the second index, notice that the constant term of the Cobb-Douglas production function would appear in both the numerator and denominator; since it enters multiplicatively, it has been canceled.

The next step is estimation of the weights for the input indices. The usual weights are the values added by the factors of production. Here the weights are the estimated coefficients of a cross-sectional production function. This production function is an aggregate one, with no exact real counterpart. The observations are generated by the geographic distribution of crops and livestock according to rainfall and elevation. The mathematical forms of these production functions are linear and Cobb-Douglas, corresponding to the two forms of the index. The linear production function implies straight-line production isoquants. This is unrealistic in that the optimal factor combination is either indeterminate or a corner solution with only one factor employed. The task then was to estimate a linear and a Cobb-Douglas production function for 1958.

The first question to be resolved was the choice of inputs. The census provides a fairly wide array of types of inputs with several levels of disaggregation. There are no data, however, for some inputs that should be included in the production function. Fertilizer has been included in the census only since 1962. Gross investment expenditures on buildings, fencing, and water control are reported, but there is no series on the stock of these real assets. In order to perform some experiments, the fifteen cross-sectional observations were pooled for the years 1956 through 1962. This provided adequate degrees of freedom to perform some trials on various levels of aggregation of inputs. The inputs chosen had to be relatively few in number because the weights for the input index are estimated cross-sectionally from only fifteen observations. The best choice of inputs seemed to be:

1. African male adults
2. African female adults
3. European and Asian male adults combined
4. land directly or indirectly used in the production process (sum of land used for permanent crops, temporary crops, temporary fallow, and uncultivated meadows and pastures)
5. wheel and crawler tractors combined

6. the stock of livestock (dairy cattle, beef cattle and sheep combined, omitting pigs, chickens, and horses).

In the annual *Statistical Abstract* of Kenya, some summary tables are drawn from the census, and it happens that the inputs chosen here are also those reported in the summary tables. Perhaps this is some justification of the choice.

MULTICOLLINEARITY PROBLEMS

A very difficult problem of multicollinearity was encountered in the estimation of production functions. In general, the magnitude and even the sign of the estimated coefficients depend on the choice of other types of inputs and their level of aggregation. The most notable example is the coefficient for livestock, which is almost always negative. This occurs over a wide range of aggregation of the livestock and other variables. A possible explanation to explore is the fact that very little distinction can be made between working capital and fixed capital in livestock. The stock of fixed capital can be augmented by simply not liquidating the working capital in the usual way (and vice versa). A negative correlation between a time series for gross farm revenue and livestock would be possible if the holdings of livestock were sharply reduced by sales, and such reductions have occurred since about 1959. The negative coefficients, however, persist cross-sectionally from 1956 through 1962, and this finding makes the stock reduction argument less than plausible. The explanation for this persistently odd result must be the econometric problem of multicollinearity.

Some insight into the location and degree of this problem can be gleaned from an inspection of the correlation matrix for these inputs for 1958. This is found in Table 1. The intercorrelations are often much higher for the logarithmic transformations of the variables.

The simple correlation coefficients in Table 1 suggest two patterns of agriculture. In the first pattern, Africans are employed extensively, with Europeans and Asians holding supervisory positions; land is used intensively; and some tractors are used. Tea, coffee, and possibly sisal and pyrethrum

TABLE 1

Correlation Matrix of Gross Farm Revenue and Farm Inputs

	1	*2*	*3*	*4*	*5*	*6*	*7*
Gross farm revenue	1.00	.90	.87	.95	.20	.63	.33
African males		1.00	.63	.91	.12	.61	.34
African females			1.00	.78	.05	.34	.11
European and Asian males				1.00	.24	.66	.45
Land					1.00	.53	.82
Tractors						1.00	.81
Livestock							1.00

are major crops produced in this way. On the other hand, the system producing grains and livestock employs a production process similar to that in the United States. This uses land extensively, relatively less labor, and more farm machinery in grain production. It seems to be in this latter group, where grain production is an intermediate good for dairy production, that the inputs are very multicollinear.

There are three ways to treat the problem of multicollinearity.[7] The first is data reduction by using factor analysis. Were this done, it might turn out that there would be two principal components, one of which would be economically identifiable as labor input. On the conviction that the advantages are too problematic to be worth the extra computation, factor analysis was not tried.

The second technique is to obtain additional information on which to base the estimates. A particular method for estimating production functions seemed possible here.[8] Assuming perfect competition and a Cobb-Douglas production function, the factor coefficient is that factor's share of output. The coefficient can be independently estimated as the geometric mean of the observations for income share to that factor. The data were such that this could be done only for labor. Continuing the assumption that the factor receives the value of its marginal product, the other coefficients could be estimated in a regression in the usual way. The dependent variable in the regression equation would be gross farm revenue minus labor costs, and the independent variables would include no labor variables. The regression results thus produced seemed to be more unstable than the others. It was not expected that this technique would be very successful because the regression estimates for African labor (which accounts for a very large share of labor costs) were relatively stable. The attempt, therefore, was not continued.

The strategy then used was to delete input variables until the coefficients were not too badly behaved (i.e. they were all positive). The result of this strategy is an improperly specified production function. To test the sensitivity of the final index to this problem, several variations of the production function were tried. These include the one with the negative coefficient for livestock. The difference in the index of productivity was comparatively slight. The results reported in this paper are those which include the inputs cited above, omitting livestock.

The cross-sectional production functions are as follows:

$$R = -56{,}632.6 + \underset{(29.7)}{112.7}\, W_1 + \underset{(29.5)}{174.4}\, W_2 + \underset{(3466.6)}{660.9}\, W_3 + \underset{(.26)}{.22}\, L + \underset{(317.7)}{509.1}\, K$$

where R is gross farm revenue,
W_1 is African males,
W_2 is African females,
W_3 is European and Asian males,
L is land as defined previously,
K is tractors.

R^2 is .982 and the standard error of estimate is 295,807.8.

$$\ln R = 6.383 + \underset{(.180)}{.526}\ln W_1 + \underset{(.084)}{.292}\ln W_2 + \underset{(.200)}{.104}\ln W_3 + \underset{(.065)}{.020}\ln L + \underset{(.105)}{.041}\ln K$$

R^2 for this regression equation is .967 and the standard error of estimate is .201.

The most striking feature of these findings is that the only variables which pass the test of significance at the .05 level are the two on African labor. Given the multicollinearity problem present in this data, all these estimates might be worthy of a little more trust than the conventional test of significance indicates. For the first regression equation, the coefficients are estimates of the value of the marginal product in Kenya pounds. (The Kenya pound was then on a par with the British pound.) For this equation only the estimate for land seems to be incorrect by an order of magnitude. The others appear to be accurate within a factor of two. The value of the marginal product for African females is consistently higher than that for African males. A word should be said about the variable W_3. This is employment of European and Asian males, and generally excludes the owner. Adding the number of farms to European and Asian employment might have produced a better estimate of the labor input of this type. What is not known, however, is what proportion of the owners are active managers. In other regressions the variable W_3 was more successful, having a value of the marginal product of about £2,000. In conclusion, we may note that the linear production function has slight economies of scale and that the Cobb-Douglas has slight diseconomies of scale.

The coefficients of the above regression equations were used as weights to construct the input index and the index of productivity, as has been described previously. These results are reported in Table 2. The results depend critically on whether gross farm revenue is deflated by the export price index or not. The more dramatic character of the deflated series suggests the possibility that the gross farm revenue is more appropriate undeflated. It seems possible that gross farm revenue may be sufficiently insulated from price fluctuations by statutory marketing boards and the procedures of estimation such that the series is not improved by deflating by the export price index.[9] A tentative conclusion is possible when based on two assumptions: that gross farm revenue is partly insulated from export price fluctuations, and that export prices have, on balance, fallen over the period. The conclusion is that the undeflated index of productivity is a low estimate and the deflated index is a high estimate of the change of resource productivity between the end years.

If one prefers the undeflated index, one can conclude that at least there has been no decline in resource productivity over the transitional period from 1956 through 1962. However, if one prefers the deflated index then one finds a substantial gain in resource productivity over that period. The sharp improvement from 1954 to 1956 is very puzzling.

TABLE 2
Index of Productivity, 1954–1962

Year	*1954*	*1955*	*1956*	*1957*	*1958*	*1959*	*1960*	*1961*	*1962*
Linear									
Index of productivity	.92	—	1.01	.99	1.00	.99	1.01	1.02	1.02
Index of productivity deflated by price index	.78	—	.91	.91	1.00	.96	.98	1.05	1.05
Index of inputs	.90	1.00	.97	.99	1.00	1.04	1.13	1.07	1.08
Cobb-Douglas									
Index of productivity	.91	—	1.01	.98	1.00	.99	1.01	1.02	1.02
Index of productivity deflated by price index	.77	—	.91	.91	1.00	.96	.97	1.06	1.06
Index of inputs	.91	.99	.97	1.00	1.00	1.04	1.13	1.06	1.07

EXTENSION OF THE INDEX

The temptation to extend the study to 1966 is very powerful. This has been done at the cost of using another, only partially correct, series for labor input. This is employment in agriculture and forestry from the annual enumeration of employment, which distinguishes only among African, Asian, and European employment. This enumeration includes employment on small farms and in forestry as well as on the large farms. For European and Asian employment this series very closely approximates that of the large farm census; but for African employment the two series are quite different. Data errors in African employment are more serious than elsewhere because African labor dominates the input index. Nonetheless, the computations were performed with a single African labor input replacing African males and African females. These results are reported in Table 3.

These findings are similar to those already reported, with the exception of the very sharp increase in productivity between 1962 and 1963. This sharp increase is due in part to a reduction of African employment from 243,500 to 217,600 (and a further decline thereafter) and a moderate increase in gross farm revenue. The results in Table 3 could be construed as a valid extension of the study to 1966 only if this reduction in African employment was shared between the large farms and the rest

TABLE 3

Index of Productivity, 1954–1966

Year	*1954*	*1955*	*1956*	*1957*	*1958*	*1959*	*1960*	*1961*	*1962*	*1963*	*1964*	*1965*	*1966*
Linear													
Index of productivity	.93	—	1.04	.97	1.00	1.02	1.06	1.07	1.11	1.26	1.29	1.22	1.31
Index of productivity deflated by price index	.79	—	.94	.90	1.00	.98	1.02	1.11	1.15	1.26	1.27	1.22	1.34
Index of inputs	.89	.99	.94	1.01	1.00	1.01	1.08	1.01	.99	.89	.84	.83	.84
Cobb-Douglas													
Index of productivity	.93	—	1.05	.97	1.00	1.02	1.05	1.07	1.11	1.27	1.31	1.25	1.32
Index of productiviy deflated by price index	.79	—	.95	.90	1.00	.98	1.01	1.11	1.15	1.27	1.29	1.25	1.36
Index of inputs	.89	.98	.94	1.01	1.00	1.01	1.09	1.01	.98	.88	.83	.81	.83

of the agriculture and forestry sector. The indirect evidence is fairly indicative that it was. There is an increase in production for sale of crops, some of which are labor intensive. The increase in gross farm revenue from this source is greater than the overall increase. On the other hand, there were fairly substantial reductions in some other inputs: land, tractors, and livestock. There were also substantial reductions in the number of farms and net capital expenditures on the farms. There were no reductions in European or Asian employment in agriculture and forestry at that time, but this is consistent with the changing size distribution of farms. The reduction in the number of farms occurred in the size range from 200–1,499 acres, with an absolute increase in the number of farms of more than 1,500 acres. It is these very large farms that would be most likely to hire Europeans and Asians. In other years the number of very large farms declined and European employment also declined. Thus, although the evidence is somewhat mixed, it is the conviction of this author that African employment on the large farms did decline at this time. If one accepts this, and if the data are to be trusted at all, it must be concluded that a substantial increase in output per unit of input did occur on the large farms between 1962 and 1963 and was maintained at that level thereafter.

CONCLUSION

This increase of productivity has special political interest, since critics of Kenya's independence predicted a decrease in farm efficiency as a result of independence. In contrast, it is the finding of this study that output per unit of input actually increased with the coming of independence. This might have been the result of growing confidence in the new government.[10]

It is difficult to know how seriously to take the findings of this study, which was beset by three types of problems: the multicollinearity in the data; the related problem of improper specification of the production function (which may have occurred because of multicollinearity or because of total lack of data on significant inputs); and finally, the discontinuation in 1963 of the appropriate employment data. All these problems render suspect the indices of productivity reported. It does seem, however, that the findings will support a general conclusion. There was a substantial improvement in resource productivity over the periol 1954–66. There was relative stagnation during the few years preceding the new government and a sudden spurt of productivity immediately thereafter.

POSTSCRIPT

For whatever it may be worth, the author constructed an index of productivity (that cannot be taken very seriously) for the early 1920s with 1958 as a base.[11] The value of exports from Mombasa is the output variable. There is no adjustment made for price changes. The input index is constructed by applying the coefficients of the linear production function for 1958 to roughly appropriate inputs found in the 1923 census. The results are reported without comment in Table 4.

TABLE 4
Index of Productivity, 1920–1923

Year	*1920*	*1921*	*1922*	*1923*
Index of productivity change	.17	.10	.14	.18
Index of inputs	.17	.22	.20	.22

NOTES

1. Single factoral terms of trade indicate the volume of imports that can be acquired in exchange for the exports produced by a given volume of productive factors; other things remaining the same, this would rise as productivity in the export industries increased.
2. Net barter terms of trade refer to the volume of imports that can be acquired in exchange for a given volume of exports.
3. It appears that estimates for nonresponse began in 1960 and were included for earlier years only for census totals.
4. Evsey D. Domar, Scott M. Eddie, Bruce H. Herrick, Paul M. Hohenberg, Michael D. Intriligator, and Ichizo Miyamoto, "Economic Growth and Productivity in the United States, Canada, the United Kingdom, Germany, and Japan in the Post-War Period," *Review of Economics and Statistics* 46: 1 (February 1964), pp. 33–40.
5. Zvi Griliches, "The Sources of Measured Productivity Growth: U.S. Agriculture, 1940–1960," *Journal of Political Economy* 71: 4 (August

1963), pp. 331–46; also, "Research Expenditures, Education, and the Aggregate Agricultural Production Function," *The American Economic Review*, 54: 6 (December 1964), pp. 961–74.

6. *Kenya Agricultural Census, 1962, Scheduled Areas and Coastal Strip, A Statistical Analysis*, 1963, p. 65.
7. For a survey of the problem and some new diagnostic techniques, see Donald E. Farrar and Robert R. Glauber, "Multicollinearity in Regression Analysis: The Problem Revisited," *The Review of Economics and Statistics* 49: 1 (February 1967), pp. 92–107.
8. Robert J. Wolfson, "An Econometric Investigation of Regional Differentials in American Agricultural Wages," *Econometrica* 26: 2 (April 1958), pp. 225–57.
9. Another explanation seems to be the differing price behavior of major exported products and those products which are largely consumed within East Africa. The prices of the major exports fluctuate greatly with a downward trend overall. The prices of the other products (wheat, meat, and dairy products) fluctuate very little and rise over the period. These latter products generally account for almost 30 percent of the gross farm revenue. Thus this differing price behavior tends to insulate the gross farm revenue from changes of export prices.
10. On the other hand, the increase might have been only a statistical artifact caused by removal from the census of farms involved in resettlement schemes. If most of these farms were of less-than-average productivity, their elimination from the data would cause the index of productivity to rise. Further investigation would be needed to establish this point.
11. Quite by accident, the author discovered in Syracuse University a small document entitled *Agricultural Census of the Colony and Protectorate of Kenya for 1923*. Although this census is not comparable to the later census used in this study, it is clearly similar in concept and execution. This early census extends from 1920 to 1938 or 1939.

Chapter 10

Rural Household Expenditures in Kenya: Consistent Estimation of Expenditure Elasticities

Benton F. Massell

In estimating Engel curves, it is common to use total expenditure in place of income as an explanatory variable. Summers has shown that least-squares estimators will then be inconsistent.[1] More recently, Liviatan has shown that using income as an instrumental variable will permit consistent and relatively efficient estimation of the expenditure elasticities.[2]

However, when the sample consists of households in a less-developed country (LDC) that produce partly for subsistence, there are further sources of bias. Estimates may be asymptotically biased because of the spread between the buying and selling price of many food items in a partial subsistence economy; a household that is a net buyer of an item is confronted with a higher effective price than a household that is a net seller. Also, the arbitrary valuation of home-produced goods introduces possibly serious errors of observation with respect to both the regressand and regressor, resulting in the usual errors-in-variables bias. This paper discusses these sources of bias, presents a method for obtaining consistent estimates of the

This article is a later version of one that was presented in a different form to the Conference on African Economic Development at Temple University. It was published under the title "Consistent Estimation of Expenditure Elasticities from Cross-Section Data on Households Producing Partly for Subsistence." in *The Review of Economics and Statistics*, 51:2 (May 1969).

parameters in the Engel relationship, and applies the method to a sample of 816 households in rural Kenya.[3]

THE MODEL

The model most frequently used to estimate expenditure (or income) elasticities, and the one used here, is the double log function. In this paper, the expenditure relationships are written (for $i = 1, \ldots, 16$)

$$X_{ij}^* = \beta_{0i} + \beta_{1i}X_j^* + \beta_{2i}N_j^* + \beta_{3i}R_j + \sum_{K=1}^{4} \gamma_{Ki}D_{Kj} + u_{ij} \qquad (1)$$

where X_{ij} = expenditure by household j on item i, $X_j = \sum_i X_{ij}$ = total expenditure by household j, N = household size, R = the ratio of subsistence to total expenditure, $D_1, \ldots, D_4$ are district dummy variables,[4] u_{ij} is the disturbance, and an asterisk denotes a logarithm. The β's and γ's in equation (1) are parameters to be estimated. The parameters β_1 and β_2 are respectively the total expenditure and household-size elasticities. The model has the advantage of considerable simplicity; in addition, a double log relationship is usually found to provide a good fit and to satisfy the assumption of homoscedastic residuals.

There are sixteen equations to be estimated, one for each expenditure item. The X_{ij} are defined as the sum of cash plus subsistence expenditure on the item in question. Subsistence expenditure is the imputed value of goods produced by the household for own consumption, using the wholesale price for valuation. Most food items and fuel are consumed in part from own production. Unfortunately, the subsistence component of other items, if any, was not recorded.

Total expenditure is simply the sum of the expenditure items. It is common to use total expenditure in place of income as an explanatory variable in the expenditure relationship because of the conceptual and measurement errors associated with observations on income. With total expenditure as a proxy for income, one can use income as an instrumental variable to obtain consistent estimates of (1).

Household size is the number of adult-equivalent consumer units present in the household. Children are weighted by one-half, and the figure is then adjusted to allow for extended absences from the area. The weighting scheme is not ideal, but appears to represent a reasonable compromise.

The district dummy variables were included to net out differences in expenditure due to interdistrict differences in relative prices. Such differences are likely to exist particularly for foods. In an LDC, inadequate and expensive transport and a relatively small market combine to restrict the interregional flow of some commodities, thereby permitting price differentials to persist. The regulation of some commodities by statutory marketing boards also contributes to the interregional price spread. If one area has a surplus and another area a shortage of some commodity, restrictions on the flow of the item between the areas impede the equalization in its price. By adding district dummy variables to the expenditure function, it is assumed that district price differentials, where they exist, shift the expenditure function iso-elastically. In the absence of further information, this assumption appears reasonable.[5, 6]

SUBSISTENCE RATIO

In the rural areas of many LDCs, and notably in the Central Province of Kenya from which our sample is drawn, a substantial part of household income consists of food grown on the farm. Most households grow the major part of the food consumed. A household's expenditure on a food item, say corn, is hypothesized to be related to the household's income and to the corn price (as well as to other variables, such as household size). The relevant price to associate with home-grown corn is the opportunity cost of this corn, i.e. the price at which the corn can be sold in the market. In a frictionless world characterized by perfect markets, the amount of corn grown on the farm would not influence corn consumption. But in an LDC like Kenya, where markets are highly imperfect, this is not the case. The price a farmer can get for his corn is less than what he would have to pay to buy corn, because of transport and other frictional costs, including marketing restrictions.

Consider Figure 1. DD′ is the household's demand curve for corn, AA′ is the selling price, and BB′ the buying price. Regardless of how much is produced on the farm, at least OM and no more than ON will be consumed. But between these two amounts, consumption will depend on the household's production. Consider two households with the same tastes, each growing corn, and each planting the same number of acres. Due to a combination of stochastic factors (weather, timing, luck, etc.) one farm obtains higher yields than the other and consequently a larger corn output. It is likely that the farm growing more will also consume more. Specifically, this will be the case unless either both households produce more than ON or both produce less than OM. The higher consumption of corn is due not only to the income difference, but also to the price effect of the higher output. As food consumption is related to food production, and as food production is likely to be related to total expenditure, the estimated expenditure elasticities will contain a specification bias.[7] This bias can be eliminated (or at least greatly reduced) by adding to the regression the subsistence ratio: the ratio of subsistence to total (cash plus subsistence) expenditure.

ESTIMATION

For ordinary least squares estimators to be asymptotically unbiased, the regressors must be independent of the disturbance term. In equation (1), however, neither X_j^* nor R_j can be assumed independent of u_{ij}. The nonindependence of total expenditure has been discussed.[8, 9] The nonindependence of the subsistence ratio is attributable to errors in measuring subsistence production. The valuation of subsistence is necessarily arbitrary. In the sample used here, subsistence was valued at the wholesale price. An item consumed from own production is valued less than an identical item purchased for cash. Both expenditure on food items, and the subsistence ratio may thus be understated, resulting in nonindependence of R_j and u_{ij}.

Consistent estimates of the parameters in equation (1) can be obtained by using two-stage least squares (TSLS) with at least two instrumental variables. The instrumental variables must be correlated with the regressors but independent of the disturbances. Liviatan argues that, for urban households. household income – even if measured with error – satisfies these conditions.[10] However, in the present case, total household income – the sum of cash income and the imputed value of

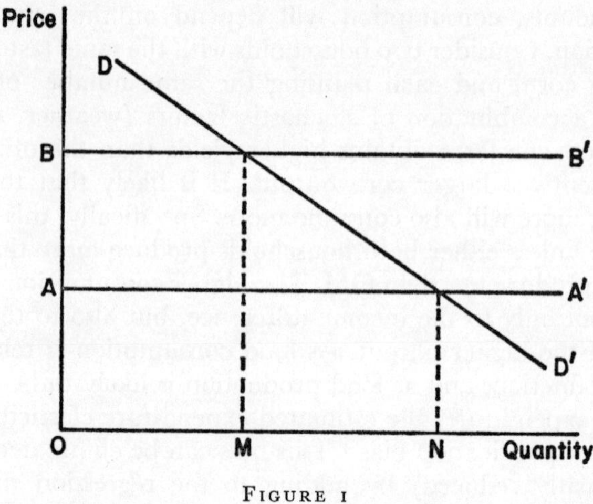

FIGURE 1

subsistence production – would not be suitable. Any errors in valuing subsistence would be reflected in income as well as in expenditure (which includes subsistence expenditure) on the item in question, thereby establishing nonindependence between income and the disturbances. However, cash income is a suitable instrument, and is used here. It is possible that the allocation of a household's resources between cash and subsistence activities is a function of the household's tastes. Thus a household that wants to spend its income on corn will tend to devote a major share of its resources to corn production; while a family wishing to consume education will grow cash crops or work for wages. If consumption decisions and production decisions are taken jointly, then cash income will not be independent of the u_{ij} in (1). In this case, if subsistence is not measured with error, one can use total income as an instrument in place of cash income. But, with interdependence of consumption and production decisions *and* with errors in measuring subsistence, consistent estimation is impossible without further information. To get around this problem, we assume that the allocation of effort between cash and subsistence activities is determined principally by the household's resources and location, and only negligibly by consumption tastes.

In a sense this problem exists for urban households as well. Although we conveniently consider income as the explanatory variable, this is not obviously the case. It is unrealistic to assume that income cannot be influenced by the individual. But if so, then surely one's income is functionally related to one's tastes, so that income decisions and consumption decisions are interdependent. A man with a taste for expensive cars – or expensive women – is likely to choose a profession which affords an opportunity to earn a high income, and is likely to work long hours as well. The exogenous variables in the system are tastes, initial wealth, and innate ability.

As an additional instrumental variable, we use farm size (i.e. acreage operated by the household). It is clear that farm size is an important determinant of both total expenditure and allocation of this expenditure between the subsistence and cash components. Moreover, it is reasonable to assume that farm size is independent of the disturbances in (1). While one may argue that farm size serves as a proxy for permanent income or wealth, which in turn may influence total expenditure, it is plausible to assume that it does not influence the allocation of total expenditure among individual items.

To formalize the preceding remarks, the model contains, in addition to equation (1), two additional equations:

$$X_j^* = a_0 + a_1 Y_j^* + a_2 T_j^* + a_3 N_j^* + a_4 D_{1j} + \ldots + a_7 D_{4j} + v_j \quad (2)$$

$$R_j = \xi_0 + \xi_1 Y_j^* + \xi_2 T_j^* + \xi_3 N_j^* + \xi_4 D_{1j} + \ldots + \xi_7 D_{4j} + w_j \quad (3)$$

where Y = cash income, T = land operated, v and w are disturbances, an asterisk denotes a logarithm, and where the other variables are defined as in (1). It is assumed that both Y_j^* and T_j^* are independent of the u_{ij} in (1).

THE DATA

The sample data were obtained from the Central Province Survey, conducted in the former Central Province of Kenya, over a one-year period beginning in mid-February 1963.[11] The survey was organized and supervised by a United Nations statistician on behalf of the Kenya Government. Households were visited fortnightly for the full year. In addition, daily visits were made to each household for a two-month period to provide detailed information on expenditure on food, tobacco, and beverages. A stratified random sample was used, with higher percentage representation of households with larger farms – and therefore with higher income. Of 1,080 returns, 816 were found suitable for inclusion in the present study. These were grouped by household cash income into 136 groups of 6 households each. Arithmetic means were calculated for all variables for each group, and these means were used as observations in the regression analysis. Grouping facilitates data processing by reducing the effective sample size. But more importantly, the original data contained zero observations on several of the expenditure variables, which were eliminated by grouping.

Mean farm size in the sample is 3.9 acres.[12] Mean income is 1,592 East African shillings,[13] 51 percent of which is derived from agriculture and the remainder from wage income and non-farm enterprises.[14] Subsistence income amounts to 32 percent of total income and 39 percent of total consumption. The average household size is 2.7 adults and 2.8 children.

Table 1 presents a breakdown of expenditure by major category. Food accounts for 56.0 percent of total expenditure, with clothing, fuel, and services next in importance. Of the foods, the most important are cereals, roots-tubers, and pulses. All of the food items except fats-oils are consumed in part from own production. Of the nonfoods, fuel is the sum of purchased fuels (kerosene and charcoal) and firewood, which is collected by members of the household. The remaining items are purchased for cash only.

EMPIRICAL RESULTS

Using TSLS, the coefficients in equations (1) were estimated for the 16 expenditure items. For each item, the residuals were examined; there was no evidence of heteroscedasticity or of nonlinearity. The double log function appears to give a good fit to the data, providing support for the hypothesis that the expenditure elasticities are at least roughly constant in the income range covered by the sample.[15]

An F-test was used to test the significance of the district classification.[16] The set of district dummy variables was significant at the 5 percent level for only one item, roots. There

TABLE 1

Expenditures by Category: Kenya Central Province Survey, 1963–1964

Expenditure Category	*Shillings*[a]	*Percent of Total*	*Remarks*
Cereals	169	12.6	Mainly corn, some wheat
Roots-tubers	116	8.6	Mainly potatoes
Pulses	111	8.3	
Milk	86	6.4	Includes butter, other milk products
Meat	75	5.6	Includes eggs
Vegetables-fruit	67	5.0	
Sugar	64	4.8	
Fats-oils	34	2.5	
Other foods	30	2.2	
Clothing	126	9.4	
Fuel	125	9.3	Firewood, kerosene, charcoal
Services	83	6.2	About equal parts transportation, medical expenses, and other services
Tobacco-beverages	78	5.8	
Education-recreation	64	4.8	Mainly school fees
Housing	46	3.4	Housing materials and paid labor for housing construction and repair
Durables	45	3.3	Furniture, bedding, utensils, equipment
Miscellaneous nondurables	24	1.8	Largest component is soap
Total Expenditure	1343	100.0	

NOTE: See text for description of the survey.

[a] East African shillings. The exchange rate is 14 East African shillings per United States dollar.

are large interdistrict differences in the production and consumption of roots due to the fact that roots grow extremely well in some districts and not in others. Leaving the district variables out of the roots regression could bias the coefficients substantially. The interdistrict differences for the other fifteen items were not statistically significant, even at the 10 percent level. As there is considerable collinearity between the district variables and the other regressors, these 15 regressions were re-run with district deleted.

Table 2 presents the estimated regression coefficients and R^2s (adjusted for degrees of freedom).[17] For roots, these coefficients were estimated net of the district dummy variables, but district was excluded from the remaining regressions. For total expenditure and household size, but not for the subsistence ratio, the coefficients are elasticities. The *t*-ratios are presented in parentheses below the respective coefficients. Single and double asterisks denote significance at the 5 percent and 1 percent level, using a two-tail test.

It is noteworthy that all the regressions are significant at the 0.001 level, using an F-test. The regression explains better than half of the variance in the regressand for all sixteen expenditure items and better than 70 percent for eleven items. The clothing regression provides the best fit.

Total expenditure is significant at the 1 percent level in 12 regressions and at the 5 percent level in an additional three regressions. Nine items, including four foods, have elasticities greater than unity, and can be termed luxuries. There are no inferior goods, items with negative expenditure elasticities. Housing and milk have the highest elasticities; fuel and the staple foods have the lowest.

The high expenditure elasticity for housing deserves comment. All families in the sample own their own housing. Housing expenditure recorded in the survey includes only cash expenditure on materials and paid labor in connection with construction and maintenance of the house, and excludes the imputed value of family labor and materials manufactured by the household. If this subsistence component of housing expenditure were recorded, it is reasonable to assume that the elasticity of expenditure on housing would be substantially lower. As it is, as income rises, there is a shift from unrecorded

TABLE 2

Estimated Regression Coefficients

	Total Expenditure		Household Size		Subsistence Ratio		R^2
Housing	2.34	(2.69)*	–.32	(–.34)	–2.30	(–.78)	.56
Milk	2.34	(5.61)**	–.59	(–1.16)	1.53	(.99)	.69
Fats-oils	1.22	(6.23)**	–.30	(–1.27)	–1.48	(–2.04)*	.85
Meat	1.20	(6.77)**	.12	(.58)	–1.08	(–1.65)	.89
Tobacco-beverages	1.12	(5.23)**	–.14	(–.53)	–.80	(–1.01)	.80
Education-recreation	1.10	(2.29)*	.55	(.95)	–2.23	(–1.25)	.60
Miscellaneous nondurables	1.09	(7.96)**	–.11	(–.65)	–.65	(–1.29)	.90
Services	1.08	(4.53)**	.08	(.29)	–2.51	(–2.84)**	.84
Sugar	1.06	(5.75)**	–.12	(–.56)	–1.40	(–2.06)*	.85
Durables	.99	(3.48)**	–.11	(–.33)	–2.02	(–1.91)	.72
Clothing	.89	(6.94)**	.37	(2.35)*	–1.07	(–2.24)*	.92
Vegetables-fruit	.79	(3.96)*	.09	(.37)	1.31	(1.78)	.55
Pulses	.79	(5.21)**	.08	(.42)	1.42	(2.54)*	.66
Fuel	.69	(7.01)**	–.08	(–.70)	1.04	(2.85)*	.74
Cereals	.59	(5.79)**	.15	(1.21)	.70	(1.83)	.79
Roots-tubers	.53	(1.59)	.15	(.56)	1.06	(.72)	.81

NOTE: Figures in parentheses are *t*-ratios.
* Indicates significance at the 5 percent level.
** Indicates significance at the 1 percent level.

subsistence expenditure to recorded cash expenditure. The high elasticity reflects the fact that higher-income households are more likely to pay cash for work on their houses and does not necessarily imply a large improvement in the quality of housing as income rises. The failure to record subsistence housing expenditure doubtless also explains the negative household size elasticity for housing. It would be hard to explain why a larger family has smaller housing needs than a small family. However the negative elasticity probably reflects the fact that there is a greater need to pay cash for housing the smaller the household labor force in residence.[18]

It is interesting that some of the food items rank high on the list. The high elasticities for milk, fats-oils, meat, and sugar suggest a substantial shift in the quality of the diet as income increases. The traditional food items – cereals, roots-tubers, vegetables-fruits, and pulses – have the lowest elasticities, as one would expect.

The high *t*-ratios for total expenditure suggest that interhousehold differences in expenditure patterns are overwhelmingly the result of differences in income (assuming that total household expenditure serves as a proxy for income). This fact is especially interesting in view of the large interhousehold differences in the subsistence ratio, and the fairly major differences in the pattern of consumption among districts. The overriding importance of total expenditure as an explanatory variable results also in high standard errors for the other explanatory variables, and explains the low statistical significance of these variables in most of the regressions.

The household size elasticities are significant in only one regression – clothing. The elasticity is positive for the staple foods, clothing, and education, for obvious reasons, and tends to be negative for the luxury items. The negative elasticity for housing is probably (as noted above) due to a conceptual error in defining this variable. The tendency for the luxuries to have negative household size elasticities may reflect the fact that a larger family places demands on a household that compete with the demand for these items. However, because of the high standard errors associated with the household size coefficients, one should not place too much reliance on the estimates themselves.

The subsistence ratio is significant at the 5 percent level in six regressions (one of these also at the 1 percent level). Because the subsistence ratio is negatively correlated with total expenditure, deleting the ratio from the regressions would bias the expenditure elasticity estimates upward for the items purchased mainly for cash and downward for the subsistence items.

As an increase in the subsistence ratio implies a substitution of subsistence for cash expenditure, it is not surprising that the nonfood items (except for fuel, which is mainly a subsistence item) have negative coefficients. In addition, meat, fats-oils, and sugar have negative coefficients; fats-oils are purchased entirely for cash, and meat and sugar are principally cash expenditure items. Of the negative coefficients, those with the highest absolute value are (in order): services, housing, education, and durables.

The items consumed mainly from subsistence have high positive coefficients. These include milk, pulses, and vegetables-fruit. Milk perhaps deserves special note. Milk is principally produced on the farm, and is one of the most valuable subsistence food items. Thus farms with a high milk production tend also to have a large subsistence income. One reason why so much milk is consumed by milk producers is because of the quota system, which limits the quantity of fresh milk that a farmer can sell. Farmers producing more than this amount can either sell the milk at a much lower price or consume the milk themselves. Therefore large milk producers tend to consume much of their milk output.

The insignificance (except for roots) of the district effect is interesting; it suggests that the observable differences in expenditure among districts is adequately explained by differences in total expenditure and the other explanatory variables. This in turn implies that our results may have a somewhat wider applicability. If the net district coefficients were significant, then it would be hazardous to use the estimated expenditure elasticities as a basis for projecting demand for rural Kenya as a whole. Significant interdistrict differences within the Central Province would imply even larger differences between this and other provinces. As it is, expenditure patterns appear to be explained largely by total expenditure and the subsistence ratio.

NOTES

An earlier version of this paper was presented at the December 1967 meetings of the Econometric Society. The author thanks Bridger Mitchell and James Rosee for helpful comments on statistical procedures; and Andrew Parnes and Henry Moore for their able assistance in processing the data. He also acknowledges indebtedness to Christopher A. Sims for especially useful and stimulating comments. Thanks are also due A. T. Brough and S. S. Heyer (Kenya Ministry of Economic Planning and Development) and S. A. A. Sundstrom (formerly with the United Nations) for providing access to the data and for giving generously of their time.

1. R. Summers, "A Note on Least Squares Bias in Household Expenditure Analysis," *Econometrica* 27: 7, 1959.
2. Liviatan, N., "Errors in Variables and Engel Curve Analysis," *Econometrica* 29: 3 (July 1961), pp. 336–62.
3. For an analysis of expenditure elasticities in urban Kenya, see B. F. Massell and J. Heyer, "Household Expenditure in Nairobi: A Statistical Analysis of Consumer Behavior," *Economic Development and Cultural Change* 17: 2 (January 1969).
4. There are five districts in all, but one district dummy variable was deleted to avoid singularity of the moments matrix.
5. Another source of interdistrict shifts in the Engel curves may be inter-district differences in tastes; it is assumed that any such differences also give rise to iso-elastic shifts.
6. With relevant price data, and with enough observations, one could insert the price data directly in the regression equation.
7. It does not matter whether one is talking about quantity consumed or the value of consumption – the effect is the same because the same price is used to value all corn grown in the area.
8. Summers, "A Note on Least Squares."
9. Livitian, "Errors in Variables and Engle Curve Analysis."
10. Ibid.
11. The data are unpublished, but were kindly made available to me by the government of Kenya. For a more extensive discussion of the survey and the data, see Kenya Government, Ministry of Economic Planning and Development, Statistics Division, *Economic Survey of Central Province—1963/64*, Nairobi, 1968.
12. The figures in this paragraph and in Table 1 refer to weighted means of the sample observations, taking account of the stratification of the sample.
13. At the time of the survey, an East African shilling equaled 14 United States cents.
14. Subsistence production of each item was valued at the average wholesale price obtaining in the district during the survey year.
15. Strictly speaking, this is not a valid test of the hypothesis of constant vs. nonconstant expenditure elasticities. It is possible that alternative

functions would provide a better fit. For a discussion of some plausible alternatives, see C. E. V. Leser, "Forms of Engel Functions," *Econometrica,* 31 : 4 (October 1963), pp. 694–703.

16. See A. S. Goldberger, *Econometric Theory* (New York: John Wiley and Sons, 1964), pp. 176–77.
17. In Table 2, R^2 indicates the proportion of the intergroup variance in the regressand explained by intergroup variation in the regressors. Because the data were grouped by an instrumental variable which is correlated with regressors, there is a presumption that the R^2's are higher than would be the case with ungrouped data.
18. A household with a small recorded size is likely to have members living off the farm during all or part of the year. Household size does not measure family size but number of consumer units, adjusted for absences from the area.

Part III

Economic Policy and Finance

In writing about economic policy, economists may be concerned with making a case for a particular approach or set of policies, with studying the outcome of policies actually followed, or with providing a setting for the formulation of policy. These are of course not the only policy issues of interest to economists, but they are the concerns of the essays in this section.

Green develops a strong brief for comprehensive economic planning in Africa. By this he means planning which encompasses, in addition to government investment, overall targets for the economy, sectoral projections including the major projects within the sectors, and an analysis of intersectoral relations. Such planning entails a considered set of goals, a coherent development strategy and set of policies, and a careful attempt to make the best use of all the resources available or potentially available. Although private-sector decisions, exports, and foreign aid are subject to only limited control by government, comprehensive planning helps government to identify the ways in which it can exercise such influence as is possible. It also makes it more possible for government to react intelligently to unexpected changes in these and other sectors of the economy. Interwoven in Green's treatment of planning are stimulating discussions of a number of related issues.

Russell McLaughlin's paper is a study of the events and processes which brought on severe balance-of-payments and financial crises in Liberia in 1962, and of the consequent Debt

Rearrangement Plan, standby financing arrangements, and program of budgetary austerity negotiated with the International Monetary Fund. His treatment of IMF-supervised policies provides some support to both supporters and critics of the IMF. On the one hand, he discusses a catalogue of benefits. On the other hand, he indicates that the austerity program caused a sharp decline in Liberian real income and employment.

Langley's essay on Nigeria provides the kind of overview necessary for intelligent formulation or understanding of policy. She traces the economic change in the country (accompanying the political change from colonial to independent status) from almost exclusive dependence on agriculture and agricultural exports to a situation in which petroleum has become increasingly important and in which there has been some growth of manufacturing. These structural changes are reflected in alterations in the actual and potential sources of finance for the development of Nigeria. The paper is a highly knowledgeable delineation of major forces and major constraints at work in the economy of Nigeria.

Chapter 11

Some Problems of National Development Planning and Foreign Financing

Reginald H. Green

NATURE OF COMPREHENSIVE PLANNING

A national development plan is – or should be – a form of budget. This has a number of implications for plan formulation, implementation, revision, and evaluation. It is of particular relevance to the relationship between comprehensive national planning and foreign financing.

A budget sets out to achieve certain aims by using a limited supply of resources in a specified manner. Two aspects of a budget are important: (1) it should cover a stated time period, and (2) its resources, allocations to specific uses, and targets should be in quantitative form. In no sense does this imply that the aims of a comprehensive development plan are purely (or even basically) economic or that they are all inherently quantitative. Ultimate national goals are not basically economic, but sociopolitical. So long as they are selected in the national interest, and with careful attention to the cost of achieving any objective in terms of other objectives foregone, it is eminently proper that national resources be allocated to achieving "noneconomic" goals.[1]

It does not follow, however, that economic considerations are minor. The attainment of any objective costs resources; the efficient allocation of scarce resources among competing goals lies at the heart of economic analysis. The goal of a better life for a majority of the population is basically social; however, its achievement requires a rise in the output of consumer goods and services, in investment, in public services of an investment nature (e.g. technical education, road maintenance, agricultural extension), and in public services of a consumption nature. Thus the allocation of resources in such a way as to attain and maintain a rapid growth in domestic output per person is essential for the effective pursuit of national sociopolitical goals. Economic advance alone is not development, but without economic advance national development cannot be maintained for long.

A comprehensive development plan, therefore, sets out its aims in the form of quantitative targets (of total domestic product, of exports, of school enrollments, of water supply points, of textile output, etc.) to be attained by the use of policy and project instruments which either direct or influence resource allocation. To be useful, a plan must be possible; that is, the use of available resources through viable projects and operational policy instruments must be capable of achieving – or at least of making substantial progress toward achieving – the stated targets. Further it must be consistent, that is the interrelationships of supplies and demands must be such that anomalies (e.g. completed schools without teachers, or new factories with no available foreign exchange to purchase raw material inputs) are avoided.

Finally, a plan must be reasonably efficient. The set of targets and the policies and projects chosen as means of achieving them must be geared to attain a more rapid rate of national development than would a different selection of targets, policies, and projects.[2]

While national development planning is – at least verbally – almost universally accepted in Africa, serious questions have been raised about the desirability of comprehensive planning. Simpler types of planning have often been employed or favored. The least comprehensive has been what may be called list-of-projects planning. This refers to a catalogue of desirable public-sector capital projects, usually compiled from lists submitted by various government agencies. The list is neither complete nor definite: the investments of some government or quasi-government agencies may not be included at all; moreover, projects may easily be dropped or added, since little attention is paid to the relations between them. "Planning" of this kind is not generally favored, even by public authorities but because of limitations in government capacity, it has often been resorted to. An integrated public-sector investment plan (or program) is more inclusive. All expected public-sector investments are included, and an attempt is made to consider the interrelations among various public programs. The strategic-sector plan is still more comprehensive. It may include an integrated public-sector investment program and may also focus on programs and policies for a few sectors of the national economy considered strategic.[3]

Part of the criticism appears to stem from a special view of a comprehensive plan – as an artifact derived from an econometric model and ineptly imposed upon an economy it does not reflect. In fact, a comprehensive plan should be based on empirical data and detailed evaluation of possibilities as well as on an overall strategic analysis, and may contain little formal econometrics. Further, plans that are labeled as comprehensive (but wrongly so) are often deprived of operational significance by being presented and left in a truncated formulation stage without carryover into implementation and evaluation. Quite clearly a plan with such characteristics is neither comprehensive nor, in most cases, even a part of any significant planning process. However, both weaknesses can arise in the other types of plans. Bad plans and bad planning are not unique to any one methodology.

More basic criticisms question the realism of comprehensive planning, which often appears to assume more significant governmental control than actually exists over private-sector decisions, export performance, and foreign aid availability. This error is seen as leading to inflexibility and inability to adjust to unforeseen external forces and events. Comprehensive planning probably is more prone than other approaches to these weaknesses. On the other hand, without the kind of overall analytical framework characteristic of comprehensive planning, it is doubtful whether such influence as is possible over the private and export sectors and over aid procurement will be identified and exercised. The public-sector investment program is unlikely to be equally effective in establishing fully the extent of the possible. Such a program, or even more, a list-of-projects plan, is doubtless easy to alter. Whether it can be altered rationally in the absence of a comprehensive projection and policy-planning framework is a very different question, especially if changes concern public projects designed to support the private sector and are made in response to unforeseen private-sector shortfalls.

It is a common mistake to equate the success or failure of a comprehensive planning effort with exact fulfillment of a plan. Thus, even a sympathetic critic has suggested that the Tanzania Five-Year Plan has had little influence on public economic actions or policies.[4] A glance at implementation results raises some doubts about this evaluation. Public-sector investment in real terms was of the order of 80–85 percent of targets, while the growth rate of constant price gross domestic product averaged about 5½ percent a year or over 80 percent of the Plan's target. In both cases the level of attainment is higher than comparable pre-comprehensive planning results.

Perhaps more significant is the distinct and cumulative change in ministerial thinking about problems and approaches to decision-making. Especially in the Planning Ministry and in the Treasury, there has been increasing emphasis on the development implications of all policy measures. It is not accidental that domestic revenue for the development budget reached the five-year target in three years and was slightly over 200 percent fulfilled for the full five years. Nor can Tanzania's steady re-evaluation and refinement of rural development policies and programs be separated from the planning effort as a whole. Equally, the Plan's emphasis on parastatal (public-owned, independently managed, directly productive) ventures has led to both (1) a sharp increase in their scale and (2) to the development of a body of experience in their operation which in 1967–68 allowed the carrying through of bank, insurance, milling, major import-export, and selected industrial nationalizations, with no major interruptions of economic activity and an increase during the years 1967–69 in attained profit levels.[5]

In the past few years planning in Africa has become more instrument and efficiency conscious, but this development has been concentrated on projects and their viability. Clearly this is an important advance: unsound projects in the public sector (including parastatal and other publicly owned but separately managed bodies and cooperatives) waste scarce resources and often hinder private-sector activity. An unprofitable national airline, for example, dissipates potential investible surplus, reduces foreign exchange available for capital goods imports, and impedes development of the road and ocean transport needed for agricultural and industrial growth. A high-cost publicly owned petroleum refinery raises the costs of all fuel-consuming industries and thus raises their prices to consumers, lowers their competitiveness with imports, and acts as a brake on their expansion.

Policies are at least as critical, however, as projects.[6] They are often more critical in attempts to induce private investment – by farmers, by consumers, by small firms, as well as by large domestic or foreign investors. Independent decision-makers can often be influenced by incentives, advice, and selective technical assistance more efficiently and effectively than they can be controlled by fiat.

PROCUREMENT AND USE OF FOREIGN CAPITAL

Procurement and use of foreign capital pose a number of critical policy questions. Wrong decisions on these matters can be extremely costly. They may reduce substantially the effective value of the foreign resources; they may alter plan focus greatly; they may affect administrative and economic efficiency, and standards of political, public, and business honesty. All too often the wrong decisions have been taken; and not, it should be stressed, simply by African politicians, but also by their civil servants and economic advisors, and by the governments of the aid-transferring countries.

Few if any African plans contain an identifiable medium-term foreign borrowing policy. Such a policy should project ceilings for debt-servicing capacity and should spell out the ceiling's implications regarding maximum allowable borrowing at alternative interest and repayment terms. It is much more common – especially in East Africa – to find ad hoc planning procedures which set rough criteria for acceptable credit and lay down general rules of thumb regarding manageable debt levels. Such an approach is limited in its potential for long-term strategy guidance. Anglophonic West African and Asian experience[7] indicate that ill-considered medium-term borrowing – either on poor terms or for marginal or poor projects – slightly alleviates present foreign-resource problems only at the cost of a permanent reduction in external debt-servicing capacity, a loss of external lender confidence in ability to repay, and an immensely aggravated future balance-of-payments position. Unfortunately, this seems to have been taken as an operational lesson elsewhere in Africa to only a limited degree.

CONTRACTOR FINANCE

Contractor finance – whether from private western firms usually backed by state export promotion guarantees or from socialist state export monopolies – almost always entails high direct and indirect costs. Repayment is normally in installments, often beginning before the contracted unit is completed, and to be completed in less than ten years. Consequently, the effective period of the full loans is usually quite short. On western (though not on socialist) contractor finance, the effective interest rate is quite often over 10 percent and sometimes over 20 percent. In both western and socialist contracts, the plant cost tends to be well above competitive levels. Early repayment makes it impossible to pay for the productive unit out of the plant's own earnings. In practice, steadily rising levels of contractor finance (and associated costs) become necessary simply to repay the initial borrowings, not to speak of raising the level of investment.

A series of West African states (with very different political and economic systems and outlooks) have opted for heavy use of contractor finance. In at least two cases the results have been disastrous; total contractor debts were piled up in excess of annual export earnings. In Ghana, senior economists (both national and expatriate) favored this policy. They advised that manufacturing investment raises exports and reduces imports rapidly enough to allow self-financing of repayments. Thus they expected that in eight years the whole structure of production and the balance-of-payments position could be transformed. This advice involved serious underestimation of the lag between initial ground-breaking and capacity operation (which probably runs three to eight years), serious underestimation of the growth of repayments demands, and serious overestimation of net import substitution and export growth. Massive finance was initially obtained, primarily from western firms backed by unselective government export guarantees that protected their profits. These guarantees had the effect of encouraging unsound investment and finance policies on the part of African governments, and of encouraging dealings with high cost (and in several cases palpably dishonest) firms, all in the sacrosanct names of "foreign aid" and "export promotion."

Soon debts could be repaid and new projects instituted only if new contractor finance per annum exceeded 30 percent of export earnings – a situation deterring any long-term lender, and leading to a panic by the short-term lenders as soon as the flow of new borrowings began to fall. The economists (who indeed changed their views on contractor finance before the crash, but still too late to avert it), the selling firms (who, by and large, had their profits), the government-export promotion bodies (who after all promoted exports and then piously protested at African claims of inability to repay on time) are not greatly hurt. The government and the development plan, however, have vanished without a trace, and the economy is now faced with a substantial foreign debt and a new investment policy as overcautious as the old was overcredulous. Capital area unemployment "boomed" from 10 percent in 1965 toward 35–50 percent in 1968–70, with the side-effect of a wholesale xenophobic expulsion of tens of thousands of long-time foreign African residents.

Much of the contractor finance was used on elaborate infrastructural and/or doubtfully viable productive projects. Nonetheless, it also provided the basic finance for additions to usable industrial plant with a capacity of up to $250–300 million annual value added. However, the resulting exchange crises, by limiting import allocations for inputs and necessitating domestic demand-curbing policies, will prevent full use of this capacity before the mid-1970s; production in 1969 appears to have been at 55–65 percent of capacity.

Contractor finance has uses, as a limited supplement to basic sources of foreign finance. If a particular project or building is believed critical to the effectiveness of a much broader operation, then a very high price, whether in terms of interest or stated price, may be worth while. To break what were considered bottlenecks, Tanzania has, for example, used contractor finance in a handful of cases, including one critical ministerial building and its initial large first-class hotel. The point is to evaluate costs, repayment schedules, and future financial implications clearly, and to recognize that to borrow short at high cost to finance long-term investment is unsound except as a method of filling minor gaps in the country's long-term financing program.

It is possible, of course, that contractor finance can be a good source of credit. The real issues concern interest, project cost and contractor selection, and repayment terms.

ADJUSTING TO PREFERENCES OF FOREIGN CAPITAL SOURCES

Foreign aid and loan sources – public and private, bilateral and international – have their own views on what projects and programs developing economies should undertake. Their reasons are mixed: economic interest, political strategy or preference, reliance on analogies from their own economic history, and disinterested technical and economic appraisal. Some of these reasons may be legitimate or partially legitimate. All are facts of world economic life. All pose problems for development plan financing and implementation.

Three methods of "reconciling" the views and interests of the aid donor on the one hand, and the plan goals on the other hand, have proved crippling to national economic development. The first is to secure a major donor's official experts to write the plan (as a number of African countries have done) with the predictable result that its overall aims are automatically suspect (not always correctly) and its national support low, even though its external financing appears substantially assured. All too clearly, neither national economic nor political development can be expected on this path, whether the plan drafter is a nation, an international institution, or a consortium.[8] A national plan can be drawn up only by experts responsible solely to national leadership.

Second, national plans can, in fact if not in name, be submitted to a limited number of aid sources for redrafting, either overtly or via "projects to be financed" selection. The plan then proceeds on the basis of the financed group of projects, which may be more closely related to the preconceived interests of the aid sources than to the goals of the developing economy. It is widely believed in Africa that relationships between the European Economic Community and certain of its member states on the one hand, and many EEC African associate economies on the other, have been of this nature. This belief underlies the central criticisms directed at the pattern of relationships between the EEC and the African Associates. The critics' basic view (perhaps a trifle too harsh) is that economic policies and plans may now be proposed in the African capitals, but they are still disposed in Paris and Brussels, with very little real influence by any Associate on crucial financing decisions.[9]

Third, national plans can be amended in the course of implementation to take account of foreign financing preferences and availabilities. This course of action is not necessarily unsound and is to some extent unavoidable. Such changes do not necessarily compromise basic plan aims. Some overseas proposals for alterations are likely to be potentially consistent, or at least compatible, with national development aspirations. Some in fact may represent improved resource allocations and program balances even from the recipient's viewpoint.

The danger, especially if the contractor finance element is high, is that alterations on an ad hoc basis will be made without reference to their impact on overall plan objectives and resource allocation patterns. The result is likely to be one of very inconsistent plan fulfillment, e.g. 150 percent in civil service offices and housing, 150 percent on main roads and bridges, 25 percent on directly productive investment at the halfway point in one major plan. Moreover, ad hoc alterations are peculiarly likely to allow, or to provide cover for, fraud and special-interest promotion. In Nigeria, an issue-by-issue approach to such policies as tariffs and a project-by-project handling of development undertakings were in fact the façade for a political system whose philosophy was that the proper purpose of holding responsible political office was the promotion of personal, family, and local interests through the misallocation of public funds. Although that government too is no longer with us, its heritage of violence, chaos, and national agony will be long in abating.[10]

A clear set of priorities can advance really key projects with domestic resources when foreign resources are not available; at the same time, the planners can develop alternative, coherent sets of desirable but less-essential projects that accord with the predilections of the sources of foreign finance, and which will therefore be able to secure foreign funds.[11] As Tanzania's 1964–68 experience suggests (following loss of a £7.5 million negotiated UK loan and the realization that Plan foreign-aid projections were unrealistically high), such an approach is complex. It makes great demands at the levels of the implementing ministry, the development-planning agency, and Treasury, but it is workable and, hopefully, perfectible. Broadening the range of programs for which foreign funds may be available is especially important for an economy seeking to diversify its foreign finance sources; it lessens its economic dependence on a handful of much larger economies, and it increases its international economic freedom of maneuver and its range of policy choices.

"Secondary" aid-transferring nations (Scandinavia, Canada, Australia, Yugoslavia, Netherlands, Italy) can be interested in a range of useful projects, including technical and personnel assistance, that can help small economies avoid depending on just a few major aid-providers. Tanzania, for example, has now developed ten substantial aid sources: China, the United States, the World Bank and the International Development Association, West Germany, Sweden, Italy, Denmark, Japan, United Nations family organizations, Canada, Netherlands. None accounts for more than about 20 percent of annual foreign resource inflows.

Because lender "tastes" differ, the total range of programs that can be financed from an array of lenders is broadened. For example, Sweden and Denmark see rural water supply development, and loan capital and personnel for parastatal productive ventures as critical areas for assistance. Diversification of funding sources permits extending the range of fundable programs so as to include almost all programs with substantial direct import content as well as certain educational and agricultural programs of special development interest.

Closed negotiations for large contracts are preferred by many (not all) international firms, by some aid-providing countries, and also by developing-economy politicians or officials who place great emphasis on tidiness and speed (or alas, on under-the-table rakeoffs). In general (as illustrated in almost every African and Asian state the author has visited) the result is to raise costs. This is especially true when contractor finance or tied aid enters the picture. It is even more true when there is corruption. But it also happens when speed or neatness motivate the negotiations for the economy. A small economy in a hurry and with limited information cannot easily solve the problems inherent in dealing with a single large firm with greater financial opportunities, better data, more expertise, and less urgency about time and place. This problem is not necessarily eased by requirement of a foreign equity stake in the venture. Intercorporate incest on construction, management, purchasing, and sales can make the equity stake a minor cost of getting the contract, not a compelling incentive to build the most suitable plant at the lowest cost or to ensure reasonably satisfactory operation.

Open tender is not always practicable; shopping among alternative builders, managers, investors, usually is. Comparisons suggest that closed negotiations can increase costs by 50–150 percent above the attainable competitive price. Oil refineries and pipelines, dams, water supply development, hospitals, highway construction, and (on a slightly different front) mineral and oil concession agreements and selective joint-venture agreements provide notable examples.

The need for freedom to bargain with alternative suppliers[12] enhances the case against heavy dependence on traditional contractor finance. The sound contract, if truly viable, can usually receive medium-term bank credit; the project that can gain only high-cost short-term money is probably a bad bargain on other grounds as well. Unfortunately, the high 1967–70 levels of money market rates have tended to increase reliance in contractor finance by making other funding more expensive and harder to secure. The reputable contractor with a viable project and a creditworthy client can be of assistance in raising medium-term finance on reasonable terms, e.g.

through a government export bank. Alternatively, industrial economy governments might consider more general use of medium-term commercial loan interest subsidies to allow fifteen-year 4–6 percent credit for viable, directly productive projects of a developing economy.

Foreign exchange and foreign high-level (and on occasion medium-level technical) manpower, like all flows of scarce goods and services and the purchasing power needed to affect their allocation, must be budgeted, not taken as a residual item to "cover" a gap. Projections of foreign exchange needs should be built up on a project-by-project basis, and then cumulated annually and over a plan period. A simplistic macro-projection appearing in a formal plan is no substitute for continuous planning aimed at securing needed flows, rephasing temporarily unmanageable requirements, and estimating potentially attainable future resource allocation.

INTERNATIONAL UNCERTAINTY AND THE NEED FOR COMPREHENSIVE PLANNING

Like all budgets, a plan is drawn up for the future. It is a projection based on evaluation of what is likely to happen, not a prediction of what will happen. The fact that a plan's policies and projects are designed to influence the course of events does not alter this. Weather, international trade and market conditions, world liquidity and aid crises, the failure of two successive United Nations Conferences on Trade and Development, and similar factors, are neither precisely predictable nor significantly within the scope of any one developing economy's influence. They do, however, affect the performances and the possibilities of each economy. Moreover, projections of trends are usually more reliable than projections for individual years.

However, one cannot realistically construct annual budgets, recurrent or capital, on the basis of average government revenues or export earnings if the initial years fall below trend before any surplus is amassed to cushion shortfalls. Herein lies a substantial cause of the inherent conservative strain in any responsible Central Bank or Ministry of Finance. Caution can be overdone, but early over-optimism that later results in drastic cutbacks surely hampers development. Initial caution permits an assured program to go forward with interim increases as, and if, resources are secured above initial anticipations. Supplementary needs are much more certain to arise than are supplementary sources of finance. Nevertheless, deliberate overcaution in resource estimation can be dangerous. A formal contingency vote (i.e. appropriation), by providing funds to meet unexpected urgent needs, might encourage publication of realistic resource estimates.

Uncertainty is never greater than in the area of external resources. Export earnings, import costs, foreign assistance, private capital flows – all are extremely volatile from year to year even when they appear to follow a satisfactory medium-run trend. All too often the trend is also unsatisfactory, and leads to increasing external account stringency.

A few examples can be taken from the 1961–67 Tanzanian experience. Over that period exports (including those of Zanzibar) rose from £56 to £87 million – a 7 percent growth trend. However, in three of the six years the actual export earnings diverged from the annual value by 10 percent or more, and the annual export increases varied from over 20 percent to minus 9 percent.

Imports grew from £55 million to £83 million. This appears to indicate a 6 percent trend, but in fact for the first three years the average increase was around 2½ percent, was then 12½ percent for three years and for the last year was negative. The range was from negative to almost 20 percent.

Aid data for (mainland) Tanzania from 1961 to 1962 through 1966–67 show sharp declines, with only 1966–67 showing the 1961–62 level of £7 million, and 1963–64 down to £2.6 million. Further, the proportion of grants has fallen from 45 percent in 1961–62 and 94 percent in 1962–63 to little over 20 percent in 1965–66 and under 20 percent in 1966–67. In absolute terms, grants attained a level of nearly £5 million in 1962–63 and have not reached £2 million in any subsequent year.

Commodity terms of trade data for (mainland) Tanzania's exports outside East Africa have fluctuated since 1961, moving generally downward. Taking 1961 (a depressed year) as a base, they stood at 91 in 1965 and fell to 85 in 1967.

Because exports are a critical sector of domestic production and imports a key source of government revenue, the erratic performance of the international sector has sharply aggravated the instability of the growth rate of domestic product and government revenue. Gross monetary domestic product from 1961 through 1967 grew 5.6 percent a year, on average, after adjusting for domestic price changes. However, the range of annual growth rates is negative (1960 to 1962) to 8.6 percent (1965 to 1966).

The combined effect of erratic tax revenue growth and foreign-aid fluctuations on public investment (and therefore development plan implementation) is self-evident. Public investment grew by more than 30 percent in 1964–65 and 1966–67, but only by 10 percent in 1956–66. 1968 and 1969 showed a sustained rise in development spending financed largely through a very considerable augmentation of local resources, although foreign resource transfers increased in 1968. Exports declined in 1968 and recovered only to 1967 levels in 1969. The continued strength of the balance of payments was due partly to increased capital inflows but was probably due more to rapid import substitution in final consumer goods. In 1968 such imports stood at approximately 50 percent of local consumption whereas in 1961 they had been over 80 percent.

Uncertainty in the international economic sector, for trade, aid, and investment alike, is a fact of life for developing economies. The existence of comprehensive external uncertainty has been advanced as an argument against comprehensive development planning in African, Asian, and Latin American economies. Given a high ratio of international trade to gross domestic product and of foreign financing to gross domestic investment (so this line of argument runs), strategic sector planning is appropriate. It would center on a few key sectors and might include an integrated government investment program, but would steer clear of overall national targets and intersectoral analysis.[13]

Superficially, this criticism of comprehensive planning sounds reasonable. The greater the degree of uncertainty about foreign earnings and capital flows, the more flexibility needs to be built into a plan that is intended for actual implementation. However, this argument against comprehensive planning overlooks three considerations. First, a comprehensive plan with overall and sectoral projections is the only framework allowing even approximate evaluation of crucial matters like probable foreign-balance trends by sector, the sensitivity of the economy as a whole to fluctuations around these trends, and the sensitivity of significant economic units to such fluctuations. Second, in the absence of a coherent analytical framework, with data on relationships among projects and among the different sectors of the economy, it would be extremely difficult to make rational project alterations, additions or deletions in response to changes in the public-sector financial situation, or to devise sound and consistent economic policies to affect private decisions regarding resource allocation and production. Third, strategic sector planning tends to make development planning an echo of the very international economy weaknesses and uncertainties it is designed to overcome.

It is true that addition or subtraction of projects from a limited number of sectoral plans – or, a fortiori from a list-of-projects plan – appears easier than working through the ramifications of international-sector changes on a comprehensive plan involving an interlocking set of policies and projects. But this "ease" conceals the problems that addition or deletion of projects may entail substantial policy changes, and that the information required for assessing the impact, the necessity and the wisdom of these policy changes is simply not available from the more limited approach to planning.

The same problem of unavailability of information necessary for evaluating alterations obtains in the case of an integrated public-sector investment program. Without a clear set of targets for the private sector, and policies relating to the private-sector policies melded with public investment to influence target attainment, alteration in the investment program will almost inevitably be excessively ex-post, unnecessarily inconsistent, and erratically ad hoc. Policies and related investments should be altered jointly and on the basis both of short- and medium-run projections and of past results. Further, when they are related to private economic activity, policies and investments should be altered in light of the demands, trends, and possibilities of influencing relevant private units. For example, an actual or projected decline in exports of a particular crop may require many policy and investment changes: greater investment in support of import-substitute manufacturing and agriculture; increased incentives to import-substituting activities; a shift in road priorities from one crop area to another; and a general reorientation of agricultural education, extension, research, credit, and input supply away from the disfavored export and toward domestic food, industrial and alternative export crops. This type of consistent, timely, and efficient alteration of resource allocation is difficult enough at best. It is almost unattainable in principle, let alone in practice, in a context of public investment programs separated from related policies and not supported by operational targets for related private economic activity.

The importance and the erratic behavior of the foreign-trade sector of the economy combine to make the best attainable projections a matter of priority for economic policy formulation. A comprehensive plan with detailed projections of the production of exports and of import substitutes and of the demand for various categories of imports can provide at least an approximation of probable export and import trends and of the need for international aid and investment flows. It is no accident that the appearance of the first three comprehensive East African Development Plans over the period 1964–66 parallels the rise of informed concern and specific policies relating to the medium-run trade, capital, and external finance aspects of Kenyan, Ugandan, and Tanzanian economic development.

While the actual balances of payments and of international transactions of Tanzania, Kenya, and Uganda between 1969 and 1971 are likely to diverge significantly from plan projections, the projections are providing far better indicators of what to expect than would ad hoc guesswork or simple extrapolation of past trends. Furthermore the same process that yields the projections helps to provide data on the probability of shortfalls or overfulfillment in various revenue and expenditure categories, and of the senstitivity of the economic structure to such contingencies.

In Tanzania and Uganda (and probably in Kenya as well), foreign balance projections on an annual and a longer-term basis have focused considerably greater attention on the external balance implications of particular policies, projects, and programs. It is possible that the 1966–67 reactions in both

Uganda and Tanzania have been slightly on the overcautious side. However, marginal initial overcaution combined with refinement of data collection and improvement of projections surely provides a firmer foundation for medium- and long-term development than do the blithe disregard for external balance considerations and dissipation of basic as well as surplus external reserves that have too often characterized anglophonic West Africa (including Liberia).

In addition to reducing the degree of uncertainty about the magnitudes of future foreign economic transactions, a comprehensive plan provides a body of data and a framework for intelligent reallocation of available foreign exchange resources when these fall short of (or exceed) expectations. The existence of the data and framework make a coherent annual operating plan possible, and allow greater flexibility in phasing projects forward or backward as resources and/or demand for them alters. Both overall plan alterations and the relative size of different sub-period programs can be altered more easily and efficiently; the choice between rephasing and alterations in absolute program size can be made on a more informed basis.

It is worth pointing out that any coherent and efficient plan built up solely on the basis of individual projects and policies, but modifying individual decisions to take account of their broader effects, does, in fact, embody an implicit comprehensive development plan and strategy. This is, however, a very difficult way to achieve consistent and efficient resource allocation. Aside from other difficulties, the fact that the project-by-project aggregation method is unlikely to yield balance-of-payments projections decreases the probability of arriving at a comprehensive plan. This is no argument against project or policy evaluation. Rather, it is an affirmation that they are most effective within a comprehensive plan which lays down a coherent development strategy, a considered set of goals, and a consistent resource utilization framework.

POLICY IMPLICATIONS OF INTERNATIONAL UNCERTAINTY

The foregoing thesis that comprehensive planning not only provides a greater degree of predictability, but also makes possible more rational adjustments to situations diverging significantly from projections involves a series of policy implications. The first set of implications relates to allocation of resource shortfalls or windfalls. Normally, all major sectors of the economy should share in the changes. The public development budget, the recurrent government expenditure level, private consumption, private investment, and the foreign balance account will all need alteration directly or through policies influencing private decisions.

The development budget poses special problems. There is a temptation, if growth in gross domestic production lags, to try to boost the development budget. As Ghana discovered, the result of trying to increase overall public investment including infrastructure out of a diminished total supply of resources will normally be popular unrest caused by falling consumer goods availability, radical deterioration of the external payments position, internal inflation, and a fall in private investment (domestic as well as foreign). In the case in point, the results included a coup and a draconic decrease in development spending below the levels which could have been sustained had lagging growth not been "met" with public investment expansion.

On the other hand, to place the main burden of adjusting to a resource shortfall on the development budget is also counterproductive. It ensures a continuation of the initial slump – vide a number of the smaller and poorer West African and South Asian economies whose public investment levels have been cut in relation to gross domestic product and whose annual economic growth rates have fallen to the 2 percent to minus 2 percent range.[14]

What is needed is a combination of broad reductions, selective sectoral cuts and increases, and an urgent attempt to speed up external-assistance flows with long repayment periods and low interest rates. The price of accelerated structural change during export stagnation will almost certainly include both austerity and inflation; but if long-term payoff, infrastructural and non-directly productive investment can be postponed (and recurrent expenditure held to a 2–3 percent annual increase), the cost may be bearable. Argentina (in the 1930s) and Brazil (in the 1950s) did attain substantial increases in real output per capita through structural change in the face of endemic foreign-balance crises. A more rational policy pattern regarding peripheral investments and recurrent expenditure would almost certainly have allowed the same results at lower costs in inflation, social malformation, and political instability.[15]

For social and political reasons, recurrent government budgets cannot normally be cut back drastically under African conditions. The more satisfactory approach probably lies in limiting growth of recurrent expenditure to a ceiling not higher than a cautious projection of average annual growth of monetary domestic product. What is to be avoided is rapid increases in good years because funds are at hand, and less rapid but positive increases in slump years as well. Runaway increases in recurrent public spending in poor countries are inconsistent with high rates of investment, significant growth of per-capita production, and sustained increases in per-capita personal consumption.[16]

Clearly, not all recurrent expenditure categories should grow at the same rate. Some are genuinely preconditions for sustained national development, e.g. education (especially post-primary and adult), health (especially preventive and nutritional), agricultural research, education and extension, and road maintenance. The same is true, most regrettably, of security for states such as Zambia and Tanzania which face border raids, espionage overflights (and the threat of worse) from Portugal, Rhodesia, and South Africa. So long as the threatened nations have no reason to feel confident that attacks on their territory will be met either promptly or effectively (much less prevented) by major power action, enhanced defense capacity will remain a national imperative.

Rational setting of growth ceilings for different types of expenditure would be greatly helped by improved budgetary procedures. Neither the inherited French nor the British public-accounts system is adequate. As a first step, program budgeting allowing allocation of costs by relevant functional programs (e.g. adult education) and their sub-units (e.g. adult education residential college) is needed. When possible, this could be supplemented by performance budgeting to identify the unit cost trend for some relevant output (e.g. teachers graduated in teacher training colleges), and to determine changes in component costs (salaries, wages, supplies, etc.).

Such a budgetary procedure would hinder neither accountability nor ministerial responsibility. It would allow for more intelligent and specific allocation of any agreed total of increased recurrent spending. It would make it possible to consider, say, agricultural extension and agricultural capital projects as alternatives for marginal agricultural funds. This would be a considerable improvement over the inherited systems, which separate the recurrent and capital budgets, and which therefore facilitate marginal comparisons between various types of recurrent expenditures (e.g. agricultural extension vs. police activities), and separate comparisons between various types of capital expenditures (e.g. agricultural investments vs. administrative buildings). Neither thinking in terms of Ministry grouped functions of very different expansion priorities nor in terms of a capital/recurrent as opposed to a development/upkeep dichotomy is conducive to effective planning or even to effective national budgeting in the narrower sense.

Private consumption must bear some of the impact of lower-than-anticipated resource availability. This is especially true when, as in virtually all African states except for a few mineral-enclave-based economies, personal consumption accounts for over two-thirds of total resource use. What can be done is to seek bearable ways of allotting cuts in private consumption among different groups of consumers by adjusting internal taxes and prices. Unnecessary cutbacks in domestically produced consumer goods should of course be avoided.[17]

Private investment is particularly hard to influence in the face of unexpected resource shortfalls. If these are expected to be brief, private investment may well rise (as in Tanzania during 1965) and help hasten recovery. Otherwise, the difficulties of devising policies adequate to the task of limiting cutbacks in private (especially foreign private) investment are grave indeed. Private foreign capital flows will normally aggravate, not smooth, a balance-of-payments crisis initially arising from export stagnation or decline. Payments problems are seen as increasing the risk that profits and capital may not be repatriatable. Moreover stagnation or decline in export-sector incomes usually harms the market for those final consumer goods in whose production the majority of foreign private investment outside of mining and plantation agriculture is interested.

Foreign balance alterations result from changes in resource availability not fully countered by changes in use. If an economy has adequate initial foreign reserves, it can, and should, meet a portion of temporary shortfalls in foreign earnings by drawing on such reserves, or by short-term borrowing. However, this requires careful distinction between short-run swings around a trend and an altered trend. It also demands recognition of the need for offsetting accumulation of international reserves in good years.

What can be done to dampen swings depends also on what new foreign resources can be attracted and on what terms. Usually a one- or two-year slump, even in the highly export-dependent and drought-prone East African economies, can be significantly dampened, at least on the development expenditure side, by judicious reserve use and medium-term borrowing (e.g. under one or another International Monetary Fund option). The balance-of-payments problem is especially acute in African states because, contrary to the bulk of recent industrial economy experience, external balance difficulties are normally associated with internal stagnation or depressed growth rates, not booms. Thus the uncritical use of standard deflationary means of dealing with balance-of-payments deficits criteria will render the economy more, not less, unstable.

Economics has been termed "the dismal science" and what has been said here may seem to justify that charge. Almost all examples have dealt with shortfalls and cutbacks. Realistically, this is the situation confronting policy-makers and planners in most African economies. Deteriorating international trade and finance conditions plus the perfectly correct goal of planning for the maximum attainable development combine to produce this result. In any event, the same principle applies to windfalls as to shortfalls; the additional resources should be so distributed among alternative uses as to make the largest possible contribution to present welfare consistent with raising significantly the pace of development.

DECENTRALIZATION OF PLANNING

The need to revise comprehensive plans comprehensively places heavy demands on economic planning, advising, and decision-making machinery. If individual decisions are prepared and taken in isolation, the sum total of ad hoc alterations soon causes a loss of any initial consistency or coherence of economic policies. This has proved glaringly evident in a number of West African planning experiences under quite different conditions, goals, and political outlooks.

However, coherent and efficient policy-making and implementation does not mean unlimited centralization. Decentralization, in plan revision as in formulation, and in policy implementation as in project proposal, is critical. Working parties involving all interested experts are a useful device for increasing available information and judgment and for diffusing understanding, as demonstrated at least partially by Uganda's experience in formulating its second five-year plan (1966–71), *Work for Progress*. They should also be valuable in providing data and advice on policy, on program progress and on the need for revision.

The foregoing is not intended to advocate unmodified adoption of the French planning mechanism. The number of sources of information and expertise available are far more limited in African states than in France. This is particularly true of the private sector. Contrary to opinion fairly widely held, it appears increasingly fair to say that in a majority of the larger African states, higher civil service personnel and their advisers (whether national or expatriate) are usually of a considerable average level of competence. They are usually distinctly superior to the majority of their local private-sector counterparts. Furthermore, the private-sector executives of foreign concerns are hampered by lack of authority to make decisions. This is to a significant degree the result of the number of branch or subsidiary private-sector units in Africa whose basic decisions are not made by the executives in the African state who would attend planning meetings. It also relates to the fact that few firms (and usually only in special circumstances) post their best senior personnel to Africa. The concept of the efficient expatriate business community in Africa and Southeast Asia is very largely a myth.[18] Lack of initiative, acceptance of "tried and true" solutions until forced to change, failure to seek maximum profit at the price of managerial leisure, acceptance of past results plus a modest growth rate as a ceiling target – these are characteristics at least as typical of the colonial business community as of the official community. They have not contributed to widespread understanding of, or consistently effective participation in, national planning, even when this would have been to the immediate benefit of the private interests concerned.

The principle of broad central decision-maker and adviser participation from all sectors of the economy in planning, including proposal-making and data provision, whether at the formulation or revision stage, is nonetheless applicable in Africa. Indeed, given the limited number of experienced first-level personnel, public or private, it is even more important that planning be broadly based than would be true in a country better supplied with high-level manpower, comprehensive data collection, and analysis mechanisms.

Regional and local development committees, including planning and implementing ministry, local government, party and public, cooperative and private enterprise members, are critical, if often also notably absent. Central bodies are not ideally situated to know of local possibilities, to formulate flexible policy applications, to publicize the plan in terms meaningful for enlisting mass support, or to respond rapidly to grassroots problems and possibilities. Local bodies, when integrated into an overall development effort, can make good at least some of these weaknesses.

Regional and local planning at all stages needs to be carried out within an overall policy frame. Only in a plan with no clear policy guidelines is it necessary for every medium and small-scale project to be channeled all the way up to ministerial and planning commission level to ensure consistency. That procedure is unsound for four reaons:

1. It thwarts local initiative, reduces the evident results of local participation, and chokes off any local interest in mobilizing resources for small projects of immediate interest to a village or district.

2. It fails to make effective use of the technical knowledge

and decision-making capacity, the local experience, or the supervisory capacity of regional and district officers, or of such technical ministries as agriculture, water development, communications, and works.

3. It clogs the central ministries with minor issues, which take up time out of all proportion to their size; this prevents careful evaluation of ongoing and new major policies, programs, and large-scale projects, and also prevents detailed attention to implementation.

4. It creates a bias against small projects because more funds can be expended if time is concentrated on a few large ones; this criterion makes economic sense only if no decentralization is possible without loss of overall direction, or if large projects are almost always more productive. The latter condition, at least, is usually contrary to fact in a majority of African rural sectors.

An experiment has been begun in Tanzania aimed at combining decentralization of project initiation and implementation, and increased local resource provision, with central maintenance of overall control. A Regional Development Fund (allocated Sh. 7, 17, and 21 million in 1967–68, 1968–1969, and 1969–70 respectively) has been created to finance small directly productive projects (e.g. small-scale irrigation, brush clearing, water supply) and small infrastructural projects (e.g. feeder roads, rural clinics). These are proposed by District Development Committees (District Council committees with district technical officers and local organizational members); they are examined by district and regional technical officers for consistency with overall planning efforts and with the criteria set out for the Development Fund program, as well as for project feasibility and viability; they are then approved by the Regional Commissioners. Enough money has been allocated so that each district making a serious effort to work up a viable project should receive funding for at least one new start each year. Districts are responsible for providing unskilled labor, whether voluntary or hired out of district levy funds, and, where possible, a cash contribution. District and regional technical staffs provide overall supervision and personnel, while skilled labor, materials, and the bulk of the cash costs are met from the Regional Development Fund.

Planning and policy are not the unique concern of only one or two ministries. If national development comprises all nationally agreed goals, and development planning is the resource allocation pattern for attaining development objectives, then a ministry or parastatal corporation with no effective planning unit is either saying that its work is irrelevant to national development or that it is technically incapable of participating effectively. Either alternative has rather far-reaching implications. Certainly planning and finance ministries should not seek to do detailed technical and technico-economic work down to the project and sub-policy level in all fields. For example, industrial studies centers and ministries of commerce and industry quite rightly deal with industrial, technical, market, and economic feasibility studies, and work out incentive and protection policy proposals within the overall national industrialization and fiscal strategies.

Decentralized involvement in planning and policy decisions requires centralized coordination and frame-setting if feasibility and consistency are to be preserved. At the center, a case exists for a single ministry combining the tasks usually divided between a ministry of planning and a ministry of finance. A logical threefold division of function would exist within such an economic policy and program ministry: planning and policy formulation (which would be central); revenue-raising; and expenditure allocation and implementation. Foreign aid and investment, for example, would fall into resource raising; detailed project feasibility studies and progress reviews would come under expenditure allocation and implementation. If combined with an effectively decentralized administration of development, such a ministry need not result in undue concentration of political or civil-service power and should be of significant value in improving the quality and coherence of economic policy and its effectuation. The central manpower policy (for the entire economy, not simply for the civil service) is logically an integral part of this functional cluster.

As suggested earlier, decentralization of activities at the regional or local level is a necessary step toward efficient central control, at least under conditions of extreme scarcity of top-level personnel. (Eastern European experience suggests this principle may hold true even for economies much less limited in personnel and data than those of Africa.) Only if detailed secondary decisions are sent out can central officers devote the time to organize broad strategies, overall project criteria, or coherent policy patterns. And only with decentralization can second-level manpower (especially outside the capital) get a chance to use its data and judgment, and to develop really relevant decision-making experience. Overcentralization thus becomes a vicious circle impeding consistency, proper attention to key issues, local initiative, efficient utilization of existing personnel, and the educational value of lower-level experience for subsequently promoted officers. Whether the Tanzanian regional development funding experiment noted above is fully successful or not, it is at the least an imaginative and well-designed attempt to break free from this spiral. So is the creation of more sophisticated project analysis units in parastatal corporations capable of making projections of the national products and balance of payments as well as projections of corporation income and expenditure.

ROLE OF FOREIGN FINANCING IN COMPREHENSIVE PLANNING

How can foreign financing be rendered more consistent with comprehensive national development planning and less contributory to uncertainty? The issues involved are complex for both the provider and the receiver of foreign resources.[19] That the present procedures are far from ideal is becoming almost an article of faith, although different analysts present different and even compatible criticisms.

Great frankness and openness to new methods and ideas is required if the general belief that something must be done is not to deteriorate into making do from year to year in the hope that something will turn up (more defaults and crises, in all probability, if that primrose path is followed). The basic reasons for which resource transfers have been sought and provided have all too often been unsound. What, for example, have $2,500 million of Western and Eastern arms and related military credits done for Indonesia? For the Soviet Union? For Western suppliers? What have Western European export loan guarantees achieved by furthering up to $200 million in often unsound or ill-considered, sometimes shoddy, frequently shady, and almost all high-cost supplier credits to Ghana? Surely not the long-term welfare of their own export sectors, the easing of their own liquidity problems, or the political or economic advance of Ghana.

Errors have not been limited to the borrowers. Countries providing resources have been quite as reckless, and self-defeating at the levels of strategy, policy, project-selection, and feasibility evaluation. Nor are failings limited to politicians on either side; civil servants and economists have a very flawed record of advice. When right, they have often not pressed hard or cogently enough for more appropriate policies (on the liquidity issue this has been so notable that as conservative and soft-spoken a source as the *Economist* has spoken of the "treason of the trimming clerks"); when wrong, they have often convinced political decision-makers only too well. Battles between planning and finance ministries at all levels have on occasion been conducted as if the maximization of ministerial power, or even of clashes won, not of national development and mutually workable procedures, was the appropriate end. True, planners are temperamentally and organizationally optimistic – perhaps especially so with regard to foreign resources and the foreign balance – and may fail to see that to attempt too much is often to achieve less than is possible, since overoptimism leads to resource misallocations, including policies and projects suddenly cut off half-achieved. On the other hand, orthodox Treasury-Central Bank conservatism can also result in failure to realize that overcaution will often divert resources into less efficient rather than more efficient uses and indeed result in failing to use at all some available resources (including aid offers).

The first step toward improving aid and other resource transfers, both quantitatively and qualitatively, is to halt their 1961–68 stagnation or deterioration. Net aid and investment flows from all sources (gross transfers less repayment, interest, and dividends) to the Third World have declined since 1961, especially if a handful of oil-rich economies are excluded. Given the "Development Decade" goal of 5 percent annual growth of national product in developing economies or the 6 percent target of the Pearson Report and the often-stated intention of industrial economies to use resource transfers to contribute to that goal, the declining net transfer record is an absurdity. A doubling of net transfers by 1975 would fit both the OECD and UNCTAD-1 goal of 1 percent of national income for aid (and a fortiori the 1 percent of gross domestic product platitude of UNCTAD-II) and would be consistent with bolstering rapid increases in internal savings mobilization in developing economies and their participation in world trade.

There is a need not only for increased foreign financing of developing economies, but also for better terms. Interest rates and repayment terms have tended to grow harsher since 1961. Conditions have certainly not improved with respect to the duration of aid commitments and the freedom from risk of sudden cancellations. While some progress in flexibility can be noted in terms of planned versus purely project-tied aid and of consortia approaches, this is by no means general; at the same time, inflexibility has also grown, in terms of aid tied to specific countries of procurement and often to particular transferrer-chosen projects as well. Improvement of the qualitative record requires attention to at least seven points: timing, "local cost" coverage, usability, terms, conditions, diversification, and liquidity creation.

Timing involves both certainty over time and flexibility within the period of an agreement. A $15 million five-year loan negotiated at the beginning of a five-year plan is much more consistent with serious and effective medium-term budgeting than a series of one-year agreements adding to the same total. Similarly the value of a multi-year loan is greater if annual drawing schedules are flexible to allow for offsetting windfalls and shortfalls in other sources of development finance or variations in physical implementation capacity.

It is not self-evident that such an approach would pose insurmountable problems for lenders. Fewer negotiations would be a blessing all round. It should not prove politically or bureaucratically unthinkable to secure budget approval for a limited number of larger, multi-year commitments, as opposed to a larger number of annual commitments adding up to approximately the same sum. Indeed this should help avoid annual parliamentary or official debates on each program and allow a more serious examination of the limited number of new commitments each year.

"Local costs" are what lenders do not wish to pay but which a developing economy believes should be financed externally. This facetious definition really is what emerges, at least de facto, from specific cases and from much general discussion of the issue. "Local costs" as usually defined are clearly a misnomer. Total cost less direct import cost of a project does not yield local costs in any meaningful sense. At least two varieties of "indirect import costs" remain.

First, there are direct project-related costs for capital project inputs not usually included in import cost calculations. For example, "local transport" represents imported vehicles, spares, fuel; only excise and customs duties and wages are likely to be truly domestic. In many developing countries all high-level manpower is fully utilized so that the marginal development project has a high foreign-expert cost component, a component largely spent on imported goods and services and on personal remittances.

Second, once true domestic cost (largely unskilled labor, local raw materials, and value added in construction and in the processing and manufacturing of construction materials) is isolated, the import multiplier effect remains to be calculated. In most developing economies this is high. Attempts to reduce it rapidly to zero would hardly be conducive to expansion of world trade, to reasonable internal price stability or, indeed, to social and political stability either. Thus a development project's payments for genuinely local factors of production will give rise to an import leakage.

The change in focus which may result from substituting true domestic costs for the standard "local cost" definition is often quite major. In the case of Tanzania, direct import costs of ministerial development projects run perhaps 50 percent. Indirect project-tied imports average another 15–20 percent. Assuming a multiplier of two on initial domestic income generation, the indirect increase in import demand is likely to be of the order of 10–15 percent of the initial expenditure.[20] In short, true import cost is not of the order of 50 percent, but of 75–80 percent.

The point is not that aid should cover 70–90 percent of all project costs. Aside from being normally unobtainable, any percentage of foreign finance significantly above 50–60 percent hands over effective control of national economic policy to "donors" and casts doubts on the seriousness with which efforts are being pursued to mobilize national resources (including increased or better-sold primary product exports). Some portion of development expenditure can and should be covered by foreign exchange made available through export promotion or import substitution. Nevertheless, evaluation of foreign exchange components of projects and plans should be both realistic and complete. The whole foreign exchange content (not just the direct physical import content) should be viewed as potentially aidworthy, with indirect import content of a project just as strong a claimant for external borrowing (at least so far as the lender is concerned) as the present more limited definition of import content.

From the developing-economy point of view, selling "indirect import content" should be easier than "local costs." Not only is the description (of the impact on imports) true, it points out to the aid-provider that there are additional export possibilities resulting from its resource transfer. Further, it poses the financial problem in terms of foreign account balance, not internal deficits, a method of presentation that industrial economies are likely to view with greater sympathy. Unfortunately, without a lasting solution to world liquidity and credit stringency and with actual or imminent threats to the external balance positions of major resource-transferring economies, the sympathy may not come to much in terms of additional resource transfers.

Usability relates to what expenditures are seen as "aidworthy." Surely foreign resource transfers should be made to finance "development" (at any rate "economic development") not only "fixed investment." It is now accepted as a truism that fixed investment alone will not bring development in the absence of other "non-investment" expenditures. Yet aid policy still promotes a malallocation of resources to construction and machinery because non-capital development expenditure, while often viewed as "grantworthy," is grudgingly, if at all, seen to be "aidworthy" for loans or general support.

Feasibility studies, surveys, statistical services, recurrent costs of technical education, agricultural extension services, disease control and pest clearance to open up new areas or increase crop yields – all are investments in development which tend to be stinted of resources in contrast to more "normal" brick-and-mortar type spending.

Some progress has been made (e.g. by the United Nations Development Program, the United States, Canada, and the Netherlands) on the survey-feasibility study front, but not enough. Permanent centers and teams, rather than once-for-all major project studies, are the basic requirement. As candidates for economic assistance, these should be as valid as the projects their work shows to be potentially viable. Initially such centers and teams require both material and human imports to a very high proportion of their total cost. Aid providers, therefore, should not allow balance-of-payments constraints to deter them from offering increased support in this field.

With respect to *terms*, it would be desirable to have a high proportion of 0–1 percent interest loans, with ten-year grace periods plus 25- to 40-year subsequent repayment periods. These should be linked to independent valuation (by whatever method) to ensure that goods transferred are of value equivalent to the loan. A loan on easy terms may be no bargain if the price of the goods provided has been doubled to "offset" the low interest and long repayment span. The principle of securing either alternative or independent appraisals to guide price negotiations is no less critical in relation to overseas public bodies than in dealing with private firms. Furthermore it is a workable principle in most cases. One can shop in Japan, West Germany, Czechoslovakia, East Germany, Italy, and India for widely overlapping ranges of machinery and construction goods and services. Similarly, it is possible to bargain with both Western parastatal (e.g. Ente Nazionale Indrocarburi – ENI) and Socialist public sector corporations if adequate economic, legal, technical, and commercial talent is allocated to this potentially "high payoff" field.

For the main body of development loans, high interest and early repayment make less than no sense to lenders as well as to borrowers. At least this is the case if the lenders seriously wish to promote the sustained growth of borrower economies. It is quite incredible that the majority of developing countries will be able to dispense with significant net resource transfers before the year 2000. This granted, repayments before that date merely hamper planning, and force the lenders to relend the same funds. The process raises apparent totals of aid voted and presumably maximizes parliamentary political problems. Interest charges have a similar effect. They merely raise the total that the developing countries must ultimately borrow, and reduce the net flow of resources resulting from any given level of gross lending. The combination of a high proportion of short-term loans with relatively high rates of interest has been a major factor leading to the present Alice-in-Wonderland aid situation in which it takes many developing countries and also many lenders all the running they can do not even to stay in the same place but to check a backward movement.

The encouragement of use by developing economies of a large volume of high-cost, short-term contractor finance (promoted by industrial economy export promotion schemes and state trade corporation credits) has been and remains misguided and unwise to the point of irresponsibility. One can only hope that the recent rash of defaults or quasi-defaults, with refinancing and moratoria on the one hand, and dislocated economies following or attempting to follow draconically depressing policies on the other, will be seen by lenders and borrowers alike as telling evidence of this.

On qualitative as well as quantitative grounds there is a case for increased channeling of resource transfers through international economic institutions – in particular the International Development Association (IDA), the United Nations Development Program (UNDP), and regional development banks controlled by developing economies (e.g. the African and East African Development Banks). These bodies do provide higher proportions of grant, low-interest, and long-term resource transfers, by their nature largely eschew source- (though not project-) tying, and have a somewhat lower level of concern with ideological considerations as opposed to project and economy viability. The Pearson Report's target of one fifth of public resource transfers via such bodies by 1975 and a funding of IDA at $1,500 million a year by that date (vs. $400 million now) represent a reasonable minimum goal.

This is not to argue that diversification of aid terms, sources, and types is unsound; it is quite the reverse, if there is careful evaluation of what resource-transfer terms fit any specific case.

Private or quasi-public medium-term credit is appropriate to some projects. The Tanzam pipeline, involving the ENI group and Mediobanca, and financed by a fifteen-year 6–6½ percent credit, is a case in point. Such a project can carry that interest rate and repayment schedule and thus tap an otherwise unusable source of external finance. Similarly a short- to medium-term commercial loan can be appropriate if the assets can really provide an appropriate profit and cash-flow pattern: as one example, the Zantam Road Services Company hauling assured petroleum product and copper cargoes between Dar es Salaam and the Zambia copper belt.

This type of imaginative case-by-case examination is especially appropriate for parastatal bodies. For example, a national industrial development corporation might borrow to finance industrial projects, partly drawing on a credit for machinery and interim management personnel and partly taking the credit in the form of finished goods whose sale during the construction period would have two beneficial effects: it would cover part of local costs, and at the same time it would build up the selling organization of the firm so that it would be ready when the firm's own production came on the market. A shoe, tire and tube, or bicycle plant might use this approach, especially if the new plant's brand name was different from that previously dominant in the market. Such an approach, if skillfully handled, could reduce the disadvantages of an "export-tied" loan to a minimum for the borrower, while also minimizing adverse balance-of-payments results for the lender.

Diversification should involve reducing dependence on any single source of foreign resources. Dependence on a single source of funds can only add to uncertainty because of the possible shifts in the source's economic and balance-of-payments position and also because of the possible shifts in its political interests. Freedom to bargain for aid terms and projects can be significantly expanded, and international trade patterns can be made less arbitrary and more economic, if resource-provision sources are varied.

For states that provide aid, the converse policy of providing significant assistance to many developing economies and dominating the aid flows to none would seem to offer advantages. For one thing it would extend the aid-provider's significant trade relations to a larger number of developing countries and would probably also help to stabilize trade patterns. For another, it would leave the industrial economy less vulnerable to sudden requests for massive aid increases if a handful of its aid clients met substantial setbacks, and less open to demands of the "if-you-don't-help-us-we-shall-surely-sink" variety. Dependence has adverse implications for the dominating power. Once committed, it is less able to argue for economic rationality and probably less able to exert influence for change except at such a draconic level of pressure as to arouse intense resentment rather than serious policy reevaluation. The record of those states whose foreign resource flows come almost entirely from either of the two largest Western aid providers suggests that such concentration is not beneficial to the developing economy nor in the long-term international economic or even political interests of the aid provider.

Conditions on aid are a vexed subject. Only two will be considered here: tying and plan versus project support. The aid provider may insist on tying aid in order to ease balance-of-payments pressures or (less reputably but nonetheless significantly in the case of at least several major lenders) in order to support declining or noncompetitive home industries. However, from the recipient's point of view tying of aid to projects in the initial negotiation phase and to exports of the transferring country at any stage are undesirable. They lower flexibility and raise costs. The greatest harm arises when project ties are linked with export ties. Then the recipient cannot purchase the project's import component in the best market nor use a tied loan on the most competitive goods available in the lender's markets.[21] This form of multiple tie should be ended. Surely aid programs are not the appropriate method for bolstering weaker sections of an industrial economy at the expense of developing states. If national industries are to be supported, it would be far better to give them subsidies allowing them to compete for aid contracts and showing the subsidy as what it is – an internal transfer payment – rather than falsely including it in external assistance.

Plan-support aid through consortia of major resource transferers offers possibilities for reducing limitations and conditions on resource use, with mutual advantage to all participating states. In such a forum, careful examination of overall goals and needs can be conducted in a pragmatic, economic context, limiting political clashes and simple misunderstandings or miscalculations. Once a number of overall commitments from industrial countries have been received, it is much easier to agree on purchase patterns consistent with efficient buying while avoiding creating serious balance-of-payments problems for any one lender. Both long-term commitments and enhanced flexibility in annual drawing schedules may well be easier to achieve via the consortium approach. While consortia are not a cure-all for the problems of foreign aid, let alone of all foreign finance, they do offer a means by which progress can be made.

Liquidity and international reserves are often mentioned in the context of aid, but not necessarily for the most appropriate reasons. There is a set of economic myths that developing countries spend any additional reserves they acquire on nonproductive investment, follow policies that maximize inflation and balance-of-payments deficits, and can best be held to a "sound" monetary path by keeping them short of reserves and borrowing capacity. With all respect, this is nonsense, and arrogant nonsense at that.

Many developing countries follow rational or even cautious policies both on the domestic and international-balance fronts. Indeed, a number of industrial economies have rather more dismal and less responsible records. A developing economy normally needs a more interventionist, more innovating, and more efficient set of economic policies than an industrial economy, if it is to attain an acceptable growth rate. The first two requirements follow from its initial economic weakness, the lack of any automatic growth dynamic, and the relative weakness of the private (particularly the domestic private) and public corporation sectors. The last flows from low levels of available resources, initial reserves, and emergency credit sources and also from a high degree of international economic openness.

It is rich, not poor, economies which spend massive sums on armaments, subsidies to inefficient or declining economic sectors, and the pursut of economic policies based either on prestige or on sustained misconceptions about the nature of their economies. One of the luxuries of being a rich country is precisely the ability to afford ill-timed, ill-considered, and ill-costed economic policies to a significant degree and over an extended period of time, without serious economic damage or really widespread official criticism.[22] This is not a luxury available to the Third World.

International reserves are needed primarily as a safeguard against short-run fluctuations in international transactions, and therefore the level of needed reserves increases as transactions grow. If developing economies are to participate in broadening and expanding world trade, they will require increased reserve holdings. A shortage of reserves does not promote responsible policies. In practice it usually leads to neo-autarchy, sky-high tariffs and tight quantitative restrictions, with resultant profiteering-corruption-administrative breakdowns, internal inflation, growing foreign-balance stringency, and often an internal socioeconomic crisis pattern threatening endemic revolution. An alternative pattern is rigid internal austerity, stringent control over most forms of external expenditure, and acceptance of a rate of growth of production less than that of population (perhaps less than zero) which is, in developing economies at least, another highroad to recurrent internal crises and governmental changes. Neither of these patterns precisely fits any definition of sound economic policy.

The basic global liquidity and credit constriction problems are well known. Space prohibits a discussion here of their implications for the developing nations, but an effective and equitable solution is of great importance to the Third World. Everything that can be achieved with respect to foreign resources through comprehensive planning that is more flexible, better-organized, and better related to a revised and improved system of international resource transfers could be wiped out by a recurrence of 1967–69's liquidity crises and/or by a continuation of the related 1968–70 pattern of high interest rates and lending restrictions – everything and more. The fall in 1968 net resource transfers, the danger of a sharper deterioration in primary product terms-of-trade, the parrot cry "but our hands are tied by balance-of-payments considerations . . ." from a majority of Western industrial nations on which virtually every significant proposal at UNCTAD-II foundered and which underlies United States rejection of the Pearson proposals – these are evidence enough of the dangers that internal and external imbalance in the industrial economies pose to any meaningful development of the Third World economies.

The emphasis in this section on improved aid quality stems from the premise that greater developing-economy reliance on national resources is essential, whatever the absolute level of external resources available.[23] The corollary should be the improvement of the quality of external resource transfers so that they form a more effective complement to national efforts and are more adequately integrated into comprehensive planning of the mobilization, allocation, and augmentation over time of scarce resources.

NOTES

1. Cf. Dudley Seers, "Why Visiting Economists Fail," *Journal of Political Economy* 70:4 (August 1962); F. X. Sutton, "Planning and Rationality in the Newly Independent States in Africa," *Economic Development and Cultural Change* 10:1 (October 1961); R. H. Green, "Planning in a Developing Economy," in *The Challenge of Uganda's Second Five-Year Development Plan* (Kampala: Milton Obote Foundation, 1967).
2. See for example W. Arthur Lewis, *Development Planning* (Methuen University and London: George Allen and Unwin, 1966); Paul G. Clark, *Development Planning in East Africa* (Nairobi: East African Publishing House, 1965).
3. Cf. Albert Waterston, *Development Planning: Lessons of Experience* (Baltimore: Johns Hopkins University Press, 1965); C. S. Gray, "Development Planning in East Africa," *East African Economic Review* (December 1966); Wolfgang F. Stolper, *Planning Without Facts* (Cambridge, Mass.: Harvard University Press, 1966).
4. G. K. Helleiner, "Tanzania's Second Plan: Socialism and Self-Reliance," *East African Journal* 5:3 (December 1968).
5. *Background to Budget 1967–68, 1968–69, 1969–70* (Tanzania: Ministries of Economic Affairs and Development Planning and of Finance) (name changed to *Economic Survey* with 1969–70 issue); *Tanzania Second Five-Year Plan*, Government Printer, Dar es Salaam, 1969, *National Accounts 1966–1968*, Central Bureau of Statistics, Dar es Salaam, 1970; *Economic Report December 1968 and 1969*, Bank of Tanzania, 1969, 1970. These sources apply also to subsequent quantitative citations in respect of Tanzania.
6. This type of point has been very well made by such writers as Gray, Stolper, and Waterston. However, none of them appears to be very

optimistic about the possibility of attaining a coordinated national comprehensive economic policy framework as opposed to a set of sectoral policy frameworks linked to integrated sectoral public investment programs.

7. See E. N. Omaboe on planning in *The Economy of Ghana*, W. Birmingham, I. Neustadt, E. N. Omaboe, eds. (London: Allen and Unwin, 1966) and *Economic Survey* (of Ghana), 1964, 1965, 1966, 1967, Omaboe, ed. (Accra: Ministry of Information and Broadcasting 1965, 1966, 1967, 1968) for more detailed discussion and comment including a shift in position. See also note 15.
8. Cf. Paul Borel and F. F. Jackson, "Some Experiences of Planning in Africa," in *Development Plans and Programmes* (Paris: OECD Development Center, 1964).
9. Cf. R. H. Green and A. Seidman, *Unity or Poverty? The Economics of Pan-Africanism* (Harmondsworth: Penguin African, 1968). pp. 150–70.
10. Cf. R. H. Green, "Nigeria: The Economics of Socio-Political Bankruptcy," *New African* (August–September 1965); "A Lament for Nigeria," *Mawazo*, Kampala: (June 1967); "Four African Development Plans," *Journal of Modern African Studies*, 3:2, pp. 249—79.
11. For a much more extensive discussion see *Problems of Foreign Aid* (Dar es Salaam: Oxford University Press, 1966), especially papers by Dudley Seers, Paul Clark, Brian Van Arkadie and Philip Ndegwa, Nicholas Kaldor, Philip Bell, and George Skorov.
12. See the Fall 1966 articles in *The Economist* on initial and final costs for the Zamtan Pipeline.
13. See references in Note 4.
14. Cf. R. H. Green, "Reflections on Economic Strategy, Structure, Implementation, and Necessity": in P. J. Foster, ed., *Ghana and the Ivory Coast* (Chicago: University of Chicago Press, 1970). (Tentative title.)
15. Cf. Dudley Seers, "A Theory of Inflation and Growth in Under-Developed Economies," *Oxford Economic Papers* 14:2 (June 1962); W. Baer, "Brazil: Inflation and Economic Rationality," *Economic Development and Cultural Change* 11:4 (July 1963).
16. Cf. Samir Amin, *Trois expériences Africaines de développement: le Mali, la Guinée, le Ghana* (Paris: Presses Universitaries de France, 1965).
17. Cf. R. H. Green, "Austerity, Participation, and Dialogue: The Triple Challenge Before Ghana," *New African*, London (April–May 1966).
18. Cf. James Puthucheary, *Ownership and Control in the Malayan Economy* (Singapore: Eastern Universities Press, 1960).
19. For a fuller discussion see R. H. Green "UNCTAD and After: The Anatomy of a Failure," *Journal of Modern African Studies* 5:2; *Partners in Development, the Report of the Commission on International Development* (Pearson Report) (New York: Praeger, 1969); Sir R. Jackson, *Study of the Capacity of the United Nations Development System* (Jackson Report) 2 vols., (Geneva: United Nations, 1962); R. H. Green, "Anatomy of Two Assizes: Pearson, Jackson and Development Partnership," *African Review* 1:2 (University College, Dar es Salaam) 1970.

20. This assumes a marginal propensity to import in the neighborhood of 20 percent.
21. Cf. G. K. Helleiner, "Trade and Aid in Tanzania," *East African Journal* 4:1 (April 1967).
22. Clearly this luxury is not one which may be purchased in unlimited quantities as the present economic problems of the United States, France, and the United Kingdom bear witness.
23. For a fuller exposition see R. H. Green, "Political Independence and the National Economy: An Essay in the Political Economy of Decolonization" in R. W. Johnson and C. H. Allen eds., *African Perspectives: Essays in the History, Politics and Economics of Africa* (presented to Thomas Hodgkin) (Cambridge: Cambridge University Press, 1970).

Chapter 12

Financing Development in Nigeria: An Appraisal

Kathleen M. Langley

In ending the civil war Nigeria enters a period of political and economic transition. Immediate problems give cause for concern but it is appropriate at this time also to review the difficulties that have plagued past economic development. The immediate national tasks are those of (1) rebuilding of war-torn areas; (2) the rehabilitation of agricultural productive capacity, especially in the eastern States; and (3) the reintegration of war-weary peoples and demobilized soldiers into a divided society. Superimposed upon these problems there is also one of a complex organizational and administrative nature. The creation of twelve States in 1967 to replace the former four regional governments within the Federation of Nigeria implies that new institutions and procedures will have to be established within the next few years. An important opportunity arises to apply the lessons of past experience and establish new relationships that otherwise might be resisted by the forces of conservatism and inertia.

Governmental reorganization and reconstruction of the economy will take place as Nigeria changes from being an economy largely dependent on agricultural exports to one where the exploitation of mineral resources may be increasingly important. At present, the country faces some short-term financial problems. War damages have to be made good, no cushion of foreign exchange reserves is on hand[1] and the problem of debt servicing due to financial follies of the early 1960s has to be faced. In addition, the repayment of war debts which have yet to be fully revealed will encumber the economy. Undoubtedly, both foreign aid and foreign willingness to re-negotiate the terms of past debts will substantially help Nigeria during the current transition period. Nevertheless, considerable economic progress can be achieved during the next decade and foreign exchange reserves built up if institutional weaknesses which threatened the country during the 1960s can be rectified. The most obvious drain on export proceeds of the last three years, namely arms purchases, should now cease and expenditures will be diverted to reconstruction and longer-term development.[2] The abundance of petroleum resources yet to be significantly exploited provides Nigeria with a substantial development asset. External forces have been and are important to the Nigerian economy but they need not constrain future development if internal rivalries can be controlled.

The administrative reorganization of the Federation has already begun and political negotiations over the exact number and boundaries of the states of the Federation of Nigeria will soon take place. A conference (postponed until the end of hostilities) of the states to settle federal-state and intra-state relationships has been a matter of declared government policy since 1967. Of particular importance will be the resolution of conflicting interests between the States on the issues of industrial, agricultural and fiscal policies. In the years before the civil-war intra-regional suspicions were intense; economic and political decisions were made with local interests in mind and the pursuit of rational economic development strategies designed for the whole nation was thwarted.

EXTERNAL FORCES AND NATIONAL DEVELOPMENT

Foreign investment and foreign relationships in Nigeria have to some extent followed a pattern made broadly familiar by the experience of many other developing countries. The political change from colonial to national independence status appears to release forces anxious to see rapid industrialization and modernization of the economy. Foreign investment is no longer desired in the traditional lines for the development of raw materials for export but only for import substitution. Industrialization in many countries has produced disappointing results; in particular, it has not led to a lessening of foreign dependence and while attention has been given to the build-up of industries, the traditional export sector has frequently stagnated. In the process of moving from a colonial economy to one of national sovereignty, Nigeria has maintained a dynamic export sector and while not escaping financial problems associated with industrialization, the country may yet be able to accelerate the pace of economic growth without becoming unduly dependent on foreign financing.

The impetus to Nigeria's entry into the economy of the modern world came from foreign investment which led to commercial production of agricultural products for export. During the first fifty years of the present century foreign investment was the motive force in the organization of Nigeria's export trade of palm products, of cocoa and of groundnuts. An essential monetary stimulus was offered to the indigenous producer and the response was positive. More land was brought under cultivation and both aggregate output and exports increased; between 1900 and 1962 export volume rose more than sixteenfold. British government loans and grants-in-aid helped to develop Nigeria's infra-structure and amounted to approximately half of the estimated total foreign investment (£N72 million) in the years between 1870 and 1936.[3] The loans were long-term, carrying relatively low interest charges.

Nigeria became an independent national state in 1960 but the marketing system of the country's export crops underwent transformation at an earlier date. There were important consequences both economically and politically. At the end of World War II and stemming from changes made during the war years, agricultural export Marketing Boards took over the export trading activities of the foreign companies. The Marketing Boards, although commodity based, were, in fact, essentially regionally specialized being concerned primarily with cocoa in the Western region, palm products in the Eastern region and with groundnuts in the Northern region.[4] During the 1950s, these Boards built up large trading surpluses ostensibly in pursuit of price stabilization policies for producers. Marketing Board legislation also permitted, however, the allocation of funds to promote broadly "the general prosperity of producers" and with the advent of national independence the accumulated surpluses were used, through numerous schemes, by Nigeria's governments to help in the financing of general development projects. In particular, the desire of each of the former regional governments to obtain "its" share of national industry led to investment in a number of injudiciously selected projects: the using-up of reserves did not hold back activities as additional external funds were obtained by means of short- or medium-term credits.

The statistics of the direction of foreign private investment show that investment in manufacturing enterprises in the 1960s took the place of former investment in trading services. In the first half of the 1950s, 30 percent of total foreign business investment entered trading activities; during 1961–66, trading services absorbed 8 percent and manufacturing concerns 24 percent of total foreign private investment.[5] Contractor-finance "deals" were dominant in the field of industrial investment and predictions were made that the enterprises financed would pay off indebtedness in five or six years. Short-term loans may be welcomed by developing countries if high profitability is expected from the assets they finance, and especially if such assets result in additional exports; but if such expectations are frustrated, and if there is inadequate financing from abroad, their attitude is radically changed. Today, the short-term debt incurred in connection with a number of the industrial projects is a matter of national concern as the suppliers' and contractors' credits were guaranteed by the Federal government.

The reliance of the sponsoring agencies, especially the regional statutory corporations, upon this form of finance was designed to minimize their initial cash disbursements and, consequently, debt-equity ratios typically were high – usually well over three to one, but repayment schedules were short. During the repayment period projects must therefore meet debt servicing burdens that are substantially greater than is normal for industrial projects in the manufacturing sector. Although their feasibility studies predicted high profitability for the concerns, the foreign promoters of the industrial plants had little or no financial or other interest in the ultimate viability of the enterprises since the highly inflated prices charged for the equipment adequately covered their apparent equity participation in the ventures. The feasibility studies on which major projects were based usually made highly inflated estimates of market demand and assumed operating rates and levels of managerial and labor efficiency similar to those found in industrialized countries. As most industrial plants in developing countries face "learning" problems in getting into viable production, the debt-servicing burden very quickly assumes awesome proportions.

It is believed that the former regional government-owned corporations, ably assisted by the sales representatives of equipment manufacturers, managed to mislocate industrial plants with total repayment costs in excess of £N40 million[6] – a sum approximately equal to the current level of published foreign reserves. The civil war in Nigeria compounded difficulties for a number of the contractor-financed projects; non-availability of raw materials and management problems disrupted activity in the eastern states and to a considerable degree in the mid-western state. A number of the projects, if they can be made operationally viable, represent productive capacity that can be utilized in the future, but numerous problems have to be overcome. Competent management must be secured and the plants require considerable sums of money as working capital. The Nigerian government is obviously faced with the problem of requesting from its creditors a moratorium, or of taking steps to arrange appropriate refinancing. One complication is that the creditors today are no longer the original equipment suppliers but rather the European banks with which the credits were discounted.

Another unsatisfactory feature of the approach to industrialization in the recent past was the regional rivalry in establishing the same industries without adequate regard for the size of market essential for viable and efficient operation. The governments of Nigeria fell easily prey to this temptation as the National Development Plan (1962–68) guideline on industrialization policy was drawn up on aggregate lines and the governments therefore struggled for each project as it was developed. The consequences for Nigeria could be extremely damaging and could produce serious misuse of resources if the industrial interests of the new States are not harmonized and attention focused on obtaining maximum economic and social benefits for the Federation as a whole.

Nigeria's attempt to accelerate industrialization has entangled the country in foreign financial commitments which would have placed a serious foreign exchange constraint on economic progress but for the inflow of substantial private longer-term capital in another direction in the export sector. Investment in petroleum exploration, while not insignificant in the 1950s became the predominant private foreign investment activity of the 1960s and accounted for more than half of the inflow of private capital funds. A rapid increase in oil company capital expenditures took place; from an estimated total of £N100 million in 1961 to £N300 million in 1967.[7] At the outbreak of hostilities, the oil companies had plans for significant further expenditures for exploration and development and these operations will now presumably go forward.

The future foreign exchange earnings from petroleum exports should provide the means whereby the country can escape from an ever-accumulating burden of foreign debt. It is not yet possible directly to compare from Nigerian trade statistics the contribution of oil export earnings with those of the country's traditional export crops. As the full proceeds from oil exports do not directly accrue to oil exporting countries, the trade statistics, as a measure of the importance of individual exports, have become distorted in recent years in Nigeria. Very little meaning can be given, for example, to the statistic that in 1966 oil exports formed 33 percent of Nigerian total exports. The major contribution of the petroleum industry (financed and managed by international companies) to the local economy is not assessed by attributing some price to the product but by the results accruing from astute bargaining on concession terms and from precision in the definition of accounting concepts.

Within the next few years, Nigeria can confidently expect to receive from petroleum exports revenues which will exceed foreign exchange earnings from any one of the country's other exports. The cutback in production in 1967 and 1968 has meant a loss of foreign exchange to Nigeria of the order of at least £N50 million.[8] The future of Nigeria as a nation of potentially significant political and economic power depends crucially on whether petroleum revenues will be used to provide development finance for the country as a whole or whether the oil-producing states will attempt to appropriate such funds for local projects (even if of "white-elephant" nature). The matter is of considerable concern as the prospective outlook for the marketing of Nigeria's traditional crops is not very favorable.

STRUCTURAL CHANGE AND THE TRADE AND PAYMENTS BALANCES

The process of economic development demands that an increase in the total volume of economic activity take place and that structural changes occur within the economy. Initially, the increased incomes generated by greater output will to a considerable extent spill over into an enlarged demand for imported consumer goods, but as the market expands it becomes feasible to establish industrial plants for the production of consumer goods and perhaps also of intermediate and capital goods within the local economy. The change in a country's structure of production is reflected in the composition of imports. Imports are made up increasingly of capital goods and raw materials. The country becomes highly dependent upon the proceeds of exports and/or an inflow of funds from abroad to finance imports which are essential if the existing level of economic activity is to be maintained and much more so if the national goal is that of accelerating economic growth.

During the years 1964–66, it is estimated that imports of capital goods and raw materials in Nigeria rose from approximately 53 percent to 64 percent of total imports.[9] A number of the country's manufacturing plants are very dependent upon imports; for example, in paper converting and in flour milling, imported raw materials exceed 50 percent of the gross value of output and far exceed their contribution to value added in manufacturing. Nigerian manufacturing industries have so far achieved only a very low degree of interdependence. Intermediate products purchased from other manufacturers probably constitute less than 10 percent of the materials used.

Since 1955, commodity exports from Nigeria have lagged behind commodity imports (Table 1). Merchandise exports covered approximately 83 percent of imports from 1955 to 1958 and 77 percent from 1959 to 1961. It is not possible to calculate precisely what proportion of imports has been met by commodity exports since that time because from 1962 onwards, the misleading inclusion of oil exports at 100 percent commodity valuation has distorted the trade statistics.[10] A study by the Central Bank of Nigeria of the period 1964–66, however, concluded that excluding oil sector operations, approximately 76 percent of commodity imports were financed by exports.[11] Imports of nonessential consumer goods were restricted during the civil war years and a corresponding improvement occurred in the percentage of imports financed by commodity exports, even when the oil sector is excluded. It may, however, be politically difficult to maintain import controls in peace time.

TABLE 1

Proportion of Commodity Imports Financed by Commodity Exports 1955–68 (£Nm)

	1950	*1955*	*1956*	*1957*[a]	*1958*	*1959*	*1960*	*1961*
Imports	61.8	139.7	155.2	151.6	166.9	179.4	215.2	222.4
Exports	85.9	121.2	127.4	126.6	135.7	135.8	164.9	173.5
Percentage	139.0	86.7	82.1	83.5	81.4	75.7	76.7	78.0

	1962	1963	1964[b]	1965	1966	1967[c]	1968[c]
Imports	203.0	207.5	242.0	262.4	237.7	206.1	179.6
Exports	168.6	189.6	182.6	200.3	191.2	170.4	175.2
Percentage	83.1	91.5	75.6	76.4	80.3	82.7	97.3

[a] 1957–63 inclusive. Federal Office of Statistics, *Review of External Trade Nigeria 1966*. (Imports and exports including oil sector.)

[b] 1964–68. Central Bank of Nigeria, *Annual Reports, 1966, 1967, 1968*. (Imports and exports excluding oil sector.)

[c] Years of import restrictions.

Foreign investment and the associated inflow of technology are extremely valuable and at times indispensable. The larger the capital inflow from abroad the larger the flow of resources available to a country over time to finance investment-stimulated growth, but, excluding the case of gifts, the higher also will be subsequent interest payments. Foreign private investors expect to recover their investment outlays in the currency in which they are made relatively quickly, and even the most generous foreign governments and international lending agencies hope to receive interest payments and eventually to recover their capital. As we have seen, the debt servicing cost of past foreign investment in Nigeria has become of national concern.

Table 2 gives some indication of the magnitude of international monetary transfers between Nigeria and the rest of the world during the years 1958–65. The table is based upon Nigerian published statistics of the balance of payments and shows (1) the balance on "basic" transactions; (2) the balance of other capital transfers; and (3) the sum of these two, which indicates a drain on the official reserves. The balance on "basic" transactions is that on merchandise goods and services (excluding dividend payments), plus the inflow of long-term private capital.

TABLE 2

Nigeria: Balance of Payments
1958–1965
(£Nm)

Year	*"Basic" balance*[a]	*Other capital transfers (including net errors and omissions)*	*Overall balance (1) + (2)*
1958	−25.6	+ 2.8	−22.8
1959	− 6.3	− 2.8	− 9.1
1960	−49.7	+11.6	−38.1
1961	−36.9	+ 3.9	−33.0
1962	−27.1	+ 2.0	−25.1
1963	+ 3.1	−31.6	−28.5
1964	−17.6	+ 9.0	− 8.6
1965	+ 7.3	−50.5	−43.2

[a] Balance on merchandise goods and services (excluding dividend payments) plus the inflow of long-term capital.

SOURCE: Constructed from data in Federal Office of Statistics, Lagos, Nigeria. *Annual Abstract of Statistics 1965*, p. 105, and *Digest of Statistics July and October 1965*, p. 62.

The outflow of other capital transfers was high and negative in 1963 and 1965. Such capital transfers included dividend remittances and also (unfortunately) "errors and omissions," which have been a substantial item from time to time in

Nigeria. However, over the whole period 1958–65, these transfers moved inversely to the basic balance and so moderated the fluctuations that needed official financing. A continuation of this trend would be very helpful to Nigeria but the outflow of funds in the years 1963 and 1965 gives a warning to the country. International capital movements in the post-World War II years have been closely correlated with a nation's political stability. Foreign exchange controls can, of course, be tightened and, indeed were tightened by the Nigerian monetary authorities in order to control an outflow of funds in the emergency situation, but controls maintained for too long would undoubtedly inhibit the transfer of private capital funds to Nigeria.

Foreign capital may supplement domestic capital formation but it cannot replace it. There is not enough of it, and it is self-reversing. In the long run, the building-up of a flourishing and flexible economy is, to a large extent, dependent upon the ability to generate locally a surplus of resources for investment. Essentially, an increase in exports is required because when imports are increasingly necessary to support productive activity, any expansion of national savings and investment capacity becomes dependent upon rising exports.

NIGERIA'S EXPORTS

Nigeria's principal exports are petroleum, groundnuts and groundnut oil, palm kernels and palm oil, cocoa and rubber. The strength of the country's competitive position in relation to the world market for these products differs markedly. Before the civil war disrupted oil operations, Nigeria was the tenth largest oil-producing country in the world (excluding North America and the USSR), but, of even greater importance, was the fact that Nigeria was a relative newcomer to the world's crude oil production and that output was on the threshold of significant expansion. Large sums had been spent by the international oil companies on exploration activity but the "pay-off" from petroleum exports on any substantial scale had yet to be realized.

Nigerian crude oil competes actively with that coming from Libya and from the Persian (Arabian) Gulf. In comparison with the crude oil coming from the Persian Gulf, two advantages accrue to Nigerian crude; (1) it is virtually sulphur-free (which reduces processing costs, especially important as concern with air-pollution grows in developed countries) and (2) it is significantly closer to Western European and South American markets. The freight advantage to Western Europe over Persian Gulf crude has been estimated to be of the order of 20 cents a barrel.[12] Libyan crude possesses the same advantages as does the Nigerian product and the freight superiority is larger (30 cents a barrel).[13] The Libyan oil sector expansion of recent years[14] indicates that the above factors are important. However, Libya is tied politically to the Arab countries and the endemic hostilities of the Middle Eastern countries make it expedient for the international oil companies to develop alternative well-located fields. Today, production from Nigeria can be relatively easily expanded and the output loss of the last few years gives the oil companies an added incentive to increase production as swiftly as possible.[15]

The prospects for an expansion of oil exports appear to be very favorable and the per-barrel "take" obtained by the Nigerian government will be greater in future than it has been in the past. Nigerian oil legislation was designed to offer attractive terms to the oil companies as exploration conditions in the Niger delta were difficult. Oil, for the calculation of income taxes, was valued at "realization prices" which were lower than the "posted prices" used as the basis for income taxation by the majority of other oil producing countries.[16] As the success of exploration in Nigeria brought increased competition for concessions, the federal government in 1967 negotiated with the companies a revision of the taxation arrangements and, in future, income taxation will be based on posted prices.

Petroleum exports do have some impact on the level of indigenous activity in the local producing areas but the impact is small in comparison with that generated in the producing areas by Nigeria's other commodity exports. The traditional commodity exports confront more difficult marketing conditions than does petroleum but the fortunes of these exports determine directly (1) the distribution of incomes and (2) local taxation capacity within the producing regions. As petroleum revenues increase, both national cohesion and political stability will be jeopardized unless these revenues are used for the overall benefit of the country.

Nigeria, since the nineteenth century, has been a major supplier of oilseeds to the world market and the exports of groundnuts, palm oil and palm kernels were the mainstay of economic activity in the former northern and eastern regions. Today, in the northern states, well over a million farmers (or between 5–7 million people) depend on the groundnut crop for their monetary incomes and groundnut production has been increasing in importance in the agricultural economies of these states. The production of palm oil products, despite (for reasons discussed below) some decline in output in recent years, still provides the livelihood of many people in the eastern states and in the mid-western state.

Oilseeds have a high degree of technical substitutability and Nigeria during the next decade will face keen competition in the world market. Crushing capacity in Western Europe has been adapted increasingly to oilseeds competitive with Nigerian products, namely, soybeans and sunflower seeds. In 1968, the EEC countries absorbed around 40 percent of the volume of oilseeds, edible fats and oils of all kinds traded internationally.[17] If Britain should join the Common Market, the privileged position that Nigerian oilseeds have long enjoyed in this important market might well cease. Further, developments in vegetable oil technology threaten to eliminate the premium that has been paid by consumers for edible groundnuts over industrial groundnuts. The premium ranged from £N8 to £N23 per ton in the years 1963–67 (Table 3). Groundnut oil was preferred by consumers as a table oil but today, oils from sunflower and soya are widely accepted for this purpose. The use of groundnut cake in the animal feed market is impeded by fears among customers of aflatoxin, a fungal poison present in groundnuts that have not been properly stored. Restrictions on the usage of groundnut cake have been introduced by a number of West European countries and Nigeria will have to fight for their removal. The fastest-growing section of the feed market, that for poultry, is effectively closed to groundnut exporters as poultry are very susceptible to aflatoxin.

Palm oil and palm kernel oil face competition from other developing countries. Coconut oil competes closely with palm

TABLE 3

Comparison of Edible and Industrial Groundnut Prices 1963–1967 (£s/long ton)

Year	*Edible groundnuts*	*Industrial groundnuts*	*Edible groundnut premium*
1963	70	62	8
1964	80	68	12
1965	91	75	16
1966	91	68	23
1967	81	66	15

SOURCE: Nigerian Groundnut Processors, Nigeria Commonwealth Secretariat, Great Britain.

kernel oil and supplies are expected to increase substantially within a few years when new plantings from the Philippines become fully productive. Malaysia, Indonesia, and Ceylon are other competing countries and palm oil from new plantations in Malaysia and also from rival African producers in the Congo and in the Ivory Coast will increase the overall supply of palm products. Keen competition for markets may be anticipated. In recent years, Nigerian production of palm oil produce for export has declined, partly because local consumption has increased and partly as a result of Marketing Board price policy. Prices offered to the farmers in the decade before the civil war were approximately 40 percent lower than the world price. If Nigeria is to maintain the country's relative share of the world market and also to increase output for the domestic market, the producer will have to be given greater production incentives. The matter is of particular concern as petroleum production has so far been concentrated in certain areas of the former Eastern Region; pressure to apportion substantial petroleum revenues to the eastern producing states will gather momentum if other economic activity is depressed.

Other important items of the Nigerian commodity export trade are cocoa and rubber. The market for cocoa is extremely difficult to forecast; the dynamics of this market seem to follow no determinate pattern. Factors exogenous to the market system such as the various difficulties in control of cocoa tree diseases influence the size of the crop from year to year and stocks accumulated by consuming countries do not seem to iron out price fluctuations. If past experience is any guide, world prices can be expected to vary widely over a decade.[18] Some market problems can be foreseen. There has been a tendency for manufacturers of chocolate confectionery to reduce the coating of chocolate when cocoa prices are relatively high and, in recent years, in order to sustain profits, thin coatings have become standard practice. In diet-conscious high-income countries, consumer preferences have moved away from all high calorific items including chocolate. Demand may increase in developing countries including Nigeria as incomes rise but the stimulation of taste is a relatively lengthy and laborious business.

Exports of rubber have brought Nigeria approximately £N10–12 million each year during the decade before the civil war (or, for example, in 1966, about 10 percent of the total value of the main agricultural commodity exports of groundnuts, palm products, cocoa, and rubber). Synthetic rubber is keenly competitive with the natural product and unless the productivity of rubber estates is high, the product has difficulty in competing effectively in the world market. Nigerian output is for the most part from small holdings where productivity is low and it is not unlikely that earnings from rubber production will fall in the future.

Exports of other Nigerian commodities may be developed, for example, of forest and livestock products but numerous difficulties have to be overcome. A flourishing livestock industry cannot be based on the present itinerant Fulani cattle and sedentary practices have yet to be accepted and shown to be profitable. Petroleum revenues, if used to finance economic development throughout the country, could help to bring about the initiation or expansion of promising alternatives to the traditional list of export commodities and help to ease any financial pressures which may affect producer incomes.

INSTITUTIONAL AND ADMINISTRATIVE PROBLEMS

The former regional marketing boards were the main progenitors of development finance for their respective regions and, inevitably as the states emerge as administrative units the question of state versus national commodity marketing institutions arises. Historical consistency seems to point to state-based produce marketing and on the division of the former Eastern region into three states, independent state marketing boards were created, each assuming the full range of powers enjoyed by its regional predecessor. The outbreak of hostilities prevented any attempt to coordinate policies. The states may well have individual marketing interests which diverge from those of the former region and these specific concerns may seem to make desirable state control of the marketing of produce. National interest, however, in the efficiency of produce marketing should require that an organization be in existence which would be concerned with all operations connected with any particular crop – from planting to the receipt of payment from overseas.

Proliferation of marketing bodies would be likely to lead to administrative chaos and economic loss. Agreement on basic matters such as pricing policies would be difficult to achieve and if a common policy did not exist, price competition along state borders to attract produce from neighboring areas could develop. Expenses incurred to prevent interstate smuggling would be a truly unnecessary burden on the ultimate payer, namely the farmer. Transactions with shipping companies would be complex and competition in selling produce could well result in lower returns to Nigeria than formerly. Matters such as research might tend to be neglected.

Harmonization of national and state interests will be difficult to achieve unless fiscal policies ensure that each state is allocated "sufficient" funds for development purposes. The sufficiency of funds must be such that the peoples of a state become convinced that they are indeed sharing equitably in national prosperity. In the past, regions have obtained revenues from the produce of the area but the principle of area derivation should not apply to revenues from petroleum. Oil royalties have so far been allocated 50 percent to the producing states but the major payments of the petroleum industry will come from the sharing of the profits attributed to crude-oil sales and these will be made to the federal government. The usage and distribution of the considerable sums involved should be directed to securing the optimum national benefits. During the next few years, the states which suffered most from war damages should probably receive special attention.

If rivalry among the states can be turned to constructive and productive ends a promising future for Nigeria can be foreseen. Genuine reconstruction and development should renew foreign confidence in the country and, when considered in retrospect, today's financial constraints will be seen to have been temporary.

NOTES

1. Foreign assets were reported by the Central Bank of Nigeria to approximate £N46 million during 1969 – down from more than £N80 million in the months before the civil war and a far cry from the mid-1950s when reserves at their height reached £N260 million, sufficient at that time to finance the equivalent of two years' imports. The level of reserves was probably maintained during the civil war years by the procedure of leaving debts, including some for armaments, outstanding.
2. A four-year reconstruction program to be launched at the end of hostilities was announced by the federal government in March 1969. The total cost was estimated at £N1,163 million, of which approximately 40 percent would be provided each by the federal government and the private sector, and 20 percent by state governments and agencies.
3. Gerald Helleiner, *Peasant Agriculture, Government and Economic Growth in Nigeria* (Homewood, Ill.: R. D. Irwin, Inc., 1966), p. 16.
4. In 1954, as part of a general move by the colonial authorities to create a strong regional system, the marketing boards were reorganized and regionally designated.
5. U.S. Department of Commerce, *Investment in Nigeria*, 1957, and estimates made by the Central Bank of Nigeria.
6. Federal Ministry of Industries, Nigeria, preliminary estimate, 1968.
7. *Petroleum Press Service*, January 1968.
8. Oil revenues, in the year ended March 31, 1967 were estimated by the federal government at £N29.5 million. Higher revenues would have been received in the next fiscal year not only because of larger oil output (approximately 50 percent increase was anticipated) but also as a result of new taxation legislation. Fiscal terms, laid down in the Petroleum Profits Tax Ordinance of 1959, were amended in January 1967 and agreements were subsequently negotiated with individual oil companies beginning with Shell-British Petroleum Development Company, producers of more than 80 percent of the country's output. The company was also liable for additional taxes for fiscal year 1966–67.

   Export receipts from groundnuts and groundnut oil, for the first time, amounted to £N50.5 million in 1966 and receipts from cocoa exports, also for the first time, exceeded £N50 million in 1967 and 1968 – years of very high cocoa prices.

9. Central Bank of Nigeria, *Annual Report, 1966*, p. 77. Oil sector imports rose from £N12 million to £N18.6 million between these years, and attributing all such imports to capital goods would reduce the percentage of capital goods and raw materials imports for non-oil sectors to approximately 61 percent.
10. Oil exports began in 1958 but it was not until 1962 that they amounted to as much as 10 percent of total exports and began noticeably to distort the simple statistic of the trade balance.
11. Central Bank of Nigeria, *Annual Report*, 1966.
12. M. A. Adelman, "Oil Production Costs in Four Areas," a paper presented at the Annual Meeting of the American Institute of Mining, Metallurgical and Petroleum Engineers (February 28–March 2, 1966), *Proceedings of the Council of Economics*. The freight costs are calculated on a comparable basis, assuming transportation by large tankers.
13. Ibid.
14. Oil production in Libya was less than one million tons a year in 1961; in 1970 the country's oilfields were producing at a rate of over 160 million tons a year and further rises in output were anticipated. *Petroleum Press Service*, January 1970. Oil revenues increased from $109 million in 1963 to $952 million in 1968. Petroleum Information Foundation, New York, 1969.
15. Despite the hostilities, one oil company, Gulf Oil (Nigeria) expanded production, mainly from off-shore sources from an average of 57,000 barrels a day in 1967 to around 200,000 barrels a day in 1969. At the beginning of 1970, it was reported that the "oil companies are now preparing for a resumption of large-scale production" and that "production in Nigeria is now above pre-war peak." *Petroleum Press Service*, February 1970.
16. Until very recently no "market price" in any meaningful sense could be said to exist for crude oil; such "prices" were for most oil companies internal (interaffiliate) transfer prices, which, with the imposition of taxes by producing countries, became important for fiscal purposes. For discussion of this issue see Edith T. Penrose, *The Large International Firm in Developing Countries: The International Petroleum Industry* (London: George Allen and Unwin Ltd., 1968), chap. 6. The "prices" posted for fiscal purposes were widely discounted in the world market during the 1960s.
17. "Implications Inherent in the World Agricultural Trading Situation." *Far East Trade and Development*, March 1970.
18. The index of Nigerian cocoa export prices during the years 1962–68 inclusive was as follows: (1963=100) 91, 100, 108, 75, 79, 119, 133. The per-unit value fluctuated from a low of £N17.75 (1965) to a high of £N31.26 (1968). (International Monetary Fund, *International Financial Statistics*: October 1969.)

Chapter 13

The Liberian Budget Crisis of 1962–63

Russell U. McLaughlin

Late in 1962, the Liberian government was confronted with a financial and balance-of-payments crisis that eventually led it to negotiate a series of standby agreements with the International Monetary Fund and to accept a fiscal austerity program designed and supervised by the Fund. As a quid pro quo for accepting the austerity budget, the Liberian government successfully renegotiated the maturities of its foreign debts.

This paper examines the causes of the 1962 budget crisis and attempts to assess the short-run and probable long-run effects of the Debt Rearrangement Plan on the Liberian economy.

BACKGROUND OF THE PROBLEM

The financial history of Liberia is a portrait of a poor, independent country borrowing in the major world capital markets on relatively costly – one might call them onerous – terms. When a combination of internal and external forces made it impossible for the country to meet its obligations under the terms of the Loan of 1871 and again under the Loan of 1912, Liberia was forced in each instance to accept a settlement imposed on it from the outside by its private creditors. In 1926, Harvey Firestone concluded a loan agreement with Liberia in conjunction with his plantation lease arrangement, the effect of the 1926 loan being to transfer the outstanding foreign debt then held by a consortium of American and European bankers to the Finance Corporation of America, a Firestone subsidiary. A particularly humiliating feature of this agreement was the presence of a customs receiver who exacted a first claim on all customs revenue to meet principal and interest obligations and of a financial adviser who held veto power over the Treasury. Despite some unpleasant moments during the early 1930s, the loan agreement with Firestone proved to be at least tolerable. The entire loan was fully retired by 1955, at which time Liberia found herself completely free of international debt for the first time in many decades.

At about the same time, the Liberian economy began to experience the stimulating effects of earlier investments made during and immediately following World War II. Among these were the Port of Monrovia, the Robertsfield airport, the services of both an economic and a public health mission, small amounts of road construction, and the Bomi Hills concession to the Liberian Mining Company. Beginning in 1950, the Liberian economy exhibited an upward although unsteady climb. Between 1950 and 1962, real domestic product increased by two and one-half times, exports rose from $28 million to $67 million and government revenues expanded from $3.8 million to $38 million. By 1962, the total inflow of foreign capital is estimated to have reached an annual rate of between $70 million and $80 million. Added to this investment rate was an annual investment expenditure by government of between $15 million and $20 million.

In 1962, total gross investment amounted to 70 percent of the national income of $139 million and 45 percent of the gross domestic product of $222 million.

A principal cause of the crisis of 1962–63 is to be found in the peculiar character of this extraordinarily large volume of investment spending:

1. While the average annual investment rate has been relatively high, it has been characterized by extreme cyclical instability. A wave of foreign private and public capital inflow dominated the economy from 1946 to about 1951. From this point to the middle of the decade, new investment shrank to a relatively small figure, but it recovered sharply in the late 1950s and early 1960s. This latter

investment surge was dominated by iron ore mining but other sectors, especially the government, also shared in it.

2. Investment has been heavily concentrated in a few sectors of the economy, the lion's share going into rubber, iron ore, transport, and other infrastructure facilities. Moreover, individual projects often accounted for the bulk of investment in each sector. One iron ore company alone invested $220 million between 1959 and 1963. Of $18 million of public building contracts reported in 1961, one structure alone absorbed $16 million.
3. A very high percentage of the government investment during the 1959–62 era was financed by contractors' notes, popularly termed "pre-financing notes." This method of financing, it will be shown, became the principal ingredient of the financial crisis of 1962.

GOVERNMENT REVENUES

The budget crisis in 1962 might be visualized as a pincer-like squeeze imposed on the Treasury, one jaw being revenues that, because of events described below, failed to increase as expected, and the other the sharp rise in debt service expenditures during the years 1959 to 1962.

Liberian government revenues are derived from two basic sources: incomes from concessions and import duties. Small additional amounts are contributed by the personal income tax and other assorted revenue sources. In 1963, for example, government income from concessions and foreign businesses amounted to about $12 million, or almost 31 percent of total revenues. Import duties and other income associated with foreign trade (consular fees, etc.) totaled $17 million and accounted for 41 percent of total revenues. Thus, almost three-fourths of total government revenue is a function of the production rate and prices of export commodities. A fall of rubber or iron ore prices has a direct impact on profit-sharing payments (on concessions) and income tax payments made by both foreign and domestic producers. Furthermore, because of a high marginal propensity to import, a curtailment of export production or of new investment activity leads directly to reduced imports and lower customs revenues.

In the early 1960s the Liberian economy experienced three major shocks that individually might have been absorbed with only minor inconveniences, but which collectively combined to curtail seriously economic and budget growth. There was, first, a major decline in both rubber and iron-ore prices. The average value of rubber exports fell from 31.4 cents per pound in 1959 to about 26 cents per pound in 1962. Although the volume of rubber exports rose from 44,500 long tons in 1959 to 45,500 long tons in 1962, the total value of exports declined from $30.7 million in 1959 to $25.5 million in 1961, rising only slightly in 1962 to $25.7 million. However, the overall decline of 18 percent in the value of rubber exports between 1959 and 1962 dealt a major blow to Liberian employment, income, and budget revenues. Even more dramatic was the 41 percent decline in iron-ore prices from $11.90 a ton in 1960 to $7.03 in 1963. Only a sharp rise in export volume from 2.6 million to 6.4 million tons made it possible for the dollar value of iron-ore exports to double between 1960 and 1963.

The second major adverse development was the slower than expected rate of growth of iron-ore production. The Liberia-American Minerals Company (LAMCO) was running about one year behind its own anticipated production schedule. In addition, a requirement in the concession agreement of this company allowed it to accumulate a reserve of 25 percent of capital out of profits before profit-sharing payments would begin. At the same time the National Iron Ore Company (NIOC) was experiencing technical difficulties in its Mano River operation, so that ore was not flowing at the rate expected from that installation. As a result of these delays, government revenues fell below their expectations in the critical years when large foreign debt payments were coming due.

The third major blow to the Liberian economy in 1962–63 was the sharp reduction in the rate of new investment. This was partly the result of price declines in iron and rubber, but it was also caused in large measure by the completion of planned installations by one company that alone had been responsible for more than half of all private investment received in the years 1959–62. This shrinkage in investment outlays was not compensated by other expenditures of a similar size. New construction activity also was seriously curtailed following the decision of the Liberian government to end deficit financing of public buildings. At the same time, an autonomous decline in construction was experienced as several large ventures reached completion, in particular the Treasury building and the Executive Mansion.

TABLE 1

Liberian Revenues and Expenditures
1959–1963[a]
(Millions of dollars)

Fiscal Year	*Revenues*	*Operating expenses and interest*	*Construction credit expenditures*	*Deficit*
1959	28.93	36.22	12.51	19.8
1960	32.72	38.58	17.06	22.9
1961	35.49	44.26	14.39	23.2
1962	36.15	42.65	20.35	26.9
1963	39.09	50.50[b]	—	11.4

[a] Fiscal Year = October 1–September 30.
[b] Budget before austerity cuts and Debt Rearrangement Plan.

DEBT REPAYMENT OBLIGATIONS

The other jaw of the financial pincer in which Liberia was caught in 1963 is explained by the structure of its debt repayment schedule.

At the beginning of 1963, the Liberian national debt stood at $124.7 million. At the time, $117 million of this debt was scheduled to be amortized over the fifteen-year period of 1963 to 1977, and the small remaining balance thereafter. As the repayment schedule then stood, a total of $33.4 million of interest was also due to be paid over the payment period. The aggregate debt retirement and interest commitments faced by the government of Liberia in 1963 stood at $158.1 million.

However, it was not the aggregate size of this debt that created budgetary problems for the government so much as the distribution of the debt among different types of creditors, the timing of the repayments, and the fact that it was virtually all externally held. The source of credit is of particular interest, since it had the effect of inflating the principal amount owed above the real value of resources actually received. A total of $61.5 million, almost one-half of the entire debt, had been contracted with private creditors. These creditors were for the most part European construction firms who accepted Liberian government promissory notes in payment for work performed and who then discounted these notes in the major money markets of Europe. As the debt increased, so did the rate of discount. Because of a contractual guarantee of a fixed payment to the contractors, the Liberian government was compelled to issue additional notes to the contractors to cover declines in current value of notes caused by rising discount rates. There is no complete record available of the total inflation of project costs due to this vicious circle, but from isolated reports, this writer estimates that, at a minimum, the final project costs were inflated by at least 20 percent over the original contracted price. We will also never know the full effect on final project costs of the excessive equipment purchases made under these contracts – equipment that was used for the project and then allowed to stand idle and deteriorate under the combined effects of Liberian sun and rain. Whatever the intrinsic value of projects financed by this technique, there is no doubt that a more costly method of financing would be difficult to find.

The original debt repayment schedule is shown in Table 2. In 1963 alone the principal and interest due amounted to $33.5 million, or about 94 percent of estimated revenues for that year. While in subsequent years the programmed repayments declined from the extremely high 1963 level, a sizeable portion of total payments was scheduled in earlier years when revenues would be at their lowest level. Between 1963 and 1967, total repayments of principal and interest amounted to $101.6 million, or 65 percent of the total sum due over the entire fifteen-year period.

It is fair to state that the financial problem was caused more by poor management of the debt than by excess borrowing in the aggregate. A principal source of difficulty was the presence of too many cooks in the financial kitchen. To appreciate this view it is necessary to understand the pre-1963 budget procedure.

The formal process of budget-making in Liberia prior to 1963 was quite simple. Each department or agency presented

TABLE 2

Original and Rearranged Debt Repayment Schedule
Republic of Liberia
(Millions of dollars)

	Original Schedule		*Rearranged Schedule*	
Year	*principal*	*interest*	*principal*	*interest*
1963	27.0	6.5	—	—
1964	13.2	5.1	3.8	6.0
1965	14.0	5.1	3.1	6.1
1966	13.6	3.6	3.5	5.9
1967	10.2	3.3	3.1	5.7
1968	8.7	1.9	4.7	5.5
1969	7.1	1.6	10.6	5.1
1970	5.5	1.3	10.3	4.5
1971	4.4	1.0	10.3	3.9
1972	4.2	1.3	12.9	3.3
1973	2.9	0.7	9.2	2.8
1974	2.5	0.5	10.7	2.3
1975	2.2	0.4	8.1	1.6
1976	1.9	0.3	7.8	1.1
1977	1.7	0.3	7.2	0.6
After 1977	5.6	0.5	6.9	0.5

SOURCE : M. A. Qureshi, Y. Mizoe, and F. D'A. Collongs, "The Liberian Economy," *International Monetary Fund Staff Papers*, vol. 11, 1964, pp. 310–11.

a line-item budget proposal to the Secretary of the Treasury. These independent submissions were then totaled with no more than a casual review of the intra-departmental allocation of funds. To the direct department allocations was added an amount equal to 20 percent of estimated total revenues, the expenditure of which was to be controlled by the Joint Liberia–U.S. Commission for Economic Development. A further substantial sum was designated as a contingency reserve; this was utilized throughout the budget year for supplementary appropriations to departments and it was allocated, for all intents and purposes, at the will of the President. In the years immediately preceding the budget crisis, provisional appropriations exceeded 10 percent of total public expenditures.

In the face of this loose and uncoordinated procedure, the competition between departments and agencies for funds was fierce. What inter-departmental planning there was took place within the Joint Commission and this was confined to the expenditure of the 20 percent share of the total budget alloted to the Joint Commission. Since there existed no central budget agency, each operating department fared in direct proportion to the power of its head to obtain direct access to the President. Not only did this procedure result in poor planning and lack of coordination between departments but it opened the way for individuals to contract external debt in the name of the government of Liberia. This happened when a department secretary, having developed a pet project, or having been sold on one by an enterprising contractor, got the President's approval. The Treasury Department was then ordered to arrange for the appropriate financing, which generally took the form of contractor notes.

For the debt explosion to occur it was necessary that a generally permissive attitude toward borrowing should prevail. The expected revenues from iron ore and other investments, coupled with an overly optimistic psychology generated by several years of rapid expansion of the economy, served to engender a presidential climate of financial leniency that was reinforced by the Secretary of the Treasury.

When the bubble finally burst in 1963, stringent measures became necessary. Several more or less simultaneous actions were taken by the government:

1. It announced an end to further short-term deficit financing of public construction.
2. It requested and received from the International Monetary Fund a standby agreement in the amount of $5.7 million to help cover the balance-of-payments deficit generated by the need to make large principal and interest payments.
3. It entered into direct negotiation with its creditors to rearrange the repayment schedule of its external debt. This action was taken with the advice and assistance of the Fund.

The outcome of these negotiations was the Debt Rearrangement Plan (DRP) of 1963. Since both the standby agreement and the refinancing activities were part of a total package, although legally separate actions, they are treated as one in this paper.

STANDBY AGREEMENT AND DEBT REARRANGEMENT PLAN

The standby agreement was requested in late 1962, and was finally concluded in May 1963. The initial standby was for one year (later extended by one month) and placed $5.7 million at the disposal of the Liberian government.

An IMF standby agreement guarantees the right to draw on its quota to a member country for a specified period of time. Standby agreements have generally been used to deal with balance-of-payments problems like a speculative attack on a currency; the Fund used this instrument to assist Liberia in meeting her domestic budget crisis because, since $9 million of the 1962–63 budget deficit was for payment of interest to foreign creditors, it considered the domestic and international financial problems to be closely intertwined. The initial standby agreement was extended until May 31, 1964. During this period actual drawings amounted to $4.1 million. Less than the full amount was used because the debt rearrangement program became operative in September 1963. Subsequent renewals of the standby agreement and drawings against this resource are given in Table 3.

TABLE 3

Liberia Standby Agreements and Net Drawings from the International Monetary Fund (Millions of dollars)

Standby agreements		*Net drawings*
May 1963–May 1964	$5.7	$4.1
June 1964–May 1965	4.4	5.3
June 1966–May 1967	6.0	3.0
June 1967–May 1968	4.4	3.3

While the standby agreement was being negotiated, the Liberian government was also consulting with the Fund about rearrangement of its scheduled debt repayments. Since such a rearrangement depended upon approval of the plan by the great majority of creditors, it was necessary that the government take steps to put its financial house in order. By presenting creditors with a realistic proposal for repayment, coupled with a program of budget control and reform to be supervised by the Fund, it was felt that agreement could be attained with virtually all creditors.

Even before working out the agreement with the Fund, the Secretary of the Treasury had become aware of the serious shortcomings of the budgetmaking process in Liberia. As early as 1961 the Liberian government requested AID to provide technical assistance to the Special Commission of Government Operations (SCOGO). With respect to Treasury operations, this aid was concentrated on the problems of budget preparation and control. A system of rigid budgetary review was established and a more modern procedure of budget preparation was inaugurated in 1963. Other supplementary measures served to tighten control over the budgetmaking process. In general, the new procedures involved the submission of firm requests by all government departments to the newly created Bureau of the Budget. Supplemental requests and interdepartmental transfers required approval by a Special Committee on Budget Allotment and were to be allowed only under conditions of extreme emergency. All departmental requests were to specify the total expenditures contemplated by the department, including those monies previously allotted to various departments through the Joint Commission.[1]

In April 1963, the government announced its proposed debt rearrangement program. This was buttressed by announced expenditure reductions totaling $2.3 million from the already severely restricted 1963 budget. A 10 percent across-the-board reduction was imposed on all departments, plus further selective budget reductions. A freeze was imposed on all salaries and on the filling of vacancies except in cases of exceptional need. At the same time, the President called for new tax revenues, and promised stricter administration of existing tax legislation.[2]

By September 1963, agreement had been reached with all but a handful of creditors. At that time the DRP was formally adopted by the Liberian government. The extent of the alteration of the debt repayment schedule is seen in Table 2. Not shown are changes that were made in the repayment schedules of specific components of the total debt. Commercial bank debt totaling $15.4 million, all due in 1963–66, was entirely postponed until 1968–74. Official and semi-official debt repayments were reduced during the early years by 90 percent of their original amounts. Lengthening of the terms of private debt was also effected. This portion of the negotiations represents a major achievement in communication; since many of the notes had been resold in European money markets, tracking down of holders of the notes at the time of the rearrangement negotiations became a tedious task.

Several principles characterized the final debt repayment settlement:

1. All interest at originally contracted rates would be paid annually. This agreement had the effect of increasing the total service cost for the entire debt by $21.5 million.
2. All creditors in each class were to be treated equally. No payments were to be made in advance of the agreed schedule without increasing the amortization payment on all other debts in that class.
3. Repayments, including interest, under the new schedule averaged less than $10 million annually for the years 1964 to 1968. In 1969 annual payments increase by about 50 per cent. This rather large jump in scheduled payments is predicated on the expectation that LAMCO will begin making profit-sharing payments in that year, and on the contracted increase in LMC profit-sharing from 35 percent to 50 percent in that year.
4. The Liberian government could contract no additional loans with a maturity less than twelve years for any purpose without approval by the Fund. Subsequent to the Debt Rearrangement Program, new loans were negotiated with the World Bank and the Development Loan Fund. In each case the loan agreement included a grace period sufficiently long to permit the Liberian government to meet its obligations under the first six years of the Debt Rearrangement Program.[3]
5. The final requirement imposed upon the government of Liberia by the International Monetary Fund was that efforts should be directed toward bringing about a general improvement in the government's internal financial management.

EFFECTS OF THE DEBT REARRANGEMENT

While it is too early to evaluate fully the import of the Debt Rearrangement Program on the Liberian economy, some tentative assessments can be made. Perhaps the most obvious and most predictable immediate impact of the new debt agreement was the sharp fall in employment and real incomes that accompanied the vigorous cutback in Liberian government expenditures. For example, many contractors who had been operating in Liberia for several years under lucrative government construction contracts slowly began to curtail operations. Several of the firms, including some of the largest, finally quit the country entirely. Still others experienced severe curtailment of their construction activities although they continued operation of their other Liberian interests.

One of the long-run consequences of the crisis and its settlement has been growing awareness on the part of Liberian government officials and planners of the value and importance of the national budget as a planning and control instrument. Other benefits also flowed from the new budget procedure. There was a growth in appreciation of the complementary relationship between material support and personnel requirements. There was also a decline in the extent of personal budget-making by the President, as measured by the reduction in the number of unilateral adjustments in departmental appropriations.

There has been a noticeable diminution in the solicitations by "confidence men" that plague all small low-income countries, and an even greater decline in the number of unsavory "sales" by such men to the government. This benefit is due in large part to the fact that the crisis hastened the acceptance of national economic planning and enhanced the prestige of the planning agency. This latter body now reviews all external proposals for concessions or investment and applies to them a strict economic evaluation. The planning agency has been reasonably successful in thwarting at least some of the more questionable proposals made by outsiders to the government of Liberia. The reduction in the number of would-be exploiters may also be attributed to the requirement imposed by the Fund that new loans must have at least a twelve-year maturity.

The most notable example of this improved climate was the decision in 1963 not to accept the Liberia National Electric Corporation (LINEC) proposal for a privately-owned hydro-electric project. Had this plan been accepted, debt repayment and interest charges, as well as power rates, would have been considerably higher than those which now prevail under the terms of the DLF loan for the same project.[4]

The budget crisis literally forced the Liberian government to undertake a complete reappraisal of all foreign-aid programs, giving particular attention to the size of Liberian contributions and to the operating costs generated by aid-financed projects. It is hopefully expected that more careful scrutiny of such projects in the future will lead to a more efficient use of this development resource.

Finally the budget pressure of the past four years has caused the treasury to reform its tax collection procedures. Tax collection is now more efficient with an attendant rise in revenues. Additional tax sources are being tapped and the tax or profit-sharing provisions of concession agreements are being more strictly interpreted. The government is negotiating a double taxation treaty with Sweden that will, when completed, give Liberia the first opportunity for LAMCO's profits.

We should not conclude too hastily that the Fund management of the debt and budget policy has had only beneficial results. It created some problems of its own and it did not cure all that existed earlier. The ban on the filling of vacancies in government departments tended to impede the efficient operation of many departments during the early days of the budget crisis. The restriction served not only to freeze the number of positions but also to hold particular people in their jobs. Since, for political reasons, firing was virtually impossible, a department with needs for more type A labor skills and fewer of type B was not able to make this rearrangement in its personnel structure. Furthermore, the arbitrary budget cuts failed to distinguish between programs with different priorities. Since the reductions could not affect personnel, they were concentrated on supplies and equipment. As a result, there occurred innumerable instances of people in government departments who were idle because of a shortage of gasoline or other supplies.

A strong resistance to the new budgeting and planning

machinery remains. There were many who prospered under the old system of personal dealings with the President, and these people are understandably reluctant to give to a more impersonal system their wholehearted support. They accept the new methods only unwillingly. The new budget system is operative, but only imperfectly, so its victory is far from assured.

CONCLUSIONS

Liberia's financial history has been that of a small and poor country caught up in the flow of world forces that from time to time have tended to overwhelm the financial and administrative capacity of the government. This most recent financial episode differed in significant respects from those of the past, however. The borrowing during the late 1950s and early 1960s was for the purpose of financing economic development. Despite tense moments when the renegotiations were in process, the economy has been left with such tangible results as schools and other useful installations. The borrowing was also predicated on the income from Liberia's natural resources, supplemented by applications of foreign capital and management. While the economy is still subject to the vagaries of external price fluctuations, there is little doubt of the capacity of this economy ultimately to carry the full debt.

In the present crisis Liberia was able to turn to an international body for assistance; she did not have to resort as in the past to a consortium of private bankers or to a private investor. Instead of being saddled with a customs receiver who took first claim on income, and a financial advisor who acted unilaterally for the Liberian Treasury, as had been the case in the past, the government in this present crisis was encouraged to use its own personnel and resources in modernizing its budgetary structure. Aid from IMF was contingent upon budgetary reform rather than upon a first claim on revenues.

The character of the IMF assistance contrasts sharply with the conditions imposed on Liberia by creditors in the past. The Fund, in approaching Liberia's financial problems, treated her as a full member of the international family in contrast to the attitudes of and treatment by earlier foreign creditors which were regarded by Liberians as humiliating. The Fund recognized that both exogenous and endogenous factors created the budget crisis of 1963, and it acted to offset the effects of the former while assisting the Liberian government to correct those over which it had control.

There are those who argue that Liberia has paid an extremely high price for its financial orgy of 1959–62. Perhaps this is so. Nevertheless, there is evidence that the economy has emerged from this situation with a more sober attitude toward borrowing and toward the entire process of economic development. Government personnel changes indicate that a new breed of young Liberians is rising to positions of political and economic power. One characteristic of this new breed is dedication to economic growth and development. New enterprises have appeared, some of them Liberian. The economy has continued to grow albeit less rapidly than in the 1950s, despite the constraints imposed upon it. Its borrowing activities are now directed to a greater degree toward long-run productive projects than toward monuments and excessive frills. It is fervently hoped that a number of lessons have been learned by Liberia's financial managers. Perhaps one of these is the realization that foreign investment can not provide the total impetus for self-sustaining economic growth. Another may be that a modern public administration committed to improvement of the standard of living of all citizens is a sine qua non for economic and social development.

NOTES

1. This provision had two effects: (1) It served to create a unified budget for all departments at a time when all expenditures required extremely careful scrutiny; (2) It also paved the way for the ultimate demise of the Joint Commission as the economic development planning agency and the assumption of the planning role by the National Planning Agency, now the Department of Planning and Economic Affairs.
2. The writer recalls the furor caused by the actual padlocking of one Monrovia business house until its taxes were paid. Despite the resentment by others of this act, the list of tax delinquents took a sudden and sharp drop.
3. AID and DLF loans totaling $33.2 million and an IBRD loan of $3.35 million, later increased to $4.25 million, were subsequently contracted.
4. The Mount Coffee Hydroelectric project.

Part IV

International Economic Relations

Development in Africa is closely related to international trade and aid, the subjects that occupy the papers in this section. The first paper is concerned with aid, in particular the aid rendered by the International Bank for Reconstruction and Development in appraising a country's economic performance. Kamarck, who is director of the economics department of the Bank, offers a knowledgeable description of the Bank's method of economic diagnosis. He describes the nature of the analytical process, the formulation of policy recommendations, and the major considerations which shape both the analysis and the policy proposals.

Harwitz, Galbraith, and Resnick deal with trade. It has been commonly believed that the short-run instability and unpredictability of export earnings of the less-developed economies are related to the degree of export specialization, and that stability could be increased by broadening the variety of export commodities. However, a series of empirical studies have cast doubt upon this commonsensible notion. Now, Harwitz's reexamination of the work already done and his analysis of the data available lead him to the tentative conclusion that there is a positive relation between export concentration and instability of export earnings for many countries, although not for all. Some commodities tend to exhibit much greater earnings stability than do others, and the stability of a country's export receipts depends partially on the degree to which its export assortment includes these stable commodities. In general, Harwitz finds that while export concentration is of some significance, factors other than such concentration may explain a considerable part of the instability observed.

The experience of the Ivory Coast demonstrates that when a country pursues its comparative advantage, trade can act as a powerful engine of self-sustaining growth. This is the major thesis of the Galbraith essay. Galbraith finds, using criteria developed by Chenery and Strout, that Ivory Coast has reached a stage of self-sustaining growth. She traces the export-led growth of Ivory Coast during the first half of the 1960s and discusses the country's export diversification strategy for the 1970s.

East African economic integration, and especially the effects of the integration arrangements on Tanzania, are discussed in the Resnick essay. With the Treaty for East African Co-operation, Kenya, Uganda, and Tanzania have moved from a position of free trade among themselves to one involving special arrangements for limited protection of Tanzanian and Ugandan industry from Kenyan competition. Kenya, the most industrial of the three countries, has accepted this arrangement in the expectation that its special concessions will be of less long-run consequence than will the benefits of economic integration. Resnick expects the treaty to promote a small increase in Tanzanian industrial production. He also expects the negative effect on Kenya to be small at worst and to be very small if, as he believes both likely and desirable, Tanzania's import substitution enterprises largely supplant imports from outside the Community rather than only those from Kenya and Uganda.

Chapter 14

Appraisal of Country Economic Performance

Andrew M. Kamarck

I would with such perfection govern, sir,
To excel the golden age.
Shakespeare, *The Tempest*

One of the principal lessons that the World Bank has learned from twenty-three years of experience is that the economic development or growth of a country depends primarily on a continuing improvement in the effectiveness with which a country uses the economic resources it possesses. The research in the universities has apparently come to similar conclusions. A series of articles by economists like Aukrust, Denison, Domar, and Solow has shown that an increase in the supply of capital and in labor of unchanging quality does not appear to explain at a maximum more than one-half the estimated growth of GNP in the many countries studied.

Simon Kuznets goes so far as to say that "while the results would clearly vary among individual countries, the inescapable conclusion is that the direct contribution of man-hours and capital accumulation would hardly account for more than a tenth of the rate of growth in per-capita product – and probably less. The large remainder must be assigned to an increase in efficiency in the productive resources – a rise in output per unit of input, due either to the improved quality of the resources, or to the effects of changing arrangements, or to the impact of technological change, or to all three."[1]

What this means is that improving "economic performance," or action to increase effectiveness in the use of resources, has to be the central focus of development policy. Economic development comes through making more effective use and improving the management of all resources – existing capital as well as new capital, manpower, land, and other natural resources. This does not mean that providing more capital is not important; in fact, it may be that a greater supply of capital is essential to make it possible to take the necessary measures to improve economic performance. (Kaldor and other economists maintain that new knowledge is mainly introduced or infused into the growth process through the introduction of new equipment.) The point is that concentration on increasing the amount of capital as the central element in the economic development process represents the wrong approach to getting faster growth.

Now, how does the World Bank Group fit into this? The contribution to a country's development made by an agency like the World Bank Group (and usually emphasized) is capital. The loan or credit is an addition to the resources available to a country, but it is often more important than the sum of money involved would indicate. It may be more valuable than an equal amount of domestic resources if the country concerned is one where the "foreign exchange gap" is more important than the "savings-investment gap." I do not think this actually applies in many of the Latin American countries. But it certainly is true of most of the African countries, since there the production structure is much less flexible and the substitutability of domestic resources for foreign resources is very low, within a reasonably short time period, that is, within a year or two. (The amount of foreign exchange available to Ghana for the purchase of machinery and equipment abroad depends mainly on how much cocoa is produced and sold abroad and how much of the foreign exchange is used to buy foreign consumer goods. A sudden increase in Ghanian saving can affect the latter amount but will have very little immediate impact on making more cocoa available for sale abroad. At the same time, having more savings for investment cannot result in immediately shifting labor from producing yams – for which demand falls because of increased saving – to producing generators, turbines, or airplanes, which the increased investment demand requires. But, of course, the labor that formerly produced yams can be used to plant more cocoa, and in three to five years result in more cocoa exports.)

The capital that comes from abroad is also often much more mobile. It can be more easily directed to the higher priority needs than the savings produced within the country which may be mobilized, for example, only for investment in real estate. However, probably the most important role for the capital that comes from the outside is that it can be used as an incentive to the government to take action to improve economic performance in the economy, or it can help the government by making it possible for the government to take measures that it would like to take and feels necessary to take but is not able to take without this additional support from abroad.

Fundamentally, improvement of economic performance is something that can be carried out only by the government and the people of the country concerned. It is not something that can be imposed from abroad, but the help from abroad can be used to facilitate or encourage the government to take actions that otherwise could not or would not be taken. The World Bank, from its inception, has had as a principal objective helping countries improve their economic performance.[2] There has been an evolution in the methods used, the scope of the area of economy affected, and even in the emphasis given to this – but not in the existence of the objective.

WORLD BANK GROUP RESPONSIBILITIES IN DEVELOPMENT FINANCE

International lending to governments, prior to the organization of the World Bank, paid little attention to the particular use that would be made of the money by the borrower. The defaults on international loans in the 1930s were widespread, and it was concluded that a principal reason for them was improper use by the borrowers of the funds they had received. Consequently, when the World Bank charter was being written, a provision was put in that Bank lending should be for projects. Essentially, this means (as was explained in the 1949–50 Annual Report) that the Bank should lend only for clearly defined and agreed purposes that would result in an increase in the productive capacity of the borrowing country, and that appropriate institutional arrangements in the recipient country should exist or should be created to ensure that the purposes of the loan would be achieved.

How this worked out in practice is clearly explained in the following excerpt from an address by the Bank officer who was most intimately involved in this evolution of Bank policy.

> We began to discover the problem with our first mission to one of our underdeveloped countries, a mission which went to Chile in 1947 to examine a proposal that we finance a power project there. The presentation of this proposal had been made in a book handsomely bound in black morocco leather, and I remember that one of the senior people in the Bank at the time expressed a belief that we would be able to make a loan for the project in about a week. But when we opened the book, we found that what we had really was more of an idea about a project, not a project sufficiently prepared that its needs for finance, equipment, and manpower resources could be accurately forecast.
>
> We found it necessary to visit Chile several times to get information about the project and its economic setting – as I remember well, since one of these visits was one of the first missions that I ever undertook for the Bank. The loan – our first development loan, incidentally – was not made until more than a year had passed. In the meantime, members of the Bank staff had made suggestions about the financial plan, had contributed to the economic analysis of the scheme, had advised on changes of engineering, and had helped study measures for improving the organization of the company which was to carry out the scheme. When we finally made the loan, the project had been modified and improved, the borrowing organization had been strengthened, and the foundation had been laid for a power expansion program in Chile which has been proceeding steadily ever since.[3]

From the beginning, the Bank has used this technique of lending as a means of securing some progress in a more effective use of resources – both borrowed and domestic – in the recipient country. The improvement in performance sought concerns more than the actual piece of investment being financed – it often extends to an entire sector and to the building or improvement of institutions. An early example of this was the 1950 telecommunications loan to Ethiopia, the first loan made in Africa by the Bank. This loan financed the import of telecommunications equipment but this, while important, was only a small part of the real contribution involved: A new organization was created and built up over the years with the help of foreign experts. It is now able to run successfully the modern telecommunications system existing in Ethiopia. Indeed, the project enabled the Ethiopians themselves to become a source of technical assistance: when teams of technicians went to the Congo to help to restore the economic life of that country, one consisted of telecommunications personnel from Ethiopia. In the same way, a loan for a power project often involves the creation of an effective power authority or improvement in the management of the existing agency. A road loan may involve an overhaul or creation of the whole road maintenance and building agency.

Over the years, therefore, even when the Bank made only a relatively small contribution to international capital flows, it made a significant contribution in improving the management of resources in at least the areas of the economies that it was directly aiding. And the Bank continues today to regard this as important; it was in fact built into the Bank administrative structure in a basic reorganization of the Bank in 1952 which has since remained unchanged. "Responsibility for judgments about the merits of individual projects was deliberately divorced from responsibility for judgments about the desirability of lending to particular countries or borrowers. Divorcing project responsibility from country and borrower responsibility built into the internal organization of the Bank a limitation on the possibility that a defective or inadequately prepared project would be pushed through because there were felt to be overriding considerations arising out of the Bank's relations with a particular country. Conversely, a project could not be pushed through merely because it was fascinating. The Bank thus protected itself simultaneously against the technocrat and the diplomat."[4]

From its earliest years, the Bank has also contributed to improvement of economic performance through the process of Bank economic analysis in cooperation with the government of the country of the development problems, needs, and possibilities for improvement of an economy. At times, this resulted from a formal invitation from a government for direct help in shaping its developmental policies or in preparing a development plan. Formal economic survey missions for such a purpose have been organized by the Bank for twenty-five countries over the years. In other cases, missions of a lesser degree of formality were charged with similar tasks. A mission to Mauretania in 1967, for example, was sent in response to a request for help in preparing a new development plan. Ireland joined the Bank not because it was going to ask for any loans, but merely because the government wanted to have a chance to discuss its development problems with the World Bank Group. A 1967 mission to New Zealand was requested for the same sort of reason. There have been many other missions of a similar type. But probably the greatest contribution in this way comes from the regular country economic missions of the Bank.

Even in the years when the Bank took a fairly limited view of its responsibilities, the process of investigation and discussion with a government of its development problems inevitably had a positive effect in making a government more conscious of its problems and the need to take action to cope with them. This process of country analysis is inevitably enlightening both for the Bank economists and the government. It is a fairly common experience for Bank economists to have an official raise a particular or general problem that had not been discussed in order to get the Bank economists' views on it. Sometimes the official will say: "We are planning to try such and such. Do you know of any experience with this? How do you think it will go?"

This "dialogue" is always therefore an important feature of the Bank work. What does it consist of?

In studying a particular country, fundamentally what has to be done is to make an adequate analysis of the way in which the national economy actually functions, to identify the constraints which influence its direction and rate of development, and finally, to identify what the development objectives of the government are and what the government can do to improve the conditions for growth either directly or through policies that stimulate the economy. In other words, as Luis Escobar has suggested in a recent article, what has to be done is "to organize study and research with a view to formulating a diagnosis which I have defined as a 'national interpretation of economic development,'" that is, "an adequate interpretation of the way in which our national economies function."[5]

To do his work well, the development economist should know the country thoroughly. Specifically, he should start by acquiring a knowledge of the economic geography of a country: its natural and human resources, its structure of production, its position in world trade and finance, its economic history. He should acquire an understanding and appreciation of the social and institutional infrastructure: the main constraints and critical preconditions to growth have to be identified. Based on this, the analyst must identify an implicit or explicit development strategy or what in very rough terms might be called a long-range development plan. This must identify what are the policies and measures in the short term that the government can take to carry out the longer-range development strategy. Finally, what the government is doing and its policy plans must be measured against the analysis of what the economy requires for development. The major test of the development policy of a government is, therefore, the assessment of the extent to which steps are actually taken or programs launched to remove or to reduce the main constraints to growth, and to create and to improve the necessary conditions and institutions for growth. (This is not to suggest that the development economist should have a rigid approach. It is important that he should be willing to reevaluate his findings if events and new facts show that it is necessary. What is, however, important is that government actions and plans should be judged with reference to the "development strategy" that is fully supported by the basic analysis.)

In evaluating a particular country's economic performance, among the specific questions that would need to be answered, most of the following would certainly be included: 1. what is happening to growth of production and income; 2. what is the extent of the mobilization of resources for development and is the national savings ratio to GNP growing; 3. how efficiently are existing financial resources being used; 4. how compatible is the social and institutional framework with development;

what policies are being undertaken to improve this; 5. is there a population growth problem; if so, what does it consist of and what, if any, effort is the government making to cope with it; 6. is development being given appropriate emphasis compared say, to defense; 7. how succesful is the country in maintaining confidence in the currency and in the future value of savings; 8. how rapidly is import capacity increasing, that is, what is the rate of increase of export and other foreign exchange earnings; 9. how efficiently is the country economizing on spending for imports; 10. how well is the balance of payments and the external debt managed; for example, does the country have an effective way of keeping track of and controlling debts incurred by government entities and enterprises; 11. how internally consistent are the development and financial policies?

What may be noted is that in this list there is no specific inclusion of a "development plan." To a large extent, of course, a good development plan would involve all these factors. A country that scored high on all these points might well be a country that would also have a good development plan: a good development plan is a result of a set of good financial and economic policies; it is not a substitute for them.

In evaluating the answers to the foregoing questions it is not justifiable to apply a standard grading system to all countries. In my view, there is no standard pattern, no one royal road to development. Each country must make its own way. It is useful to know what other countries have done; it is useful to know what other countries are doing; but it would have to be a very special case where one country could follow exactly the same road that another had pioneered in the past, or fit into exactly the model applicable to another country. Consequently, what one can reasonably expect of a country must differ from country to country.

The approach is not that of Procrustes. What must not be done is to take an actual or mental model that has been worked out for a developed country, apply it to the developing country and, where the developing country does not fit, prescribe the changes that will make it conform to the model.[6] There is a song from an old musical *The Belle of New York*, which describes exactly what the approach of an economist coming from an industrialized country should not be. It goes as follows:

Our virtues continue to strike us
as qualities magnificent to see.
We know that you never can be like us,
but be as like us as you're able to be.

It is also wrong to work out a set of quantitative tests and grade all developing countries by how well they do in these tests. For example, it is useful to have, for analytical purposes, a set of comparative country statistics such as capital/output ratios, the ratio of savings to GNP, tax revenues to GNP, and so forth. But, the temptation must be resisted to apply these mechanically and to conclude that if a country falls below the average or the optimum levels it is falling in economic performance. This approach is fundamentally wrong because it does not take into account the very different stages of development that countries are in; it does not take into account the very different natural resource endowments that they have, and the very different natural, historical, and institutional obstacles that they face.

There is also no unique role for government in fostering economic development. There are cases like that of Hong Kong, where there is a very creative and energetic private sector. The "right" government role in a country like Hong Kong may simply be to provide the basic utilities and then get out of the way and let the private economy boom. On the other hand, there may be cases, for example like Malawi in Central Africa, that are at the other extreme. In Malawi, the bulk of the population is still largely in a subsistence agricultural economy; there is little in the way of manufacturing, and no mining. In Malawi, economic development depends almost entirely on the stimulus given by government through finding suitable crops and improving them through research, teaching farmers how to grow them, and providing suitable incentives.

Other countries fall somewhere in between. It follows from this that while in some circumstances the actual rate of growth of GNP may be an important indicator of economic performance, it is not necessarily so. In some countries, even with the best will in the world, the economy may not be able to grow very rapidly. Malawi is again a good example. If government action and policies were perfect and no mistakes were made, without external help the economy would still grow very slowly. On the other hand, there are cases, particularly countries that have a stable structure of the economy and society (or one that is changing only very slowly) reasonably suitable for economic growth, and that have a reasonably good natural resource endowment, where the rate of growth of income and production may be a very good indication of how well the government is doing its job.

But, in most developing countries, development entails changing the structure of the economy. It is perfectly possible that a government may be doing an excellent job in changing or facilitating a change in the structure of the economy and the society to provide the necessary basis for growth in the future, but in the meantime, no perceptible growth may be seen in the statistics. In such a case, even though economic statistics may show no growth, one could reasonably conclude that the performance of the government is optimum.

An example of this might be that of Tunisia between 1956 and 1960. When Tunisia became independent in 1956, the bulk of the modern sector (commercial farms, factories, public utilities, banking system) was essentially a foreign enclave – owned, controlled, and managed by foreign settlers. During the next four years the Tunisians took over most of this sector, absorbing it into the Tunisian national economy. The fact that there was little or no growth shown in the economic indicators during this period cannot be taken as a conclusive sign of bad economic performance.

Another example of the same type is the case where a country needs to carry through a fundamental land reform to provide the basis for future growth. Examples of this might be the Republic of China on Taiwan and, perhaps, Iran in recent years. If during the period that such a fundamental transformation of the structure is taking place the economy does not register growth in its GNP figures or other purely economic indicators, this cannot be taken as prima facie evidence that the economy is not performing well. The focus, in other words, should always be on the particular country, its special problems and possibilities.

As the magnitude of the resources that the World Bank Group disposes of has increased, and as other suppliers of capital have joined in a greater coordination of lending under the World Bank's consortia and consultative groups, the need to devote more and more attention to the use of resources in an economy outside of the particular sectors directly financed by the Basic Group has become much more important. In a number of developing countries the World Bank Group has become the principal lender and the leading supplier of external capital. The number of consortia and consultative groups for the developing countries has now increased to around a dozen. In these cases, even though the World Bank Group may not be the principal lender, it is called on to chair the group and to provide periodic analyses of the position, prospects, and performance of the country. These groups now cover over 40 percent of the total flow of capital from the industrial countries to the developing countries. At the same time, the World Bank has gradually discontinued lending to the higher income countries, and its activities have become concentrated on the developing countries alone.

WORLD BANK GROUP ASSISTANCE IN NATIONAL ECONOMIC PERFORMANCE

Along with this growth of the greater responsibility of the World Bank Group in development finance, there has also been growth in the sentiment for more positive action to secure better country economic performance. In part, this has stemmed from the economic research in the universities that was mentioned earlier; in part, from a feeling of disappointment in the progress made by the developing countries so far, and consequently, the desire to modify the way in which economic aid has been given.

A very important force in this evolution was the creation of the International Development Association (IDA) in 1960 to make capital available on soft terms, that is, with a very large grant equivalent, to the poorer developing countries. As long as there was only the IBRD proper, it was easy to overlook the fact that the World Bank loans included a subsidy element (with the credit of the richer countries behind the Bank, the Bank was able to borrow and to lend at rates generally below what the developing countries would otherwise have had to pay). It was easier, therefore, to be influenced by the feeling that the World Bank was a bank and, overlooking the practice of securing better performance in the projects and sectors financed, conclude that the economic performance of the borrower's economy was outside of the World Bank's interest. With the addition of IDA and the provision by IDA of credits which at the present terms are equivalent to a grant element of 80 percent of the face value of the credit (calculated at a discount rate of 10 percent), it becomes very obvious that what is involved is something quite different from normal investment banking – that, in fact, the World Bank Group is engaged in development finance, and inescapably must be concerned with the performance of the economy as a whole.

The justification for project and sector lending, in fact, always included the hope that improvement in one project or sector would act as a leaven for wider areas of the economy. But it was also realized that "the fundamental limitation on the effectiveness of project lending is that although investment consists of projects, in the sense of discrete decisions that have to be executed within some organizational framework, be it ministry or enterprise, investment does not consist only of projects. It certainly does not consist only of projects considered eligible by outside lenders and donors. There are in addition expenditures which are not identifiable as projects, or may not be readily identifiable at all. Total capital requirements moreover include one, often crucial, non-project item, namely debt service. Project financing, no matter how well conceived and executed, will thus always be incomplete as a means of financing development."[7]

The rational alternative is to base financing on total capital requirements, supporting a development plan for a period of years ahead. This the Bank has in theory been willing to consider. In the 1949–50 annual report, the statement was made "the Bank would prefer to go further, wherever that is feasible, and base its financing on a national development program, provided that it is properly worked out in terms of the projects by which the objectives of the program are to be attained." But it has done so in only a few isolated cases, and one could interpret the impact of the consortia and consultative groups as also being equivalent to this to a partial extent. On the country side, the record has been that most plans so far have not consisted of the realistic well-worked set of investment projects and appropriate development policies that would deserve blanket long-term support.

Another point that also must be mentioned here is that economic development is a much broader field than the conventional economics of a developed society comprehends. To secure progress in a developing country the government may have to devote considerable attention to such noneconomic variables as reform of the civil service, enforcement of effective taxation, and land reform. It may also be true that more economic growth may come from parts of what is conventionally labeled as "consumption" (i.e. government expenditure on agricultural extension workers or on the eradication of debilitating disease) than from some of the items that are conventionally labeled "investment" (i.e. construction of a presidential palace).

Consequently, when one thinks of securing improvement in economic performance beyond the particular project or sector that happens to be externally financed, consideration must be given to picking out the strategic items in the whole spectrum of government policy that would affect the most important constraints on growth and that are amenable to action. In a few cases, this might affect a whole investment program of a government; in most cases, it would be something quite different. Essentially, the approach has to be pragmatic and directed as far as possible to what is most desirable and practicable.

As a result, in the last few years, there has been a further major evolution in bank policy in that consistent and deliberate analysis of country economic performance has been made a major objective of the Bank Group's economic work and the Bank's lending program has been more specifically and more deliberately designed to help countries improve their economic performance.

The earlier Staff Economic Committee, which in large part tended to focus on credit worthiness questions, has been replaced by an Economic Committee, chaired by the Economic Advisor to the President, which has directed its main focus to evaluation of economic performance and formation of bank policy to secure better economic performance. In this process, the staff of the International Monetary Fund now also participate and contribute their country experience and expertise. The Bank economic staff has also been considerably strengthened, but not yet sufficiently to fully attain the objective set. There are also still many corollary questions of policy which have not yet been fully worked out.

The present position, therefore, is that in all of the World Bank Group's lending: 1. the Bank directly attempts to improve the use of resources in those projects or sectors or institutions where Bank finance is directly involved through attaching conditions to the loans; 2. it also always tries to make a basic analysis of the economic problems and prospects of a country in cooperation with the government of a country. The next step is the most difficult one. It varies from country to country depending on ascertaining what it is that is holding up faster growth and that the government, by appropriate action within its capability, can correct, and what the World Bank Group can reasonably expect to achieve with the government in securing improved performance in this respect.

At one extreme, there are countries where the role of the World Bank Group is very small. This may be because the country concerned has reached the stage where it needs very little help from abroad, or because the political or governmental situation is such that the government is relatively helpless to accomplish anything much in improving economic performance, or because the bulk of its external capital comes from a source that is not interested in whatever economic conclusions this group may come to in its economic analysis. In such cases, if anything can be done at all, the World Bank Group may have to limit itself to the influence of the basic economic analysis process or the improvements it can secure through financing a particular sector or succession of sectors. At the other extreme, there are countries where the Bank Group is the predominant source of external capital, and there are sufficient elements in the government that are both eager to take and capable of taking action to improve economic performance in a number of ways, if they are supported by the World Bank Group in getting the government officially to agree to such measures. In these cases, the World Bank Group may agree with the country, in a more or less formal form, on a lending program in a number of sectors together with understandings on the policy actions the government will take to improve performance in significant fields. Most countries, of course, lie between these two extremes.

What measures to improve performance are economically desirable and possible vary from country to country. As the focus is always on the particular country, its problems and its potential, what needs to be emphasized consequently varies from country to country and from time to time in a particular country. The World Bank Group has to look at the whole of the development process, and in the course of the economic analysis conclusions have to be reached as to which are the areas or sectors which are most important at the particular time in which progress should and can be made. In some countries, the most important measure may be to have a more stable price level or a better monetary or fiscal policy. In these countries, the Bank works in parallel with the Fund, and what the World Bank and the Fund try to accomplish may be identical or may supplement each other. In other countries, other measures in quite different sectors may be the strategic ones. In one country in Africa, for example, the Bank analysis came to the conclusion that the most important immediate measure to be taken was raising the price paid to the farmer for peanuts, the most important export of the country. Because the government had maintained the price its market board paid to the farmers at too low a level, the farmers had cut down on their production. The result was that the foreign exchange at the disposal of the government to be used for financing imports of equipment was too low. Here the most important item was the price of peanuts, and this is what the World Bank Group devoted its attention to. In another case, the crucial policy improvement needed and feasible may be the general arrangements for management of industry, the financing of public utilities or agriculture, etc.

In spite of the experience of the World Bank Group in this area, which in some respects goes back for over twenty-three years, there remain a number of open questions on which the World Bank and its member countries are still feeling their way. Take, for example, the very difficult problem of population growth. In the Bank analysis of an economy, the dynamics of population growth and the population policy of the government are now included as topics to be covered. The Bank does not, however, use population policy as a condition of lending. There are quite a few development economists who would definitely feel that population policy may be the most important test that one could apply to a country's economic performance. They point out that the rates of population growth in the developing countries are higher than anything the present industrial countries experienced at any period of their history; second, that the phase of rapid population growth in the industrial countries came only after the industrial countries had embarked on their rapid economic growth and the process of industrialization which came at a time when it was easier to handle and did not cut into the rate of per-capita income growth as much as it does now in the developing countries. In the European countries, moreover, when in their phase of rapid economic growth they also had rapid population growth (although well below that of the developing countries today) their problems were mitigated by the fact that there was large-scale emigration to the United States and to other countries, which helped them meet their population problem even more easily. The rate of population growth in the developing countries today is unique in the world's history, and one can hardly argue that it is a positive factor for economic growth; but how and in what respect an economic performance test could be applied to this is still to be worked out.

The trend of policy in the Bank and the needs of the developing countries both point to a further deepening of the cooperation between the World Bank Group and the governments of its member countries in trying to continue to improve the effectiveness of the use of resources in the member countries' economies. How this will evolve is still unclear, but it is obvious that there are still many problems in this process which will have to be solved.

> What's past is prologue; what to come,
> In yours and my discharge.
>
> Shakespeare, *The Tempest*

NOTES

1. Simon Kuznets, *Modern Economic Growth* (New Haven, Conn.: Yale University Press, 1966), pp. 80–81.
2. "Economic performance" can be taken to mean the behavior of certain national economic indicators (such as the rate of growth of gross national product, savings as a ratio of GNP, export earnings) or the actions the government takes to influence or direct the economy. It is in the latter sense of economic management that the term "economic performance" is used in this paper.
3. S. Aldewereld, "The Challenge of Development Aid," May 6, 1966.
4. J. H. Williams, "International Bank for Reconstruction and Development" (Paper presented at Bretton Woods, 1967).
5. Luis Escobar Cerda, "An Economist's View of the Role of Social Sciences in Latin America," in *Social Science in Latin America*, ed. Bruce Woods and Manuel Diegues, Jr. (New York and London: Columbia University Press, 1967), p. 58.
6. For a more comprehensive statement of this point, see Dudley Seers, "The Limitations of the Special Case," in *The Teaching of Development Economics*, ed. Kurt Martin and John Knapp (London: Frank Cass & Co., 1967).
7. Williams, "International Bank for Reconstruction and Development."

Chapter 15

Measuring Export Instability: Theory and African Experience

Mitchell Harwitz

Since World War II, discussions of the economic problems of poor countries have frequently focused upon their experience as trading nations. One of the aspects of this experience that was less than satisfactory was their regularity of export incomes. The short-run unpredictability and instability of export earnings was thought to be sufficiently widespread and serious among poor countries to deserve special efforts at correction. The language of this discussion and the empirical content of the assertions were both rather imprecise. It seems fair to say that the discussion entailed the following:

1. Poor countries export more primary goods than do rich ones, as a percentage of total exports;
2. Poor countries have more unstable exports than do rich countries;
3. The exports of countries selling to many customers are likely to be more stable than the exports of countries with few buyers;
4. The exports of countries are more stable the greater the number of distinct commodities they sell abroad.

These brief statements are crude in many ways. They do not, in themselves, define their terms: instability, primary products, poor countries, and so on. Nor are they evocative in the way that the policy-oriented formulations of the literature were. The policies justified by the truth of these propositions would run something like:

1. Poor countries should try to export more industrial goods;
2. Rich countries should try to stabilize the exports of poor countries;
3. Poor countries should diversify both the commodity and
4. composition and the geographical concentration of their exports.

Much of the debate over "stabilization policy" ran along these lines. The validity of the underlying empirical assertions was hardly questioned until the early 1960s.

In 1962, Joseph Coppock published a wide-ranging study, *International Economic Instability*,[1] intended in part to summarize the relevant facts concerning instability and its correlates. Among other things the study attempted regressions of an index of instability upon indices of geographical and commodity concentration for a sample of 66 to 83 countries (depending on the regression). The hypotheses quoted earlier ought presumably to have led to some statistically significant results. Remarkably, there were no regression coefficients large enough to reject a null hypothesis of independence. The relations could have been random! A series of other studies confirmed this lack of relation in cross-sections.[2] The results of these studies may be summarized as follows:

1. On the average, rich countries have somewhat more stable export earnings than do poor ones, the difference between mean instability being statistically significant;
2. Poor countries specialize more heavily in primary exports than do rich ones, but primary exports as a whole are not markedly more unstable than industrial exports;
3. Cross-section correlations of export instability and primary-product specialization are insignificant;
4. Multiple regression of export instability indices on commodity and geographic concentration indices shows only one significant result, that geographical concentration is negatively related to instability.[3]

The uniformly weak associations noted in these results called into question the lines of reasoning that ran from concentration to instability. It seemed true that poor countries had greater export instability, but no obvious explanations appeared to hold.

This paper considers the results of a more precise formulation of the conventional position. The mathematical problem is to specify the algebraic relation between instability indices on the one hand and concentration indices on the other. The connected statistical problem is to derive a statistical model, preferably in the form of a regression equation, representing the mathematical model in measurable form. The second section of the paper summarizes the results of these studies.[4] Briefly, the conclusion of this section is that the existence of any functional relation between instability and concentration indices depends on two hypotheses, both of which can be tested to some degree.

The first hypothesis is that the instability of (de-trended) sales of a particular export is a constant with respect to the commodity in question or the country buying. The concept of instability used here must naturally be dimension-free, or relative, so that absolute volumes of sales do not affect the measurement. The hypothesis can in principle be checked by calculating instability measures for detailed export data. For purposes of empirical analysis, it must be retained as a logically necessary hypothesis. Without it, there need be no functional relation at all between concentration and instability.

The second hypothesis is that the time-series of de-trended export sales of particular commodities by one country are mutually uncorrelated. The matrix of correlation coefficients of these time series with each other should be a unit matrix. This assumption gives a simple mathematical form to the function relating instability and concentration. In the third section of this paper, tests of this hypothesis carried out on data for ten African countries whose exports the writer has studied intensively are reported on. The hypothesis is rejected. This leads to the conclusion that a functional relation between instability and concentration, if it exists, is neither linear nor multiplicative. It is, instead, positive but non-linear. The elasticity of instability with respect to concentration will be positive and generally not unity. This contrasts with the multiplicative (log-linear) results of independence, when the elasticities are unity. In the fourth section, these conclusions are used in the analysis of regressions across countries. At the end of the third section the results of some exploratory studies of the reasons for the failure of the independence hypothesis are analyzed. Little positive information is gleaned, but a negative result is that the causes of fluctuations in de-trended residuals do not cluster on particular types of commodities.

The fourth section of the paper uses the results of the preceding two to reexamine some of the published regression studies and some hitherto unpublished extensions. The results of the second section show that a possible cross-section equation has the form

$$\log I = b_0 + b_1 V + b_2 \log C_m + b_3 \log C_n$$

In this equation, I is an index of instability, C_m is a Gini index of commodity concentration, and C_n is a Gini index of geographical concentration. The variable V is a measure of export instability fulfilling the requirement of multiplicative separability from C_m and C_n. Attempts to fit this log-linear equation to available data suffer from the absence of data on V. However, even in the presence of bias due to the omission of V, this estimating equation performs better than simple linear forms. The earlier analysis also suggests that a sample of countries should lead to a cross-section regression with positive coefficients. Negative coefficients indicate either mis-specification or the inclusion in the sample of countries where the assumed functional relation is false. The possibility that the independence hypothesis is false helps to explain why the estimated coefficients differ significantly from unity. The use of new variables as estimators for V should in principle improve estimation of b_2 and b_3; the unpublished results of Massell agree with this hypothesis.

To sum up, the empirical studies published so far, reestimated on the basis of detailed theory, suggest:

1. A positive connection between instability and concentration is not found in all countries, but may be in a large number;
2. Studies that use only concentration indices as explanatory variables are mis-specified and lead to impossible signs of coefficients;
3. Diversification into stable commodity types always reduces instability;

4. The importance of constant terms in the reestimated regressions suggests that factors other than concentration explain much of observed instability.

Some theory of instability indices

There are five distinct indices in the literature I have surveyed. They are:

1. Average annual percentage deviations from a five-year moving average (MacBean);
2. The antilog of a "logarithmic-variance" measure (Coppock);
3. A UN measure of average percentage year-to-year change based on the ratio of year-to-year change to the higher of the two annual values involved;
4. The normalized standard deviation of export series residuals about a linear trend, normalizing on the average level of export for the period of observation (Massell);
5. The average annual percentage rate of change in imports, corrected for linear trend (Massell).

It can be shown that the third and fifth of these measures do not have clear statistical properties, so that they are best left alone. The remaining three can be shown to be rather similar to each other. Of them, the fourth is the most tractable. It can be characterized algebraically. Let there be T observations on exports for one country: E_t, $t=1, \ldots, T$. Let U_t be the measured deviation $U_t = E_t - (b_0 + b_1 t)$, where b_0 and b_1 are fitted least-squares trend coefficients. Then the fourth index is

$$I = \left(1/T \sum_{1}^{T} U_t^2\right)^{1/2} \Big/ (1/T) \sum_{1}^{T} E_t. \qquad (1)$$

The "theory" of this index can be developed by assuming that the de-trending of E_t by $b_0 + b_1 t$ is correct. For then E_t is a sum of a non-stochastic element

$$M_t = b_0 + b_1 t \qquad (2)$$

and a stationary stochastic element x_t which can be assumed to be normally distributed with zero mean and variance σ^2 independent of time. U_t in (1) is an estimate of x_t.

The sample statistic, I, has an asymptotic expectation. It can be shown that this expectation, denoted by $\hat{I}$, is given by

$$\hat{I} = \sigma/\bar{M}, \tag{3}$$

where σ is defined above and

$$\bar{M} = 1/T \sum_{1}^{T} (b_0 + b_1 t). \tag{4}$$

The error in using the right side of (3) for a sample of size T is not larger than $1/T$.

The next task is to analyze the instability of total exports of a single country in such a way as to develop a mathematical relation between instability and concentration. To this end, let me divide the total exports of one country into exports by commodity class and by receiving country, so that

$$E_t = \sum_{i=1}^{m} \sum_{j=1}^{n} E_{ijt} \tag{5}$$

for each t. Here, i indexes commodities and j indexes the receiving countries. For each value of i and j, we have a time series $\{E_{ijt}\}$, to which may be attached an instability index I_{ij}, exactly analogous to I as it is attached to $\{E_t\}$. Let us assume that every one of the time series $\{E_t\}$ and $\{E_{ijt}\}$ for each i and j, can be treated as we have already treated $\{E_t\}$ in deriving I_4. From (5) we see that E_t is a sum, and from (3) we see that

$$\hat{I}^2 = \text{var. } E_j/\bar{M}^2 = \sigma^2/\bar{M}^2 \tag{6}$$

where the variance of E_t is on our assumptions the variance of its random component σ^2. The analogous index for $\{E_{ijt}\}$ is

$$\hat{I}^2_{ij} = \sigma^2_{ij}/\bar{M}^2_{ij}. \tag{7}$$

The formula I want consists in representing the right-hand side of (6) in terms of the right-hand side of (7).

The first step in the procedure is to define a connection between $\bar{M}_{ij}$ and $\bar{M}$. To this end, I introduce weights w_{ij}, defined by

$$w_{ij} = \bar{M}_{ij}/\bar{M}. \tag{8}$$

Evidently, these weights are "mean shares." After detrending all export time-series, one would calculate the w_{ij} operationally by calculating $\bar{M}_{ij}/\bar{M}$ for all the time series at the respective mean values. For any given sample, the w_{ij} are fixed. They are, algebraically, a set of probabilities, and we shall define for further use the marginal values of the "density table":

$$w_{i.} = \sum_{j=1}^{n} w_{ij}, \qquad i = 1, \ldots, m; \tag{9}$$

$$w_{.j} = \sum_{i=1}^{m} w_{ij}, \qquad j = 1, \ldots, n, \tag{10}$$

$$\sum_{i,j} w_{ij} = \sum_{i} w_{i.} = \sum_{j} w_{.j} = 1. \tag{11}$$

These weights lead directly to concentration coefficients, for the numbers

$$C_m^2 = \sum_{i=1}^{m} w_{i.}^2. \tag{12}$$

and

$$C_n^2 = \sum_{j=1}^{n} w_{.j}^2 \tag{13}$$

are the squares of Gini coefficients of concentration of export sales by commodity and country, respectively. Note that these coefficients should be calculated at the point of means, though in practice they are usually calculated for one "typical" year. Finally, note that available data do not usually permit the calculation of w_{ij} directly. It is usually necessary to use the marginals, which are available, so as to derive the weight w_{ij} from the formula

$$w_{ij} = w_{i.} w_{.j}. \tag{14}$$

This relation will be seen below to lead to very convenient algebra.

Having developed the connection between $\bar{M}$ and $\bar{M}_{ij}$, it can be shown that the general relation between I^2 and its components is

$$\hat{I}^2 = \sum_{i,j} \frac{\sigma_{ij}^2}{\bar{M}^2} + \sum_{ij,hk} \frac{\sigma_{ij}\sigma_{hk}\rho_{ij,hk}}{\bar{M}^2} \tag{15}$$

$$= \sum_{i,j} w_{ij}^2 \hat{I}_{ij}^2 + 2 \sum_{ij<hk} \rho_{ij,hk} w_{ij} w_{hk} \hat{I}_{ij} \hat{I}_{hk}.$$

In this formula, w_{ij}, $\hat{I}_{ij}$, $\hat{I}$ are already defined, and

$$\rho_{ij,\,hk} = \frac{\text{Covariance }(\chi_{ij}, \chi_{hk})}{\sigma_{ij}\sigma_{hk}}. \tag{16}$$

Here *ij* and *hk* denote two values (not necessarily distinct) of the classificatory indices for commodities and receiving countries. The general formula doesn't get us very far. The formula (15) defines $\hat{I}^2$ as a quadratic form with matrix

$$\underline{R} \equiv \| \rho_{ij,\,hk} \| \tag{17}$$

and variables $w_{ij}\hat{I}_{ij}$ and $w_{hk}\hat{I}_{hk}$. There is, in general, no functional between Σw_{ij}^2 and $\hat{I}^2$. There is a functional relation between $\hat{I}^2$ and $\Sigma w_{ij}\hat{I}_{ij}$, for the former is a non-decreasing function of the latter.

To go farther, let us use one of the two hypotheses mentioned in the introduction; let us separate $\hat{I}_{ij}$ from w_{ij} by assuming that $\hat{I}_{ij}$ is a constant, say V, for all i and j. This amounts to the assertion that the relative variability (variance-over-squared-mean) of each export time series is fixed. Then (15) becomes

$$I^2 = V^2(\Sigma_{i,\,j}\, w_{ij}^2 + \Sigma_{ij,\,hk}\rho_{ij,\,hk}w_{ij}w_{hk}). \tag{18}$$

Now we have at least a non-linear formula in which instability, $\hat{I}^2$, depends on a non-negative quadratic form with w_{ij} as arguments and $\underline{R}$ as matrix. The next step is to induce the quadratic form to depend in a measurable way upon the concentration indices C_m and C_n. Since any quadratic form with $\underline{R}$ as matrix will be positive semi-definite, the quadratic form in the parentheses does depend positively on the sum

$$C^2 = \sum_{i,\,j} w_{ij}^2. \tag{19}$$

This is not yet a concentration index for commodities or receiving countries, however.

The direct influence of the indices C_m and C_n can be established if it is assumed that $w_{ij} = w_{i.}w_{.j}$, for then

$$C^2 = \sum_{i,\,j} w_{i.}^2 w_{.j}^2 = C_m^2\, C_n^2. \tag{20}$$

Thus, the parenthetical expression on the right-hand side of (18) is a non-linear and non-decreasing function of C_m and C_n, which are Gini coefficients.

Finally, a simple equation can be derived if the correlations

$\rho_{ij,hk}$ are all zero when $ij \neq hk$. That is, the form is simple when the covariances of the residuals χ_{ij} are zero. It is

$$\hat{I}^2 = V^2 C_m^2 C_n^2 \tag{21}$$

or

$$\hat{I} = VC_m C_n. \tag{22}$$

Thus, a linear regression in the logarithms of V, C_m, and C_n can be derived from the basic model, on the assumptions made above.

It is important to compare the conclusions of the analysis leading to (18) with those leading to (21). Using (18) and (20) together, one has a non-linear but positive relation between C_m^2, C_n^2, and $\hat{I}^2$. Given that $\underline{R}$ is not a unit matrix, the coefficients of a log-linear form should differ from unity. If (21) holds, then $\underline{R}$ is a unit matrix and there is a log-linear relation with coefficients equal to unity.

To recapitulate briefly, it is essential that the indices $\hat{I}_{ij}$ be separable from weights w_{ij}. Otherwise, no functional relation between instability and concentration need exist. The "conventional wisdom" can only conclude that diversification decreases instability if the new commodities or customers are less unstable than the old, or if the new weights w_{ij} shift sales in the direction of more stable export commodities or buyers. That is hardly a startling conclusion! If the algebraic "removal" of V is possible, then the further assumptions of "independence" in the density table of the shares ($w_{ij} = w_{i.}w_{.j}$) and independence of residuals lead to (26) and (28). I remark here that precisely analogous reasoning, confined to commodity classification alone, or to country classification alone, leads to the formulae

$$\hat{I} = VC_m = wC_n, \tag{23}$$

which are analogous to (22). Note that only the assumptions leading to (20) can justify using C_m and C_n together in a regression.

TESTS OF THE HYPOTHESIS OF INDEPENDENCE

The independence hypothesis was shown earlier to be fundamental to the derivation of a simple relation between C_m or C_n and I. Two approaches to tests are taken here. The first is to study sums of variances. The second is to study correlation matrices. The basic data are generated by detailed study of ten African countries which have export data by commodity from 1951 on. These countries are listed in Tables 1 and 2. For each country reasonably reliable time-series exist for total exports and for most individual commodities at the 3-digit level. The calculations were based on the period 1951–63. Table 1B lists the major exports of each country in 1963. Reexamination in the light of later data is probably not worthwhile at this time, for reasons to be noted.

The first approach mentioned above is a test of the null hypothesis that the de-trended export time series should be independent. On the null hypothesis, the variance of the de-trended total export series for any one country should equal the sum of the variances of the commodity export series that are the components of total exports. This is just an application

TABLE 1A

Instability and Concentration Indices

Country	*I*	*Rank*[d]	*One*[e]	*Rank*	*Top 3*[f]	*Rank*	*Rank*[g]
Cameroun	0.1273	3	32	6½	71	4	5
Ethiopia[a]	0.0770	7	50	4	70	5	4
Ghana	0.0799	5	67	1	84	1	1
Malagasy Rep.[b]	0.780	6	29	8	49	9	9
Morocco	0.0629	9	24	9	42	10	8
Nigeria	0.0707	8	32	6½	60	6	6
Rhodesia[c]	0.0883	4	53	3	77	2	3
S. Africa	0.0470	10	37	5	51	8	7
Sudan	0.1614	2	57	2	72	3	2
Tunisia	1.0622	1	20	10	53	7	10

Rank correlations, Kendall's tau: $|\tau| \geq .49$ entails 5 percent significance
$\tau 2, 4 = .1333$ . . . $\tau 27 = .111$ . . .
$\tau 2, 6 = .333$ . . .

[a] and Eritrea before it was absorbed
[b] Madagascar
[c] Federation of Rhodesia and Nyasaland and then Malawi, Rhodesia, and Zambia as a group
[d] highest to lowest rank for all ranking
[e] percentage of total export sales accounted for by most important export commodity, 1963
[f] percentage of total sales accounted for by three most important commodities
[g] Rank of Gini coefficients

TABLE 1B

Country	Major Commodity	SITC Code	Percent Total Exports 1963
Cameroun	Cocoa	072	32
	Coffee beans	071	20
	Aluminium	684	19
Ethiopia	Coffee beans	071	50
	Oilseeds, nuts, kernels	221	12
	Vegetables	054	8
Ghana	Cocoa	072	67
	Gold		10
	Wood, round	242	7
Malagasy Rep.	Coffee beans	071	29
	Sugar and honey	061	11
	Sisal	265	9
	Spices	075	8
	Rice	042	7
Morocco	Calcium phosphate	271	24
	Citrus fruits	051	13
	Fresh tomatoes	054	5
	Preserved fish	031	5
Nigeria	Oilseeds, nuts, kernels	221	33
	Cocoa	072	17
	Mineral fuels	331	11
	Vegetable oils	421	8
Rhodesia	Copper	682	53
	Tobacco, unmanufactured	121	20
	Asbestos	276	3
South Africa	Gold		37
	Wool and hair	262	8
	Diamonds	275	6
	Maize	044	6
	Uranium ores, etc.	286	4
Sudan	Cotton	263	57
	Oilseeds, nuts, kernels	221	13[a]
	Gum arabic	292	7
Tunisia	Alcoholic beverages	112	20
	Olive oil	421	19
	Nature phosphate	271	14
	Wheat and coarse grain[b]	041	12
	Phosphate fertilizer	271	6

[a] Cotton seed 5 percent
Groundnuts 8 percent

[b] Wheat 7 percent
Semolina 4 percent

TABLE 2

Country	*Number of SITC 3-digit series*
Cameroun	13
Ethiopia	13
Ghana	14
Malagasy Republic	27
Morocco	27
Nigeria	16
Former Federation of Rhodesia and Nyasaland (Malawi, Rhodesia, Zambia as a group)	22
South Africa	23
Sudan	19
Tunisia	26

of the argument used to derive equation (21) in the second section. In the present context, it produces a test of independence. From the de-trending operation of fitting a linear trend, one has, for a given country, a time-series of residuals for each commodity group: $u_{i1}, \ldots, u_{iT}$ $(i = 1, \ldots, m)$. This series has simple average zero (because of the technique of fitting the regression) and a variance that is essentially the variance of the regression estimate (square of the standard error).

This variance is known to be a X^2 variate with $T - 2$ degrees of freedom. In a notation analogous to that used in section 2, let s_i^2 be the sample variance of the u_i calculated from the residuals $u_{i1}, \ldots, u_{i,13}$. The sum $\sum_{i=1}^{m} s_i^2$ is, on the null hypothesis, a sum of independent variables each of which is $\frac{1}{(T-1)}$ times a X^2 variate. Thus $(m-1)(T-1)\sum_{i=1}^{m} s_i^2$ is a X^2-variate with $(m-1)(T-2)$ degrees of freedom, where m is the number of independent commodity series in the statistics of total exports. The number is given in a column to the right of the list of countries in the sample. Because the number of degrees of freedom exceeds 100 in every case, a simple approximate test can be applied. We may construct a 95 percent confidence interval around $(\Sigma_{i=1}^{m} s^2)^{1/2}$, since this variable is distributed much like a normal variable with mean $s = (\Sigma_{1=1}^{m} s_i^2)^{1/2}$ and standard deviation $s/\sqrt{2(m-1)(T-2)}$.

The standard error of the residuals of the de-trended total export series is another estimate of this variable s. The two should differ, on the null hypothesis, only because of sampling fluctuations in the estimates of the s_i and the standard error for the total. Thus, the standard error of the residuals of total exports (s_E, say) should fall within a 95 percent confidence band around with probability .95.

Table 3 below gives the results of the test. In interpreting this table, the reader should be aware that:

(*a*) the units of measurement are local currencies, so comparisons between rows cannot be made;

TABLE 3A

Country	s_E^2 [a]	s_i^2	s_E	S	*Standard deviation of s*
Cameroun	7,054,091.63	4,140,176.06	2,035.8	2,651	125.2
Ethiopia	199,140,359.12	264,160,208.96	16,253.0	14,111	1000.4
Ghana	101,218,515.06	78,854,802.00	8,880.0	10,068	525.1
Malagasy	1,852,222.21	2,202,939.00	1,484.2	1,361	62.8
Morocco	8,407.4176	4,299.663	65.58	91.69	2.743
Nigeria	128,668,868.83	108,986,808.74	10,440.0	11,343.0	574.68
Rhodesia	284,711,965.00	160,541,982.00	16,141.0	16,873.0	750.97
South Africa	38,464,936.5	42,504,232.52	6,519.6	6,202.0	296.48
Sudan	103,283,926.64	85,535,977.41	9,248.8	10,163.0	464.76
Tunisia	112,662,090.78	26,212,584.25	5,119.9	10,613.0	218.31

TABLE 3B

Confidence Interval, 2 *s.d.* about *s*

Country	Minimum	Maximum
Cameroun	1,785	2,285
Ethiopia	14,253	18,253
Ghana	8,355	9,405
Malagasy	1,421	1,547
Morocco	62	68
Nigeria	9,865	11,015
Rhodesia	15,390	16,892
South Africa	6,222	6,816
Sudan	8,784	9,714
Tunisia	4,902	5,338

(*b*) columns (3), (4), and (5) of part A are computed with 5-place logarithmic accuracy.

Given these limitations, it is still clear that only one of the values of s_E, that for Rhodesia, actually falls within the confidence region, and even this observation is very close to the upper limit of the region. With a confidence coefficient better than .97, one can reject the null hypothesis of independence for nine of the ten countries. For Rhodesia, the confidence coefficient is at best .90.

The second test is less reliable than the first because it depends on the calculation of correlation coefficients. Under the null hypothesis of independence, the matrix of correlation coefficients of the residuals $u_{i,1}, \ldots, u_{iT}$, $i = 1, \ldots, m$, for any one country should be diagonal, with unity on the diagonal. Any sample correlation coefficient r_{ij}, $i \neq j$, is distributed about zero with a variance depending on the number of independent pairs of observations (i.e. independent pairs (u_{it}, u_{jt})). Table 4 lists the results of the significance tests with the number of independent pairs reduced by one to allow for known dependencies among the u_{it}. At the 5 percent level of significance, the observed r must exceed .576 in order to reject the null hypothesis $r_{ij} = 0$ when there are 12 independent pairs of observations.[5] The number of significant correlations is in all cases higher than the 5 percent one must allow at this level of significance. I have, therefore, another reason to reject the null hypothesis.

Given that the correlation matrices of the residual did not exhibit independence, I tried to determine whether there were natural groupings among commodities that might suggest explanations for the dependence among the time series of residuals. I computed a factor analysis of the correlation matrices, using a correlation matrix as input for each country. I shall here simply sketch the fact that the initial estimates – essentially principal components estimates – are not particularly revealing for future work.

Table 5 lists the dimensions suggested for each matrix by the principal components solution that is a by-product of the factor analysis program I used.[6] A scientist trying to reduce his data would hope to explain at least 50 percent, preferably more than 75 percent of the total generalized variance through his first principal component (pc). He also has to trust the correlation matrix and the residuals he uses.

A check of table 4 and the original data suggest that three of the correlation matrices, those for Ghana, Malagasy, and South Africa, contain anomalies caused by some short underlying time series. These conditions don't really affect our previous two tests, but they do destroy any possible meaning for a factor or principal components analysis. In the case of South Africa, I was able to deal with a reduced matrix of residuals, different from the one on which the initial tests were performed. In the cases of Ghana and Malagasy there has been no such opportunity, so I must exclude them from further comment. For the remaining matrices, the first principal component explained about 35 percent of variance in three cases, and between 25 percent and 30 percent in the other five cases. The second principal component – which one would hope explains less than half the variance explained by the first – explained between 20 and 25 percent of variance in all countries but one (Tunisia). One is therefore led to suspect that the natural groupings, if they exist, are limited in scope and do not classify residuals into any dominant pattern.

TABLE 4

Country	*Possible Correlations*[a] *P*	*Significant Correlations*[b]	*Percent*
Cameroun	91	15	16
Ethiopia	91	10	11
Ghana	105	25	24
Malagasy Rep.[c]	378/104	97/15	27/14
Morocco	350	37	11
Nigeria	136	15	11
Rhodesia	253	33	13
South Africa[d]	1080	245	23
Sudan	190	19	10
Tunisia	350	53	15

[a] $p = \frac{1}{2}m(m-1) - m$, where m is the number of 3-digit classes

[b] Null hypothesis $\rho = 0$, corrected for degrees of freedom

[c] Larger matrix includes time series of six observations; the smaller does not

[d] Larger matrix includes time series of seven observations; smaller matrix excludes these series, which are not important exports

However, a check of the weights of the eigenvectors themselves in the eight matrices of interest led to the observation that the larger weights in the important vectors went to disjoint groups. For example, in Cameroun, the elements of the first pc that have weights in excess of .3 are all different from the elements of the overlaps in the data on Cameroun. On the basis of this kind of examination, I would suggest that this "block-orthogonality" holds for most of these countries if one makes an arbitrary distinction between weights. The imposed orthogonality of the components is reflected in the commodity groupings of largest weights.

TABLE 5
Factor Analysis

Country	*Principal components Absorbing 75 Percent of variation*	*Approximate rank of correlation matrix*	
Cameroun	4 pick up 81%	12 or 13	(13)[b]
Ethiopia	4 pick up 75%	12 or 13	(13)
Ghana	3 pick up 77%	11 or greater	(14)
Malagasy Rep.	4 pick up 81%	15	(27)
Morocco	5 pick up 75%	16	(27)
Nigeria	4 pick up 73%	11	(16)
Rhodesia	4 pick up 78%	14	(22)
South Africa	4 pick up 77/67%	22/14[a]	(47/24)
Sudan	4 pick up 73%	13	(19)
Tunisia	4 pick up 75%	15	(26)

[a] First number refers to full matrix, second to smaller one (See Table 4 above)
[b] Parenthetical number is dimension of correlation matrix

The pattern of association within these main groups escapes me. Except to note that coffee and cocoa always move together in the exports of any country that sells them both, it is very hard to see groupings by the nature of the commodity in these block-orthogonal collections. One finds, regularly, a mixture of perennial and annual crops, field and free crops, foods and minerals. While there are "groupings," small groupings of like commodities almost never occur in isolation; the inter-class mixture almost always appears.

The negative character of the result cannot be overemphasized. If dependence were based mainly on commodity types, these fractured results would not occur. Orthogonality would not require linear combination of many different commodities. Each component would be based heavily on narrow, exclusive groups.

REGRESSIONS REEXAMINED

In this section, the application of the results of the two preceding sections to empirical regression studies are discussed. The exposition is in three steps: (1) a review of the results, given "ideal data"; (2) a discussion of what could be done when data on V are absent; (3) a résumé of empirical hypotheses and their tests in view of the preceding.

"Ideal data" in this problem means the availability of a sample of countries for each of which there are given values of V, C_m, C_n, and I. Since these are all estimates, one might argue that the appropriate treatment is via errors-in-variables. The resultant estimation problems are so great that one must proceed as if the disturbing influences are all additive. The standard regression model, with errors-in-the-equations, has to be used if any tests are to be made. To begin with the most restrictive hypothesis, the regression equation derivable from (22) is

$$\log I_s = b_0 + b_1 \log V_s + b_2 \log C_{m,s} + b_3 \log C_{n,s} + e_s, \quad (24)$$

where the b's are least-squares estimates and e_s is the estimated residual. The sample of countries is of size S and so $s = 1, \ldots, S$. On the hypotheses leading to (22), the true values of b_0, b_1, b_2, and b_3 are 0, 1, 1, and 1, respectively. If the independence hypothesis is not satisfied, so that the matrix $\underline{R}$ in (18) is not a unit matrix, the relation between C_m^2 C_n^2 and $\bar{I}^2$ is such that the slopes in (24) cannot be unity. Thus, if (24) is estimated across a sample of countries, the resulting estimates of b_2 and b_3 must be positive but need not be unity. If the sample of countries includes some for which the variable V is not multiplicatively separable, "noise" will be introduced into the regression, since the empirical data for these countries may show any sign and magnitude whatever for the regression coefficients. The resulting estimated equation might show slopes of the wrong sign. With "ideal data," incorrect signs lead to the conclusion that there is no functional relation between instability and concentration for a significant minority of the sample.

The data available in all previously published regression studies do not include observations on V for any country. Indeed, even a more detailed set of statistics, like those underlying the third section does not provide a direct measure of V. To measure V, given the requisite time series, one must accept as a maintained hypothesis that V exists, that it is multiplicatively separable, and that it is the expected value of all measured indices $\hat{I}_{ij}$ for a given country. Then it can be estimated as a sample average from the available series for each country. In the absence of the needed series, there is no measure of V. The effect of this omission is to exclude a variable from the regression equation, with the usual effects on the results. The estimates of b_2 and b_3 will be biased. The direction of the bias will depend on the sample correlations of V with C_m and C_n.

If the correlations are both of the same sign (e.g. positive), the bias will also have that sign. Thus, if (24) is approximately a correct model and if the conventional wisdom means that V is positively correlated with C_m and C_n in the sample, then the regressions in the literature should all give misleadingly large coefficients for C_m and C_n.

Several studies already published introduce new variables, so that the regressions are of the form

$$I_s = c_0 + c_1 C_{m,s} + C_{n,s} + c_3 X_{1s} + \ldots + c_n X_{ks} + e_s, \qquad (25)$$

where $\underline{X}_1, \ldots, \underline{X}_k$ are vectors of observations on other explanatory variables. From the present point of view, these new variables can be regarded as proxies for V. The better they function as estimators of V, the less bias will there be in the coefficients of C_m and C_n. It is notable that a log-linear form is never used in the cited studies. This is unfortunate, since the use of natural numbers, rather than logarithms, will tend to reduce regression coefficients by reducing the absolute size of every observation. The reason is that the logarithms in question are logarithms of decimal fractions.

The preceding discussion suggests that the available empirical studies suffer from two defects. The first is that, since diversification need not stabilize, the expected result ought not to be confidently expected. The second is that, even if diversification does stabilize, the available studies produce estimates of the slopes that are probably biased. The use of additional variables may counteract this bias somewhat. The importance of the omitted variable can be checked by looking at the constant term in the estimated regression equation when *V* is not used. If it is large, *V* is important.

The first study by Professor Massell can be used to examine the possible features of empirical regressions, since the basic data are given in the article. Professor Massell has since written two further papers that will be used as sources of further hypotheses.[7] The original study, in linear form, produced the results listed in Table 6, part A. The basic data are listed in Table 7. A linear regression of instability against commodity concentration alone leads, first, to results highly sensitive to the content of the sample. Removal of just one country, Malaya, reduces the regression coefficient to the level of insignificance. The linear regression of instability on commodity and geographical concentration produces an incorrect sign for the coefficient of geographical concentration, but also has a value not significantly different from zero. In all these equations, the constant term is significant and accounts for a great deal of the total sum of squares. The explanatory variables are significant in the one-variable regressions, but are not jointly significant in the second estimated equation.

What happens when logarithms are used, according to equation (24)? The dummy variable for *V*, which will be explained below, helps very little. Each coefficient of the explanatory variables is significantly different from zero with a one-tailed *t*-test, in all the equations of Table 6, part B. Furthermore, the explanatory variables log C_m and log C_n are jointly significant at the 1 percent level, the computed *F* value being 10.63. The new equations fit the data better and explain more of the variation they are supposed to explain. However, the mean correction – that is, the constant term – is still far more important in both equations than the other terms. For example, the total sum of squares in equation (1), part B, is 178.062, and the sum of squares explained by the constant term is 174.17. In equation (2), the relevant sums of squares are 140.532 and 138.268. It is easy to see that the

TABLE 6A

Sample dependent variable	*Independent variable*	
36 Countries I	C_m	
(1) coefficients	.05979	
(standard error)	(.03059)	
36 countries I	C_m	C_n
(2) coefficients	.055	–.043
(standard error)	(.027)	(.033)
35 countries	C_m	
(3) coefficient	.03730	
(standard error)	(.02368)	
28 countries I	C_m	
(4) coefficient	.10233	
(standard error)	(.02565)	

TABLE 6B

Sample dependent variable	*Independent variable*		
36 countries log I	dummy V	log C_m	log C_n
(1) coefficients	–.0690	.38102	–.29712
(standard error)	(.14565)	(.12819)	(.16331)
36 countries log I		log C_m	
(2) coefficient		.24708	
(standard error)		(.10097)	
28 countries log I		log C_m	log C_n
(3) coefficients		.45419	–.25109
(standard error)		(.09864)	(.13939)
28 countries log I		log C_m	
(4) coefficient		.37726	
(standard error)		(.09270)	

NOTE: Logarithms are to base *e*.

transformation to logarithms does not reduce the cost of omitting observations on V.

The dummy variable for V was developed as a result of further work by Professor Massell. In the cited reexamination of the 1964 data, it was noted that Malaya and the seven smallest countries of the sample of thirty-six were all outliers from the regression: Malaya because of its extreme instability,

TABLE 7

Country	C_m	C_n	I
1. Mauritius	.991	.847	.113
2. Trinidad and Tobago	.810	.461	.060
3. Colombia	.780	.705	.184
4. Panama	.740	.967	.082
5. Iceland	.715	.322	.103
6. El Salvador	.704	.483	.106
7. Ghana	.704	.393	.136
8. Malaya	.697	.347	.284
9. Burma	.691	.330	.138
10. United Arab Republic	.685	.264	.123
11. Ceylon	.640	.390	.132
12. Brazil	.568	.465	.125
13. Thailand	.490	.324	.129
14. Dominican Republic	.490	.593	.108
15. Cyprus	.455	.454	.164
16. New Zealand	.449	.619	.095
17. Nigeria	.439	.571	.118
18. Malta	.428	.500	.152
19. Australia	.427	.387	.166
20. Philippines	.414	.611	.085
21. Finland	.373	.336	.158
22. Argentina	.303	.340	.150
23. India	.280	.347	.108
24. Ireland	.365	.814	.091
25. Belgium–Luxembourg	.264	.328	.097
26. Sweden	.252	.291	.111
27. Austria	.242	.352	.084
28. Portugal	.237	.285	.103
29. Norway	.233	.321	.111
30. Canada	.227	.601	.057
31. Japan	.215	.354	.101
32. France	.214	.280	.134
33. Italy	.207	.270	.087
34. United Kingdom	.195	.212	.063
35. Netherlands	.170	.334	.061
36. United States	.160	.292	.099

SOURCE: Massell, "Export Instability and Concentration," p. 51 for I and p. 53 for C_m.

NOTE: Countries 1, 2, 3, 4, 5, 6, 8, 15, and 18 were excluded by Massell in his re-study as being outliers. In dividing the group into less-developed and developed countries, the 15 developed countries are all the last 12 but Portugal, plus Australia, Finland, Ireland, and New Zealand.

and the others because of large deviations from predicted values. The result of excluding these countries in the simple linear regression was to increase the regression coefficient of C_m (from .06 to .10, or by two-thirds) and to reduce its standard error sharply. The same treatment of the sample with log-linear regression, equation (2) of part B, leads to an even larger increase in the coefficient (from .25 to .38, or about 50 percent), but to a very small fall in the standard error. The computed F value for the two explanatory variables considered jointly increases from 4.64 in equation (1) to 10.63 in equation (3) of part B, as one would expect when a sample is "trimmed" of its outliers.

The net result of these reexaminations is to suggest that V might vary among countries, and that a dummy for V, applied to the outliers in the full sample, might shed light on V. This proved to be a false hope, as some reflection might show. The importance of the constant term in all equations and the presence of a theoretically impossible sign in the multiple regressions suggest that the model is seriously mis-specified. Professor Massell's most recent paper[8] offers strong confirmation of this hypothesis. The equations fit better than any prior estimates, and all estimated coefficients have the right sign. A continued improvement due to "trimming" the small countries again suggests that these observations have a non-separable V.

Various ad hoc hypotheses have been put forward in the literature to explain the "weakness" of estimated regressions. They can be tested on the available data, though rejection is not complete because the tests accept a mis-specified model essentially. The hypotheses are: (a) that the most "concentrated" traders exhibit a clearer relation than do the others; (b) that the less developed countries (LDC's) show a clearer relation than do the developed ones (DC's).

Table 8 makes it clear that neither of these hypotheses agrees with Massell's data. The twelve "most concentrated" show no significant relation at all. One might note that this group includes six of Massell's eight outliers. The fifteen DC's and thirteen LDC's in the sample both show significantly positive coefficients, and Chow's test for a difference between the coefficients does not reject the hypothesis that the true slopes are in fact equal.

TABLE 8

Regression Results

Dependent variable		C_m Independent variable (standard error in parentheses)	t-value
Most concentrated 12 countries	I	−.09751 (.17227)	−.56602
Next 24 countries	I	.15168 (.051791)	2.92897
Pooled sample (28 countries)	I	.10233 (.02565)	3.98931
15 DC's	I	.18591 (.08181)	2.27258
13 LDC's	I	.07941 (.03368)	2.35767

CONCLUSION

A mathematical analysis of the theory of instability indices leads to the conclusion that measured instability is essentially a measure of the coefficient of variation of export sales about their trend. The theory goes on to show that there need not actually be a functional relation between measured instability and measured concentration. If such a relation does exist, it should generate a log-linear regression with positive coefficients. The most important aspect of the theory for empirical work is that there must be a measure of instability partly uncorrelated with concentration indices, measurable independently of them, and used as an explanatory variable. If such a measure is omitted from the estimating equation, the model is misspecified and the coefficients will be biased. Finally, independence among residuals in export time-series leads to a special log-linear form with coefficients equal to unity.

A study of African data shows that the hypothesis of independence is not acceptable. The estimated empirical coefficients of regression equations need not cluster around unity. Reexamination of earlier studies by Massell shows that the log-linear form does improve the fit of the equations and tends to give significant coefficients. The omission of an independent instability estimator shows in a comparatively low F-statistic for the coefficients of the regression (other than the constant term, which is always significant). The constant term in these equations tends to explain a lot.

Finally, it may be guessed, from the possibility of "trimming" samples to improve the fit, that a minority of countries belong to a type where instability and concentration are simply not related. The policy conclusion of all this remains from the early discussions: diversification into comparatively stable export markets must help the stability of the diversifying country.

NOTES

1. Joseph Coppock, *International Economic Instability* (New York: McGraw-Hill, 1962).
2. These studies were: M. Michaely, *Concentration in International Trade* (Amsterdam: North-Holland Press, 1962); B. F. Massell, "Export Concentration and Export Earnings," *American Economic Review* 54:2 (March 1964), p. 47; A. I. MacBean, *Export Instability and Economic Development* (Cambridge, Mass.: Harvard University Press, 1966).
3. All these statements can be verified in MacBean, *Export Instability*, pp. 34–45.
4. The mathematical and statistical details will be published elsewhere.
5. The significant points of r are tabled in Fisher and Yates, *Statistical Tables for Use in Biological, Agricultural and Medical Research* (Edinburgh: Oliver and Boyd, 1942).
6. Eight tables showing the principal components of variance of exports for the countries listed in Table 5 are available from the author upon request.
7. B. F. Massell, "Export Instability and Concentration: A Re-examination" (October 1968), and "Export Instability and Economic Structure" (November 1968), both unpublished. I owe thanks to Professor Massell for allowing me to see these essays.
8. "Export Instability and Economic Structure."

Chapter 16

Trade as an Engine of Growth: The Ivory Coast

Virginia L. Galbraith

> Not only has the Ivory Coast reached the second stage of growth, according to the classification of Rostow, but she has passed it, and she has already entered the third stage, that of "demarrage," of the takeoff.
>
> M. Pierre Roques, President-Director General,
> International Bank of West Africa

In the controversy among economists, national planners, aid officers, and United Nations officials over the role of foreign trade in developing national economies, the successful plan of the Ivory Coast has been largely ignored. Yet here is a country which has with full intent and purpose pursued its comparative advantage and has proved beyond doubt that foreign trade can act as a powerful engine for growth.

The Ivory Coast's Development Plan for 1960–70 was written in 1962 by Father J. L. Fyot, a Jesuit priest of the *Institut pour le Développement Economique et Social* in Abidjan, under the supervision of the then Finance Minister Saller and with the participation of the present Minister of Planning Diawara. International Bank officials have characterized this plan as one of the most realistic and the result achieved under it one of the most impressive seen in either Africa or Latin America. The Plan's success is indicated by the fact that in its first six years its objectives were either met or surpassed. The Plan's target rate of growth for gross domestic product was 7.2 percent for 1960–65. The actual growth rate was 10 percent annually. Per-capita income grew by over 7 percent.

The Plan is based firmly on an export drive in two stages. The first stage called for an increase in the volume of traditional agricultural exports aimed at increasing foreign exchange earnings and incomes of peasant farmers from whom domestic savings could be extracted for domestic public investment. The second stage calls for diversification of agricultural exports and increased processing of products for export to raise the value-added content. By 1965 the first stage had been accomplished. The period 1965–70 is viewed as a pause in the economy while it is prepared by public and private investment to enter the second stage of export-led growth. During the pause the planners revised downward the target rate of growth to 5.9 percent.

"TAKEOFF" – 1960–65

To determine whether or not Ivory Coast has achieved a position leading to self-sustaining growth, we have put it to the test developed by Chenery and Strout.[1] This model sets up three criteria for judging economic performance: an investment criterion, a savings criterion, and a trade criterion. The

TABLE 1

Indicators of Self-sustaining Growth 1960–65, Ivory Coast

Capital Inflow	*Investment performance*			*Saving performance*		*Trade performance*			*Growth in GDP*
F_0/V_0	$k\bar{r}$	I_0/V_0	i	α_0	α'	E_0/m_0	ϵ	u'/u_0	r
.025	.103	.159	.197	.192	.198	1.22	.128	1.014	.101

Symbols:
r = GDP growth rate
$k\bar{r}$ = ratio of investment to GDP needed for 7.2 percent growth rate
I_0/V_0 = ratio of investment to GDP
i = rate of growth of investment
α_0 = ratio of savings to GDP[a]
α' = marginal savings/GDP ratio[b]
E_0/m_0 = ratio of export to import
ϵ = export growth rate
u'/u_0 = ratio of marginal to average import/GDP coefficients
F_0/V_0 = ratio of capital inflow to GDP[c]

All indicators average annual 1960–65 except:
[a] omits 1964
[b] omits 1964–65
[c] annual average 1963–65

relationships among the economic parameters for Ivory Coast were calculated as described in Table 1.

The investment criterion states that in the first phase of growth, the rate of growth of investment must be greater than the target rate of growth. Thereafter, the ratio of investment to Gross Domestic Product (GDP) must be able to sustain the target rate of growth.

$$I/V \geq k\bar{r} \tag{1}$$

Ivory Coast, with a target rate of growth of 7.2 percent, met the investment criterion.

$$.159 > .103$$

The incremental capital-output ratio (k) was only 1.43, indicating that increments to output were obtained by labor-intensive techniques. This was possible because the largest absolute increments to output came from the agricultural sector where, by drawing in a substantial number of laborers from neighboring countries, conditions for growth with an unlimited supply of labor were created. This feature of Ivory Coast's growth will be discussed at greater length below.

According to Chenery and Strout's savings criterion "the marginal savings rate must be greater than the target investment rate unless the average rate of saving is already above this level."[2] Working with gross domestic product (GDP), rather than gross national product (GNP), so that total resources available to the country are considered,[3] we find, in appraising Ivory Coast's performance that it has easily met this criterion for self-sustaining growth.[4]

$$\alpha' \geq k\bar{r} \tag{2}$$

The average savings rate is nearly identical with the marginal rate. Ivory Coast met this criterion for growth.

$$.198 > .103$$

The trade criterion calls for either the growth of exports to exceed the target rate of growth of GDP or else the marginal import ratio must be reduced below the average import ratio of the base year.

$$\frac{u'}{u_0} \geq \frac{(E_0/m_0)(1+\epsilon)^P - 1}{(1+\bar{r})^P - 1} \qquad (3)$$

Again, Ivory Coast meets the test:

$$1.01 < 2.95$$

The growth of exports (.128) exceeded $k\bar{r}$ (.103) while the marginal import ratio (.225) was kept nearly the same as the average ratio in 1960. Hence, even though the income elasticity of imports was unity, the growth rate of exports was sufficiently large to allow a comfortable trade account.

Ivory Coast used its traditional exports to increase its rate of growth of output. It successfully channeled increments to income into domestic savings and avoided both domestic inflation and balance-of-payments difficulties. Its increased savings were, for the most part, channeled into public investment in infrastructure and the agricultural sector. Private investment was responsible for the manufacturing and service sectors. We turn now to an explanation of how this success was achieved.

EXPORT-LED GROWTH

Ivory Coast, like most newly independent African states, is an agricultural economy with a low ratio of capital and labor to land. Its traditional exports are coffee and cocoa, which enjoyed preferences in French markets and were sold at prices guaranteed above world levels. Two facts, however, limited this arrangement as a source of growth for Ivory Coast. First, French markets for coffee and cocoa were growing slowly and France was unwilling to take increasing amounts of these commodities at high guaranteed prices. Second, the Agreement of Yaoundé between the European Economic Community and the eighteen Associated African States called for dismantling the French price-support system and generalizing preferential entry to all six of the Community members. If Ivory Coast was to enjoy export-led growth, it was incumbent on her to seek new markets for her traditional exports. France encouraged and, indeed, helped to finance this effort. In addition, Ivory Coast had to make as certain as possible that limitations on the supply side did not inhibit the export drive.

Turning to the demand side first, Ivory Coast ran into some luck. The United States was rapidly expanding its demand for soluble coffee, which for reasons of both taste and cost can be made with robusta type beans grown in Ivory Coast. Brazil, acting under terms of the International Coffee Agreement, bore the brunt of stockpiling arabica types, which resulted in a drop in volume of her exports of coffee and in small annual rises in price. The price differential between the two types of coffee, plus the fact that Ivory Coast was a relatively small producer in world markets and without quota restrictions under the Coffee Agreement until 1962, allowed Ivory Coast to move into an expanding market. In volume, Ivory Coast nearly doubled its coffee sales to the United States while those to France stabilized between 1960–66. France remained the biggest customer but took a decreasing proportion of Ivory Coast's coffee. In value terms, Ivory Coast again ran into luck between 1962 and 1965 as robusta prices rose in New York, mainly because of poor harvests in Brazil. This allowed France in July 1964 (sooner than necessary under the EEC agreement) to abolish quotas and guaranteed prices for Ivoirien coffee. In 1965, for the first time, Ivory Coast had to limit its production of coffee and face up to its own importance in the world coffee market. The government ordered production stabilized at 250,000–300,000 tons a year and stated that new plantings would be destroyed.

Turning to the supply side, production of coffee rose from 131,485 tons in the harvest of 1959–60 to 272,566 tons harvested in 1965–66. Ivory Coast went from supplying 4 percent of the world's exportable coffee in 1959–60 to 8 percent between 1963–66. It also gained ground as a supplier of African coffee.

This impressive increase in supply was achieved by price incentives to peasant farmers who increased acreage planted to coffee and increased productivity per acre. The interesting fact here is that government investment in the agricultural sector lagged well behind the Plan's target. The ratio of realization of investment in the public sector as a whole for 1960–66 was 46 percent of its 1960 target, but in agriculture the ratio was only 27 percent.[5] How can one account for increases in agricultural output (not coffee alone) of the magnitude indicated and the disappointing realization of public investment in agriculture? We can best explain this paradox by turning to Lewis' model of growth with unlimited supplies of labor.[6] This model may appear at first glance to be the least useful in explaining growth in an African country the size of France but with a population of only 3.8 millions. However, in the initial growth of Ivory Coast, wages in the agricultural sector were kept down to a subsistence level by a vast influx of foreign workers from Upper Volta, Mali, Guinea, Dahomey, and Ghana. No one knows the numbers of these workers, but the Ministry of Planning estimated that in 1965 there were 360,000 Africans living temporarily in Ivory Coast, of whom 220,000 were males employed in agriculture. Working on their own account in agriculture were 1,650,000 Ivoiriens and other Africans living permanently in Ivory Coast. This estimate takes no account, furthermore, of large numbers of Africans who live close enough to the border of Ivory Coast to commute back and forth to work in its agricultural sector.

What seems to have happened, then, is something like this. Between 1960 and 1965 the Ivoirien government increased the absolute price of coffee paid to the producer (although this price fell as a percentage of export prices of coffee) sufficiently to induce him to expand supply in the traditional way, by labor-intensive means. Workers came from surrounding countries, lured by prospects of money wages denied them in their own countries. The supply of workers was sufficient to hold real wages constant. There was, however, a sizeable amount of investment in agriculture, and technical progress did take place. Instead of these gains in productivity going into increasing wages, they were divided between the peasant farmer, as higher prices for his crop, and the government, as the difference between the export price of the crop and that paid to the farmer. This distribution of income, as we shall see shortly, provided the domestic savings from which investment could take place. The central fact is that the growth of output in agriculture was labor-intensive with a sufficiently elastic supply of workers to allow an income distribution which favored savings. With a large foreign trade sector the government was well situated to take a large percentage of marginal income without creating disincentives to output.[7]

We have described growth in the agricultural sector by looking at demand and supply of coffee, Ivory Coast's most important crop and export. However, similar expansion occurred in other agricultural products. Some space must be given here to the development of timber and wood products as an export. Between 1960 and 1965 Ivory Coast exports of wood grew from 443,000 to 1,566,000 metric tons. Moreover, by 1965 there were sixty sawmills transforming 700,000 metric tons. Ivory Coast quickly became the chief supplier of tropical woods to West Germany. Private capital moved in to develop this industry further by adding facilities for pulp. Again Ivory Coast exploited its comparative advantage for export-led growth.

We turn now to the second step taken to achieve self-sustaining growth: channeling the increments to income into increased savings and investment.

SAVINGS AND INVESTMENT

Ivory Coast, like all African countries, relies heavily on indirect taxes for government revenues, with import duties and export taxes accounting for 57 percent of its revenue. A value-added tax modeled after the French version accounts for another 20 percent of revenue.[8]

Import duties and value-added taxes serve to restrain imports and to transfer income from consumers to government. A further effect is to give priorities to imports for development purposes by differentiating duties. The fact that the income elasticity of imports has been held down to one attests to the successful manipulation of these taxes by Ivory Coast.

Export taxes are essentially income taxes on Ivoirien farmers. Table 2 shows for the case of coffee how the government, in the four years for which these data are available, extracted savings from coffee producers and still provided incentives to farmers. A slower rate of growth during the initial export drive would have made it difficult to achieve both revenue for the government and incentives for farmers.

The structure of taxes as well as the level of rates made it possible for the proportion of government receipts to national income to rise automatically as income rose in Ivory Coast. The current budgetary surplus rose from 6.45 billion CFA

TABLE 2

Exports of Coffee and Prices Received by Government and Producer

Year	*Volume of exports (thousand tons)*	*Price, f.o.b. Abidjan (CFA francs per kilo)*	*Price paid to producer (CFA francs per kilo*	*Percent of price f.o.b. paid to producer*
1960	149	—	—	—
1961	156	—	—	—
1962	143	133	80	60
1963	182	134	80	60
1964	204	155	90	58
1965	246	139	75	54

francs in 1960 to 16.03 in 1965. The total current budgetary surplus for 1960–65 was 58.66 billion CFA francs compared to total capital expenditures by the Ivoirien government of 78.42 billion CFA francs (Table 3). Foreign grants, mainly from France, totaled 14.94 billion CFA francs for the same period. The deficit between domestic public savings plus grants and public capital expenditures was only 4.82 billion CFA francs

TABLE 3

Government Savings and Investments (billions of CFAF)

	1960	*1961*	*1962*	*1963*	*1964*	*1965*	*Total period 1960–65*
Total revenue of the central government	22.96	28.41	30.75	33.25	42.53	46.61	204.51
Total current expenditures	*16.51*	*20.51*	*23.99*	*26.27*	*27.99*	*30.58*	*145.85*
Total savings of the central government	*6.45*	*7.90*	*6.76*	*6.98*	*14.54*	*16.03*	*58.66*
Total investments of the central government	9.86	11.09	10.92	11.14	17.79	17.62	78.42
Savings gap: Total (public)	3.41	3.19	4.16	4.16	3.25	1.59	19.76
As percent of total investments	*35%*	*29%*	*38%*	*37%*	*19%*	*10%*	*25%*

NOTE: Based on official data of Ivory Coast.

made up of loans and supplier credits. The amount of self-financed public investment is impressive in a country beginning its development. Ivory Coast overachieved its public investment targets in all categories of economic infrastructure, general education, health, and other social investments. Only in agriculture, as noted above, did investment fall short of target. However, this was more likely a failure due to overestimating the need for capital in agriculture to achieve growth than a failure of realization.

Thanks to Ivory Coast's liberal government, substantial amounts of foreign private savings have gone into private investment in the country. In order to encourage these investments, Ivory Coast has a number of fiscal incentives. First it has the *régime fiscal de longue durée* which provides for stabilizing all tax rates at the rate in effect when the enterprise is approved for an extended number of years, for exemption from changes in assessment or collection procedures, and for exemption from new taxes.[9] Second, Ivory Coast has entered into a number of Enterprise Agreements provided for in the CFA system. These agreements for new investment projects must be approved by the Ministers of Finance and Planning and must follow the priorities of the Plan. Although these agreements carry the same fiscal incentives as in the first case above, they go further by giving nondiscrimination and juridical guarantees, as well as guarantees for repatriation of capital and profits, and remission of import duties on capital goods and raw materials necessary to the enterprise. In addition, where called for, an enterprise may be exempted from 50 percent of export duties for ten years and given a tax holiday from income taxes for five years. The latter two devices are especially useful in encouraging investment in agricultural exports.

All the Enterprise Agreements implement Ivory Coast's Plan. They range from an agreement with Société Africain de Cacaos to expand cocoa exports to one with the Intercontinental Hotel Chain to develop a hotel-tourist complex in Abidjan to recent agreements for paper and cellulose factories to process timber.

Ivory Coast, it can be concluded, has been able both to extract domestic savings and to attract foreign private investment. Its domestic savings have not been squandered in current expenditures by government but rather have gone into public investment. Where short-falls in investment have occurred, the results have not impeded growth.

BALANCE OF TRADE AND PAYMENTS

Ivory Coast's balance of trade has consistently remained in surplus since 1960. Furthermore, annual increments to exports were larger than increments to imports, 1960–65, resulting in increasing surpluses on trade account. These were achieved despite a rise of about 25 percent in import prices. The composition of imports changed in favor of equipment goods, raw materials, and energy, and against foodstuffs and finished products for consumption.

Despite this excellent performance on trade account, Ivory Coast's current account shows sizeable deficits. Repatriated earnings from investment and private transfers abroad are sufficiently large to wipe out the trade surplus. Nearly two-thirds of investment income repatriated went to France and about one-half of private transfers were to France, the remainder being African workers' remittances. The size of these deficits can be appreciated by examining Ivory Coast's 1964 balance-of-payments with France.[10] Interest and dividends to France totaled 3.6 billion CFA francs and private transfers to France were 3.5 billion, a total of 7.1 billion CFA francs. By contrast, 3.6 billion CFA francs came from France as private long-term capital and 1.5 billion were government transfers from France. Ivory Coast paid out some two billion more CFA francs to France than it received in private investment and government aid. Nevertheless, the total balance on capital accounts was sufficient to overcome the deficits on current account.

The size of repatriated earnings and capital transfers to France obviously plagues Ivory Coast's balance-of-payments. In 1963, the government took steps to discourage repatriation of profits. It instituted the National Investment Fund which requires that 10 percent of business profits and 16 percent of net real estate revenue be put into NIF certificates which are reimbursable by several methods, the most important being local investment. Holders of these certificates are reimbursed upon approval of a proposed investment for at least three times the amount of the certificate and of a minimum size. In 1963, only about 20 percent of the certificates were used for local investment but by 1965 over 40 percent were being used in this way. Unless this method or new ones are successful, Ivory Coast will continue to be dependent on growth of private long-term investment and on aid from abroad to make up for its current payments to France and its transfers to French private citizens. So far, fortunately, private investment continues to expand (except for a small dip in 1965) and French grants and loans are stable.

The United States, although second only to France as a trading partner of Ivory Coast, has invested very little in the country. However, since 1965 American banks have acquired interests in the financial sector and the Ivoirien government hopes that there will be a large expansion of American participation in Ivory Coast's economy. This, along with growing investments from West Germany and aid from the European Economic Community, would reduce the dependency on France.

THE SECOND PHASE OF GROWTH: DIVERSIFICATION

The first phase of Ivory Coast's Plan for export-led growth is complete and was, for the most part, a success. The second phase now begun calls for well-planned agricultural diversification to end dependence on coffee and cocoa. Both public and private investment are being relied on to expand output and exports. Two products in particular are being developed: palm oil and wood.[11]

Since 1964 the government, with European aid, has financed the development of 38,500 hectares for oil palm plantations. It expects to raise this to 78,000 by 1970. To process this product, the government hopes to enter into an enterprise agreement for oil palm crushing plants. This would be in line with Ivory Coast's emphasis on processing its agricultural products to add value to its exports. (There are six coffee-processing plants in Abidjan.) Since forecasts by the EEC indicate future expansion in world demand for oils, and since Ivory Coast has a comparative advantage in palm oils, this part of the Plan is sound and is going well. Forward linkages are being promoted.

On the other hand, the Plan's expansion of wood products has encountered serious obstacles. Between 1960 and 1966, Ivory Coast tripled the value of its exports of wood. More importantly, local industry processed 33 percent of total production in 1966 as compared to only 17.4 percent in 1964. In 1966 the number of sawmills went from sixty-two to seventy and three new companies signed enterprise agreements for further processing of wood. But the rate of exploitation of timber appears to have been excessive and reforestation was insufficient. In 1965 and 1966 the government issued a series of decrees aimed at a new forestry policy. For the first time, Ivory Coast tried to rationalize use of its timber resources by classifying its forest lands, defining rights to their use, and establishing forms of exploitation. The government hopes to regulate exploitation in conformity with the objectives of the Plan by fixing the volume of cuttings and by assigning quotas to local industry. New permits to cut will be granted only if investment furthers concentration and integration of the wood industry. Uncontrolled cutting by individuals who practiced no reforestation made it essential for Ivory Coast to adopt this forestry policy. But greater concentration and integrated companies will afford lower costs as well. Recent studies by the FAO indicate that there is great opportunity for African nations to export pulp and paper as well as to use it for future domestic needs.[12] At the present time, twenty companies account for 80 percent of exports of undressed timber.

As a result of investment in primary products which can be economically processed, Ivory Coast expects exports of transformed products to make up 50 percent of all exports by 1975. Externalities from this sector's growth will be exploited. The major externality will be widening of the internal market, making production for domestic consumption profitable. Plants of efficient size to produce consumers' goods would be able to compete on a cost basis with imports. Thus the development of import substitutes would take place as a natural consequence of profitability rather than as forced industrialization in a protected market. In this regard, it should be noted that no heavy industry is planned in Ivory Coast. It intends to trade for those products in which it has no comparative advantage.

The promotion of new high-valued exports with growing

international demand, and of domestic substitutes for imports with high domestic income elasticities, could avoid balance-of-payments difficulties in the future. Ivory Coast's Plan calls for exports to grow at a 7.5 percent annual rate between 1965–70 and imports by 6.6 annually. However, between 1970–75 the annual rate of export growth is expected to slow down to 5 percent and of import growth to 4.5 percent. If these targets are met, the trade balance would be twenty-four billion CFA francs in 1970 and thirty-three billion CFA francs in 1975. Repatriated earnings and private transfers can be expected to grow more slowly as profitability of investment in Ivory Coast increases. This strategy for development is sound. It is not unrealistic in its assessment of demand and supply parameters. This does not mean, however, that barriers to its achievement do not exist. We refer to our thesis accounting for Ivory Coast's progress so far: rapid export growth with unlimited supplies of labor.

IMMIGRATION

Without the immigration and temporary migration of neighboring Africans to work as unskilled laborers in agriculture, Ivory Coast could not have expanded its total production of exports at the rate it did. Furthermore, real wages would have increased well above rural subsistence levels had Ivory Coast relied on its own supply of labor. This, in turn, would have distributed more of the gains in income to consumption rather than to public savings. Investment for development purposes would have been curtailed.

There are, however, costs as well as benefits from immigration. The savings effect of immigration, which we have stressed so far in Ivory Coast's early growth, can be outweighed by an investment effect from immigration. As more immigrants swell a population, investment of resources to care for them rises. Moreover, many forms of investment required for their care carry high incremental capital-output ratios, such as housing in cities. Therefore, larger amounts of savings would have to be diverted to investment of this type and output per unit of investment could be expected to fall.

What we have in mind here is a concept of an optimal immigration rate. This optimum may be solved for by relating rates of growth of income and rates of growth of immigration. At some rate of growth of the latter, the rate of growth of income reaches a maximum, after which it falls. Income per capita would reach a peak before the turning point of the income growth. Therefore, in terms of Ivoirien welfare, immigration would at some point have to be restricted.[13]

Where immigrants go is as important as their numbers to Ivory Coast. To the extent that immigrants replace Ivoiriens in rural areas who migrate to cities, rural wages are kept down and the savings effect is strong. But immigrants going to cities require a much greater amount of investment per head than in the rural sector, given African living conditions. Hence, immigration to cities probably affects investment more than savings. Data from the 1965 study of population show that there is a concentration of foreigners in the south of the Ivory Coast and especially in the urban environs of Abidjan. Half of all foreign-born persons resided in 1965 in the southern urban department.

TABLE 4

Distribution by Department and Place of Residence of Persons by Foreign Origin (in thousands)

Department	*Rural*	*Urban*	*Total*
East	22	17	39
Center	66	81	147
Center-West	26	28	54
North	20	28	48
West	36	22	58
South (except Abidjan)	100	70	170
Abidjan	—	154	154
TOTAL	270	400	670

SOURCE : Côte d'Ivoire, *Population*, Études régionales 1962–65, Ministère du Plan, p. 159.

The implications of immigration and rural-urban migration for Ivory Coast's future welfare cannot be probed in this short paper. However, some possible effects may be indicated. The second phase of the plan for development, as we have noted above, leans heavily on diversification of exports and forward linkages of industry. The planting of new strains of short-statured and high-yielding palm trees by the government will bring into agriculture a crop with higher productivity per unit of land and per unit of labor than traditional products. Since the government is parceling out this newly planted land into family-sized farms to Ivoiriens, rural prosperity of peasants can be expected to grow, as in the past. Migrant labor will still be needed, but not in the numbers of the past. Settlement on this land by foreigners will be impossible, thus acting as a depressant to immigration. Since the new oil palms require less labor, increments to incomes from this source should raise per-capita peasant incomes and favor peasant savings. Reduction in immigration, and the relative increase in attractiveness of rural employment, should also reduce investment requirements. In this respect, the plan to open up the southwest of the country to new industry linked to processing agricultural inputs will take the strain off the cities, especially Abidjan, and ameliorate the high cost of immigrants (and hopefully rural migrants). One would have to know a great deal more about patterns of movement of people in the Ivory Coast before any precise assessment of these benefits and costs of immigration could be undertaken.

CONCLUSION

At the beginning of this paper we saw that the incremental capital-output ratio for Ivory Coast was relatively low during its first phase of growth. This cannot continue. New types of investment in industry and agriculture, as well as the need for investment in social overhead, will substantially raise the incremental capital-output ratio. For this reason, the Plan has lowered the target rate of growth from 7.2 percent between 1960 and 1965 to 6.2 percent for 1970–75 and calls for the ratio of gross investment to gross domestic product to reach 20 percent by 1970. The export sector is planned to lead this growth but with significant changes from the earlier export-led growth. We quote from the working paper on the new Plan.

> Exports will go from 47 billion (CFA) francs in 1960 (prices 1965) to 220.7 billions in 1980. They will thus

multiply by 4.7 in twenty years, an average annual rate of increase of 8 percent.

These results will be possible only at the price of profound changes in the internal structure of exports during this period. The latter will result, on the one hand, from a policy of diversification of crops which will begin to bear fruit at the beginning of 1970 and, on the other hand, from the development of industrial production oriented toward exterior markets . . . Briefly, while in 1960 only 11 percent of exports were industrially processed, nearly one half of them will have gone through factories in 1980.[14]

The second phase of growth no longer depends on exports based on an infinite supply of labor, but on exports based on processing of a variety of materials in which Ivory Coast has a comparative advantage.

However, much will depend on the development of social and economic conditions in surrounding countries. The Ivoirien demand for immigrant labor should decline; but, if present economic trends continue, the potential supply of immigrants is likely to increase. This imbalance could create tensions and jealousies within the area which might submerge the growth of per-capita income in the Ivory Coast under floods of unwanted immigrants.

NOTES

1. H. B. Chenery and A. M. Strout, "Foreign Assistance and Economic Development," *American Economic Review* 56:4 (September 1966), pp. 679–733. All data on Ivory Coast are from *Situation économique de la Côte d'Ivoire*, 1964, and *Projet de Loi Plan, 1967–69, Rapport de Présentation.*
2. Chenery and Strout, "Foreign Assistance," p. 705.
3. GDP differs from GNP in that the latter consists of output and income attributable to the *nationals* of a country while the former refers to that attributable to *residents*. In most less-developed economies, part of the GDP is produced with the help of foreign-owned factors of production. Income attributable to such factors must be deducted from GDP in calculating GNP. In Ivory Coast the difference is large because of the substantial economic role of French nationals.
4. The marginal savings ratio out of GDP has been calculated here. This relates increments in savings by nationals and foreign factor-suppliers to increments in GDP. If, however, the marginal savings ratio out of

GNP had been calculated (relating increments in saving by nationals only to increments in GNP), the marginal savings rate (α') would be .099, which falls just short of meeting the Chenery-Strout criterion. This indicates that Ivory Coast's growth has been quite dependent upon French investment and other factor inputs. This dependence, however, has been decreasing. This feature of Ivory Coast's growth is discussed further in the subsequent section on the balance of payments.

5. Total value of investment, however, was exceeded only by buildings and road and bridges construction. Out of a total investment of 93.2 billion CFA francs, agriculture accounted for 11.1 billion CFA francs, 1960–66.
6. Lewis, W. A., "Economic Development with Unlimited Supplies of Labour," *The Manchester School* 22:2 (May 1954), pp. 139–91.
7. The case of Ivory Coast is similar to that of postwar Western Europe where migration to the north kept down real wages and allowed the distribution of income to favor capitalist savers. See Charles P. Kindleberger, *Europe's Postwar Growth: The Role of Labor Supply* (Cambridge, Mass.: Harvard University Press, 1967).
8. For a description of Ivory Coast's tax systems, see A. Abdel-Rahman, "The Revenue Structure of the CFA Countries," *IMF Staff Papers* 12:1 (March 1965).
9. For a full description of this and other features of Ivory Coast's tax incentives to investment see George C. Lent, "Tax Incentives for Investment in Developing Countries," *IMF Staff Papers* 14:2 (July 1967).
10. Ministère de l'Économie et des Finances, République de Côte d'Ivoire; *Balance des Paiements*, 1964. Tableau B, Partie 1 et 2.
11. The discussion which follows owes its facts to *Rapport d'Activité 1966*, Banque Centrale des États de l'Afrique de l'Ouest, pp. 183–84 and 190–93.
12. United Nations Food and Agriculture Organization, *Pulp and Paper Development in Africa and the Near East*, Rome, 1966, Secretariat Paper 5.
13. Data to forecast the turning point of benefit vs. cost of immigration are poor and our attempt to do so is worth only a footnote. To obtain annual numbers of immigrants we interpolated at an increasing rate the foreign-born from the census of 1960 to 1965. Plotting the rates of growth of GDP against the rates of growth of immigrants, we fitted a least-squares parabola. The turning point was an annual immigration rate of 6.5 percent, which was reached in our interpolated figures in 1963–64. However, due to wide fluctuations, the standard error for the GDP variable was 5.569. Our interpolated immigration variable had a standard error of .023.
14. *Plan Quinquennial de Développement, 1971–75*, Document de Travail à l'usage des Commissions de *Planification*, Ministère du Plan, République de Côte d'Ivoire, pp. 18, 19.

Chapter 17

East African Economic Cooperation: The Impact on a Less-Developed Participant

Idrian N. Resnick

Economic integration among the three East African countries of Kenya, Uganda, and Tanzania[1] has been occurring since the second decade of this century. However, there was no formal treaty governing the relationships among the members until December 1967, when the *Treaty for East African Cooperation*[2] came into force. It is a curiosity of the history of integration that this treaty provides for an apparent increase in trade restrictions[3] among integrating parties. The *raison d'être* for these provisions is correction of an imbalance between Kenya, on the one hand, and Tanzania and Uganda, on the other, with respect to the net benefits of the common market. The chief aim is to increase radically the latter's share in East African manufacturing output and trade. This goal and the use of restrictions to accomplish it raises serious theoretical questions which, while they have not been neglected in the literature on integration, need to be examined carefully in relation to East Africa.

Consequently, after the presentation of background material on the history of the East African Common Market and the economic relationships among the three countries, the theoretical implications of the treaty will be explored. Finally the consequences of the restrictive aspects of the treaty will be examined with respect to Tanzania, particular emphasis being placed on their effects on interterritorial trade.[4]

Tanzania is the focus of the paper because it was most critical of the pre-treaty arrangements, and the new restrictive measures were designed mainly to placate Tanzania.

BACKGROUND

As early as 1917 Kenya and Uganda were united in a free trade area to which Tanganyika was joined in 1923. In 1927 the three territories became a customs union, although a common external tariff had been adopted in 1922.[5] In general, this tariff has been maintained as a unified barrier, although members were never formally obligated to maintain the same rates against foreign imports. In addition to the common tariff, relatively free movement of capital, and, to a lesser extent labor, takes place within East Africa and the three countries maintain broadly the same tax structure. Until 1965 a common currency, the East African shilling, was used in these countries – as well as in Aden and Zanzibar – and the East African Currency Board was the central monetary authority for the area. From 1926 to 1948 various services common to the three countries evolved under joint control and in the latter year these came under the formal auspices of the East African High Commission (now known as the East African Common Services Organization).[6]

From the early days of the common market there was a growth of industry in Kenya, which sold to the entire market under the protection of the common tariff. Owing to the presence of a relatively large white settler class in Kenya, the favorable location of its capitol Nairobi with respect to the rest of the market, a vigorous colonial government receptive to the wishes of the settler class, and a higher level of purchasing power in the monetary sector than in the other two territories, East African industrial growth occurred almost exclusively in Kenya until the later part of the 1950s. In 1948 industrial licensing was introduced and resulted in the granting of exclusive rights of production in East Africa to single firms, most of them located in Kenya.[7]

During the 1950s Tanganyika and Uganda reopened a discussion which had lain dormant since the 1920s[8] concerning their losses from membership in the market. They argued that they lost customs revenues by importing goods from Kenya rather than from the rest of the world, tax flexibility through the necessity of avoiding differentials in corporate taxes, and lost industrialization opportunities because protected Kenya industries had precluded the possibilities of the most obvious import substitutes.[9]

As a result of the controversy, two attempts were made before the introduction of the Treaty in 1967 to create a mechanism which would alleviate some of the losses on the part of Uganda and Tanganyika. In 1961, following the recommendations of the Raisman Commission,[10] a scheme was worked out to redistribute tax revenues to provide compensation for loss of customs revenues.[11] In 1964 the Kampala Agreement[12] was drawn up with the aim of redressing some of the imbalances existing in the market. Specifically, the agreement was designed to decrease the trade deficits between Tanzania and Uganda, on the one hand, and Kenya, on the other, and to correct the imbalance of industrial activity. This was to be accomplished by granting monopolies in the production of certain products to each country and by permitting the introduction of interterritorial quotas to protect infant industries. The agreement failed because it was never ratified by Kenya[13] and because it attacked only the question of industrial production, ignoring the many other problems of integration which were undermining cooperation.[14]

Before examining the third attempt (the 1967 Treaty) to put economic integration on a sound footing in East Africa, it is desirable to review briefly the context within which cooperation has been taking place.

In many ways the three East African economies are quite similar. They have roughly similar population sizes (between eight and twelve million), their per-capita incomes are low and about the same (£24–£31 per annum), they rely heavily on exports of primary products, and have experienced average growth rates in monetary GDP (gross domestic product) of between 5 and 6 percent per year since 1960.

However, there are significant differences among the three countries, several of which have led to tension during the past ten years, culminating in the "corrective" measures embodied in the 1967 Treaty. Table 1 presents some of these differences.

The main bone of contention centers around manufactures; in 1965 Kenya produced twice the value of Uganda and three times that of Tanzania. Kenya's total manufactured exports were not extraordinarily greater than those of its common market partners,[15] but its interterritorial manufactured exports were more than double Uganda's, and nearly six times Tanzania's, and Tanzania and Uganda purchased a much larger proportion (almost double) of their manufactured imports

TABLE 1

East Africa: Comparative Economic Data 1965 and 1966
(£ million)

	1965		
Economic Indicators	*Tanzania*	*Kenya*	*Ugand*
Population (in millions)	10.2	9.4	7.6
Monetary gross domestic product	197.5	222.3	150.8
Per-capita gross domestic product (in £)	24.0	31.0	30.0
Agricultural production[a]	64.9	44.5	59.3
Manufacturing production	11.1	32.0	16.2
Construction	7.9	4.9	4.6
Transport and power	12.7	33.2	9.7
Gross capital formation	41.9	38.2	32.3
Trade	*1966*		
Exports plus re-exports	89.3	92.4	77.5
East African exports	4.6	30.1	10.4
Manufactured exports[b]	12.3	15.8	11.3
to East Africa	2.2	12.5	5.4
Imports[c]	80.7	123.5	60.3
East African imports	16.4	11.1	17.6
Manufactured imports	55.4	77.3	40.0
from East Africa	7.9	6.7	7.4
Trade Balance			
Overall	8.6	-31.1	17.2
East Africa	-11.8	19.0	-7.2

[a] Monetary sector only; also includes livestock, forestry, fishing, and hunting.
[b] SITC Sections 6, 7, and 8.
[c] Includes re-exports and inter-East African exports.

SOURCE: United Republic of Tanzania, *Background to the Budget, 1967–68* (Dar es Salaam: Government Printer, 1967); Republic of Kenya, *Economic Survey 1966* (Nairobi: Ministry of Economic Planning and Development, 1966); United Nations, *Yearbook of National Account Statistics, 1966*, Sales No. E.67, 17:14 (New York: 1967) and East African Common Services Organization, *Annual Trade Report, 1966* (Mombasa: Customs and Excise, 1967).

from East Africa than did Kenya in 1966. However, from 1959 to 1966 Kenya doubled its share of purchases of East African manufactured exports. This represented an increase in import value of more than 500 percent. During the same period, Tanzania expanded its interterritorial manufactured imports 300 percent, but only slightly increased its already large share to 40 percent.[16]

Furthermore, Kenya runs a sizeable overall trade deficit (£31 million in 1966) which is reduced 40 percent by its East African trade surplus. The reverse is true for Tanzania and Uganda.

The level of protection in East Africa has yet to be fully analyzed,[17] but there is some indication that Kenyan exports to the common market enjoy a much higher level of effective protection than do those of Tanzania or Uganda.[18]

TANZANIA AND THE EAST AFRICAN COMMON MARKET

In the aggregate, East Africa is not an important market for Tanzanian exports. Table 2 shows that far less than 10 percent of the country's exports typically go to its common market partners. Although their importance increased after independence, it was not until 1964 that these exports exceeded the proportion of total exports that they attained in 1958. Tanzania's interterritorial exports expanded six-fold between 1954 and 1965. After 1962 there was a rather marked upsurge in interterritorial exports, but in 1966 the trend was sharply reversed. Imports from Kenya and Uganda also declined in 1966 after having increased in importance steadily (with the exception of a slight decline in 1959) from 1955 to 1965.

The importance of interterritorial trade for Tanzania is less than it is for Uganda and Kenya. Uganda has sent about 13 percent of total exports to the East African market and has imported about 29 percent of total imports. This has been relatively constant in recent years. Nearly 80 percent of Uganda's interterritorial exports have gone to Kenya and over 90 percent of such imports have been from Kenya.

Kenya, on the other hand, is closely linked with Uganda and Tanzania from the point of view of export markets (more then 35 percent of its total exports has gone to these two

TABLE 2

Tanzania: Interterritorial Trade 1960–66
(£000)

Year	*Exports to:*		*Total Inter-territorial exports*	*Total exports*[a]	*Total as % of inter-territorial exports*	*Imports from:*		*Total Inter-territorial imports*	*Total imports*[b]	*Total as % of inter-territorial imports*
	Kenya	*Uganda*				*Kenya*	*Uganda*			
1960	1875	450	2325	57148	4.1	7608	1574	9182	46999[c]	19.5
1961	1844	390	2234	50901	4.4	8901	1704	10605	53150	20.0
1962	1954	437	2391	53632	4.5	10017	1669	11686	54864	21.3
1963	2915	508	3423	66976	5.1	10365	1993	12358	56736	21.8
1964	4110	1021	5331	75443	7.1	13299	2403	15702	63599	24.7
1965	4569	1346	5915	68693	8.6	14087	2592	16679	70316	23.7
1966	3806	842	4648	83754	5.5	13282	3120	16407	80658[c]	20.3

SOURCE: East African Common Services Organization, *Annual Trade Report*, 1960–66 (Mombasa, Kenya: East African Customs and Excise).

[a] Domestic exports plus interterritorial exports.

[b] Net imports plus interterritorial imports plus valuation adjustments for charges incurred between off-loading at Mombasa and entry into Tanzania.

[c] Does not include valuation adjustment.

countries), but it buys most of its imports (about 91 percent) from outside East Africa. These import proportions have been fairly constant since 1960, while exports to East Africa became less important after 1963. Kenya exports about the same amount to Tanzania as to Uganda but buys 70 percent of its East African imports from the latter.

Tanzania has imported considerably more from its East African partners than it has exported to them. In fact, while Tanzania experienced export surpluses with respect to its non-East African trade in all years from 1960–66 except 1962, it encountered deficits in interterritorial trade in all seven years; and in 1961 and 1965 these were large enough to turn the external surpluses into overall deficits in commodity trade.

Table 3 shows that Tanzania's interterritorial exports have been composed mainly of food and manufactured goods.[19] Food exports have tended to rise, particularly to Kenya, since 1960 when they were 50 percent of the 1964 level; for the most part these act as supplements to Kenya's food production.[20] Manufactured exports (mainly Section 6), on the other hand, showed a marked expansion after 1962 as new products were introduced in Tanzania which were then exported to Kenya and Uganda. This is primarily a supply, rather than a demand phenomenon.

By comparison, Kenya's interterritorial exports in 1966 showed a surprising similarity in structure to Tanzania's. Food, beverages and tobacco (Sections 0 and 1) accounted for about 30 percent of Kenya's interterritorial exports by value, and manufactured exports (Sections 6–8) represented only 41 percent of Kenya's East African exports, while accounting for 47 percent of Tanzania's. Although there were marked differences in the relative importance of Sections 2 and 4, these are accounted for by Kenya's importation of oil seed and vegetable oils from Tanzania. With only two exceptions – beverages and tobacco, and fuels – the structure of Kenya's interterritorial trade has not altered in recent years; and these exceptions resulted from import substitution in Tanzania which substantially reduced the importance of Sections 1 and 3 in Kenya's East African Trade.

Tanzania's interterritorial imports (Table 4) are spread over SITC Sections 0, 3, 6, and 8.[21] Growth of interterritorial

TABLE 3

Tanzania: Interterritorial Exports by SITC Section
Selected Years 1960–66
(£000)

	1960		1962		1964		1966	
Section[a]	*Kenya*	*Uganda*	*Kenya*	*Uganda*	*Kenya*	*Uganda*	*Kenya*	*Uganda*
0	737	193	956	170	1077	256	842	182
1	348	38	68	10	412	13	397	14
2	331	23	257	111	349	20	427	29
3	62	—	50	—	14	—	5	—
4	143	146	139	96	349	228	353	122
5	70	18	38	4	76	3	91	5
6	126	27	188	43	1315	398	1248	412
7	1	—	2	—	7	—	63	42
8	54	3	252	2	504	102	371	35
9	3	1	4	1	7	1	10	1
TOTAL	1875	449	1954	437	4110	1021	3807	842

	Percentage of total		
Section[a]	*1954*	*1960*	*1966*
0	34	40	22
1	6	17	9
2	30	11	10
3	4	3	—
4	16	12	10
5	6	4	2
6	1	7	36
7	1	—	2
8	1	2	9
9	1	—	—

SOURCE: East Africa Customs and Excise, *Annual Trade Report*, 1954 and 1960–66 (Mombasa, Kenya: East Africa Customs and Excise).

[a] 0. Food
1. Beverages and tobacco
2. Crude materials, inedible, except fuels
3. Mineral fuels, lubricants, and related materials
4. Animal and vegetable oils and fats
5. Chemicals
6. Manufactured goods, classified chiefly by material
7. Machinery and transport equipment
8. Miscellaneous manufactured articles
9. Miscellaneous transactions and commodities, n.e.s.

TABLE 4

Tanzania: Interterritorial Imports by SITC Section
Selected Years 1960–66
(£000)

	1960		*1962*		*1964*		*1966*	
Section[a]	*Kenya*	*Uganda*	*Kenya*	*Uganda*	*Kenya*	*Uganda*	*Kenya*	*Uganda*
0	2330	175	2836	230	2724	233	2518	375
1	1476	700	1837	352	1740	454	850	198
2	88	25	95	14	87	38	160	58
3	5	—	13	—	1521	—	2187	7
4	214	188	142	121	74	98	54	51
5	469	112	980	55	1687	265	1930	78
6	1884	356	2425	857	2860	1238	3861	2194
7	53	3	58	18	92	10	181	11
8	1038	16	1554	22	2426	65	1487	146
9	52	1	76	1	88	2	53	2
TOTAL	7609	1576	10016	1670	13299	2403	13281	3120

	Percentage of total		
Section[a]	*1954*	*1960*	*1966*
0	32.0	27.0	18.0
1	48.0	24.0	6.0
2	2.0	1.0	1.0
3	—	—	13.0
4	4.0	4.0	0.6
5	2.0	6.0	12.0
6	6.0	24.0	37.0
7	—	0.6	1.0
8	6.0	11.0	10.0
9	—	0.4	0.4

SOURCE: East Africa Customs and Excise, *Annual Trade Report,* 1954 and 1960–1966 (Mombasa, Kenya: East Africa Customs and Excise).

[a] For definitions see Table 3.

imports of the various SITC Sections has been fairly steady since 1960.

Kenya's interterritorial imports are markedly different from Tanzania's. In 1966, the former spent 21 percent of its East African import outlays on food; Tanzania spent only 18 percent. Kenya's fuel and lubricant imports were only 4 percent of the total, while they were 13 percent for Tanzania. Chemicals were 33 percent more important for Tanzania than Kenya and miscellaneous manufactures (Section 8) twice as important.

However, the trends are moving in the same directions in the two countries.

The percentages, of course, do not tell the whole story. Not only are the export values of various sections substantially higher for Kenya, the breadth of exports is much wider than Tanzania's. In 1966, for example, only six manufactured products in Section 6 showed an interterritorial export value of £50 thousand or more for Tanzania; these represented about 60 percent of Tanzania's East African exports in that section. For Kenya, twenty-one manufactured goods secured interterritorial export receipts of £100 thousand or more and together represented 94 percent of the total exports of that section. This is indicative of Kenya's higher level of development and, therefore, of its more complex industrial base.

The most significant change in the structure of Tanzania's interterritorial imports and exports occurred over the years from 1954 to 1966. In 1954 food, beverages and tobacco (SITC Sections 0 and 1) accounted for 80 percent of Tanzania's imports from Kenya and Uganda and food and crude materials (Sections 0 and 2), mainly oil seeds, made up 64 percent of its East African exports. By 1960, however, manufactured imports (Sections 6–8) were nearly 36 percent of the total (compared with 12 percent in 1954) but still only 9 percent of the country's interterritorial exports. The period from 1960 to 1966 brought about further major changes in the composition of interterritorial trade. Primary products declined in importance (although there was a shift from using an overseas source to Kenya as a supplier of lubricants before 1966) on the import and export side, and manufactured goods took a more prominent place. It should be pointed out that the manufacturing industries in East Africa are protected; it is not known whether or not they could survive foreign competition even in the long run. Consequently, it is not possible to conclude from these trends that Tanzania and the rest of the East African common market is moving into a phase of development in which manufacturing will play an increasingly important role. For, unless the new industries can survive, unless the market can support them, this trend will not continue.

Finally, it will be noticed from Tables 3 and 4 that the vast majority of Tanzania's interterritorial trade is carried on with

Kenya. Moreover, this link between the two countries has been increasing over thirteen years from 1954.[22] In fact, in both value and percentage terms, Uganda represents a very unimportant trading partner for Tanzania.

EFFECTS OF UNMODIFIED INTEGRATION

In order to understand the Treaty for East African Cooperation, it is necessary to delineate the impact of unmodified economic integration, particularly in Kenya and Tanzania. East African industrial production is highly concentrated in Kenya and would be even more concentrated were it not for the restrictive measures taken in Tanzania after the Kampala Agreement. Kenya's advantages stem primarily from external economies to its manufacturing sector (a better harbor, the presence of a more developed banking and insurance system, a larger number of entrepreneurs, a concentration of industry, etc.), and from the fact that many of its industries have experienced internal economies and have rid themselves of many of the kinks often found in the early years of production. Kenya sells its industrial production to the entire East African market and imports relatively little from its partners. Kenya's balance-of-payments deficits with the rest of the world are financed by its surpluses with Tanzania and Uganda, while the reverse is true for Tanzania.

Under conditions of unqualified integration, Kenya's advantages in terms of internal and external economies tend to increase its rate of economic growth at the expense of Tanzania. Existing industrial firms generally expand their operations in Kenya as East African demand grows, rather than setting up branches in Tanzania. Similarly, new firms, attracted by the external economies, set up their operations in Kenya. Unmodified integration between two underdeveloped economies of significantly different levels of development leads to a widening of the gap between them.

If the function of Tanzanian policy is to reduce the trade and industrial production gaps, there are two main courses which come to mind as policy solutions. First, measures may be taken to create the social overhead capital necessary to put new industries in Tanzania on an equal footing with new industries in Kenya. Such a step would stimulate directly productive investment and help reduce costs in existing industries but would not overcome differentials due to internal economies; that is, it would not eliminate the need for infant industry assistance. The second course (not exclusive of the first) would be artificially to shift relative prices in Tanzania's favor by use of trade restrictions. This is the choice embodied in the *Treaty for East African Co-operation.*

TREATY FOR EAST AFRICAN CO-OPERATION

After the failure of the Kampala Agreement there was a period of deterioration in East African economic cooperation.[23] Nevertheless, in spite of public invective, a fundamental desire for partnership prevailed and the East African Common Services Authority formed the East African Commission in 1965 to examine the common market, money and banking, and the common services, and to recommend ways in which East African cooperation could be strengthened. Under the chairmanship of Mr. Kjeld Philip, former Minister for Finance in Denmark, the commission ultimately recommended that economic arrangements among the East African countries be embodied in a treaty.

The Treaty for East African Co-operation, which came into force on December 1, 1967, formalizes for the first time the details, principles, and direction of economic integration in East Africa. It becomes immediately clear, upon reading the treaty, that the problems which beset the market, at least since Tanzania became independent in 1961, arose out of the static nature of the informal agreement. That is, the failure to organize cooperation on the basis of agreed-upon goals constituted a de facto acceptance of the existing structure and the direction in which the market was moving. However, events showed that this structure was not in fact acceptable to members, so that conflicting policies were thus pursued. The treaty clears up these conflicts and provides a dynamic framework – the economic development of each country – within which integration can take place.

The treaty, in force for an initial period of fifteen years, mobilizes East African cooperation on three broad fronts:

1. economic policy; 2. common institutions; and 3. the common market.

With respect to economic policy, the members agree to: coordinate fiscal policies in order to achieve maximum industrial development; harmonize monetary policies so as to facilitate the smooth operation of the market and the maintenance of convertibility among the three currencies at least for current account payments; cooperate in the formulation of transport policies, economic plans, and commercial laws so as to maximize the contribution of resources towards development; and to work out a common agricultural policy so that these products may be produced and marketed efficiently within the market as a whole.

Although the self-contained common services are converted to corporations by the treaty, and their headquarters decentralized and spread more evenly among the three countries, the substantive institutional innovation contained in the treaty is the establishment of the East African Development Bank. The Bank will act as a source of financial and technical assistance for industrial development in East Africa as a whole, but, for at least ten years, its efforts will be directed toward correcting the industrial imbalance which now exists among the three countries. To this end, Tanzania and Uganda will each receive $38\frac{3}{4}$ percent of its resources and Kenya $22\frac{1}{2}$ percent during the first ten years of its operation.

Regarding the common market, the treaty attacks the problems on two fronts – the relations of the members to the outside world, and interterritorial trade and production. The treaty formalizes the customs union, includes Zanzibar for the first time, and affirms the maintenance of a common external tariff.[24] Members must receive all the concessions accorded to an outside country in any agreement between a member and a nonmember country. And they agree not to make barter arrangements with nonmembers for imports of goods that compete with manufactured commodities produced in East Africa.

In order to bring about more equal levels of industrial production in the three countries, interterritorial trade restrictions are provided for in the treaty. Industrial licensing will be continued for a period of twenty-two years but no new industries may be added to the scheduled list.

With the exception of certain agricultural products "which are basic staple foods or major export crops, subject to special marketing arrangements,"[25] quantitative restrictions, which were allowed by the Kampala Agreement and used extensively by Tanzania, are not permitted on interterritorial trade.[26] Instead, an interterritorial tariff, called a "transfer tax" by the treaty, may be applied by a market member to manufactures imported from the other two nations. Although no new transfer taxes will be permitted after 1985 and each tax may be applied only for a limit of eight years, the entire system will be reviewed in 1972 in order to determine whether or not it is bringing about the industrial balance it is aimed to promote. Furthermore, since it is implicitly assumed by the drafters of the treaty that the current interterritorial imbalance in trade in manufactures is the chief indicator of the different levels of industrial development in the three countries, the total value of goods taxed must not be greater than the taxing country's interterritorial deficit in manufactures. And when the interterritorial manufactured exports of a tax-imposing country are equal to 80 percent of its interterritorial manufactured imports, no new taxes may be introduced.

In order to ensure that the transfer taxes actually stimulate industrial production, the treaty requires that goods chosen for taxation be produced in the tax-imposing country at the time of the imposition of the tax, or three months thereafter. However, an industry may receive this protection only if it has the capacity to produce in the year immediately following the introduction of the transfer tax 15 percent of the consumption of the product in its country or an ouput at least equal to two million shillings (ex-factory). Finally, at any point that the protected industry exports at least 30 percent of its sales to the rest of East Africa, the tax will be revoked.

With a view to avoiding any serious disruption of production and trade within the East African market as a whole, the treaty insists that there must be no diversion of imports from interterritorial to external sources in the taxing country and that the importing member must take steps to correct such diversions should they take place. And since taxes may not be higher than 50 percent of the external tariff, there is a ceiling on the price increases which will result from this new protection.

Thus, the East African community has moved from a laissez faire system, where the economies adjusted to the static institutional framework, to a policy-directed system, where the economies within the community are expected to grow in specified ways and the institutional dimensions will be changed in order to facilitate the achievement of goals. In general, the treaty is founded upon the goal of a more equal distribution of the benefits of economic integration. In effect, Kenya has agreed that unequal rates of industrial development – whatever their origin – cannot continue, but obviously believes that the benefits of association are worth the short-run sacrifices it might incur.

It is important to point out that the treaty does not attempt to bring about a reallocation of resources but, rather, a reallocation of growth, and, therefore, of new resources. That is, it is not that Tanzania and Uganda are to receive some of Kenya's industrial plant and equipment but that new investment will be induced, through the Bank and the use of the transfer tax, to locate in those countries. The treaty indirectly argues that free trade – even within a limited area such as East Africa – is not necessarily beneficial to all participants. What is planned for East Africa is a movement away from free trade to restricted trade and ultimately back to free trade within the market.

IMPACT ON TANZANIA

Whether or not the treaty will have a net positive effect on Tanzania's economy depends upon a number of factors, the dimensions of which are not immediately obvious from the terms of the treaty. In particular, it is not clear whether the transfer tax will result in a larger or smaller volume of interterritorial trade, or will promote the economic development of Tanzania. The system aims at spurring industrial import substitution and industrial growth by raising the price of industrial imports in Tanzania. The effects may be divided into short- and long-run changes.

In the short run, protection can be secured only by existing firms in Tanzania which have the capacity to supply 15 percent of the market. Assuming that prices of protected products rise despite efforts to prevent this, the greater the elasticity of supply in these plants the larger will be their share of the total demand for that product in Tanzania after the tax is applied. (This proportion may be increased by default if the cross-elasticities of demand are high in particular products, i.e. if there are large shifts from the increased-price products.)[27] In any case, barring totally inelastic demands, the quantity demanded of the protected products will fall and the relative impact of the decrease on foreign and interterritorial imports will depend upon the relative supply and demand price elasticities for the products coming from these two sources. East Africa might bear the trade brunt of Tanzania's import substitution, ceteris paribus, if the price elasticity of demand is lower for foreign imports than for interterritorial imports. However, even if elasticities are of this nature (and they may prove to be the opposite) under the agreement diversion to foreign imports is supposed to be prevented. Moreover, the effects of the supply elasticities might outweigh those of the demand elasticities. The elasticity of supply of foreign imports is probably virtually infinite; foreign suppliers probably will not absorb any of the additional tariff. But interterritorial imports, particularly from Kenya, are almost certainly produced under supply-inelastic conditions and, therefore, might be expected to absorb part of the tax in the form of lower prices.[28] Given these considerations, it is not clear that the short-run impact of the transfer tax system will be to reduce Tanzania's industrial import surplus with East Africa. The short-run impact on Tanzania's real income will be negative if the prices of industrial products rise. There will be a redistribution of income, however, from consumers to producers in the form of higher profits, and to workers in the form of wages to the newly employed.

In the long run the impact may be somewhat different. Inasmuch as taxed goods may receive protection from East African competition for a maximum of eight years, interterritorial price differentials will eventually disappear. However, the fragmentation of industries within the common market, resulting from the transfer tax system, may prevent economies of scale from being experienced on an industry-wide basis and thus continue the necessity of maintaining protection against foreign competition. To the extent that this occurs in the long run, the system will not result in lower prices for industrial products.

At first more inputs will be imported and, owing to the high import content of plant and equipment, total imports are likely to rise. Eventually, however, the balance of trade will tend to move in Tanzania's favor, particularly if economies of scale in specific industries permit exports to the rest of East Africa. It is not clear, however, which and how many industries will experience such economies of scale. And until producers can market their outputs at prices competitive with East African imports, Tanzanian consumers will experience direct income losses.

The transfer tax system and economic growth will be positively correlated with: 1. the value-added; 2. net investment increases; and 3. backward and forward linkages. First, the greater the value-added in the protected industries, the higher will be their contribution to development. Second, high growth rates tend to attract more investment, simply because the opportunities for profit are likely to be positively associated with rapid development. Furthermore, external economies are generally created, particularly during the early stages of industrial change – as in Tanzania – during phases of rapid growth which induce further investment. And third, the more extensive the forward and backward linkages in the protected industries, the greater will be the impact on growth. However, these linkages must not simply be technical (in the sense that many industries are involved in the vertical structure of production and the product is used in many other industries) but must be economic (in that it is or becomes possible and profitable to establish the links in the country) in order for the effect to be felt. Thus, for example, a product which has a high import content, even though the linkages may be great, may contribute less to growth than products with lower linkages having less import content.

There is no guarantee, however, that industrial production will show a net increase in excess of what it would have been without the tax system. Investment may simply shift (ex ante) from non-protected industries to sheltered industries. In general, industrial production will show a net increase if any or all of the following occur: 1. savings increase and are invested in these industries; 2. saving is greater than investment before the tax and investment increases, owing to an expanded marginal efficiency of investment; and 3. foreign investment increases. There is most likely excess saving in Tanzania, particularly in the Asian community. The opportunity to produce under protected conditions will undoubtedly draw some of these funds into investment channels. Direct foreign investment will probably show some increase but more likely Kenyan investors, particularly in industries affected by the tax, will set up tariff factories in Tanzania. There should also be some increased investment in protected industries by the National Development Corporation, securing funds by floating bond issues on foreign markets.

It is possible to quantify some of the impact of the transfer tax system on Tanzania. One of the chief aims of the treaty is to bring about equal levels of industrial production in East Africa. From 1960–65 Kenya experienced an average annual growth in manufacturing output of 8 percent, although 21 and 10 percent increases were recorded in the last two of those years. Tanzania's annual growth in manufactures was 10.6 percent from 1960–66 with a 15.2 percent increase in 1966. Were those rates to continue, given the 1965 output of £33 million in Kenya and £11 million in Tanzania, it would be forty-seven years before manufacturing output was equal in the two countries. On the other hand, if the growth rate in Kenya fell to 5 percent compounded (entirely possible with the losses in manufactured exports to Tanzania), a compounded rate of 10 percent per year in Tanzania would bring its output level with Kenya's in 1986. Considering the rather low levels of development of the two countries and the provision in the treaty that no new taxes may be applied after 1982, it may be desirable to form a non-linear picture of the impact of the transfer tax.

The treaty lists twenty-eight industries involved in the processing of primary (agricultural included) products and all industries in SITC Sections 5, 6, 7, and 8 as those which may apply for protection from East African competition. These products accounted for 95 percent of Tanzania's total retained imports and represented 88 percent of interterritorial imports in 1966. Obviously, however, not all these products would be possible import substitutes, even if the required investment resources were available to produce them. The initial question, which must be answered before industries can be evaluated for relative profitability, their effect upon foreign exchange stocks, their contribution to growth, employment, etc., is whether or not the domestic market is large enough to justify the establishment of the minimum size operation. This is essentially a process of eliminating industries and narrowing the alternatives; it is not the choice of industries which should or will actually be started.

Since the transfer tax is designed to bring about import substitution in products traded within the Common Market, goods which are imported in large quantities from outside East Africa but which are not prominent in interterritorial trade need not concern us. An examination of the Annual Trade Report for 1966 indicates that, with very few exceptions, Tanzania's interterritorial imports of each taxable item totals over £30,000 or under £20,000. If we choose £30,000 as the (arbitrary) minimum interterritorial imports required before considering an industry for establishment with a transfer tax, fifty-two industries qualify on the basis of the 1966 figures.[29] Thirty-nine of these either exist in Tanzania or the market is known to be large enough to justify their establishment.[30] Of the remaining thirteen, most were excluded because it is not known whether or not the market is large enough; others were left out because they are known to be unprofitable under present conditions. These thirteen represented 15 percent of Tanzania's imports in "taxable" items in 1966.

Table 5 contains a list of the thirty-nine industries most likely to apply for the application of a transfer tax in the near future. The list does not imply that all thirty-nine will be established, or will be able to meet the minimum requirements for protection if they are established. These industries accounted for 36 percent of total taxable retained imports and 78 percent of interterritorial imports in taxable products in 1966. The interterritorial trade imbalance (in all products) in that year was £11.8 million, while these thirty-nine industries accounted for £11.2 million of imports from Kenya and Uganda.

Table 5 shows that twenty-five of the thirty-nine industries

TABLE 5

Tanzania: Import Substitution and the Transfer Tax
(£000)

SITC	*Product*	*Total retained imports*	*Interterritorial imports Kenya*	*Uganda*	*Industry exists (E) is planned (P) or market is large enough for local production (L)*	*External tariff (percentage)*	*Maximum price increase from tax (percentage)*	*Diversion index*
012 10	Bacon and ham	50,749	45,288	3,265	L	37½	18¾	29
021 2, 9, & 023 01	Milk, cream and butter	534,742	197,977	—	E	37½	18¾	421
048 41	Biscuits	211,794	108,891	97,844	E	50	25	48
053 31	Jams and marmalades	33,494	24,597	874	L	50	25	160
055 59	Vegetables, canned	68,919	39,313	25	L	50	25	281
06 200	Confectionary sugar	235,639	73,864	2,930	E	50	25	449
081	Feeding stuff for animals	86,134	71,734	11,098	L	30	15	21
112 30	Beer	516,958	438,000	10,000	E	19/– per imperial gallon	9/50 per imperial gallon	89
33	Petroleum and petroleum products	703,318	2,161,152	6,825	E			
122 20	Cigarettes	195,413	163,000	23,000	E	55/– per lb.	22/50 per lb.	32
34	Gas, natural and manufactured	66,647	25,940	190	L	2½ cts per lb.	1¼ cts. per lb.	405
421 30	Cottonseed oil	102,396	51,305	50,993	L	30	15	1
533 39	Paints, varnishes, etc.	158,517	53,171	996	E	37½	18¾	448
541	Medicines and pharmaceuti-	1,443,225	329,744	8,032	E	30	15	510

553	Perfumes and cosmetics	540,272	389,384	8,735	L	$66\frac{2}{3}$	$33\frac{1}{3}$	175
554	Soaps and polishes	939,517	624,370	16,512	E	$37\frac{1}{2}$	$18\frac{3}{4}$	100
581	Plastics	450,212	38,030	101	E	30	15	606
599 20	Insecticides	1,021,948	223,738	350	E	30	15	522
611	Leather	57,868	52,804	966	P	30	15	56
629 11 & 15	Bicycle tires and tubes	213,876	76,650	96,715	L	1/– per lb.	/50 per lb.	126
631 20	Plywood	35,459	32,203	3,256	E	30	15	0
632 4	Builders' wood	59,269	44,721	1,235	L	30	15	150
642	Paper articles	1,162,886	790,923	2,571	E	30	15	212
651 30 & 41	Cotton yarn	502,393	36,833	45,522	E	40	20	557
651 60	Synthetic yarn	576,180	223,124	—	E	$33\frac{1}{3}$	$16\frac{2}{3}$	409
652	Cotton fabrics	7,109,260	1,438	1,568,664	E	40	20	519
653, 53, 54, 55	Synthetic textiles	2,262,739	329,111	5,359	E	40	20	569
656 11, 12 & 19	Bags and sacks	1,366,009	186,682	—	E	30	15	624
661 21	Portland cement	803,120	803,120	—	E	1/50 per 400 lbs.	/75 per 400 lbs.	0
665 10	Glass bottles	144,945	103,601	—	L	30	15	187
691 11	Steel doors and windows	1,041,270	157,065	106	L	30	15	568
695 11	Hoes (jembes)	353,277	14,501	66,239	E	Free		514
697 25	Aluminum ware (domestic)	101,494	69,592	6,709	E	30	15	165
729 11	Auto batteries	128,964	31,018	—	L	15	$7\frac{1}{2}$	506
821 02	Metal furniture	264,260	197,682	771	L	30	15	166
821 03	Mattresses	116,418	98,588	407	L	30	15	100
841	Clothing	1,007,679	164,828	4,641	E, L	$33\frac{1}{3}$	$16\frac{2}{3}$	555
851	Footwear	816,036	606,991	6,032	E	30	15	166
899 32	Matches	129,383	15,138	104,225	E	10/– per 7200	5/– per 7200	52
TOTAL:		25,612,679	9,096,111	2,155,188				

are already established (one of these, leather, is planned) although it is not known whether they have the capacity to produce 15 percent of local consumption (the requirement for transfer tax protection). External tariffs range from 15 percent, on auto batteries, to 66⅔ percent for perfumes and cosmetics. Most, however, are between 30 and 40 percent ad valorem.

Since the transfer tax is calculated on the basis of the external tariff and may be at a maximum of 50 percent of that tariff, then 50 percent of the external tariff will be the largest price increases that will result directly from the imposition of the tax. Such increases are shown in Table 5 for each product.[31] In many cases (goods with external tariffs of 40 to 50 percent), domestic prices will be 60 to 75 percent higher than they would be without any import duties; except for cotton yarn, these high duties apply to consumer goods on the list; for dairy products, cotton yarn and cotton and synthetic textiles (goods consumed by the poor) the effect of such taxes is regressive. Seven of the thirty-nine industries are producers of intermediate inputs and the price increase (a maximum of 15 percent in most cases) will have the effect of increasing costs of production. The price elasticities of demand for pork, biscuits, jams, canned vegetables, and cottonseed oil are likely to be high and substantial price increases, therefore, may contract the quantity demanded to an extent which makes it difficult for such industries to be profitably established even with protection. Other products, such as matches, footwear, clothing, cement, medicines and pharmaceuticals, cigarettes, beer, dairy products, and sugar, almost certainly face highly price-inelastic demands and will, therefore, find the price increases do not eat significantly into total demand. However, these effects work two ways. In the first instance, high elasticities may act to shift demand from taxed imports to domestic products, particularly if the latter are sold at less than the former. In the second instance, low elasticities may act so as to keep demand from shifting from imports to domestic substitutes, particularly, as is typically the case in early years of production, if the domestic quality is not comparable to that of imports.

Finally, the thirty-nine industries in Table 5 present some interesting information with respect to the effect of the transfer tax system on the pattern of Tanzania's imports and the impact of Tanzania's import substitution choices on the rest of the common market. It will be noticed that a surprisingly large number of these – sixteen of the thirty-nine – are currently primarily imported from outside East Africa. And in all but eleven of the thirty-nine, external imports account for at least 25 percent of the total. This means that, in the absence of countermeasures, a transfer tax applied on an import from Kenya or Uganda would shift the relative price of the good in favor of the external import, even though it contains a tariff. The net effect could very easily be an increase in external imports with no significant increase in the consumption of the Tanzanian-produced good. However, the treaty provides that when the application of a transfer tax results in such shifting, the taxing country (in conjunction with the other market members) "must take measures to counteract such deviation." Although the treaty does not spell out what "measures" shall be taken, presumably it means that the taxing country shall apply an equal addition to the external tariff for those products.[32]

In practice, therefore, the system as it will be applied in nearly all cases in Tanzania will involve import substitution in general and not simply substitution for imports now coming from the rest of East Africa. The question arises, however, as to whether the impact of the higher tariffs will be upon external or interterritorial imports. In other words, will the domestic production be sold to buyers of external or interterritorial imports? If interterritorial supply is not highly inelastic, substitution will most likely involve decreases in East African, rather than external, imports because Tanzanian substitutes will probably be closer in quality to the former than the latter. However, although such a process would not qualify as a "deviation" from East African to external imports under the terms of the treaty, in substance it would be just that. For so long as products are imported from both East Africa and from outside, import substitution which results in a decrease in East African imports with little or no change in the purchase of external imports has the same effect on the common market partner as shifts resulting from relative price changes.

Furthermore, it would be better for the market as a whole if substitution eliminated external imports before eating into interterritorial trade. For the purpose of the transfer tax system is not to harm existing East African industries but to provide protection which will lead to an expansion of industrial production in the relatively industrially backward areas.

From the point of view of the spirit of the treaty, as well as the economic aims of the community, the transfer tax system ought to result in the replacement of external, before East African, imports. The "diversion index" in Table 5 is designed to show the implications for interterritorial trade if external imports are replaced before East African. The index is simply the ratio of external imports to the value of 15 percent of total imports of the products.[33] It is assumed, for the purpose of simplicity, that total demand is equal to total retained imports in each product.[34] Thus, the index shows external imports as a percentage of 15 percent of domestic demand. An index of 100, for example (soaps and polishes), means that external imports are exactly equal to 15 percent of total demand; a zero index indicates that the entire demand is met from interterritorial imports. The difference between the index and 100 shows the proportion of minimum protected output (i.e. 15 percent of demand) which will replace imports from East Africa. For biscuits the index is 48. This means that 48 percent of the import replacement stemming from domestically producing 15 percent of demand would be from external imports and 52 percent from interterritorial imports. Where the index is greater than 100, it means that domestic capacity would have to be greater than 15 percent before East African imports would be affected. Domestic production of synthetic yarn, for example, would have to be just over four times 15 percent of demand before East African imports would be diverted.

Of the thirty-nine industries examined, eleven would involve immediate diversion of interterritorial imports;[35] and two of the remaining twenty-eight – soaps and polishes and mattresses – are right at the margin. Three of the goods causing immediate diversion are food and beverages, while four of the others are also foodstuffs. Six consumer goods would be diverted and fourteen would not. Sixteen industries would have to supply over half of the total demand before interterritorial imports would decline and eleven of these would require as much as 75 percent supplied domestically.

Of the eleven products which would involve immediate

diversion from East Africa, biscuits, cottonseed oil, and matches are major Uganda exports to Tanzania, and if East African imports are not accorded preference over external imports, then cotton fabrics, hoes, cotton yarn, and bicycle tires and tubes must be added to these three. Consequently, it is possible that the transfer tax system, designed essentially to promote industrial output in Tanzania and Uganda, will work to contract major Ugandan industrial exports to Tanzania. On the other side of the picture, Tanzania exported nine products to Uganda, at values of £30,000 or more, for a total of £498,000 in 1966. These exports could be affected by Uganda's use of the transfer tax.

The effect of the transfer tax system on Tanzania's trade balance with Kenya will not be very great in the near future. For, even assuming that all thirty-nine industries were created and produced the 15 percent necessary for protection, and further, that the entire 15 percent were diverted from interterritorial trade, only £3.2 million would be deducted from Tanzania's East African imports.[36] Furthermore, over £1.2 million of this figure would be reductions in imports from Uganda, leaving £2 million to come off the import bill with Kenya. And if only those industries were taxed in which less than 15 percent of total imports comes from external sources the reduction in interterritorial imports would amount to a little over £300,000.

On balance, therefore, there is no reason why the application of the transfer tax system should result in a significant contraction of East African trade for the immediate future. Consequently, although Tanzania may experience more industrial development than it has in the past, there is little to indicate that its balance of trade with Kenya will be significantly altered.

CONCLUSION

The latest attempt to put East African cooperation on a solid footing holds promise in several senses but leaves a critical problem unresolved. On the one hand, it is finally clear where East Africa wants to go and the manner in which the countries wish to travel together – development with an equal distribution of the benefits. This is important, for Tanzania and Uganda have won their argument for equality, even at the possible cost of lower overall East African growth. To Tanzania, at least, this position is a logical extension of its domestic economic policy; a policy of socialist development with an extremely heavy weight placed upon equality. Tanzania's chief gain from the new arrangements will lie in being able to expand its industrial production while remaining within the market. Investment should increase and thereby expand employment in the monetary sector, raise income through growth, and generally provide a spurt to development. However, the gains in this area should not be overemphasized since they may be small; the treaty will not bring about an industrial revolution in Tanzania. Yet, it is still a consistent step for Tanzania to take – more so in light of its external political philosophy than in relation to its economic goals. Pan Africanism, even on a limited scale, holds a high priority to Tanzania.

On the other hand, there is not much to indicate that the treaty will bring about a significant reduction in Tanzania's imbalance of interterritorial trade in the foreseeable future. Although the secondary effects of the transfer tax system – an expansion of interterritorial exports – may be expected to be positive, on the whole the impact should be on Tanzania's external balance of trade. While a casual reading of the treaty suggests that import substitution will displace East African imports, detailed analysis indicates that external rather than interterritorial imports will be displaced. Given the aims of growth and integration, this is as it should be. What is now clear is that the "critical" problem of import surpluses with Kenya and Uganda is not really a serious problem for Tanzania after all.

NOTES

1. Tanzania is comprised of Zanzibar and former Tanganyika, but references to Tanzania in this paper are only to the latter.
2. East African Common Services Organization, *Treaty for East African Cooperation* (Nairobi: Government Printer, 1967).
3. More precisely, the equivalent of customs duties, in the form of transfer taxes, may be imposed. However, quantitative controls which had arisen in the preceding period were forbidden except in stipulated circumstances.

4. The term "interterritorial" trade is used to refer to trade between Tanzania, Kenya, and Uganda, while "external" trade refers to dealings with other countries.
5. Goods imported from outside East Africa could not move freely within the area until 1927.
6. The services are divided into two groups – "self-contained" and "nonself-contained." The former include the railways and harbors, the airways, and posts and telecommunications, while the latter encompass the departments administering customs and excise, income tax collection, meteorology, locust control, and some thirty research divisions. For a concise description of the common services, see J. Banfield, "The Structure and Administration of the East African Common Services Organization," in C. Leys and P. Robson, *Federation in East Africa* (Nairobi: Oxford University Press, 1965).
7. For a description of the licensing system see H. E. Smith, *Industrial Development in Tanzania* (Dar es Salaam: Institute of Public Administration, 1966), pp. 86–90.
8. P. Ndegwa, *The Common Market and Development in East Africa* (Nairobi: East African Publishing House, 1965), pp. 94–96.
9. Ibid., pp. 98–119. See also: International Bank for Reconstruction and Development, *The Economic Development of Uganda* (Baltimore: Johns Hopkins University Press, 1962), pp. 82–95; and International Bank for Reconstruction and Development, *The Economic Development of Tanganyika* (Baltimore: Johns Hopkins University Press, 1961), pp. 238–40.
10. United Kingdom, *Report of the East African Economic and Fiscal Commission*, Cmnd. 1279, H.M.S.O. (London, 1961).
11. For an analysis see Ndegwa, *The Common Market*, pp. 104–8.
12. United Republic of Tanganyika and Zanzibar, *Kampala Agreement* (Dar es Salaam: Mwananchi Publishing Co., 1964).
13. Kenya had agreed to the provisions on the condition, among others, that a single currency be maintained in East Africa. Tanzania created its own central bank and announced plans to introduce its own currency in June 1965.
14. Among these were the organization and location of the common services headquarters (all in Kenya), the lack of monetary policy machinery, the relations between market members and nonmarket countries (specifically with respect to trade agreements), and the common pooling of foreign exchange which historically had come to be used to finance Kenya deficits with the rest of the world.
15. Diamonds make up 90 percent of Tanzania's manufactured exports to non-East African countries.
16. See A. Roe, "The Reshaping of East African Economic Co-operation," *East African Journal* 4:5 (August 1967), p. 13.
17. See Dudley Kessel, "Effective Protection and Industrialization Strategies in Tanzania," unpublished Ph.D. thesis, Cornell University, 1969.
18. See Dharam Ghai, "Territorial Distributions of the Benefits and Costs of the East African Market," in Leys and Robson, *Federation in East Africa*.

19. Interterritorial manufactures include a variety of products ranging from cotton, yarn, and shirts to plywood and boxes and radios. Since 1963 corrugated plates have figured prominently and aluminum products have been exported to Kenya since 1964.
20. Thus, in 1966, when that production was particularly large, Section of exports fell from the 1965 level by about 40 percent.
21. Imports in these sections are mainly meat and dairy products, biscuits, beans, and tea; motor spirit and engine oils; paper bags, textiles, bicycle tires, sisal bags, cement, and asbestos; and clothing, footwear, and matches.
22. On the import side, 71, 20, 13, and 19 percent of Sections 0, 1, 4, and 7 respectively, came from Kenya in 1954; by 1966 these percentages had increased to 87, 81, 51, and 94 percent, respectively. Of Tanzania's exports to East Africa, 77, 47, 42, and 70 percent of Sections 0, 1, 4, and 8 respectively, went to Kenya in 1954; in 1966 these percentages had increased to 82, 97, 74, and 91, respectively.
23. Quantitative trade restrictions were introduced, bilateral trade agreements were made without consulting East African partners, and monetary cooperation was sharply reduced after the establishment of separate currencies in each of the three countries in mid-1965.
24. Members may diverge from the common tariff in specific instances with the agreement of the other members.
25. *Treaty for East African Co-operation*, Article 13.
26. The one exception to this rule is when a member has balance-of-payments problems which have not been corrected through other policies. Quantitative restrictions used for this purpose may not be applied discriminately against a market partner.
27. This could cause difficulties in determining and blocking – as required by the treaty – shifts from East African to foreign imports.
28. However, Kenya is forbidden to absorb the tax in this way unless it lowers its domestic prices as well.
29. Industries are defined here somewhat loosely. In some cases only a single product constitutes an industry, while in others, such as "dairy," many products are involved.
30. In 1964 the Continental-Allied Company of the United States undertook an industrial analysis in Tanganyika and identified 126 possibilities for industrial expansion. These were used as a guide to choosing possible import substitutes among the fifty industries where production was not already under way or planned. E. Tannenbaum, *Tanganyika Five-Year Industrial Plan*, Continental-Allied Co., Inc. (Washington, 1964).
31. A tariff or price increase is not shown for petroleum and petroleum products because it varies with different products. Total retained imports in this division are less than interterritorial imports because re-exports are greater then net imports (imports, including re-exports, from outside East Africa). Thus, some interterritorial imports are subsequently re-exported, particularly because of the Zambian oil line.
32. In order to avoid the goods coming in through Kenya and Uganda,

they would have to be taxed at the Tanzania border, even when they were re-exports from those two countries.

33. It will be recalled that the treaty requires that an industry be able to meet 15 percent of domestic demand before a transfer tax will be granted.
34. This is obviously incorrect for industries that are already operating in Tanzania, but even in these cases demand is often largely met by imports.
35. Petroleum is included, although it was not possible to calculate an index owing to the negative value of retained external imports.
36. This assumes further that none of the import requirements for these new industries would be bought in Kenya and Uganda.

Contributors

Virginia L. Galbraith has concentrated her research on francophone West Africa. She traveled through this area in 1966 and returned in 1968 to Ivory Coast to research its planned economic accomplishments and projections in preparation for a forthcoming book. She is the author of *World Trade in Transition*, a work which examines the efficiency and equity arguments for changes in commercial policies of developed countries toward less-developed economies. She has also written a number of articles on the foreign aid programs of France and the European Economic Community countries in West Africa. Dr Galbraith is professor of economics at Mt. Holyoke College, where she teaches a seminar in economic development that focuses on the economies of Ivory Coast and Ghana.

Peter C. Garlick, who took his doctorate at the University of London, lived for twelve years in Africa, ten of them in Ghana, where he taught at the University of Science and Technology and at the University of Ghana. Upon leaving that country, Professor Garlick taught economic development at the University of New England, New South Wales, Australia, and at Howard University in Washington, D.C., before taking his present post as professor of economics in the department of African Studies at New York State University College, New Paltz.

Reginald H. Green has, since 1956, studied plans and planning in nearly a score of African and South Asian economies, and has been more recently a consultant and advisor on various aspects of development policy and planning in East Africa. At the present time he is serving as economic advisor to the Treasury Department of the United Republic of

Tanzania and as honorary professor of economics at University college, Dar es Salaam.

John R. Harris is associate professor of economics and associate director of the special program for urban and regional studies for developing areas at the Massachusetts Institute of Technology. His previous experience included teaching at Northwestern University and serving as an associate research fellow of the Nigerian Institute of Social and Economic Research in 1965. During 1968–69, Professor Harris was a visiting research associate of the Institute for Development Studies at the University of Nairobi, Kenya. His current research and teaching activities center around problems of urbanization and regional development in developing countries. His articles have appeared in many major professional journals.

Mitchell Harwitz was on leave between 1969 and 1971 from his position as associate professor of economics at the State University of New York at Buffalo to serve as visiting professor at the Universtiy of Nairobi, Kenya. He has had earlier experience in Africa, too, and was in 1967–68 the recipient of a faculty fellowship in economics from the Ford Foundation. Dr. Harwitz was coeditor with Melville Herskovits of *Economic Transition in Africa*, Northwestern University Press, 1964. He is also the author of a number of articles dealing with the economic development of Africa and of other underdeveloped economies.

Andrew M. Kamarck completes a sabbatical leave on February 1, 1972, from the International Bank for Reconstruction and Development (IBRD, or World Bank), a leave which he is spending as a member of the development advisory service of the Center for International Affairs at Harvard University. He will return to the Bank as director of its Economic Development Institute. Dr. Kamarck has also served with the Federal Reserve Board and the United States Treasury Department. At the World Bank he has been chief of the Africa Section; economic advisor to the Department of Operations for Europe, Africa, and Australasia; and chief of economic missions to the United Kingdom, France, South Africa, Southern Rhodesia, and Zambia (including the Kariba Mission), Nyasaland, Tunisia, Ghana (Volta

Mission), Sudan, Sierra Leone, Liberia. He was chief economist of the Uganda Survey Mission, and also headed the United Nations Special Fund "Mekambo" Mission to Gabon. From 1965–71 Dr. Kamarck directed the economics department of the World Bank, where he is also director-designate of the Economic Development Institute. Dr. Kamarck is a Fellow of and has served as a member of the Board of Directors of the African Studies Association. He has been a lecturer on African Affairs at the School for Advanced International Studies of Johns Hopkins University. In 1964–65 he was Regents Professor at the University of California at Los Angeles. A summa cum laude graduate in economics of Harvard University, where he also took his master's and doctoral degrees, Dr. Kamarck is author of *The Economics of African Development*, Praeger, 1967, rev. ed., 1971. He is co-author of *The Economic Development of Uganda*, published for the International Bank of Reconstruction and Development by the Johns Hopkins Press, 1962.

KATHLEEN M. LANGLEY has been on leave during 1970–71 from her post as associate professor of economics at Boston University to be a visiting research associate at the University of the Philippines. Her experience in Africa began in 1967 as a research associate at the Nigerian Institute of Social and Economic Research, and as a visiting faculty member at the University of Ibadan. During 1969 she participated in a conference on Nigerian postwar reconstruction and development sponsored by the Nigerian Federal Ministry of Economic Development, in conjunction with the Ford Foundation. Dr. Langley has had two articles published in *The Nigerian Journal of Economic and Social Research*: "The External Factor in Nigerian Economic Development" in July 1968, and "Production Functions in Eastern Nigeria: A Comment" in November 1967.

BENTON F. MASSELL, a professor and economist at the Food Research Institute of Stanford University, worked in Kenya from 1965 to 1967 as a field staff member for the Rockefeller Foundation. During that period he organized and directed a social science research program at the University of Nairobi. While serving as a research economist for the RAND Corporation during 1962–63, Professor Massell carried on field work in Kenya on the East African Common Market, and in Rhodesia on the economics of production in African agriculture. In this country he has taught a graduate seminar on African economic problems at the University of California at Los Angeles. He has written two monographs and several articles relating to African economic problems.

RUSSELL U. McLAUGHLIN is professor of economics at Drexel University in Philadelphia, teaching graduate and undergraduate courses in economic development and international business. He has done field research work in Liberia and from 1963 to 1964 was a member of a USAID team assisting the Office of National Planning (now the Department of Economic Planning and Development) in Monrovia. He is the author of *Foreign Investment and Development in Liberia*, Praeger, 1966.

PETER F. M. McLOUGHLIN is a specialist in international development economics and currently professor and chairman of the department of economics at the University of New Brunswick. He has served as an administrative officer in Tanzania and has held teaching positions at the Universities of Khartoum (Sudan), California (Los Angeles), Santa Clara, and Toronto. Before his present appointment, Dr. McLoughlin was a research economist with the World Bank in Washington, D.C., and was there concerned primarily with agricultural projects and activities in sub-Saharan Africa. He has served subsequently as economic consultant to a number of private organizations on agricultural projects and programs in Iran, Sudan, Colombia, Ivory Coast, and Central Africa. Under Ford Foundation auspices, he was also economic advisor to the East African Development Bank. A Canadian, Dr. McLoughlin holds degrees from the Universities of British Columbia, Oxford, and Texas.

MARVIN P. MIRACLE is chairman of the African Studies program and associate professor of agricultural economics at the University of Wisconsin. He has worked in Africa on special research grants and as consultant and advisor on development projects in Ghana and Ivory Coast. His major publications include *Maize in Tropical Africa*, University of Wisconsin Press, 1966, and *Agriculture in the Congo Basin*, University of Wisconsin Press, 1967. He was guest editor of special issues of *African Urban Notes* on "Markets and Market Relationships in Africa," 5: 2 (Summer 1970), and 5:3 (Fall 1970). On his campus he teaches both a course and a seminar on the economies of Tropical Africa.

E. WAYNE NAFZIGER, assistant professor of economics at Kansas State University, is at present a visiting Fulbright professor at Andhra University in India. In 1964–65, he was a Midwest Universities Consortium Research Fellow at the Economic Development Institute of the University of Nigeria. In 1969 and 1970 he was based at Zaria and Ibadan, Nigeria, while on research grants from Kansas State University and the Social Science Foundation. His publications on Nigeria have dealt with entrepreneurship, the capital market, education and economic development, interregional economic relations, and economic aspects of the civil war.

JAMES E. PRICE took the Ph.D. degree at the Massachusetts Institute of Technology and then went to Syracuse University, where he is now associate professor and chairman of the economics department. In 1963–64, Dr. Price was a visiting lecturer in the department of economics at University College, Nairobi. For several years he has taught a graduate course on East Africa at Syracuse. Professor Price's interest in African agriculture led to his co-authoring (with Dan M. Etherington) the article "The Paradox of Surplus Agricultural Labor and Positive Marginal Productivity of Labor," in the *Indian Economic Journal* (1966).

IDRIAN N. RESNICK has been, since 1970, senior economist at the Ministry of Economic Affairs and Development Planning in Tanzania. From 1964 until 1967 he was a member of the economics department at University College, Dar es Salaam. Dr. Resnick has also taught African and economic development courses at Princeton, Columbia, Howard, and Boston Universities. Dr. Resnick took his Ph.D. degree in economics at Boston University, in the African Studies Program. He has published some fifteen articles in the field, and has edited two books, including *Tanzania: Revolution by Education.* His research has concentrated on foreign trade and payments, and on manpower and educational development problems in Africa.

GILBERT L. RUTMAN is associate professor of economics at

Southern Illinois University. He has done field research in eastern and southern Africa, and has delivered several papers at meetings of the African Studies Association. His publications include *The Economy of Tanganyika*, Praeger, 1968, and articles in scholarly journals both in this country and in Africa.

SAYRE P. SCHATZ, the editor of this volume, is professor of economics at Temple University, where he teaches courses on less-developed economies, and on African economic development, courses which he has also taught at Columbia University and at Brooklyn College. He has spent more than four years on the African continent, carrying on economic research as a Fellow of the Ford Foundation, a Senior Research Fellow of the Nigerian Institute of Social and Economic Research, and on a grant from the Social Science Research Council. He served as treasurer of the Nigerian Economic Society and a member of the executive council for three years. Dr. Schatz is the author of two books and a number of articles on economic development of both African and other less-developed economies. His articles have appeared in the *American Economic Review*, the *Quarterly Journal of Economics*, the *Oxford Economic Papers*, and in other scholarly publications.

ROBERT L. WEST is professor of international economics at the Fletcher School of Law and Diplomacy, Tufts University. He served on the faculty of the University of Ibadan in 1963–64. Additionally, Dr. West has traveled extensively throughout Africa as a member of the research liaison committee of the African Studies Association and served in Kinshasa (Congo) as a member of the Agency for International Development of the United States government. Dr. West has written a number of articles on Africa's economic development. His co-author here, E. E. Ekpenyong, was his student research assistant at the University of Ibadan. Mr. Ekpenyong died during the Nigerian civil war.

Index